D1566336

Bashō and His Interpreters

Selected Hokku
with Commentary

Bashō and His Interpreters

Selected Hokku
with Commentary

*Compiled, Translated,
and with an Introduction
by Makoto Ueda*

Stanford University Press   1991
Stanford, California

FRONTISPIECE: Portrait of Bashō by Ogawa Haritsu
(1663–1747), an artist who studied poetry under him.
Reproduced by permission of Bashō Memorial Museum,
Ueno, Mie Prefecture.

Stanford University Press, Stanford, California
© 1992 by the Board of Trustees of the
Leland Stanford Junior University
Printed in the United States of America

CIP data appear at the end of the book

Preface

This book is intended to serve two main purposes. One is to present in a new English translation the representative hokku (or haiku) poems of Matsuo Bashō, a seventeenth-century Japanese poet who is generally considered the most influential figure in the history of the genre. The poems are arranged in chronological order, so that the reader will be able to see how Bashō grew as a poet over time. I tried to trace that growth in a chapter of my earlier book, *Matsuo Bashō* (1970), but space limitations prevented me from doing so as fully as I would have liked. In addition, Bashō studies in Japan have made considerable progress in the last twenty years, and I should like to update the information I gave earlier.

The other purpose of the book is to make available in English some of the more interesting comments made by Japanese scholars on Bashō's individual hokku. As is well known, this seventeen-syllable verse form demands the active participation of those who read it. The poet leaves the poem unfinished, so to speak, and each reader is expected to "complete" it with a personal interpretation. It is instructive, then, to see how other readers have gone about interpreting specific poems. Bashō's poetry, in particular, is famous (or notorious) for its ambiguity and has attracted hundreds of commentators, including some of Japan's leading minds. Of course, today's readers are still free to read a Bashō poem in whatever way is most meaningful to them. A look at other interpretations, however, may reveal aspects of the poem they had not thought of before.

Obviously, this book is not for someone who reads Japanese with proficiency. Those who do should read Bashō in the original and experience his superb mastery of the language, especially his subtle use of particles and verb endings. For critical commentary, they are advised to consult Iwata Kurō's *Shochū hyōshaku Bashō haiku taisei* (Variorum commentary on Bashō's hokku, 1967), in which most of the noteworthy interpreters of Bashō up to that time are represented. Still better, they should go to the original sources. This book contains only the highlights of what the commentators said; indeed, I should apologize to them for any injustice that I may have done to their views by quoting them out of context.

I am indebted to a great number of people in the compilation of this book. My thanks are due, above all, to the critics and scholars whose comments make the book distinctly different from an ordinary anthology of poetry. Those whom I was able to contact kindly gave me permission to publish their comments in translation, many of them without even asking to see which passages I had selected. I am also grateful to the National Institute of Japanese Literature in Tokyo, which invited me as a visiting professor in 1986–87 and allowed me access to its rich collection of books and microfilms in Japanese literature. The National Diet Library, the Museum of Haiku Literature, and the Bashō Memorial Museum, all located in Tokyo, and the East Asian Collection of the Hoover Institution at Stanford University helped me to secure other books and materials I needed. J. M. B. Edwards read the entire manuscript from a general reader's viewpoint and gave me valuable suggestions not only on my translation but on the overall scheme and organization of the book as well. A more scholarly critique prepared by the anonymous reader for Stanford University Press was also very helpful in improving the manuscript. Last but not least, I wish to thank Helen Tartar of Stanford University Press, who encouraged me to go ahead with the project when it was little more than a vague notion.

Contents

Bashō and His Interpreters

Selected Hokku
with Commentary

Introduction

As is well known, the Japanese verse form called hokku or haiku consists of three phrases (often referred to as "lines" in English) of five,
seven, and five syllables. Historically it evolved out of *renga*, a major
form of Japanese poetry that flourished especially in the fourteenth and
fifteenth centuries. Renga, literally meaning "linked poetry," was usually
written by a team of poets under a set of prescribed rules. First the team
leader, normally the honored guest at the gathering, would write a
hokku ("opening verse") in the 5-7-5 syllable pattern and including a
word implying the season of the year. Next the host poet would write a *wakiku* ("accompanying verse"), using the 7-7 syllable form and extending
or modifying the meaning of the preceding verse in some interesting way.
This would be followed by the third poet's three-phrase, seventeen-
syllable verse, then by the fourth poet's two-phrase, fourteen-syllable
verse, and so forth, the two different syllabic forms always alternating
with each other, until the poetic sequence reached its thirty-sixth, forty-
fourth, fiftieth, or, as was most commonly the case, one hundredth verse.
On certain special occasions, poets went on to compose a renga sequence of one thousand or even ten thousand verses.

In the sixteenth century, as more Japanese became literate and began
participating in poetic activities, a variety of renga called *haikai*
emerged and gradually gained popularity among all classes of people.
Haikai, literally meaning "playful style," was a lighthearted type of
linked poetry that allowed more freedom of imagery and diction and a
more relaxed aesthetic in general. The early haikai poets in particular
aimed at eliciting laughter through the use of puns, witticisms, parody,
slang terms, or vulgar subject matter. They produced no great literature,
but they did help to democratize poetry. They also prepared the ground
for the emergence of a major poet who, with his great innovative talent,
would elevate haikai to a mature art form. Such a poet did indeed appear in the seventeenth century, namely Matsuo Bashō (1644–94).

While haikai was still establishing itself, hokku was steadily becoming
more independent of the rest of the poetic sequence. The first renga anthology, compiled in the fourteenth century, had already separated

hokku from other verses and collected them in a special section, but early renga poets always wrote them as "opening verses," expecting wakiku to follow. As more renga anthologies appeared, and as poets had more opportunities to see hokku singled out in them, that expectation gradually lessened. Some hokku written in the late fifteenth century read almost like self-contained lyrics, expressing personal emotions the poets felt on specific occasions.

The popularity of haikai among the masses in the sixteenth century further accelerated the trend. Many amateur poets found it easier and more enjoyable to write hokku than any other verse in a haikai sequence. Hokku, being the opening verse, could be written without paying attention to the bothersome rules of linkage. The game of matching individual hokku in a contest, which became widespread in the seventeenth century, also helped hokku to be viewed as autonomous poems. Although Bashō once intimated that he had more confidence in composing haikai than hokku, the fact remains that he compiled a hokku contest book in his youth and went on to write a number of hokku with no wakiku to follow. Yosa Buson (1718–83) and Kobayashi Issa (1763–1827), two major poets in the post-Bashō era, poured their creative energy more into hokku than into haikai. It can be said that in the eighteenth and nineteenth centuries the writing of independent hokku was just as popular as, and often more popular than, the composition of haikai.

It was natural, then, that in the late nineteenth century the poet Masaoka Shiki (1867–1902) should come to advocate distinguishing between the hokku as the opening verse of a haikai sequence and the hokku as an independent, self-contained poem. To make the distinction clear, Shiki gave the name *haiku* to the latter type of hokku. The new name became prevalent in subsequent years, and all autonomous poems written in seventeen syllables today are called haiku. This has created a problem, however. What should we call a 5-7-5 syllable verse that Bashō wrote to start a haikai sequence, but that we now read and appreciate as an independent poem? Until about ten years ago, it was more common to call it a haiku. In today's Japan, the situation seems to be the reverse. In this book, therefore, I have used the term "hokku" to designate all seventeen-syllable verses written before the end of the Edo period (1600–1868), regardless of whether they actually opened haikai sequences. The word "haiku," as employed in this book, denotes an independent 5-7-5 syllable poem written in the modern period.

It must be remembered, however, that Bashō himself did not distinguish between the two types of hokku as clearly as Shiki did. In Bashō's mind, a hokku was *at once* an autonomous poem and a verse that could begin a haikai sequence. As a matter of fact, there are instances where he wrote a hokku spontaneously in response to a specific scene or incident and then, at a later date, used it as the opening verse of a haikai sequence. Conveniently, the Japanese language has the all-inclusive word *ku*, which designates a haiku, a hokku (in both of its senses), or any haikai verse. Commentators on Bashō's work make frequent use of the word, thereby keeping the semantic ambiguity intact. Needless to say, the term has no English equivalent, for the word "poem" implies a self-contained piece of composition, while the term "verse" usually refers to a stanza or section of a poem. In this book, then, I have translated *ku* as "poem" when the commentator is clearly treating the hokku as an independent entity and using the term in that sense. In all other cases, I have employed the word "verse." A "verse" in my usage, therefore, covers a wider area of meaning than it normally does in English, for at times it has to signify something halfway between a poem and a stanza. The notion may seem a little nebulous to those who are used to making a clear distinction between a part and a whole, but it is integral to the basic nature of hokku.

THE SIGNIFICANCE OF BASHŌ

The historical significance of Bashō is obvious. He demonstrated, to an extent never known before, the poetic potential of the seventeen-syllable form. Prior to his time, haikai had been more an urbane game or pastime than serious poetry, and hokku was part of it. With his keen literary sensitivity and superb command of the language, Bashō explored all the potential that had been dormant in the verse form. He was a daring explorer: he used slang terms, he borrowed from classical Chinese, he wrote hokku in eighteen, nineteen, or more syllables. Even more important, he endeavored to make hokku true to actual human experience, to what he saw, thought, and felt, with all sincerity and honesty. He never completely rejected the playfulness characteristic of haikai, but he demonstrated that hokku was capable of embodying, in its brief form, all the various sentiments and moods of human life. In brief, he created serious poetry out of what had largely been an entertaining game.

Bashō's significance as a poet, however, is more than historical, for what he poured into his poetry has universal and lasting appeal. Readers have tried to explain that appeal in different ways, but they tend to agree that Bashō's poetry, seen in its totality, reveals his lifelong effort to find a meaning in life. Born in a family just below the ruling class and failing early in his attempt to climb up to that class, he went through a period of youth ridden by self-doubts, anxiety, and even despair. Yet, living in a postmedieval age, he had too much confidence in human potential to turn to a self-abnegating religion. In his extensive search for a viable scheme of salvation, he probed deep into Taosim and Zen Buddhism. Eventually he found, or thought he found, what he sought in what he called *fūga*, an artist's way of life, a reclusive life devoted to a quest for eternal truth in nature. The sincerity with which he pursued *fūga* is deeply moving. Nonetheless, it is interesting to note that he had lingering misgivings about its redemptive power. To his last days, he did not seem able to merge poetry with belief completely.

The inflow of European literature into Japan since the late nineteenth century has not diminished the appeal of Bashō's poetry. Rather, it has helped the Japanese to reappraise his writings from new perspectives. Romantics in early modern Japan, who tried to write in the manner of Wordsworth and Byron, conceived Bashō as a kind of Childe Harold, a solitary wanderer who would travel to many distant towns and evoke people and events of the past wherever he went. Symbolist poets following the footsteps of Baudelaire and Mallarmé thought of Bashō as their Japanese predecessor, a poet who probed into the mysteries of nature and gave them literary expression through subtle, evocative images. Autobiographical writers, who thought they were emulating European naturalist literature, valued Bashō's tireless efforts to be honest with himself, to improve himself as both man and poet, and to record his spiritual quest with the utmost candor.

With the increasing interest in hokku and haiku outside Japan, the appeal of Bashō's poetry is now international. Early in this century, Anglo-American poets associated with the imagist movement were attracted to the poetic language of Bashō and his followers for its objectivity and precision as well as for its ability to present what Ezra Pound called "an intellectual and emotional complex" in a fraction of time. Such language also caught the eye of Sergei M. Eisenstein, because it seemed to utilize the same technique of montage with which he was experimenting in his film work. He called hokku "montage phrases," and the first example he cited was Bashō's famous poem on the crow. Many poets of the Beat Generation were drawn to Bashō's poetry, primarily because they thought hokku were literary expressions of Zen. That view is still held by some Western admirers of Bashō today, but, in general, images of Bashō in the West have grown much more diverse. Recent readers have detected in him something of an existential philosopher, a psychological realist, an alienated intellectual, and a religious mystic. There is no doubt that many more portraits of Bashō will be drawn by his readers in and outside Japan in the years to come.

Ultimately, the greatest charm of Bashō's poetry resides in the scope and depth with which it represents human experience. He contains multitudes, so that his readers can see in him whatever they want to see. And yet they often feel they have not seen the whole of what they wanted to see, since a Bashō poem refuses to simplify the experience it represents. Because of its brevity, a hokku tends to be ambiguous, but even more so when the author is Bashō, for he tried to present life with all its complexities, pointing his finger at its mystery and depth but avoiding the attempt to force an analytical intellect on it. While that may or may not be a sign of greatness, it has proved to be a steady source of attraction to readers for the last three hundred years.

CRITICAL COMMENTARY ON BASHŌ'S HOKKU

Not surprisingly, a great many readers have been moved to record their feelings about Bashō's hokku. The amount of such critical commentary accumulated over the years is more massive than that found for any other Japanese poet. It must be noted, however, that a long history of interpretive criticism had existed prior to Bashō's time. *Man'yōshū* (The collection of ten thousand leaves, 8th c.), the earliest surviving anthology of Japanese poetry, already includes explanatory notes following some of the poems. Early books on the art of poetry also contain author's comments on the wording and style of the poems cited. One such example is the commentary accompanying the poems quoted in the famous preface to *Kokinshū* (The collection of ancient and modern poems, 905), although neither its authorship nor its date of composition is known. Commentary became more pointed and evaluative when poetry contests gained popularity during the Heian period (794–1185). In such contests

a *waka*, a thirty-one syllable poem that by then had become the dominant verse form, was matched with another waka on the same topic,
whereupon a referee decided which poem was the winner. Naturally, the
referee had to explain the reasons for his decision, and he often did so in
writing (or else his oral explanations were recorded by someone else).

By the late Heian period, earlier anthologies such as *Man'yōshū* and
Kokinshū had come to be regarded as literary classics worthy of scholarly attention. At the same time, a number of expressions appearing in
those anthologies had become obsolete and incomprehensible. Thus
scholars in the eleventh century, many of whom wrote poetry themselves, began to annotate archaic words and phrases for the benefit of
less learned readers. They also studied earlier customs and manners in
order to reveal the poems' social background. They were especially eager
to seek out any specific work of Chinese or Japanese literature to which
a given poem alluded, for that allowed them to display their erudition to
the fullest extent. The practice of writing scholarly commentary was well
established in the twelfth century, opening a path for many excellent
books of waka annotations to appear in later centuries.

When renga replaced waka as the most viable poetic form in the fourteenth century, critical remarks on linked verses began to appear in books
on the art of renga as well as in records of renga contests. The commentators' focus of attention initially tended to be on the manner in which
two sequential verses were linked to each other, because that was where
the central interest of renga poets lay. But, with the increasing independence of hokku, critics gradually began to pay more attention to the
opening verse—especially after haikai became the mainstream of renga.
Comments and discussions on hokku proliferated even further when
hokku contests came to be held frequently in the seventeenth century.

Indeed, the earliest comments on Bashō's hokku that survive today are
found in a hokku contest book compiled by Bashō himself. Entitled *Kai
ōi* (The seashell game, 1672), the book includes two samples of young
Bashō's work in the 5-7-5 form, each followed by a critical comment he
made as the contest referee. In his mature years, however, Bashō seldom
wrote about his own poetry in a formal manner. He did make some casual remarks about it in the letters he sent to his friends and disciples.
Also, he seems to have discussed his verses in conversations with his students, and a good number of the comments he made have been recorded
in the students' writings. Of those, the ones by Mukai Kyorai (1651–

1704) and Hattori Dohō (1657–1730) are the most reliable. Bashō's remarks cited in other disciples' books should be read with caution, because they may have been distorted by the author for one reason or another. These comments by Bashō and his students are valuable, as they often reveal something about the process by which a poem was created. Knowing the circumstances of composition is helpful, especially when the poem is only seventeen syllables long.

A large amount of critical commentary on Bashō's hokku appeared in the next two centuries. Mostly written by haikai poets, it shows two main characteristics. First, it reflects a major effort by the commentators to seek out classical sources and allusions. Obviously they were aware of the earlier interpretive tradition that had been established by scholars on waka and renga; they also knew that Bashō was well read in Chinese and Japanese classics. Thus such commentators as Ishiko Sekisui (1738–1803), Shoshian San'u (18th c.), and Moro Nanimaru (1761–1837) searched far and wide to discover poems, passages, and phrases to which a given hokku by Bashō might have alluded. Although they sometimes went too far in this direction, their work is valuable in making us aware of hidden references and connotations in a hokku and enriching our appreciation of it. Second, those premodern commentators were prone to overpraise Bashō's poetry, consciously or subconsciously shutting their eyes to its flaws. To them, Bashō was a poet-sage whose work was beyond reproach. Indeed, partly because of their effort, the Shinto hierarchy deified him in 1793, and the imperial court granted a similar honor thirteen years later. To say something derogatory about his work became quite literally sacrilegious.

The situation changed radically toward the end of the nineteenth century, when Western literature flowed freely into Japan and dazzled the Japanese. In the new age, Bashō was no longer a divine poet but merely a major world poet, one who showed weakness as well as strength in his work. Thus, such critics as Masaoka Shiki and Naitō Meisetsu (1847–1926) began to publish candid, sometimes adverse remarks on Bashō's poetry; Shiki especially came to be well known for his attacks on Bashō. It should be remembered, however, that the attacks were based on Shiki's Western-inspired notion of poetry and had the effect of showing that Bashō's work was universal enough to be discussed in the context of world literature.

This recognition of Bashō's universality also led to his liberation from the small world of haikai and hokku, inviting a wide variety of readers to study his poetry and make comments on it. One notable result of this was the formation of a discussion group by leading Japanese intellectuals, such as Abe Jirō (1883–1959), Abe Yoshishige (1883–1966), and Watsuji Tetsurō (1889–1960), who took up Bashō's hokku one by one and scrutinized them at regular meetings held over a period of four and a half years. Novelists like Akutagawa Ryūnosuke (1892–1927) and Murō Saisei (1889–1962) and free-verse poets like Hagiwara Sakutarō (1886–1942) and Noguchi Yonejirō (1875–1947, known as Yone Noguchi outside Japan) also published essays showing their intuitive understanding of Bashō's hokku. Even those who were known primarily as haiku poets, such as Ogiwara Seisensui (1884–1976) and Katō Shūson (b. 1905), wrote comments on Bashō's hokku from a broad, humanistic viewpoint not restricted by the past haikai tradition.

In the meantime, the introduction of Western literary studies helped Bashō scholars to make rapid progress in textual and biographical criticism. Verses that had been mistakenly attributed to Bashō were carefully weeded out. Of the variant versions, the one that seemed to be Bashō's final draft was selected through a rigorous process of scholarly authentication. Scholars also aimed at maximum objectivity in determining dates and places of composition by scrutinizing the historical and biographical evidence that had survived. Their critical comments on Bashō's hokku help us to see the poems in terms of the situation in which they were written. A great many scholars made contributions in this area, most notable among them being Shida Gishū (1876–1947) and Ebara Taizō (1894–1948).

Japanese studies on Bashō's hokku reached a peak with the work of Yamamoto Kenkichi (1907–88), who was neither a poet nor a novelist nor a resident of academia. His brilliant book *Bashō: sono kanshō to hihyō* (Bashō: Appreciation and criticism of his work), which was published in three volumes in 1955–56, selected 147 representative hokku and attempted a detailed explication of each. Well versed in world literature, Yamamoto derived his basic methodology from the works of the New Critics in the West, basing his comments on scrupulous textual analysis. He did not reject historical and other methodologies; rather, he incorporated them into his approach. Ultimately, however, the strength of his commentary lies in his incisive intellect, keen literary sensibility, and rich knowledge of both Eastern and Western literature, all of which he applied to unraveling the complex mind of Bashō.

Insightful commentary on Bashō's hokku, made by such scholars as Imoto Nōichi (b. 1913) and Ogata Tsutomu (b. 1920), continued to appear after Yamamoto's monumental work. Yamamoto himself published a new book on Bashō's hokku in 1974, this time choosing a far greater number of poems for study but considerably shortening his comment on each. In general, however, Bashō's hokku do not seem to have attracted as much critical attention in the last several decades. Some scholars even assert that the peak period of Bashō criticism has passed, as far as his hokku are concerned. Current scholarship pays more attention to his works in other genres, which, with the exception of travel journals, had not received due attention before. Also, the huge accumulated mass of past commentary on Bashō's hokku is enough to intimidate any scholar. Probably those who have the greatest potential to contribute at present are non-Japanese readers of Bashō's hokku, who have been reared in a radically different cultural tradition. In order for their comments to be valuable, however, they need to be thoroughly familiar with the Japanese language and culture, and they should be capable both of synthesizing the past Japanese commentary and of adding to that synthesis their own insights. The task would not be easy, but I believe it can be done.

TRANSLATIONS INTO ENGLISH

Bashō's hokku, together with those of other Japanese poets, began to appear in English translation around the end of the nineteenth century. It seems that the earliest translator to publish Bashō's hokku was Lafcadio Hearn, who, in his book *Exotics and Retrospectives* (1898), introduced the famous poem about a frog jumping into the old pond (Hearn saw more than one frog in this poem, however). He also included hokku by Bashō in subsequent books, such as *Shadowings* (1900) and *Kwaidan* (1904). W. G. Aston's *A History of Japanese Literature* (1899) contained eight Bashō hokku in translation, together with a brief biographical sketch and an interesting—but unauthenticated—anecdote about the traveling poet. Basil Hall Chamberlain, who thought of hokku poems as nothing more than "a litter of bricks, half-bricks in fact" in comparison with Tennyson's great Palaces of Art, nevertheless went on to translate some thirty hokku by Bashō. His long essay entitled "Bashō and the Japanese Poetical Epigram" (1902), which included those translations, was the first in-depth treatment of hokku to appear in English and, if one can discount his Victorian literary taste, is still worth reading for its many perceptive comments.

Already in those early days the style of translation varied considerably with the translator. Consider, for example, the treatment of Bashō's well-known hokku on *sémi* (cicada), a relatively simple poem as far as its meaning is concerned.

Never an intimation in all those voices of sémi
How quickly the hush will come—how speedily all must die.[1]

The cry of the cicada
Gives no sign
That presently it will die.[2]

Nothing in the cicada's voice
Gives token of a speedy death.[3]

Evidently the three translators understood Bashō's meaning in the same way, but the result was three different poems!

In the years that followed, as more people tried their hands at translating hokku, stylistic variations proliferated still further. On the whole, each translator's style seems to have been determined by two main factors: his conception of the basic nature of hokku and his choice of English poetic models. To use the same Bashō hokku for illustration, Harold G. Henderson, who saw the essence of hokku in its rigid, condensed, tension-filled form, rendered it as

So soon to die,
    and no sign of it is showing—
        locust cry.[4]

[1]Lafcadio Hearn, *Shadowings* (Boston: Little, Brown, 1900), p. 100.
[2]W. G. Aston, *A History of Japanese Literature* (London: Heinemann, 1899), p. 295.
[3]Basil Hall Chamberlain, "Bashō and the Japanese Poetical Epigram," *Transactions of the Asiatic Society of Japan* 30 (1902). Reprinted in Chamberlain, *Japanese Poetry* (London: John Murray, 1910), p. 220.
[4]Harold G. Henderson, *An Introduction to Haiku* (Garden City, N.Y.: Doubleday, 1958), p. 43. Reprinted by permission of the publisher.

while Frank Livingstone Huntley, who recognized in this hokku what he called "an arc of Zen," came up with

Busy cicadas chirp and cry
On brilliant August days,
Zzurr, zzurr—
In this ignorant haze
They think they'll never die.[5]

In the final analysis, translation is a form of literary criticism as well as artistic creation, and no matter how hard the translator may try to become transparent, some presence inevitably shows through.

The same may be said of my translations that appear in the following pages. They reflect both my idea of a hokku and my predilection for a certain English poetic style. To put the matter briefly, I believe that a hokku, when appreciated by itself, is a short, three-phrase poem intended to charm the reader into contemplating an aspect of nature or the human condition, usually through the help of a seasonal image. I also share the view that the seventeen-syllable poem presents an observation or sentiment in all its immediacy, before it is intellectually conceptualized. In my translation, therefore, a hokku neither begins with a capital letter nor ends with a period. The style should not seem entirely alien to readers of modern American poetry, which includes works by poets like e. e. cummings and William Carlos Williams. I am also influenced by the practice of contemporary American haiku poets, the majority of whom seem to favor a terse style that makes minimum use of punctuation marks. Ideally, however, individual readers should attempt their own translations according to their own tastes and preferences. It is for this reason that, after each hokku I have rendered into English, I have added the original Japanese poem in roman letters and a word-for-word translation. In addition, when a Japanese word seems to call for an explanation, I have put a note in the section that follows. I have refrained from making my own comments on the meaning of the poem, so that individual readers can, like spectators of an abstract painting, freely speculate on the implications of the work before them.

A note on the problem of lineation is due, since it has become a con-

[5]Frank Livingstone Huntley, "Zen and the Imagist Poets of Japan," *Comparative Literature* 4 (1952): 175. Reprinted by permission of Mr. Huntley and *Comparative Literature*.

troversial issue in recent years. Some translators have argued, against the objections of others, that one should not translate a hokku into a poem of multiple lines because premodern Japanese poets had no notion of lineation as a poetic device. I do not agree. I am not necessarily opposed to one-liners, but I feel it is wrong to maintain that a hokku must always be translated into a monolinear (or nonlinear) poem. My main reason is a simple one derived from the basic nature of translation. In my opinion, to insist that a hokku should be a one-line poem in English because the original Japanese poet had no sense of lineation is tantamount to insisting that no English grammatical article, such as "a" or "the," should be used in translating Japanese sentences because the Japanese language includes no concept of articles. Translation means a transference of thought and feeling from one linguistic convention to another; since each convention is different, there is necessarily a limit on the number of conventional devices that can be carried over. Where to draw the line is up to individual translators, who will make a decision based on their idea of hokku on the one hand and their sense of English style on the other.

GENERAL NOTES

Format. This book contains 255 selected hokku written by Bashō. The poems are arranged in order of composition and are grouped by year (except for three longer groupings before 1675) within five general phases of the poet's career that constitute the five chapters. Each group of hokku is introduced by a brief description of happenings in Bashō's life during that year. Within the group, each hokku is presented in English translation, preceded by the poem's original headnote if there is one, and followed by the romanized original and word-for-word translation. Often a "Note" section follows, giving background information about the poem, such as the date and place of composition or some Japanese word that requires explanation. The final "Commentary" section includes selected interpretive remarks made by past Japanese readers, whose names follow their remarks. Information on these commentators is given in the Notes on the Commentators, at the end of this book.

Dates. The dating of Bashō's hokku has been a challenge to scholars throughout the years, and problems still remain for a number of poems. In this book, I have followed the order of composition determined by Kon Eizō in his *Bashō kushū* (Collected hokku of Bashō, 1982), one of the most authoritative editions of Bashō's hokku available today. I have, however, converted all the dates to their equivalents in the Gregorian calendar, for the lunar calendar used in Bashō's day does not convey the passage of time as we know it. For example, as we read his poem on autumn's unobtrusive approach, the notation "the twenty-first day of the sixth month in the seventh year of Genroku" does not give us the sense of the season, whereas "August 11, 1694" does. On the other hand, the reader may be puzzled to find that many of Bashō's hokku on the year's end were written in February, because the lunar New Year often arrived early in that month. Obviously such conversion of dates has its advantages and disadvantages, and there does not seem to be a clear-cut solution.

There is also the problem of determining the year of composition for some winter hokku. Whereas winter in Bashō's time was normally contained in a continuous three-month period of a single year, with the modern calendar it spans a period from December to March across parts of two different years. It is difficult to decide whether a given Bashō poem was written before or after January 1, unless the exact date of composition is known. Such season words as *hatsushigure* ("first winter shower") and *susuharai* ("year-end cleaning") give helpful clues, but there are a number of cases where I have had to make arbitrary decisions.

Headnotes. Bashō's hokku as published in premodern texts often have headnotes, but it has been difficult to determine how authentic they are. Different texts also carry different headnotes. In this book I have followed Kon, who has selected only those headnotes known to have been written by Bashō himself.

Texts. For the hokku texts, I have again relied on Kon's collection cited above. His basic principle was to collect all the hokku that can be proved to have been written by Bashō and to choose, from among the variant texts, the one that can be determined to be the final draft. Those who wish to go from my translation to the original poem in Kon's book or in any other modern text will find it easy to do so, since all the standard texts have indexes of opening phrases.

Word-for-word Translation. The literal translation that follows the original shows only the most basic meaning of each Japanese word. It should be noted that Japanese nouns have no singular or plural form, and that Japanese particles are postpositional—that is, they follow the words they modify. The abbreviation "[nom.]" indicates a nominative particle; "[acc.]," an accusative particle. The particle *kana*, which emphasizes the speaker's emotion without specifying its nature, is left untranslated. Japanese verbs are inflected in accordance with their grammatical function; here, they have been translated into their "dictionary meaning" in English. The only exception is when verbs take a continuative form, in which case they have been rendered as present participles. At all events, one should remember that the word-for-word translation is no more than a very rough approximation of what the original words say, since in no case does a Japanese word correspond exactly to an English word. Still, the translation will be helpful to the reader in learning the order of images in the original poem.

Commentary. Each critical comment cited in this book is not a summary but a direct quotation from the most crucial part of the original commentary, which is often quite long. These selected comments are arranged in roughly chronological order—roughly, because the comment may first have been published in a journal and later included in a book. In translating the comment, I have aimed at preserving the tone and flavor of the original through equivalent English phrases rather than a literal translation. I am sure, however, the result suffers from the same limits of translation I mentioned earlier. For the benefit of those who read Japanese and who wish to read the comment in its entirety, the sources are included in the Notes on the Commentators.

Literary Terms. Some Japanese literary terms are impossible to translate into English. To avoid distorting the meaning by a forced translation, I have chosen to leave the problematic word in italics in romanized Japanese and to explain its implications in the Glossary at the end of the book.

Personal Names. In this book I use the normal Japanese order for names, with the family name first, followed by the given name. However, poets and other men of letters are customarily known by a *haigō* ("haikai name") or *gagō* ("elegant name"). Thus Matsuo Bashō is called Bashō (haigō), and not Matsuo (family name), whereas Akutagawa Ryūnosuke is called Akutagawa (family name), and not Ryūnosuke (given name).

CHAPTER ONE

The Making of a Poet

1644-1677

1644-1665

It is generally believed that Matsuo Bashō was born in 1644 at Ueno in the province of Iga (the modern Mie Prefecture), some thirty miles southeast of Kyoto. No extant record gives the exact date of his birth, although one recent theory sets it at September 15, with the harvest moon. He was called Kinsaku at first but gained several other names later, since it was the custom of the day to change names periodically during one's childhood. His father, Yozaemon, seems to have been a *musokunin*, a landed farmer who was allowed some of the privileges of a samurai, such as having a family name. Nothing is known about Bashō's mother, except that her parents had migrated from Iyo Province (Ehime Prefecture) in Shikoku. She and her husband already had a son and a daughter when Bashō was born, and they were to have three more daughters later.

Yozaemon died on March 13, 1656. Within the next several years young Bashō, now known as Munefusa, entered the service of Tōdō Yoshikiyo, a relative of the daimyo, or feudal lord ruling the province. No record remains of his work in the service, an omission that suggests his official rank was low and his duties minor. Whatever work he may have done officially, he soon joined the circle of Yoshikiyo's son, Yoshitada, who was two years his senior and who wrote haikai as a pastime under the pseudonym Sengin.

One of the earliest surviving documents referring to Bashō shows that he, under the haikai name of Sōbō (a Sinified reading of Munefusa), participated in a haikai gathering headed by Sengin on December 19, 1665. Sengin's haikai teacher, Kitamura Kigin (1624–1705), sent a verse to the gathering. Kigin belonged to the Teimon school of haikai, the most influential one at the time. Founded by Matsunaga Teitoku (1571–1653), it aimed at an elegant, humorous style made up of allusions to classical court literature, wordplay, and witty associations. It was this type of haikai that Bashō learned and practiced when he began to write poetry.

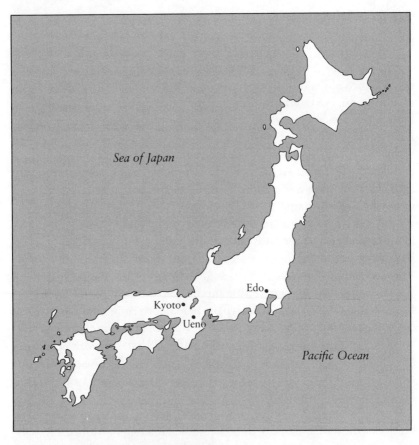

Sea of Japan

Edo●

Kyoto●

Ueno●

Pacific Ocean

It is generally believed that Matsuo Bashō was born in 1644 at Ueno, some thirty miles southeast of Kyoto.

Because spring started on the twenty-ninth

was it spring that came
or was it the year that went?
the Second Last Day

haru | ya | koshi | toshi | ya | yukiken | kotsugomori
spring | ? | came | year | ? | went | Second-Last-Day

NOTE

The oldest of Bashō's datable poems, having been composed on February 7,
1663. According to the lunar calendar, which was in use at the time, that day
was the twenty-ninth of the twelfth month and so was known as the Second Last
Day. In a normal year spring would officially start on the lunar New Year's Day,
but in a rare year, as was the case here, the first day of spring arrived one or more
days earlier. Since olden times Japanese poets had been amused enough at such
an occurrence to write poems, the most famous of which was a waka by Ariwara
Motokata (888–953) that appears at the beginning of *Kokinshū*:

Before the year	toshi no uchi ni
is gone, spring has come.	haru wa ki ni keri
Those remaining days—	hitotose wo
what shall we call them,	kozo to ya iwamu
the old year or the new year?	kotoshi to ya iwamu

Bashō's hokku furthermore alludes to another waka included in *Ise monogatari*
(The tales of Ise, 10th c.), a poem sent by a woman to her lover after their night
together:

Was it you who came	kimi ya koshi
or was it I who went?	ware ya yukikemu
I do not remember . . .	omōezu
Was I asleep or awake,	yume ka utsutsu ka
was that dream or reality?	nete ka samete ka

COMMENTARY

The only noteworthy feature of this hokku is its bantering tone. The poem gener-
ates no power that appeals to the heart. *– Shūson*

The poet's skill in parodying the sense of one classical poem and the form of another is admirable. — *Kon*

A thing is not necessarily one and the same; everything depends on the way it is looked at. Hidden behind life, there is death; the passing of this year implies the coming of the next; there is daytime because there is nighttime. True perception means looking at a thing from more than one point of view. If we read this poem in this light, we see Bashō wondering whether today meant the coming of the new year or the passing of the old year. He was reluctant to choose one way of looking at a day. Here we see Bashō trying to follow the *Kokinshū* tradition that encouraged a poet to see time from multiple viewpoints. — *Akahane*

the moon will guide you . . .
this way, traveler; please come
into the inn here

tsuki | zo | shirube | konata | e | irase | tabi | no | yado
moon | ! | guidance | this-way | to | please-enter | travel | 's | lodging

NOTE

Written probably in the autumn of 1663. The hokku alludes to the lines in the nō
play *Kurama Tengu* (Tengu in Mount Kurama): "The blossoms will guide you.
This way, sir; please come in." There is a pun on *irase tabi* ("please come in")
and *tabi* ("travel").

COMMENTARY

The poem creates the impression that the person guiding the traveler is an elegant woman. — *Komiya*

The essence of this hokku lies in the wit of the poet who borrowed from a nō
text a phrase that expresses an innkeeper's call for customers. — *Ebara*

With its reliance on borrowing and wordplay, the poem follows the Teimon style
closely. Yet a somber tone, probably deriving from the author's personality, steals
in somewhere. — *Iwata*

the old-lady cherry
is blossoming—in her old age
an event to remember

ubazakura | saku | ya | rōgo | no | omoiide
old-lady-cherry | bloom | : | old-age | 's | remembrance

NOTE

Written in the spring of 1664. The cherry tree referred to is of a kind that blossoms before its leaves come out. The hokku compares the blossoming tree to Saitō Sanemori (?–1183), an aged samurai who, in the nō play *Sanemori*, says: "I'm certain I'll be dying in action. No event in my old age will be more memorable than that." He is then killed on the battlefield.

COMMENTARY

An extremely childish, trite motif. – *Sokotsu*

Of the two possible readings—"The tree is blossoming beautifully so that it can remember its prime after it grows old" and "The tree is blossoming beautifully in old age to create a memorable event"—I prefer the latter. – *Kōseki*

The device of personification is characteristic of the Teimon style. – *Kon*

The author, amused by the name of the tree, likened it to an old woman with heavy makeup, such as one sees everywhere. – *Hori*

1666-1671

On May 28, 1666, Bashō's master Tōdō Yoshitada died suddenly in his twenty-fifth year. According to early biographers, young Bashō was so shocked that he resigned from the service and embarked on a life of wandering. Several modern scholars have speculated that he became a Buddhist monk and studied Zen at a monastery in or near Kyoto, which was the capital of Japan at the time. There is, however, too little evidence to support this or any other speculation on his whereabouts for the next five years. Although it is conceivable that he moved to Kyoto, it is more likely that he continued to live in Ueno, occasionally visiting the capital and other cities nearby. In any case, there is little doubt that he maintained some connection with his hometown, because some of his poems surviving from this period identify the author as "Sōbō of Ueno in Iga Province." The only verifiable fact is that he kept on writing poetry. His verses were published almost every year—at least four in 1666, thirty-two in 1667, six in 1669, two in 1670, and three in 1671. All of them appeared in various haikai anthologies compiled by reputed masters and duplicated either by handwriting or through woodblock printing.

here in Kyoto
ninety-nine thousand people
out to see the blossoms

Kyō | wa | kuman-kusen | kunju | no | hanami | kana
Kyoto | as-for | ninety-nine-thousand | crowd | 's | blossom-viewing | kana

NOTE
Written probably in the spring of 1666. The city of Kyoto was traditionally said to have ninety-eight thousand households. The second phrase also echoes an idiom, *kisen kunju*, "all classes of people."

COMMENTARY
The poem is about a huge mass of people crowding the streets of the capital city in spring. Although the number ninety-nine thousand has little significance in itself, the repetition of the consonant "k" creates a certain rhythm, adding to the poem's appeal. — *Momota*

By beginning with "here in Kyoto," the poet seems to be trying to suggest not only his amazement at the great number of blossom viewers but also his admiration for their fine clothes, which looked like a multitude of blossoms. — *Shūson*

autumn wind
through the opening of a door—
a piercing cry

akikaze | no | yarido | no | kuchi | ya | togarigoe
autumn-wind | 's | sliding-door | 's | opening | : | sharp-voice

NOTE

Written in 1666. *Yari* of *yarido* ("sliding door") has a second meaning, "lance," as does *kuchi*—both "opening" and "mouth."

COMMENTARY

The autumn wind, described as "sharp" because it feels so cold, is a metaphor for the voice of a samurai guarding the doorway. — *Ōsha*

The poem's only interest is that the sound of the autumn wind blowing at the door is personified and compared to a sharp voice, but the specific phrasing somehow makes the reader feel the wind's sharpness. — *Sokotsu*

At the house of a person whose child had died

bending low—the joints,
the world, all upside down—
bamboo under the snow

shiore I fusu I ya I yo I wa I sakasama I no I yuki I no I take
withered I bent I ! I world I as-for I upside-down I 's I snow I 's I bamboo

NOTE

Written in 1666. *Yo* means both "joint" and "world." *Yo wa sakasama* is a common expression meaning "The world is upside down." The poem probably alludes to *Take no yuki* (The bamboo under the snow), a nō play featuring a mother who mourns over her child who has died in the snow.

COMMENTARY

A skillful poem of condolence. – *Rika*

The use of a common saying is typical of the old Teimon way of writing verse, but—unusually for the day—the poet here tried to express a genuine feeling of sorrow. – *Yamamoto*

The poet brought images of nature into this poem on human life with the hope of giving a little consolation to the resident of the house. More important, however, is the fact that he identified himself with the other person's feeling and made his sympathy the main ingredient of the poem. – *Komiya*

do those blossoming faces
make you feel bashful?
hazy moon

hana I no I kao I ni I hareute I shite I ya I oborozuki
blossom I 's I face I at I coyness I doing I ? I hazy-moon

NOTE
Written in 1667.

COMMENTARY

At the sight of beautiful blossoms, the moon felt too shy to show itself through the haze. —*Rika*

The poet may have had in mind the chapter "Hana no en" [The blossom festival] in *Genji monogatari* [The tale of Genji, 11th c.]. —*Shūson*

Bashō added humor to this poem by personifying the moon and hinting at the scene of a bashful man covering his face when confronted with a beautiful woman. The hokku contains something that suggests the young poet's talent. —*Iwata*

blossoms on the waves . . .
snow returning to water
and blooming out of season?

nami | no | hana | to | yuki | mo | ya | mizu | no | kaeribana
wave | 's | blossom | as | snow | also | ? | water | 's | unseasonable-flower

NOTE

Nami no hana is an idiom designating the caps of waves that look like white blossoms. The hokku centers upon a play on the word *kaeri*, which means both "returning" and, in combination with *-bana*, "flower blooming out of season."

COMMENTARY

The poet is merely playing with words to amuse himself. — *Sokotsu*

The waves were rolling in the ocean under the dark cloudy sky. Then it began to snow. The poet, gazing at the white waves, wondered if the snow was returning to the water it came from. As he watched the whiteness appearing and disappearing, he tried to transform the moment into a poem. — *Abe J.*

It need not be snowing. We need only visualize whitecaps on the ocean under the cloudy winter sky. Looking at the waves, the poet wondered if snow had descended to help unseasonable flowers come into bloom. — *Abe Y.*

1672-1674

On February 23, 1672, Bashō dedicated a poetry contest book to a Shinto shrine in Ueno. Although none of the original copies survives today, it is assumed that the book was handwritten and bound by Bashō himself or by someone he knew who was skilled in bookmaking. Entitled *Kai ōi* (The seashell game), the book paired sixty hokku composed by thirty-six local poets as well as by himself. He served as the referee, passing judgment on all thirty matches. His remarks in that capacity and the two hokku of his own included in the book reveal that Bashō had by this time acquired a very large vocabulary, including words and phrases used by the most advanced urban sophisticates of the day.

The dedication of *Kai ōi* may have been his way of bidding farewell to his native town. In the spring of that year Bashō moved to Edo (renamed Tokyo in the nineteenth century), located some two hundred miles east of Ueno. His motive for the move is not clear, but the fact that he took *Kai ōi* with him indicates he had an interest in becoming a *haikaishi*, a professional haikai master who was socially sanctioned to take students and correct their verses for fees. Compared with Kyoto, where Kigin and many other famous masters lived, Edo must have seemed an easier place to get himself established as a poet. By this time he had befriended several Edo residents, among them Sugiyama Sanpū (1647–1732), and although no concrete evidence survives today, presumably those friends helped him to settle down when he arrived in the new city. He seems to have worked, at least temporarily, as a scribe for Takano Yūzan (?–1702), a haikai master originally from Kyoto. As a struggling young man, Bashō must have taken many such odd jobs to survive, while trying by every means to gain a foothold in Edo literary circles. In 1674 he somehow secured from Kigin the privilege of copying an important book on the art of haikai. He also managed to get *Kai ōi* published.

come and look!
put on a Jinbei robe
and admire the blossoms

kite | mo | miyo | Jinbe | ga | haori | hanagoromo
come | ! | see | Jinbei | 's | robe | flower-garment

NOTE

Published in *Kai ōi*. The hokku's first two phrases are taken from popular songs of the day. *Jinbe ga haori* is a short sleeveless robe split at the lower back, a garment fashionable among young men at the time. The poem includes two examples of wordplay: *kite*, which means both "come" and "wear," and *haori*, which means both "robe" and "surrender oneself to admiration."

COMMENTARY

The hokku is poorly tailored, and its words are badly dyed, too. All this is due to lack of craftsmanship on the poet's part.* – *Bashō*

In essence, the poem revolves around a play on the phrase *kite mo miyo*, with its double meaning of "Try on the robe and look at yourself" and "Come and look at the blossoms." – *Kōseki*

Making use of phrases from popular songs—that is the sum and total of this poem and what Bashō was proud of. – *Imoto*

*Bashō, serving as the referee of the contest, judged this hokku to be the loser in the match.

beyond the clouds
a wild goose, parting forever
from a friend!

kumo | to | hedatsu | tomo | ka | ya | kari | no | ikiwakare
cloud | as | part | friend | ! | : | wild-goose | 's | living-separation

NOTE

Written for a friend, Jō Magodayū, shortly before Bashō left for Edo. The poem
was either pasted on Magodayū's gate or enclosed in a letter left for him. There
may be a play on the word *kari*, which can at once mean "wild goose" and
"temporary." Wild geese are migrant birds that leave Japan in spring and come
back in autumn.

COMMENTARY

Superficially the poem is about a wild goose, but in the subtext the poet compared the goose to himself and gave vent to his feelings. — *Sokotsu*

The reference to the clouds may imply an itinerant monk's life, which is often
compared to a floating cloud and flowing water. — *Kakei*

Bashō is a wild goose, and so is Magodayū. The poem expresses the sentiment of
those two "geese," who used to fly together in the sky, now taking two different
paths separated by clouds. — *Keion*

Though the pun on *kari* indicates the usual Teimon type of composition, the
poem contains something that sounds sincere because its subject is parting. It is a
little different from the playful verses of earlier years. — *Imoto*

1675

In late spring of 1675 Bashō was introduced, probably by Yūzan, to the famed haikai master Nishiyama Sōin (1605–82), who was visiting Edo at the time. Under the new pseudonym of Tōsei ("green peach"), Bashō took part in a haikai gathering held in the master's honor. Sōin was the founder of the Danrin school which, in reaction to the courtly Teimon style, advocated a more plebeian type of poetry that freely used mundane subject matter and nonsensical comparisons to produce a more surprising, zany type of humor. Although Sōin lived in Kyoto, the Danrin school was becoming popular in Edo, a less traditional city, and undoubtedly Bashō had a strong inclination to join the new school and write poetry in the most fashionable style of the day.

Also through Yūzan, Bashō was able to make the acquaintance of Naitō Yoshimune (1619–85), a daimyo who wrote haikai under the name of Fūko and who was noted for his patronage of literature. The lord's mansion in Edo had become something of a salon for literati, and Bashō came to know a number of poets there. By this time he had begun to take students, too, among whom were Takarai Kikaku (1661–1707) and the aforementioned Sanpū.

for a town doctor
the mansion sends a horse—
a royal reception!

machi-ishi | ya | yashikigata | yori | komamukae
town-doctor | : | mansion-resident | from | horse-reception

NOTE

Machi-ishi is an ordinary town doctor as distinguished from the prestigious physicians a daimyo would retain. *Komamukae* refers to an annual court ceremony in which the emperor received select horses from provincial lords. It is a poetic theme often mentioned in Heian literature.

COMMENTARY

A steed, no matter how excellent it might be, could not gain fame unless it was discovered and brought to the capital. A town doctor was in a similar situation. For such a doctor, therefore, the call from a daimyo's mansion was felt like one from the royal palace. – *Kōseki*

The humor lies in the sense of incongruity that arises from an imperial ceremony being treated on the same level as plebeian life. Something of the Danrin flavor is beginning to emerge here. – *Shūson*

What we have here is a juxtaposition between the elegant life of the Heian period and the more mundane life of the Edo period. – *Yamamoto*

Musashi Plain—
no more than one inch,
a deer's call

Musashino | ya | issun | hodo | na | shika | no | koe
Musashi-Plain | : | one-inch | approximately | 's | deer | 's | voice

NOTE

Musashino is the modern Kantō Plain, the largest plain in Japan, which extends
from Tokyo to its neighboring prefectures in the north and west.

COMMENTARY

In order to suggest the vastness of the Musashi Plain, the poet made the deer as
tiny as possible, even specifying its length as one inch. The technique is that of
Danrin-style comparison. It also implies that the deer's call reaches no farther
than one inch. – *Kon*

1676

In the spring of 1676 Bashō joined Yamaguchi Sodō (1642–1716) in writing two haikai sequences, each of one hundred verses. Later published as *Edo ryōgin shū* (Two poets in Edo), these verses are strongly marked by the influence of Sōin and his school; in fact, the opening verse of each sequence honors Sōin by alluding to his pseudonym. It almost seems as if Bashō wanted to get himself established as a youthful standard-bearer of the Danrin school.

Probably feeling that he had settled down well enough in the new city, Bashō decided to pay a visit to his native town for the first time since his move to Edo. He arrived in Ueno on or around July 30 and stayed there until August 11. Local poets seem to have been a little reserved in welcoming this radical Danrin poet, but they did invite him to several haikai gatherings. On his return journey to Edo, he took with him a nephew named Tōin who was in his sixteenth year at the time. For the rest of his short life, the young man was to remain in Bashō's care.

on the scales
Kyoto and Edo in balance
this everlasting spring

tenbin | ya | Kyō | Edo | kakete | chiyo | no | haru
scales | : | Kyoto | Edo | weighing | thousand-generations | 's | spring

NOTE

Kakete has a double meaning of "weighing" and "matching equally." In those days a balance was most often seen at a merchant's store.

COMMENTARY

The poem celebrates the happy, peaceful New Year's season in which Kyoto and Edo—namely, the emperor's court and the shogun's government—are in perfect harmony with each other. – *Kōseki*

The poet feels that with the New Year an "everlasting spring" has come to Kyoto and Edo alike. This expansive, large-scale view of the world is interesting. A similar viewpoint is often observable in Bashō's later poetry. – *Komiya*

Underneath the surface the poem may allude to the equal prosperity of branch stores in both Kyoto and Edo. Major commercial firms had stores in these two cities. – *Ōtani*

The poem pivots on the meaning of *kakete*. Furthermore, it offers a novel comparison by placing two thriving cities on a balance. But that is about all it does. – *Imoto*

Two cities weighed on a balance—a surprising comparison typical of the Danrin school. – *Kon*

the summer moon
coming out of Goyu—
into Akasaka already!

natsu I no I tsuki I Goyu I yori I idete I Akasaka I ya
summer I 's I moon I Goyu I from I exiting I Akasaka I !

NOTE

Goyu and Akasaka were two of the fifty-three post towns along the highway
from Edo to Kyoto and were located closer to each other than were any other
two cities on the way. Literally Goyu means "honorable oil" and Akasaka "red
slope." Bashō apparently liked this hokku: almost twenty years later he is reported to have said it was "a verse I am tempted to show off even now."

COMMENTARY

On the short night of summer the moon appeared to move as quickly as a traveler reaching Akasaka from Goyu. The description suggests no ordinary imagination, deeply impressing us. – *Donto*

Even a summer night could not have been as short as the time it took to travel
from Goyu to Akasaka. But the poet said so, resorting to his usual poetic hyper-
bole. It makes us visualize a traveler trekking under the summer moon. I think
this is an interesting poem. – *Meisetsu*

To describe the summer moon, the poet utilized the sense of color implied in the
place names, Goyu and Akasaka. The technique is not at all original; indeed, one
could blame it for being too commonplace. But aurally the poem creates a calm,
leisurely effect, suggesting something of the traveler's state of mind. – *Akutagawa*

The oily darkness of night, the bright, red, round moon—the poem's meaning
would become too obvious for its own good if it is explained this way, but undeniably a colorful scene of a highway under the summer moon is here vaguely
evoked. The vision is probably supported by the actual experience of the poet,
who once traveled this one-mile distance at night. – *Yamamoto*

The moon, personified here, walks the distance from Goyu to Akasaka. The
hokku suggests the shortness of the summer night by means of a Danrin-type
comparison. – *Kon*

1677

Partly because he now had Tōin to support, Bashō began working for the waterworks department in the local government of Edo, probably as a part-time official who did administrative work in the office. The employment was to last for the next four years. Around this time he moved to a rented house in the Odawara district in downtown Edo.

Late in 1677 Bashō contributed twenty verses to a colossal poetry contest, known as *Roppyakuban haikai hokku awase* (The hokku contest in six hundred rounds), that was sponsored by Fūko and entered by a total of sixty poets. Well-known haikai masters of the time, including Kigin and Saiganji Ninkō (1602–82), served as contest referees. Bashō won in nine of the matches, lost in five, and tied in six. His record was one of the best among the participants, placing him in the same rank as established masters like Yūzan. Around the end of the year he and Sodō joined Itō Shintoku (1633–98), a poet from Kyoto, to compose a haikai sequence of one hundred verses. The threesome were to meet again to write two more sequences in the following spring. The sequences were later published as *Edo sangin* (Three poets in Edo, 1678).

Cat in love

the lover cat
over a crumbled stove
comes and goes

neko | no | tsuma | hetsui | no | kuzure | yori | kayoikeri
cat | 's | mate | cooking-stove | 's | crumble | from | frequent

NOTE

Included in *Roppyakuban haikai hokku awase*. The hokku alludes to a story in *Ise monogatari* that describes how Ariwara Narihira (825–80) went to see his secret lover, an empress known as the Consort of the Second Ward. It begins: "Once upon a time there was a certain man who had a mistress living in the Gojō district of Kyoto. Because he was not to be seen by anyone in her house, he could not enter through the gate; he went in and out over a crumbled part of the earthen wall trampled on by children."

COMMENTARY

Those words allude to Narihira secretly going to see the Consort of the Second Ward. Accordingly, the cat in the hokku must be male. The scene of a crumbling earthen wall that appears in a courtly tale is here transformed into a scene featuring a broken-down cooking stove and a cat. It must be said that here is a humor typical of haikai. – *Nobutane*

I prefer a female cat to a male here. The poet changed a wall to a cooking stove and brought in a she-cat. The poem comes to contain a greater amount of haikai spirit when it is read this way. – *Chikurei*

For the word *tsuma* all the variant texts use the Chinese character signifying "wife." I think there is humor implied in the fact that when cats fall in love the female goes to the male while in human society the case is the reverse. The poem resorts to the usual Danrin technique of vulgarizing a classical theme.* – *Shūson*

---

*As one of the ways to produce laughter, Danrin poets ridiculed the aristocratic life and sensibility of Heian courtiers. Courtly love, a favorite motif in Heian poetry, was often given a ridiculously mundane setting by them, as is the case here.

long seasonal rain—
lighting dragon candles
a municipal guard

samidare I ya I ryūtō I aguru I bantarō
seasonal-rain I : I dragon-candle I offer I city-guard

NOTE

Included in *Roppyakuban haikai hokku awase* and refereed by Ninkō. *Ryūtō* refers to the mysterious fiery dots—probably a mirage—that people reported seeing far out on the sea at night. These were popularly believed to be lighted candles offered by a dragon to the sea gods.

COMMENTARY

A flood scene during the rainy season is skillfully described in the haikai style here. This should be the winning verse. – *Ninkō*

The lanterns under the eaves lighted by a watchman are here made part of the world of the dragon palace under the sea. The metaphor depicts a scene of seasonal rain bespattering the ground and creating a mist that extends as far as the eyes can see. – *Yakumu*

Red lights are seen high up in the dusk of a rainy evening. Under them is a guard post, where voices are heard. The poem makes one visualize a wet, desolate scene. – *Sokotsu*

The hokku focuses on the comparison of seasonal rain to the sea and of lights at a guard station to dragon candles. It is a poem characteristic of the Danrin style. – *Ebara*

Lanterns hanging high on the eaves of a guard station are here compared to dragon candles. Such a scene is difficult to imagine for a modern reader who does not know how dark the town streets were in those days. And those were the streets that looked like the sea during the rainy season. – *Yamamoto*

felling a tree
and gazing at the cut end—
tonight's moon

ki | wo | kirite | motokuchi | miru | ya | kyō | no | tsuki
tree | [acc.] | cutting | cut-end | see | : | today | 's | moon

NOTE

Motokuchi, a term used by lumbermen, refers to the end of a log that is closer to the root. It may have had a more general meaning of "origin" or "source" in Bashō's day.

COMMENTARY

I think this is a scene of moon viewing at a house near the beach. Some trees are standing alongside the sea, interrupting the view of the moon. The poet is saying, playfully, that he would like to cut down the trees and see the moonrise, "the moon's source." One should note the whimsical reference to the cut end of a tree. That is because the end is shaped like the moon. – *Ōsha*

The moonlight is pale but dazzling, with a tinge of blue. In the poet's imagination there emerges a vision of a pale, freshly cut end of a tree looming in the moonlight. It is a fascinating vision. – *Watsuji*

The roundness of the moon is here compared to the cut end of a tree. The vividness of the poem derives from the originality and truthfulness of that comparison. – *Iwata*

oh, nothing's happened to me!
yesterday has passed—
fugu soup

ara l nani l tomo l na l ya l kinō l wa l sugite l fukutojiru
oh l anything l ! l is-nonexistent l ! l yesterday l as-for l passing l fugu-soup

NOTE

Fukutojiru is a soup made of *fugu*, a kind of puffer fish that is famous for its delicious taste but whose intestines contain a deadly poison. The hokku's opening phrase was borrowed from an idiomatic expression that frequently occurs in the nō drama.

COMMENTARY

Human life is full of danger. — *Bakusui*

The poet ate fugu soup with a good deal of apprehension, but now he is able to say that was what he did yesterday. He now knows he has been fortunate enough to have escaped poisoning. The hokku, using a device of inversion, suggests the poet's relief. — *Mukō*

The tone of the poem suggests that the poet, now having completely recovered from his anxiety, feels like laughing heartily at himself. — *Seisensui*

Implied in the last two phrases is the sense of relief that one feels when a feared event is over with no damage done, and the sense of slackened tension that one feels when one's misgivings go unfulfilled. For a Danrin poet, such feelings probably seemed too simple to make into a poem. Accordingly Bashō introduced a nō idiom in the hokku's opening phrase and let its strong tone accentuate the feelings. — *Shūson*

CHAPTER TWO

Haikai Master in Edo

1678-1683

1678

It appears that on February 21, 1678, which was the lunar New Year's Day, Bashō for the first time in his career distributed *Saitanchō* (New Year's verses), a small collection of haikai verses he had written for the New Year with the help of his friends and disciples. Because only a recognized haikai master could do this with impunity, it indicates that Bashō had by this time sufficiently established himself as a poet and wanted to declare that fact to the world. Another event publicizing his new start took place that spring: the composition of ten thousand verses to celebrate his professional independence. A great many poets seem to have participated in the event, but except for one hokku no record of the verses has been preserved. Because *Saitanchō* has not survived either, one may conjecture that all these verses were deemed occasional compositions, not worth keeping for posterity.

Throughout the year Bashō seems to have been extremely active, associating with a great many poets, regardless of the haikai schools they belonged to. He wrote verses with them, he sent hokku to their anthologies, he served as a referee in their poetry contests. One motivating factor for such activities may have been his feeling of indebtedness to other poets who had helped him in writing those ten thousand verses. Another factor may have been his strained relationship with his mentor Yūzan, though there is no conclusive evidence to prove animosity between the two. In any case, he was now an independent haikai master responsible for a sizable number of students, and he had to work hard for that reason alone.

the Dutch consul too
is prostrate before His Lordship—
spring under His reign

kabitan | mo | tsukubawasekeri | kimi | ga | haru
captain | also | is-prostrate | lord | 's | spring

NOTE

Kabitan, a word derived from the Portuguese *capitaō* ("captain"), refers to the
Dutch consul in Nagasaki who, during much of the Edo period, paid a courtesy
visit to the shogun in Edo every spring.

COMMENTARY

Usually a Westerner sits in a chair and does not prostrate himself. But even he is
prostrate before His Lordship in the Japanese manner because of the lord's great
power. — *Sokotsu*

The reader senses a sentiment typical of an Edo bourgeois under Shogun Tsunayoshi's reign,* who felt that the shogun was great, that Japan was the finest and
strongest nation in the world, and that foreigners were weak, despicable barbari-
ans. — *Komiya*

Of all the verses written by Bashō, none shows so vulgar a taste as this one.
— *Saisei*

The poet's main purpose lies in praising the shogun's power and celebrating the
Japanese New Year. He has mentioned the Dutch "captain" only to underline
that purpose. More than anything else, the exotic sound of that foreign word
must have appealed to the poet. Danrin poets, always fond of novelty, had no
hesitation in using topics and words imported from the West. — *Abe M.*

*Tokugawa Tsunayoshi (1646–1709) became shogun in 1680 and remained in that post
until his death. His reign saw the rapid rise of the merchant class, which had been accumu-
lating wealth during the many years of peace under the Tokugawa rule.

rainy day—
bounding the world's autumn
Boundary Town

ame | no | hi | ya | seken | no | aki | wo | Sakaichō
rain | 's | day | : | world | 's | autumn | [acc.] | Sakaichō

NOTE

NOTE

Sakaichō was an amusement district of Edo where many theaters and geisha houses were located. The name of the town literally means "boundary town," hence Bashō's play on words.

COMMENTARY

In the quietly falling autumn rain the whole world is permeated with loneliness except this Sakaichō, where there is a great deal of merrymaking. It is as if there were a boundary line marking off the rest of the world. – *Chikurei*

It is autumn everywhere else, but this district brims with good cheer even on a rainy day. In saying this, the poet is showing off what a man about town he is. – *Keion*

Autumn rain touches one's heart, but that does not apply in Sakaichō. The implications of the poem are the same as:

dark night—   yami no yo wa
only in Yoshiwara   Yoshiwara bakari
the moonlight   tsukiyo kana*
                              – *Rohan*

Lively Sakaichō, as presented here, has not only its bright side but also its dark side, for it is juxtaposed with "the world's autumn." While some consumers had a good time in large cities, the people in general were in extreme poverty at this time. In 1674 there were deaths from starvation; in 1675 many samurai were so hard pressed that they had to be given a special ration of rice; in 1677 the government issued a decree prohibiting all extravagance; and in 1679 general poverty reached an alarming level. Bashō did not deliberately hint at such social conditions here, but the reader can sense them when he reflects on the fact that the

---

* Yoshiwara was a licensed quarter in Edo. The poem is one of the better-known hokku by Kikaku.

literature of the time was being supported by a small number of prosperous merchants, while samurai and farmers were impoverished. At this time Bashō too was one of those poets who derived their support from such merchants, but he could not completely become one of them. Such an image of Bashō looms vaguely in this poem, I think. — *Shūson*

1679

In the autumn of 1679 Bashō took part in writing a couple of hundred-verse haikai sequences to honor two poets setting out on a journey to Kyoto. Otherwise he does not seem to have been as active poetically as he had been the previous year. According to a haikai book published in this year, he had already shaved his head and become a lay monk. Perhaps he was beginning to feel his lifestyle had to change.

Hollanders too
have come for the blossoms—
saddle a horse!

Oranda | mo | hana | ni | kinikeri | uma | ni | kura
Hollander | also | blossom | for | has-come | horse | on | saddle

NOTE

The Hollanders in the hokku refer to a procession of the Dutch consul and his at-
tendants who came from Nagasaki to Edo to pay respects to the shogun in the
spring. The hokku's first two phrases were borrowed from a well-known passage
in the nō play *Kurama Tengu*, which had in turn utilized a waka by Minamoto
Yorimasa (1104–80):

When the blossoms bloom,	hana sakaba
will you let me know? I had asked	tsugemu to iishi
the forest ranger . . .	yamazato no
Now that I hear him coming,	tsukai wa kitari
put a saddle on my horse!	uma ni kura oke

COMMENTARY

The annual spring visit of the Dutch was an event that added color to Japanese
life. The hokku draws on it and says the foreigners also have come to see Japanese blossoms. There is an interesting juxtaposition between cherry blossoms
and a Dutchman skillfully riding a horse. – *Donto*

Blossoms are mentioned only as a season word; they are fictional and probably
stand for the nation's prosperity. – *Tosai*

Although it has borrowed words from a nō, the poem has not fallen to the level
of mere wordplay; on the contrary, the borrowing has enriched its aftereffect.
– *Ebara*

According to a journal written by the physician Engelbert Kaempfer, who traveled with the Dutch mission between Nagasaki and Edo in 1691 and 1692, so
many restrictions were placed on the foreigners' behavior that they practically led
a prisoner's life during their stay in Edo. It goes without saying that they were
not permitted to go out for blossom viewing. The words "for the blossoms" in
this poem therefore mean something like "to this thriving city of Edo during the
blossom season." – *Imoto*

Instead of a forest ranger, a Dutchman has come all the way to Edo to see the blossoms, riding on a saddled horse. By saying that even a strange-looking European has come, the poet implicitly praises the beauty and prosperity of Edo in springtime. Superimposed on that image is the phrase of the original waka—"put a saddle on my horse!"—the superimposition adding the meaning "I too will saddle a horse and set out for blossom viewing in Edo." – *Yamamoto*

on the blue ocean
waves smell of rice wine—
tonight's moon

sōkai | no | nami | sake | kusashi | kyō | no | tsuki
blue-sea | 's | wave | rice-wine | smell | today | 's | moon

NOTE

There is a pun on the word *tsuki* ("moon"), which can also mean "wine cup"
when written in a different character. The images of the blue ocean and the autumn moon have been borrowed from the nō play *Shari* (Sarira), where they appear in a strictly religious context.

COMMENTARY

The harvest moon was about to rise above the ocean. It resembled a red-
lacquered wine cup being lifted from a washbowl. The ocean looked like the
bowl, which smelled of wine. This is a subjective poem based on an objective observation. — *Kōseki*

Since it was the full moon, the poet rowed out to sea for moon viewing. The sea,
which had been blue in the daytime, was also blue at night because there was the
moon. The waves smelled of rice wine. That was because the poet, stretching his
hand from the boat, had washed his cup in the sea a number of times. It is an exaggeration to say that the sea smells of wine because it has been used for a washbowl. But what we have here is poetic exaggeration, and for that reason it has
turned into poetic truth. — *Seishi*

1680

Bashō's school published two books in 1680, thereby demonstrating its success as well as the solidarity among its students. The first, entitled *Tōsei montei dokugin nijikkasen* (Twenty solo kasen sequences by Tō-sei's disciples), was a collection of twenty-one haikai sequences (one was appended later, hence the discrepancy with the title), each sequence consisting of thirty-six verses written by a student alone. Bashō's leading disciples, such as Kikaku, Sanpū, and Hattori Ransetsu (1654–1707), all contributed their works. The quality of the poetry was uneven, but the book publicized the fact that Bashō's school already had more than twenty students whose work was publishable. The second book, called *Haikai awase* (Haikai contests), comprised "Inaka no kuawase" (The rustic hokku contest) by Kikaku and "Tokiwaya no kuawase" (The evergreen hokku contest) by Sanpū. Each contest consisted of fifty hokku matched in twenty-five rounds, to which Bashō added a referee's commentary. The book helped to establish the reputation of his two leading disciples. And, more importantly, it also showed that his school was beginning to abandon Danrin-type poetry in favor of verses with a Chinese flavor in theme and wording.

That winter Bashō moved to a house in the Fukagawa district of Edo on the eastern side of the Sumida River. Located in a quieter, more rustic area, the new residence was a sharp contrast to his previous home downtown. The move also meant that he would no longer correct verses for a fee, a practice that was the biggest source of income for a haikai master. Bashō did not explain the reason for his move, except to cite the lines of a poem by the famous Chinese poet Po Chü-i (772–846):

> Since antiquity Chang-an has been a place for those seeking fame and fortune,
> a place rough for a traveler empty-handed and penniless.

To Bashō, Edo must have seemed like Chang-an. Just when the years of hard work in Edo had begun to bring him fame if not fortune, he may have realized that was not what he wanted.

spider—what is it,
what is it you are crying?
autumn wind

kumo | nani | to | ne | wo | nani | to | naku | aki | no | kaze
spider | what | thus | voice | [acc.] | what | thus | chirp | autumn | 's | wind

NOTE

May have had the headnote "Insect." The hokku probably alludes to a passage in
Makura no sōshi (The pillow book, 10th c.) recounting the sad fate of a bagworm, which was popularly believed to cry for its mother when the autumn
wind begins to blow. A bagworm is the larva of a certain kind of moth; it does
not cry.

COMMENTARY

Most poets writing on the topic "Insect" would refer to an insect's singing, but
Bashō here has gone beyond normal expectations. By pointing at a spider, he has
distilled the loneliness of the autumn wind. – *Nanimaru*

The hokku's first two phrases have the tone of someone who, talking to another
person, asks successive questions—"What about a spider?" "On what occasion
does it sing beautifully?" "With what voice does it chirp?" Also implied is a feeling that, regardless of what the spider or anyone else may say, the poet feels autumn's arrival because of the wind. The repetition of the word "what" creates an
impression of Zen-type dialogue, too. This is a poem loaded with meaning.
– *Sokotsu*

The hokku tactfully makes the reader visualize a desolate house with a spider's
web, through which the lonely autumn wind is blowing. It is a fine poem.
– *Chikurei*

This spider, as seen by the poet, is not the cruel spider that catches small insects
and devours them. It is the spider that crouches, forever silent, listening to the
gay chirping of autumn insects. Perhaps Bashō himself is muttering here. Yet, although his questions seem to be loud and animated, the poem has an intimate
quality, as if he has learned the spider's secrets and is talking to it from within. It
is the spider's heart that he addresses—and his own, too. The effect is a strange
one, since the poem relies primarily on a Danrin technique. – *Shūson*

The hokku's middle phrase is no academic inquiry into the cries of insects—a cricket's for instance. Rather, it inquires why a spider does not try to plead aloud. Such a question, being rhetorical, looks into the poet's heart, the lonely heart that has a great deal to plead but lacks the opportunity. The poem has elements of parody in its motif and of Danrin-type humor in its wording, but it is more than a comic poem that depends on wordplay; it is a metaphorical poem with a multilayered form and meaning. – *Yamamoto*

night . . . silently
in the moonlight, a worm
digs into a chestnut

yoru | hisokani | mushi | wa | gekka | no | kuri | wo | ugatsu
night | stealthily | worm | as-for | under-the-moon | 's | chestnut | [acc.] | bore

NOTE

One text has the headnote "The later harvest moon," which denotes the moon of
the thirteenth night of the lunar ninth month. It was also known as "the chestnut
moon" because it was the custom to offer chestnuts to the moon on this night.
The hokku alludes to a line of Fu Wen's poem, "The night rain silently digs into
the moss on the rocks." Nothing is known about the Chinese poet Fu Wen. Bashō seems to have read the line in a popular eleventh-century anthology entitled
Wakan rōeishū (The collection of Japanese and Chinese verse).

COMMENTARY

One cannot overlook the fact that Bashō, in departing from the Danrin style,
was for a time inclined toward the use of difficult Chinese words as well as serious literary themes. This hokku can be said to foreshadow that transition. – *Seihō*

Although what the poem says is not the impression of an eyewitness, there is a
sense of the pale moonlight penetrating the heart of things. The poet's imagination is extremely precise. – *Seisensui*

The poet has tried to emphasize the serene tranquillity of the later harvest moon by
eliminating everything that moves, except a tiny worm single-mindedly digging
into a chestnut. The poetic eye that captured this quiet scene is very sharp.
– *Shūson*

The poet first established a setting of moonlit tranquillity and then, in typical
haikai manner, presented a worm noiselessly boring a hole in a chestnut. The
poem shocks the reader by bringing out the unexpected. That element of surprise
is reminiscent of the Danrin style, yet the poem not only surprises but deeply stirs
the reader with its image of the bright moon of the thirteenth night and its suggestion of all things under it reposing in calm. – *Imoto*

As I read this hokku, I see in my mind an open chestnut bur on a branch bathed
in the moonlight. Then I hear, in a world that reposes in total quietness, the extremely faint sound of a worm eating into a chestnut. – *Komiya*

on a bare branch
a crow has alighted . . .
autumn nightfall

kareeda | ni | karasu | no | tomarikeri | aki | no | kure
bare-branch | on | crow | 's | is-perched | autumn | 's | evening

NOTE

There survive three paintings on which Bashō wrote this hokku. The one assumed to be the earliest depicts seven crows settled on a leafless tree, with twenty
others flying in the sky. The other two paintings show only one crow perching on
a branch of a bare tree.

COMMENTARY

The modern style. – *Takamasa*

As a leader of the Danrin school Bashō had been having a hard time, when
Kigin, feeling sympathetic, came for a visit and had a talk with him and Sodō
over a cup of tea. The three masters discussed possible ways in which to soften
the excesses of the Danrin style, and in the end Bashō was urged to take leader-
ship in the matter. Thereupon he wrote the crow poem, saying it might point in a
new direction. – *Ritō*

The poet, tired of viewing spring flowers and autumn leaves, distilled the dusky
loneliness of the fall season in the image of a crow. On a desolate autumn evening, his soul alighted on the crow. – *Donto*

Mindless, natural. – *Bakusui*

A legend says that Kigin, Bashō, and Sodō talked over a cup of tea with the intent of launching a new poetic style, but I doubt the authenticity of the legend
because in actuality Kigin and Sodō never met. – *Somaru*

Sankashū [The collection of the mountain hut, 12th c.] by the monk Saigyō
[1118–90] includes the waka [no. 997]:

On a tree standing	furuhata no
by the cliff in an old farm	soba no tatsu ki ni
a dove . . .	iru hato no
How lonely its voice	tomo yobu koe no
calling for a friend this evening!	sugoki yūgure

on a bare branch
a crow has alighted . . .
autumn nightfall

One of the two later
paintings on the poem.
Calligraphy by Bashō;
painting by his disciple
Morikawa Kyoriku
(1656–1715).
Reproduced from
Zusetsu Nihon no
koten: Bashō Buson
(Shūeisha), by
permission of Idemitsu
Art Museum.

The hokku creates an effect similar to that waka, but it is more purely descriptive and internalizes loneliness to a greater extent. One can see the essence of haikai here. – *Tosai*

I do not understand why this hokku has been said to represent the ultimate of *yūgen* and of the Bashō style. I would not deny the fact that the poem rings true in presenting a desolate scene of late autumn. The manner of presentation is not bad, either. Yet the poem is a direct translation of the Chinese phrase "a chilly-looking crow on a bare tree," a phrase one hears so often from scholars in Chinese. I feel this is a plain, ordinary poem, the like of which could have been written by many poets other than Bashō. However, if it is found that such a phrase or scene was not widely known in literature and art in Bashō's day, the hokku would increase in value and have to be placed several ranks higher. – *Shiki*

Although this can be read as a poem of *shasei*, it also contains something different from *shasei*—an aesthetic of "loneliness" handed down from the medieval waka tradition. One might say that that aesthetic is too obvious, too forced, or too deliberate, but in my opinion Bashō was trying to produce a model verse for the haikai of the future. – *Mizuho*

This is a poem of *shibumi*, the kind of poem which emerges when the subject is stripped of all its glitter and reduced to its bare skeleton. – *Handa*

A chilly-looking crow perched on a bare tree is the kind of picture one is likely to find in Chinese art, and simply combining it with autumn nightfall cannot be construed as displaying the poet's great craftsmanship. However, among contemporary Danrin verses that make much of novelty, this hokku does stand out distinctly. It was in Bashō's later years, and after he became more confident in his art, that he said: "Poetry of other schools is like colored painting. Poetry of my school should be written as if it were black-ink painting." Whatever led Bashō to such a position may have had its origin in this poem. – *Seihō*

This hokku is not a mere sketch but expresses the poetic spirit of Bashō the eternal traveler. His tears express a wanderer's loneliness and the helpless solitude of all human life. In short, an exemplary lyric. – *Hagiwara*

At a glance a reader may find it difficult to decide whether the bare branch in the poem is alive or dead. But when he appreciates the poem more deeply he will naturally come to conclude that it is dead. Bashō's own painting that accompanies the poem also supports this reading. – *Shida*

The aesthetic which the poet discovered in writing this hokku can be said to be a revival of the principles of *hie*, *yase*, and *karabi*, which Shinkei advocated as the ideals of renga. In this sense one may say that the poetic spirit cherished by the Zen monks of the Five Mountains was transmitted to Bashō by way of Shōtetsu and Shinkei.*_Hakuhatsushū_ [The white hair collection, 1563?] cites a renga verse as an example of _hie_ and _yase_:

evening crow—   yūgarasu
in a bare tree on the mountain peak   mine no kareki ni
a voice   koe wa shite

This verse aims at a simpler effect. Indeed, if it were a hokku, Bashō's poem would surely be blamed for being too close to it. – _Yamamoto_

*Shōtetsu (1381–1459), a leading waka poet of his time, developed a unique poetics of his own and expounded it in his writings. Shinkei (1406–75), a poet who wrote both waka and renga and a disciple of Shōtetsu, spent much of his life in traveling; his writings on the art of renga exerted a good deal of influence on later poets. The Five Mountains refer to five major Zen temples in and around Kyoto. During the fourteenth and fifteenth centuries, monks living on those mountains wrote a great number of poems in Chinese.

where is the shower?
with an umbrella in his hand
a monk returns

izuku | shigure | kasa | wo | te | ni | sagete | kaeru | sō
where | winter-shower | umbrella | [acc.] | hand | in | carrying | return |
monk

NOTE

Alludes to a passage in Chang Tu's prose poem: "As the endless expanse of misty rain begins to clear, there emerges a heron standing on a winter shore. Where many folds of mountain fog end, a monk returns to an evening temple." Little is known about Chang Tu, although this and other citations from his poetry appear in *Wakan rōeishū*.

COMMENTARY

An evening scene with mountains nearby. – *Bakusui*

The poet is probably asking the monk whether he has succeeded in gaining satori after wandering through the provinces. – *Tosai*

The poet wondered where the shower might be, for he noticed a monk carrying an umbrella with him. The image of the monk goes well with the winter shower. It should be counted among Bashō's finer hokku written before the Genroku period [1688–1704]. – *Rika*

Rika's reading ignores the fact that the monk had been rained on. I think the poet wrote the hokku when he observed a monk who, having met a shower, carried a dripping umbrella in his hand. The poem sounds more attractive when it is taken as describing a scene *after* the shower. – *Mukō*

This is no longer the world of Danrin-type humor. The poet's predilection for *sabi* is already evident. – *Ebara*

The poem is distinguished by the superior craftsmanship with which the poet clearly identified the nature of a winter shower, falling unpredictably wherever it may choose. The poet must also have prided himself on the stroke of imagination that made the image of a returning monk follow immediately on that of a desolate winter shower. It is an image charged with the type of beauty seen in Chinese poetry. The word "returns" evokes the mood of nightfall without saying so explicitly. – *Hori*

After living an austere life in the city for nine springs and autumns, I have now moved to the Fukagawa district. Is it because I am poor and wretched that I share the feeling of someone who said, "Since antiquity Chang-an has been a place for those seeking fame and fortune, a place rough for a traveler empty-handed and penniless"?

toward the brushwood gate
it sweeps the tea leaves—
stormy wind

shiba | no | to | ni | cha | wo | konoha | kaku | arashi | kana
brushwood | 's | gate | at | tea | [acc.] | tree-leaf | sweep | storm | kana

COMMENTARY

The poet's hut is so humble that its gate is nothing more than brushwood strung together. There is nothing especially attractive there, except a tea plant whose leaves have fallen in the storm and are waiting to be cleaned up. Here is a scene of winter coming to a tea plant and scattering its leaves. — *Sokotsu*

The sincerity of this poem has an undeniable power. There is still a trace of Ba-shō's early style—the storm wind "sweeping" tea leaves—but the trace is so faint that the reader does not notice it unless he deliberately looks for it. We see the poet's eyes gazing squarely at nature. — *Shūson*

Probably at the entrance to Bashō's house in Fukagawa there was a tea farm where a considerable number of tea plants grew, and every winter dead leaves were scattered everywhere in the area. — *Komiya*

The poem brings together two images: that of the poet gathering fallen leaves for boiling tea water, and that of the winter storm gathering leaves into a drift. Although the language is of Danrin type, the poem aims to suggest a life of *wabi* in the modest hut. — *Abe K.*

The storm wind is gathering dead leaves for the indigent resident of the hut in order that he can, without effort, start a fire, boil water, and make tea. That is the way the poet, seeing the leaves driven by a strong wind, described the scene. — *Abe M.*

Sentiment of a winter night in Fukagawa

the sound of an oar slapping the waves
chills my bowels through
this night . . . tears

ro | no | koe | nami | wo | utte | harawata | kōru | yo | ya | namida
oar | 's | voice | wave | [acc.] | beating | intestine | freeze | night | : | tear

NOTE

Ro no koe, literally "an oar's voice," may refer either to the squeak of an oar in the oarlocks or the sound of an oar beating the water. Bashō made the meaning no clearer when, later on, he wrote two *haibun* that end with this hokku. One, probably written in 1682, starts with a quotation from the Chinese poet Tu Fu (712–70):

"Within the window frames, a western peak capped with snow of one thousand
   years old.
Outside the gate, an eastern boat that has come ten thousand leagues across the
   sea.
I recognize the poem but do not see what it means. I yearn after its *wabi* but have not tasted its delight. I excel Master Tu Fu only in the number of illnesses I suffer from. In the shade of banana leaves at a modest hut, I call myself an old beggar."

The other piece, which has been preserved in a book published in 1800, says: "Near the river's fork in Fukagawa I live a lonely life at a modest hut, viewing snow-capped Mt. Fuji far away and ocean-bound boats nearby. In the morning I watch white waves in the wake of a boat leaving the harbor, and in the evening I feel the wind coming through withered reeds. Sitting in the moonlight, I grumble over my empty cask; going to bed, I worry over my thin quilt."

COMMENTARY

The number of syllables is excessive and the language is unpolished, yet the emotion is calm and peaceful. – *Yasuyoshi*

The poet, unable to go to sleep, must be pondering over time that has passed and time that is to come. – *Tosai*

An oar squeaks when plied. In spring or summer the squeak may sound pleasant or cool to the ear, but it is felt to be sad on a winter night. As the sound hit the waves its reverberation pierced the poet's ears, its sadness going through his body and moving him so deeply that he felt as if his tears were frozen. – *Rika*

At times Bashō attempted to give vent to his emotions in this kind of rugged style, which is reminiscent of Chinese poetry. This is a fine meditative poem expressing a delicate emotion in powerful language. – *Momota*

The internal rhythm, which demands a broken form, emerges clearly from the grandiose means of expression. The tone is poignant and touching; neither the squeak of the oar nor the sound of waves is a mere external object but has been integrated into the poet's inner landscape. – *Yamamoto*

Undeniably, the poem contains a degree of exaggeration and artifice, but it makes the reader visualize the profile of the poet, now in his thirty-seventh or thirty-eighth year, sitting alone in a rustic hut and pondering various things in life. – *Imoto*

Rich people enjoy themselves by eating the finest meat, and aspiring youths sustain themselves by chewing vegetable roots. As for myself, I am a poor man.

the morning of snow—
all alone, I chew
dried salmon meat

yuki I no I ashita I hitori I karazake I wo I kami I etari
snow I 's I morning I alone I dried-salmon I [acc.] I chew I can

NOTE

In Japan at that time dried salmon was considered an ordinary food item, neither especially extravagant nor especially modest. As appears below, some commentators believe the headnote alludes to a famous remark by Wang Hsin-min, a Chinese philosopher who lived during the Sung dynasty.

COMMENTARY

Because vegetables are buried under snow in winter, there is neither anything green in the soup nor anything new in the main dish day after day. That dreary feeling is suggested in the image of dried salmon. – *Donto*

That morning the poet was fortunate enough to have dried salmon, which he usually did not have. Chewing the salmon meat, he was able to admire the snow scene. The hokku vividly conveys the sense of Bashō's lonely life, the sense of his being satisfied with it, the sense of his feeling excited on a snowy morning, and the sense of his being proud of eating salmon meat. This is a forceful poem. – *Sokotsu*

The poem presents the life of *wabi* as led by a haikai poet, which is distinctly different from that of a rich man or of an aspiring youth. – *Kōseki*

"I" in the headnote can, but need not, be identified as one of the "aspiring youths," and that ambiguity leads to two different interpretations. The poem may embody the sentiment of a poet who, not being rich, chews dried salmon meat and considers himself a struggling young man with plenty of ambition. Or it may be read as depicting a haikai poet who, being neither a rich man nor an aspiring youth, chews dried salmon meat and lives a life of *wabi*. As far as I have been able to determine, more readers subscribe to the latter interpretation. But I dare to take the former view. — *Shūson*

Like the crow poem, this hokku suggests the temperament of a recluse as seen through Chinese poetry; indeed, the hokku's last two phrases carry the tone of actual Chinese language. But that passion for the hermit's life has not yet become instinctive; rather, it still includes elements of dandyism. — *Imoto*

The headnote is indebted to Wang Hsin-min's words: "A person who can get along just by chewing vegetable roots all the time will be able to achieve hundreds of things." The hokku implies that the poet, not being an aspiring youth, is chewing not vegetable roots but dried salmon meat—and is therefore achieving very little. In rugged, Chinese-type language the poet is suggesting his true motive for moving into the humble hut. — *Yamamoto*

The poet had been trying not to envy the wealthy or emulate the ambitious, and yet he found himself not completely succeeding in that attempt. Realizing that, he reconfirmed to himself the resolutions he had made at the very beginning. Something of that reconfirmation is contained in this hokku, I think. No doubt Bashō used such direct language as "I chew" in the poem because he did not want the austerity of his resolve to be softened by the lyricism with which he expressed it. — *Hori*

1681

In spring Bashō received a banana plant (*bashō* in Japanese) from a student named Rika as a gift for his new home. According to his own description, the plant grew so well in his yard that its large leaves "dwarfed my garden and almost hid the eaves of my hut." Neighbors began calling the house "the Bashō Hut" and its resident "Master Bashō." The poet liked the nickname and adopted it as his pseudonym, although he never completely abandoned the name Tōsei. The earliest surviving evidence for his use of the new name is his signature to a letter dated September 7, 1681.

Although he no longer corrected verses for fees, Bashō did not discontinue teaching poetry. Indeed, his new life-style itself taught students what the life of a poet should be. From time to time he also hosted a verse-writing party, a poetry contest, or some such event in his hut. Verses written there on one of those occasions were published in September as part of a book he had compiled under the title *Jiin* (Sequel verses). He chose this odd title because he considered the book a sequel to *Shichihyaku gojū-in* (Seven hundred and fifty verses), a haikai collection which had been compiled by Itō Shintoku and published in Kyoto six months earlier. Bashō had admired Shintoku's anthology for its Chinese flavor and wanted to emulate the style in his own work. Actually, he and the three students of his who contributed to *Jiin* went beyond their model, for their verses succeeded to a greater extent in capturing the spirit of Chinese poetry, thereby transcending the world of Danrin-type humor.

Bashō seems to have been attracted to Chinese poetry for two main reasons. One was his interest in Taoism, which he thought might lead him away from the turmoil of everyday life and into the world of nature where he could regain his true self. He became an avid reader of *Chuang-tzu*, a Taoist classic attributed to Chuang-tzu (traditional dates 369–286 B.C.), so much so that he even called himself Kukusai at times, deriving the name from a word appearing in it. Both the opening and closing verses of *Jiin* allude to *Chuang-tzu*, and a number of verses and passages he wrote on other occasions at around this time show Taoist influence, too. The other element of Chinese poetry that appealed to Bashō was Zen Buddhism. The realm of satori promised by Zen was a little different from what Taoist recluses aimed to attain, but it equally seemed to provide a means of transcending the mundane. Conveniently for Bashō, there was a Zen monk living in his new neighborhood. Butchō (1642– 1716), head of a Zen temple in Hitachi Province (Ibaraki Prefecture), was temporarily staying in Fukagawa because of a lawsuit involving his parish. Bashō practiced Zen meditation under the monk's guidance, although no record surviving today specifies when and where he did so. His commitment to Zen was a serious one, for he was later to recall "at one time I thought of confining myself within the doors of a monastery." Allusions to Zen are scattered through his poetry and other writings, even though it is sometimes difficult to tell whether they refer directly to Zen or are simply reflections of Japanese culture, which had assimilated Zen by Bashō's time.

under the waterweeds
whitefish swarm . . . they would fade away
if put on my palm

mo | ni | sudaku | shirauo | ya | toraba | kienu | beki
waterweed | at | swarm | whitefish | : | if-taken | disappear | should

NOTE

Shirauo, literally "whitefish," is a kind of icefish, a small, slender fish that lives in the waters near China and Japan. Two to three inches long, it looks almost transparent in the water but turns to silvery white once out of the water.

COMMENTARY

The lovely, delicate shape of a whitefish stimulated the imagination of the poet who, watching the fish swarming in the waterweeds, fancied that they would melt away the instant he scooped them up in his hand. — *Kōseki*

This poem is markedly different from Bashō's earlier verses, which could be appreciated only by a reader who knows what they allude to. Clearly it is focused on the impression of the whitefish itself. — *Seihō*

If one ponders over the hokku's opening phrase and then the remainder, one will notice each part has a waka-like expression. The entire poem is composed to resemble waka in outlook. — *Shūson*

Man'yōshū has a waka that reads:

White dew will fade away	shiratsuyu wo
if put on my palm . . .	toraba kenubeshi
Now, gentlemen,	iza kodomo
let us compete with the dew	tsuyu ni kioite
and enjoy viewing the bush clover.	hagi no asobi semu*

The wording of the two poems is so similar that a coincidence is out of the question. Yet, while the image of white dew immediately leads to the words "will fade away," the transition from a whitefish to "would fade away if put on my palm" shows something of haikai, not of waka. When one hears of white dew

* *Man'yōshū*, no. 2173. One of the nine anonymous waka collectively introduced by the headnote "On dewdrops."

disappearing on the palm of a hand, one thinks of it as a plain, ordinary happening. But when one hears that whitefish "would fade away if put on my palm," one vividly visualizes a swarm of icy, transparent, clean, and lovely fish near a seashore in early spring. The hokku affords us a glimpse of Bashō's rich poetic talent—of the sharpness of sensory perception with which he captured his subject. —*Imoto*

Rika gave me a banana plant.

by my new banana plant
the first sign of something I loathe—
a miscanthus bud

bashō I uete I mazu I nikumu I ogi I no I futaba I kana
banana-plant I planting I first I hate I miscanthus I 's I seed-lobe I kana

NOTE

Little is known about Rika, a student of Bashō's, although a good number of his
verses have been preserved. The miscanthus referred to here is a variety of reed, a
strong weed that grows fast in a low-lying, swampy area like Fukagawa.

COMMENTARY

Up until that time Bashō's yard had looked lonely, with nothing but miscanthus
growing there. All there had been for the poet to enjoy was the sight of miscanthus buds, which were beginning to come out in spring. Now there was a banana
plant he had received for a gift. The plant looked so fresh and new in his yard
that the miscanthus did not look as attractive as before. He no longer cared for
the miscanthus. Instead, he wanted healthy growth for the banana plant; he was
sure that the gift plant, when larger, would add beauty to his hut. This poem is
Bashō's thanks to Rika for the gift. – *Sokotsu*

The poet had planted the banana but was afraid its growth might be obstructed
by the roots of the miscanthus seen everywhere in that riverside area. In this
poem, then, the poet is saying he detests even a miscanthus bud. I have another
interpretation that may seem a little dogmatic. The tone of the hokku's first two
phrases makes me wonder if the banana plant may not stand for a bachelor and
the seed lobes for a married couple. The poem then could be read as a praise for
the carefree life of a single man. – *Higuchi*

In his yard the poet had planted a banana plant given him by Rika, and was
looking forward eagerly to the sight of its cool green leaves. But, even before the
plant began to grow, he saw a miscanthus shoot coming up because it was near
the river. Its leaves were shaped like banana leaves, only much smaller, and the
poet did not like that. – *Kōseki*

What makes the poem interesting is the way it distinguishes clearly between love and hate. — *Ebara*

This hokku can be said to provide good source material for judging Bashō's character. Bashō certainly did not hate a miscanthus for what it was. But he could not help hating it for being able to spoil his banana plant. Bashō must have been a person whose love of good (or beauty) and hatred of evil (or ugliness) admitted no compromise in all matters like this. Having no supporting document, I cannot say for certain what his love for the banana plant led him to do with the miscanthus bud. To judge from the force of this poem, though, I imagine he immediately uprooted it. — *Komiya*

As if writing in a diary, the poet took note of a trivial happening in his life and made it into a hokku. — *Yamamoto*

The poet had planted a banana and been praying for its healthy growth when miscanthus buds began to invade the area, as if they had only been waiting for the wind to blow. Although they were still buds, the poet was disturbed to sense what they were feeling. Banana leaves are easily torn in the wind, whereas miscanthus are admired for the rustle of their leaves, as evidenced by such a common phrase as "a wind over the miscanthus" in classical poetry. The theme of the poem lies in this irreconcilable conflict between the demands of these two poetic subjects. — *Hori*

in the seasonal rain
a crane's legs
have become short

samidare | ni | tsuru | no | ashi | mijikaku | nareri
fifth-month-rain | in | crane | 's | leg | short | have-become

NOTE

Draws on a passage in *Chuang-tzu* which, in advising that things be left in their natural state, says: "A wild duck has short legs, but it would be distressed if they were to be lengthened. A crane has long legs, but it would be saddened if they were to be shortened."

COMMENTARY

A crane has long legs. But they looked shorter in the water, which had become deeper during the rainy season. The poet described that sight by making a subjective assertion. – *Kōseki*

The humor in this hokku has its source in Chuang-tzu's allegory; therein lies the poet's pride as well as a characteristic feature of his haikai at this time. – *Ebara*

This is not a descriptive poem saying that a crane's legs look shorter because of deeper water during the rainy season. Rather, it is an allegorical poem implying that a crane's legs look shorter but have not been cut off. Readers will miss its humor unless they know Chuang-tzu's allegory. – *Yamamoto*

The poet is poking fun at Chuang-tzu by saying that a crane has broken the law of nature. The hokku has an abnormal syllable pattern of 5-5-7. – *Kon*

a fool in the dark
grabs a bramble—
firefly hunt

gu I ni I kuraku I ibara I wo I tsukamu I hotaru I kana
folly I in I dark I bramble I [acc.] I grab I firefly I kana

NOTE

Kuraku, as in the English word "dark," can mean either physical or metaphorical darkness.

COMMENTARY

Unable to see in the darkness of night and absorbed in an exciting firefly hunt, a man accidentally grabbed a bramble. Reading this hokku, we should remind ourselves of those pleasures that will do us harm if we are too absorbed in them. – *Donto*

This hokku seems to satirize a person who falls into an error because of his own greed. – *Tosai*

The poet saw a firefly that had settled not on a soft blade of grass but on a thorny bramble. Thereupon he speculated that the firefly must be none too brilliant during daylight hours, although at nighttime it flits about freely by its own light. That, I think, is what the poet meant by the hokku's opening phrase. – *Komiya*

The meaning of the poem centers on the loss of judgment suffered by a person who was too intent on catching a firefly. The lesson can be applied to life in general. The poem utilizes an allegorical device borrowed from *Chuang-tzu*, a device that was central to the art of the Danrin school. – *Shūson*

An allegorical poem on the folly of a person who is too preoccupied with one thing to reflect on other things. Probably self-derision. – *Kon*

moonflowers so white
at night, alongside the outhouse
in the light of a torch

yūgao | no | shiroku | yoru | no | kōka | ni | shisoku | torite
moonflower | 's | white | night | 's | outhouse | at | torch | holding

NOTE

Alludes to a scene in the chapter "Yūgao" (Moonflower) in *Genji monogatari*,
where Prince Genji reads Lady Moonflower's poem by torchlight. *Kōka*, literally
"hindhouse," is a Zen term for an outhouse, which was usually located behind
the monastery.

COMMENTARY

Moonflowers bloom at night. The poet, carrying a torch in his hand, went to the
outhouse and was surprised to find moonflowers blooming on the roof. In the
torchlight, the flowers looked indescribably beautiful. This is a hokku written by
a master; a poet of lesser talent should not try to emulate it. – *Donto*

A scene at an inn. – *Bakusui*

In a setting like this it would be more effective, I think, to show a woman going
to the outhouse, but I suppose it was the poet himself in this hokku. – *Sokotsu*

Moonflower vines had climbed up a fence by the outhouse. The poet, about to open
the door, happened to cast his eyes toward the fence and saw white flowers looming dimly in the torchlight. The poem is impressionistic and refreshing. – *Komiya*

With a meter that follows a 5-3-3-4-3-3 syllable pattern, the poem uses what
may be called an extra-long haiku method. – *Seisensui*

If we read the poem as presenting a scene from Heian court life, we should imagine an elegantly beautiful lady—like Lady Moonflower—with an attendant carrying a torch for her. If we take it to be a scene from the Edo period, we should
visualize, dimly in the torchlight, the face of a daughter of an illustrious house
going to the outhouse. Or she could be a geisha of the Yoshiwara or Shimabara
district in Edo. The rhythm of the poem is deliberately rugged in the Chinese
manner, but the scene is classical and elegant. – *Yamamoto*

The juxtaposition of moonflowers and a torch suggests the influence of the Yūgao chapter in *Genji monogatari*, but the insertion of an outhouse belongs to the
art of haikai. The poem works on the mental associations of contemporary readers who would, at the mention of the word "torch," immediately be reminded of
how strange they felt walking torch in hand to an outhouse at night. – *Hori*

What I feel in my grass-thatched hut

banana plant in the autumn gale—
the sound of rain pattering
in the tub tonight

bashō I nowaki I shite I tarai I ni I ame I wo I kiku I yo I kana
banana-plant I autumn-gale I doing I tub I in I rain I [acc.] I hear I night I
   kana

COMMENTARY

The image of a tub recreates the lonely mood of the Bashō Hut in the depth of
night. The reader should visualize a small hut with a bamboo door leading out
to a narrow yard where, under eaves covered by banana foliage, a washing tub is
placed against the wall. The word "tub" is irreplaceable. All the images suggest
the mood of *wabi* that envelops the grass-thatched hut. The hokku might have
something in common with the following waka by Fujiwara Norinaga:*

In the autumn gust	akikaze ni
torn leaves on the banana plant	au bashōba no
there one moment	kudaketsutsu
and not there the next	aru ni mo aranu
as is known to happen in this life.	yo to wa shirazu ya
	– Nobutane

There was the sound of banana leaves fluttering in the wind. Then there was the
sound of raindrops falling into a tub, which had been left outside the hut. The
poem presents the lonely, cold feeling of the place. *– Abe Y.*

I had taken it for granted that the tub was inside the hut. Having heard others
insist that it was outside, I still prefer seeing it indoors. With banana leaves flapping in the gale, the patter of rain outdoors would have been mixed with the
sound of the wind and made it impossible to tell whether the patter was coming
from the tub or the storm door. Bashō had been extremely distressed at the
sound of torn banana leaves fluttering in the gale. Then he heard rainwater drip-

---

*Fujiwara Norinaga (1109?–80) was a court nobleman well known for his skills in poetry
and calligraphy. The waka cited here is the poem no. 13648 in *Fubokushō* (Selected poems
from the Land of the Rising Sun), an anthology compiled in 1309 or 1310.

ping from a nearby leak. When the leak is a bad one, we lose the sense of our house protecting us from the elements. Doesn't this poem express the sentiment of the poet who, hearing the flapping of banana leaves outdoors and the patter of leaking rain indoors, felt that his home was no longer a place of rest? – *Watsuji*

If the tub had been there to catch the leaking rainwater, the poem would not have the charm that it does. It must have been an outdoor tub for washing one's hands. The poet had always heard the patter of rain on banana leaves, but now that the plant had succumbed to the gale, he heard rain pattering in the tub. – *Rohan*

Sitting indoors safe from the rain this stormy night, the poet heard the banana leaves flapping in the wind outside and the drip of rain leaking into a tub inside. The poem conveys the sense of a violent storm at night by leading the reader into a world of sound. – *Nose*

Clearly, what we have here is a sense of loneliness, the kind of loneliness that makes it seem as if the poet himself were swaying with the banana leaves in the gale. – *Yamamoto*

Fukagawa, known as "the sea-level lowland" even today, was a newly reclaimed area on the delta of the Sumida River, an area exposed to the constant attack of the sea wind from Tokyo Bay as well as to the danger of tidal waves from the ocean. The typhoon that assailed the area that autumn was especially devastating, so much so that the government, fearful of flood damage, issued a decree to evacuate some residents the following spring. Living alone in his hut there and going through such harsh experiences, Bashō gained a new perspective on life. The hokku's first phrase, which describes banana leaves torn to pieces in the gale, can also be taken as depicting a man as helpless as the leaves. In the violent environment of his new residence Bashō experienced such helplessness and, delving into the world of poetry and communicating with past poets, he elevated that helplessness into a new poetic ideal. This hokku marks the founding of that ideal, *wabi*. – *Ogata*

I buy water at this grass-thatched hut.

ice, tasting bitter
in the mouth of a sewer rat,
quenches his thirst

kōri | nigaku | enso | ga | nodo | wo | uruoseri
ice | bitter | sewer-rat | 's | throat | [acc.] | have-moistened

NOTE

Because the Fukagawa district produced no good water, residents had to buy it from sellers who came by boat. The hokku draws on a passage in *Chuang-tzu* which, in teaching that one can attain happiness only by living within one's means, says, "A sewer rat drinks from a large river, yet the amount of water he takes is just enough to quench his thirst."

COMMENTARY

The poet compared himself to a sewer rat and suggested how small the amount of commercially sold water he had in his hut. There is *sabi* in the word "bitter." That the poet was content with such an austere life, from which pleasure seeking was banished, shows his pure, virtuous heart—an object of emulation indeed. — *Tosai*

The poem probably expresses the poet's own sentiments in comparing himself to a sewer rat and being content with his present lot. But its central meaning has to be related to the headnote. The poet is saying that, his residence being what it is, even a sewer rat would find the water tasted bitter and would drink no more of it beyond moistening his throat. The poet used the word "ice" instead of "water" here partly because he needed a season word and partly because the image of ice would enhance the lonely feeling. — *Seisensui*

The hokku seems to have been written during the poet's illness. The words in the beginning phrase give out the impression—although they do not spell it out—that the poet, living a lonely life day after day, came to loathe the world for some reason. — *Momota*

This is not a poem expressing a satisfied, serene state of mind on Bashō's part. The rat in this hokku is different from Chuang-tzu's rat. The poet is here reflecting on his austere life by comparing himself to a rat that lives hidden from people's eyes. Just as the rat sneaks out to the edge of a river to drink water, the poet, who lives a secluded life at a modest hut in the remote Fukagawa district, quenches his thirst by sucking a piece of bitter-tasting ice since there is no drinking water. What the poem embodies is not a satisfied state of mind; the reader detects even a tone of self-derision in it. – *Imoto*

This is a hokku written on the topic "Buying water," and not one poetizing the austere beauty of life in the hut. Hence it is more important for the reader to grasp how insecure the poet must have been if he had to boast of his happy life by referring to a passage in *Chuang-tzu*. – *Hori*

1682

The publication of *Jiin* seems to have further increased Bashō's poetic fame. A collection of New Year's hokku, written by major Edo poets and published in that city in February 1682, featured him by placing his verse at its very beginning. A haikai book published in Kyoto at around the same time also had him among the six masters selected from Edo. Another book, intended for Kyoto readers who wanted to know about current poetic trends in Edo, not only opened with Bashō's verse but highlighted him and his disciples so prominently that it looked as if his school dominated the Edo poetic scene. That book, called *Musashi buri* (Eastern trends), is also significant in that it is the first publication in which he used his new pseudonym Bashō.

As Bashō's reputation spread more widely, amateur poets outside Edo began to ask for his guidance by correspondence. One such poet was Takayama Biji (1649–1718), the chief retainer of a certain feudal lord who had a fief in Kai Province (Yamanashi Prefecture). Bashō's letter to Biji, dated June 20, is one of the oldest remaining documents containing his teachings on the art of haikai. In it he says: "Even if you have three or four extra syllables—or as many as five or seven—you need not worry as long as the verse sounds right. If even one syllable stagnates in your mouth, give it a careful scrutiny." Although Biji lived in Kai, he traveled to Edo on official business from time to time, and Bashō saw him on such occasions. On September 15 Bashō, together with Sodō and Shintoku, went to a moon-viewing party hosted by Biji. Bashō had retired to rustic Fukagawa, but he was far from being a reclusive poet.

In response to Kikaku's firefly poem

with morning glories
a man eats breakfast
—that is what I am

asagao | ni | ware | wa | meshi | kū | otoko | kana
morning-glory | to | I | as-for | meal | eat | man | kana

NOTE

The poem Bashō referred to in the headnote was based on the proverb "Some worms eat nettles":

within the grassy gate	kusa no to ni
a firefly eats nettles	ware wa tade kū
—that is what I am	hotaru kana

COMMENTARY

Master Bashō's hokku was written in response to Kikaku's firefly poem, and as such it is a foil to the kind of poem that tries to produce a shocking effect. This hokku has nothing that is shocking. – *Kyorai*

Kikaku was a heavy drinker who drank day and night. Once, after drinking all night, he wrote the firefly poem at dawn. Master Bashō, wishing to warn against his disciple's dissipation, copied the priest Hōnen's pledge against drinking, added this hokku to the end, and sent it to Kikaku. – *Sanga*

Whereas Kikaku wrote a clever poem with artful wording, Bashō responded with an extremely plain poem that says nothing out of the ordinary. And yet, interestingly enough, Bashō's poem is definitely more forceful than Kikaku's. – *Abe Y.*

If I may add a superfluous comment, the poem also implies that a man who has a hangover does not know the taste of a breakfast that is eaten before morning glories lose their fresh beauty. – *Watsuji*

In answer to Kikaku, who said he enjoyed night and preferred a bitter taste, Bashō stated that he could not live that kind of abnormal life, that he was an ordinary man who slept at night, awoke early in the morning, and took a plain meal instead of liquor. His statement has a savage, biting sarcasm. Even someone like Kikaku must have been nonplussed. – *Ebara*

We must not overlook the fact that the image of the morning glory enlivens the poem not so much because the early morning flower reminds us of an early riser as because it has a quiet, pure, and wholesome type of beauty in itself. – *Shūson*

the crescent moon—
a bud on the morning glory
swelling at night

mikazuki l ya l asagao l no l yūbe l tsubomu l ran
third-day-moon l : l morning-glory l 's l evening l bud l seem

COMMENTARY

The poet imagined that the crescent moon in the evening must be preparing itself
to swell into a full moon in due time, just like a morning-glory bud which pre-
pares itself to swell into an open flower the following morning. – *Kōseki*

Bashō's love for both the crescent moon and morning-glory buds took a concrete
form in this poem. – *Komiya*

The poet is saying that the crescent moon is a morning-glory bud swollen in the
evening. The moon, which is shaped like a morning-glory bud in its early phases
but later becomes perfectly round, is here compared to the bud, which begins to
swell in the evening and opens into a large, round flower the following morning.
– *Ōtani*

Su Tung-p'o, slanting his traveler's hat, would look up toward the cloudy sky, and Tu Fu, wearing a hat heavy with snow, would roam faraway places. Since I have plenty of time here at the grassy hut, I have made a rainproof paper hat with my own hands in imitation of the hat Saigyō wore in his lonely wanderings.

life in this world
just like a temporary shelter
of Sōgi's

yo | ni | furu | mo | sarani | Sōgi | no | yadori | kana
world | in | spend-time | also | indeed | Sōgi | 's | lodging | kana

NOTE

Artists in China and Japan often painted pictures of the Chinese poet Su Tung-p'o (1037–1101) admiring a snow scene. In such a picture, Su usually wore a traveler's hat and rode on a donkey. Both Tu Fu and Saigyō spent most of their lives on the road. Iio Sōgi (1421–1502) was another such poet, and his renga verse

life in this world	yo ni furu mo
just like a temporary shelter	sarani shigure no
from a winter shower	yadori kana

inspired Bashō to write this hokku. Sōgi's verse, in turn, draws on a waka by Lady Sanuki (1141?–1217?):

Life in this world	yo ni furu mo
abounds in suffering	kurushiki mono wo
yet how lightly	maki no ya ni
the winter's first shower	yasuku mo suguru
passes over this shingled roof!	hatsushigure kana

In all three poems there is a play on the word *furu*, which can mean either "to spend time" or "to rain."

COMMENTARY

A philosophical poem. — *San'u*

Bashō borrowed from Sōgi's verse and suggested that his sympathies were entirely with Sōgi. – *Donto*

The hokku embodies Bashō's admiration for Sōgi as well as his wish to be Sōgi's poetic successor. – *Abe Y.*

In my opinion, the hokku means "Living in this world is, as Sōgi said, precisely like taking shelter during a winter rain. Nevertheless I can endure such life because I am able to rest at Sōgi's shelter." In the hokku, therefore, Bashō is thanking Sōgi for founding what was later to become haikai and thereby helping him to endure this forlorn life. – *Komiya*

Sōgi, reinterpreting Lady Sanuki's waka, intimated that because he had no ambition in this world and led the carefree life of a traveler who carried just a hat and a staff, he could stay cheerful while waiting out a winter shower in a lodging place. Bashō, making a hat, compared himself to Sōgi and wished he too could share that carefree mood when he took shelter from a shower. A person who seeks little from the world can always live a peaceful life. – *Kobayashi*

Bashō amused himself by trying his hand at hat making, caring little about the quality of the end product, and showing a poet's carefree spirit. This hokku and its accompanying prose show such a spirit—a whimsical man smiling at himself. That is haikai. No such spirit can be found anywhere in Sōgi's renga. – *Imoto*

Bashō changed just one Japanese word, and yet that change transformed the gloomy, damp tone of Sōgi's renga to the sonorous, clear, and even humorous tone of haikai. – *Yamamoto*

1683

On January 25, 1683, the Bashō Hut burned to the ground in a fire that destroyed a large part of Edo. According to Kikaku's account, Bashō "barely managed to survive in the smoke, after submerging himself in the water and covering his head with a rush mat." Kikaku went on to speculate that this unexpected disaster awakened him to the transitory nature of human life. The speculation somewhat overstates the case, because, to judge from the evolution of his poetry, Bashō's pessimistic view of life seems to have originated earlier and proceeded to take a clearer form with passage of time. Yet there is also no doubt that the disaster helped to reconfirm his religious outlook on life. He must have become aware, more than ever, that man is an eternally homeless creature, a traveler who wanders from one temporary shelter to another. Be that as it may, Bashō did not even have a temporary shelter after the fire and had to accept Biji's invitation to come and stay in Kai Province. Thus he spent the following several months in Yamura, some seventy miles west of Edo.

Bashō returned to Edo in early summer, partly to review the first full-scale anthology of his school, edited by Kikaku, before it went to press. The book, which came out in August, had the title *Minashiguri* (Shriveled chestnuts), implying that the verses collected therein were like small, misshapen chestnuts no ordinary person would pick up. To Bashō and his disciples, those "chestnuts" had the most delicious taste. In his postscript Bashō specifically pointed out their four main "flavors": lyric beauty in the work of Chinese poets Li Po (701–62) and Tu Fu; the Zen spirit of the T'ang-period monk Han Shan's verse; the *wabi* and *fūga* of Saigyō; and romantic love in Po Chü-i's poetry. The list well elucidates the ideals of Bashō's haikai at this time, even though much of the actual poetry collected in the anthology, representing the work of some 110 poets, inevitably falls short of these standards.

On August 12, Bashō's mother died in his hometown of Ueno. He did not attend the funeral. Most likely he could not, lacking the financial means to travel to Ueno at that time.

In autumn, Kikaku, Sodō, and other students of Bashō's began collecting donations to provide their teacher with new living quarters. A total of fifty-two people responded, donating money, bamboos, reed mats, a hollowed gourd, and other household articles. In winter, Bashō was able to move into the new Bashō Hut, which actually was an apartment in a tenement house located near his former residence. According to a description given in an eighteenth-century book, the apartment had two cooking stoves and an alcove where an image of Buddha was placed. On a pillar in the kitchen there hung a large gourd, and students who visited their master saw to it that the gourd was always filled with rice. Bashō had a new home, but his life in it seems to have been as austere as ever.

New Year's Day

first day of the year—
as I ponder, a lonely
nightfall in autumn

ganjitsu | ya | omoeba | sabishi | aki | no | kure
year's-first-day | : | when-think | lonely | autumn | 's | end

COMMENTARY

The poet felt the loneliness of late autumn while the whole world was celebrating the coming of spring. Everyone some time or other experiences a moment of sadness in the midst of pleasure. I wonder, however, if the hokku's middle phrase does not create an overly didactic tone. — *Ebara*

The hokku's last two phrases indicate that the poet made a distinction between the loneliness of the New Year and that of late autumn. It is quiet on New Year's Day, but there is something happy in that quietness. There is a sense of things beginning to move and open. In contrast, the quietness of late autumn carries with it a sense of things declining and falling with the approach of winter. — *Shūson*

The hokku's middle phrase implies, not that New Year's Day is lonely, but that late autumn is lonely. It was not that the poet detected loneliness in the gaiety and liveliness of New Year's Day. As a contrast to the gaiety and liveliness of New Year's Day, he thought of a late autumn day and felt that that was what human life was all about. He wrote this hokku to give form to that feeling. — *Komiya*

New Year's Day is here compared to an autumn evening. The comparison is a little odd, showing the lingering influence of the Danrin school with its love of surprise. — *Kon*

is that warbler
her soul? there sleeps
a graceful willow

uguisu | wo | tama | ni | nemuru | ka | taoyanagi
warbler | [acc.] | soul | as | sleep | ? | graceful-willow

NOTE

Alludes to a passage in *Chuang-tzu* describing a daydream in which Chuang-tzu's soul became a butterfly and flitted out of his body. Bashō seems to have coined the word *taoyanagi* by analogy to *taoyame*, "graceful lady."

COMMENTARY

Almost any poet, on seeing a willow tree hanging its branches as if in sleep, might compose a poem alluding to the butterfly in Chuang-tzu's dream. But Bashō changed the allusion and referred to a warbler. In other words, he made use of the allusion but was not used by it. He deserves to be called the Chuang-tzu of haikai. – *Ryōta*

The poem seems to depict a willow tree standing outside a bedroom on a calm spring day. The amorous undertone of the expression "graceful willow" creates the image of a lovelorn soul wandering about in a romantic dream. – *Tosai*

Although warblers also sing in the morning, the impression I get from the hokku is that this is a scene of high noon on a spring day, when the sun is balmy and there is no wind moving the willow branches. As the poet watches the tree, he becomes absorbed by it and feels as if he were hearing a warbler's song in a dream. He cannot tell the difference between the warbler and the willow. I think this is an extremely well-crafted poem—perhaps overly so, but it is among the more successful ones. – *Abe Y.*

Perhaps it is in the morning, but the willow tree is still asleep, and the warbler is flying around. There is a popular belief that when a man is sleeping his soul flies about. The willow is asleep, with its branches hanging down, yet its heart is flying around like a warbler. The willow's soul and body have been separated from each other during its sleep: the soul, having become a warbler, is flying about while the body remains a tree and continues to sleep. – *Keion*

The graceful shape of a willow tree, looking as if it were asleep, led the poet's mind to the legend of Chuang-tzu and his dream, but the poet, in composing the hokku, replaced the butterfly with a warbler, a bird that has something in common with a willow in color and gracefulness. —*Shūson*

Comparing a willow tree to Chuang-tzu, and a warbler to his butterfly, the poet wondered if the soul of the willow had not turned into the warbler. By adding the image of a warbler, he made the elegance and grace of a willow tree even more beautiful and dreamlike. Written in Bashō's early style, the hokku nevertheless shows poetic beauty, not just craftsmanship in wording and conception. —*Iwata*

On a painting
"*That hatted man on horseback,*" *I say,* "*looks like a monk. Where did he come from, and why is he wandering like that?*" "*That,*" *answers the man who painted the picture,* "*is a portrait of you on a journey.*" *If that is the case, let me tell you, clumsy horseman who roams this wide world,* "*Be careful and don't fall from the horse!*"

my horse ambles along . . .
I see myself in a painting
of this summer moor

uma I bokuboku I ware I wo I e I ni I miru I natsuno I kana
horse I amble I I I [acc.] I picture I in I see I summer-moor I kana

NOTE

A headnote to what seems to have been an early draft of this hokku says: "Written with difficulty on the way to a place called Gunnai in Kai Province." Some scholars read the first six syllables as *uma hokuhoku*. Both *bokuboku* and *hokuhoku* are onomatopoeias for the sound of a horse's hoofs, with no established difference between the two in the effects they give to Japanese readers.

COMMENTARY

It is very interesting that the poet, looking at a painting, should write a poem which in itself says he saw himself in a painting. Or one may take the hokku for the sketch of an actual observation, in which case the poet is saying he feels as if he were looking at a painting of a Chinese on horseback. This reading also creates a profound impression. – *Tosai*

As his horse slowly ambled across the green summer moor, the poet's mind left his body and immersed itself into the moor, until he saw himself as part of a painting that depicted the moor. The hokku's middle phrase welled up spontaneously from this state of mind. There is an exquisite harmony here between language and emotion, and the poem is a pleasure to read. – *Abe Y.*

In my opinion, the word *hokuhoku* not only suggests the rhythmical movement of the horse and the man on it, but clearly indicates a pleasant feeling produced by the rhythm. And I concur with Abe in believing that this summer moor is a green moor with a pleasant breeze blowing over it. – *Komiya*

I agree that *hokuhoku* suggests the rhythm with which the horse and its rider move, but I do not believe that that rhythm has anything to do with a pleasant or refreshing feeling. The horse is ambling at an extremely slow pace, so slow that it is almost irritating, and this is happening on a moor in summertime where the grass is reflecting the heat. Because there is nothing pleasant or refreshing in his actual experience, the poet wishes to "see myself in a painting." – *Watsuji*

This hokku expresses how comfortable Bashō felt as he traveled across the summer moor on horseback. Although the hokku's middle phrase sounds a little sentimental, this is an interesting poem that differs from others in that the poet here has objectified himself. – *Handa*

All that the poem says is that the poet, ambling across the summer moor on a horse, saw himself in a painting, but it embodies the tranquillity of a mind that looks at itself from a distance. – *Ebara*

It was not yet midsummer when the hokku was written, but the lunar fifth month in Kai Basin must have been hot enough to make a traveler suffer. I agree with Watsuji's interpretation and see a pained expression on the poet's face. When Bashō said "Written with difficulty" in his headnote, he was referring, I believe, not to the process of composing the hokku, but to his suffering on horseback that eventually produced the hokku. There is even a touch of self-derision in the headnote. The poet was irritated by the stupid, lazy nag that, plodding along the hot country road, stopped at times to eat the grass by the wayside. That irritation was reflected back on himself and became self-ridicule, as he realized what an awkward kind of wayfarer he must have looked atop that nag. It is true that he objectified himself as a figure in a painting, but at the same time he made a caricature of himself and saw his own stupidity in the horse's.
– *Yamamoto*

The extra-long first phrase, with its slow tempo, helps to add a leisurely, humorous flavor to the poem. Is this because Bashō's mind had become profound enough to attain the realm of *karumi*? – *Ogata*

Having settled in the new Bashō Hut

the sound of hail—
I remain, as before,
an old oak

arare | kiku | ya | kono | mi | wa | motono | furugashiwa
hail | hear | : | this | self | as-for | former | old-oak

NOTE
The oak tree mentioned in the hokku is of a variety that keeps dead leaves on its branches throughout the winter.

COMMENTARY
The poet, hearing the sound of hail and feeling the piercing cold as he sat in the hut, mused that he was the same old oak. Probably he heard the patter of hail on an oak tree and wrote this poem. The hokku may also imply the sentiment of the poet, who felt he was like an old oak in having lived a useless life for too long.
—Higuchi

The hokku laments the poet's inability to detach himself from past patterns of thinking. *—Kōseki*

The Bashō Hut had been newly set up, and *Minashiguri* had initiated a new poetic trend. In the midst of all this, Bashō muttered, "I remain . . ." and expressed an emotion that had been weighing on his heart. When he said "as before," he was addressing himself to things that were "not as before," things that had acquired a new aspect. *—Shūson*

The hokku compares the poet to an old oak, which creates a rather artificial impression. Still, the poet's melancholy comes through to the reader, over and above the artificiality of the wording. *—Abe M.*

Oak leaves are large and thick, and make a dry sound in the wind. The sound of hail hitting those leaves is loud, too. The oak reminded Bashō of his forlorn life. Yet, having settled in the new hut, he also had a feeling of relief, and that feeling led to a period of quiet reflection during which he heard the sound of hail.
—Yamamoto

CHAPTER THREE

Two Western Journeys

1684-1688

1684

In late September of 1684, Bashō embarked on a long western journey that resulted in his first poetic journal, *Nozarashi kikō* (The journal of a weatherbeaten skeleton). The aim of the journey was multiple: to pay homage to his mother's grave, to visit his students in Ōgaki, to discipline himself through the hardships of travel. He was accompanied by one of his disciples in Edo, Naemura Chiri (1648–1716), whose native town was located in a province next to his. He was not to return to Edo for the next seven months.

Bashō and Chiri trekked westward along the Tōkaidō, the main highway that roughly followed the Pacific coastline. At Atsuta, near Nagoya, they took a ferry to Kuwana across Ise Bay, then traveled southward along the bay until they reached Yamada, the modern city of Ise. Bashō visited one of the Grand Shintō Shrines there on October 8. He and his companion left Yamada after about ten days, Bashō for his hometown of Ueno, and Chiri for his of Takenouchi in Yamato Province (Nara Prefecture). Bashō arrived at Ueno on October 16.

Although it had been more than eight years since his last homecoming, Bashō left Ueno after a stay of only four or five days. He first headed southwest to call briefly on Chiri in Takenouchi. Then he turned south and climbed Mt. Yoshino to admire the exquisitely tinted foliage of the cherry trees. From there he traveled northward to Kyoto by way of Nara, and then eastward to Ōgaki, where his old friend Tani Bokuin (1646–1725) and several of his students had been waiting. During his sojourn in Ōgaki, Bokuin and two other local poets joined him in writing a *kasen*, a haikai sequence of thirty-six verses. In November he and Bokuin took a riverboat down to Kuwana, then a ferry to Atsuta. Bokuin parted with him there to return to Ōgaki; Bashō, however, stayed in the area until late January 1685. While there, he also visited haikai poets living in nearby Nagoya.

Bashō's visit to Nagoya was an especially fruitful one, for it was there that he led a team of local poets to produce five kasen that later formed the bulk of the book *Fuyu no hi* (The winter sun). The new type of haikai Bashō created with the Nagoya poets was distinctly different from the style that had characterized *Minashiguri*, for he made no special attempt to draw on Chinese poetry, nor did he try to break with the

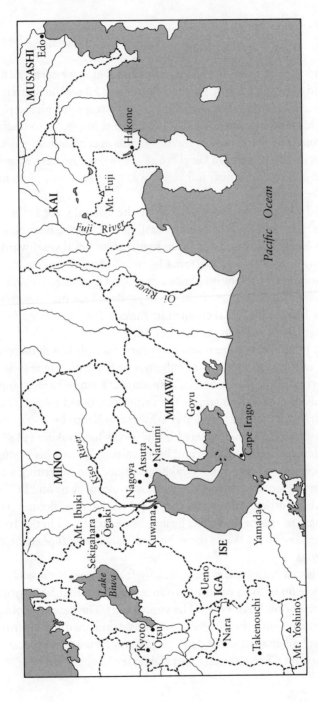

In late September of 1684, Bashō embarked on a long western journey that resulted in his first poetic journal, Nozarashi kikō.

ordinary prosody by using extra syllables. More than anything else, he endeavored to create poetic beauty through an implicit attitude of liberation from worldly concerns, and through a plain language that avoided artifice, pedantry, and overdependence on wordplay. Because he was working with amateur poets whom he had met for the first time in Nagoya, not all the verses collected in *Fuyu no hi* can be said to have attained the ideal poetic beauty he had in mind. Nevertheless, the book was the first significant work that displayed the direction in which Bashō was trying to go in his effort to create his own poetic style.

spring begins—
new year, old rice
ten quarts

haru I tatsu I ya I shinnen I furuki I kome I goshō
spring I begin I : I New-Year I old I rice I five-shō

NOTE
Written probably on February 16, which was the lunar New Year's Day. One *shō*
is roughly equivalent to two quarts.

COMMENTARY
Master Bashō recalled: "Initially, I began this hokku with the phrase 'how fitting!' That was shameful of me." He changed it to read "spring begins." His *tanzaku,** which still remains today, has the poem in that revised form. – *Dohō*

In the Bashō Hut there was a gourd that had a capacity of five *shō*. It is said that
the students added rice whenever the gourd began to look empty. Here is the
New Year as welcomed by a leisurely recluse—an enviable life indeed. – *Ryōta*

By five *to*[†] or five *shō* people in old days meant not exactly such an amount but
an amount that was about right for the occasion. The poet is here saying that he
has just about the right amount of rice to celebrate the New Year. – *Donto*

Although the New Year calls for everything to be new and plentiful, the poet is
here celebrating the occasion with nothing but five *shō* of rice. The poem gives a
helpless, forlorn impression. Needless to say, it also implies another sentiment:
the poet is satisfied with—or even amused by—that type of life. – *Meisetsu*

The lunar New Year's Day was February 16 by the Gregorian calendar. It was
ten days after the official start of spring. The poet had been happy with the arrival of spring; then the New Year came and made him doubly happy. And there
was as much as ten quarts of rice remaining from the old year. What blessings!
The poem expresses this kind of modest contentment, I think. – *Komiya*

If it were to open with "how fitting!" the hokku would sound a little conceited.
With "spring begins" it becomes a poem that expresses contentment and happi-

---

* *Tanzaku* is a thick, rectangular piece of paper especially made for writing a poem. The
poet usually gives it to someone for a gift.
[†]*To* is a measure of volume equal to ten *shō*, thus about twenty quarts.

ness as well as budding hope for future growth. There is no element of affectation in the revised hokku. – *Nose*

The hokku's middle phrase involves a rhetorical device juxtaposing the old and the new. Five *shō* is a scanty amount of rice, but the poet was content with it and transformed that feeling into a poem. The word "old" also suggests that such an austere life had its hardships. – *Kon*

In the eighth month of the first year of Jōkyō, I left my dilapidated hut on the riverside. The autumn wind was blowing with an unaccountably chilling sound.

weatherbeaten skeleton
haunting my mind, how the wind
pierces my body!

nozarashi I wo I kokoro I ni I kaze I no I shimu I mi I kana
weather-exposed-skeleton I [acc.] I mind I in I wind I 's I pierce I body I kana

NOTE
The first hokku that appears in *Nozarashi kikō*.

COMMENTARY
The poet was mentally prepared to die on the road, and yet his body felt the piercing wind. By saying so in the poem, he expressed the sadness of parting.

Having forsaken	yo wo sutete
this world, I think nothing	mi wa naki mono to
of my body, and yet	omoedomo
on a day when it snows	yuki no furu hi wa
how cold I feel!	samuku koso are*

The hokku embodies the sentiment implied in this waka. – *Donto*

Old man as he was, the poet feared he might die somewhere on the road and be reduced to a skeleton lying in the field. As the image of the bones entered his mind, he felt as if the autumn wind were piercing his body. Yet he was not truly fearful of becoming a weatherbeaten skeleton; rather, he found something appealing in that prospect. – *Meisetsu*

For a traveler—someone who is expected to befriend clouds—Bashō seems to have had a sensibility that was too delicate and too ingenuous in the face of natural phenomena. Haunted by the image of a weatherbeaten skeleton, his mind had been far too active in imagining the hardships of a long journey. No sooner had he left his hut than he was overcome by the piercing wind. – *Saisei*

* Author unknown.

A man of delicate constitution, Bashō probably could not decide to go on a journey without preparing mentally for death. That death-defying determination, rushing up from his subconscious like an autumn wind, pierced his whole body. Indeed, he felt as if it were an autumn wind piercing his body. And, in that feeling of his, there was no dichotomy between the external, tactile sense of the season and the internal, psychological sense of what was happening in his life. The two evoked each other and responded to each other, together producing a single mood. – *Shūson*

Ever since receiving the news of his mother's death the previous summer, Bashō must have been longing to return to his hometown. But, when he took to the road, his heart was troubled by something else that made him feel even greater urgency and discontent: here he was, a poet who, already over age forty, still had not secured his own claim to artistic uniqueness. Clearly, this hokku contains an exaggeration. It is not a descriptive poem, nor does it necessarily imply that the poet was prepared to die in a literal sense. Nevertheless there is no doubt that Bashō created that fictional situation out of something real within himself.
– *Yamamoto*

For Bashō, travel was where poems were born and where a poet disciplined himself. Through sheer willpower he became a traveler, although he knew it might well mean his being reduced to a skeleton. He had to feel apprehensive. That apprehension was not slight, either, since by nature he was a sensitive, delicate man, the kind of man whose senses deeply felt "how the wind pierces my body!" This hokku displays those two sides of Bashō. – *Utsubo*

This hokku is saying: "Intellectually, I was resigned to fate and prepared to leave my bones on the open field. But now I find myself unable to prevent the chilly autumn wind, together with various sorrows of human life, from penetrating and chilling my mind through and through." The words "my mind" in the poem serve as an intermediary that promotes a move from the realm of intellect to that of the senses. The last phrase of the hokku presents the poet caught in a crevice between the two realms and being looked at through the eyes of his other self. About to start on an aimless, penny-pinching journey, Bashō tried to dress himself up for a grandiose pose. Yet as he did so he had to notice the eyes of his other self watching, with a wry smile, a gap between his intellect and his sensibility that could not be covered over. That wry smile is what gives this poem a haikai flavor. – *Ogata*

Bashō at this time was a follower of Chuang-tzu, to whom a wind was the breathing of the great earth. Through his mind's ear, he tried hard to listen to the breathing of the universe hidden in the autumn wind. – *Hori*

It rained on the day when I passed through the Barrier, and all the mountains were hidden in the clouds.

in the misty rain
Mount Fuji is veiled all day—
how intriguing!

kirishigure | Fuji | wo | minu | hi | zo | omoshiroki
mist-rain | Fuji | [acc.] | not-see | day | ! | interesting

NOTE

NOTE

The Barrier in the headnote refers to a government checking station at Hakone. Such stations had been set up at strategic spots on major highways throughout Japan, mainly for the purpose of catching criminals at large and illegal goods in transit. The one at Hakone, located on a high mountain pass, was famous for its beautiful view of Mt. Fuji.

COMMENTARY

Because Bashō loved Mt. Fuji and had kept his eyes on it ever since he left Edo, he had paid no attention to other parts of the landscape along the road. This day, however, Fuji was hidden in the mist, thereby making other scenes look appealing to him. Also, there is a passage in *Tsurezuregusa** that says, "One is not to admire cherry blossoms only when they are in full bloom, or the moon only when it is uncovered by the clouds." Bashō, seeing nothing but the whiteness of the mist, might have longed for the invisible figure of the mountain or looked forward to seeing a clear sky the following day, and he might have thought that Mt. Fuji behind the clouds was fascinating because it awakened this longing. – *Donto*

Mt. Fuji exposes itself far too much to the eyes of the people. It undersells itself. Bashō was not being sarcastic in this poem. How fascinating Mt. Fuji looked to him when it remained invisible for the entire day! – *Noguchi*

Bashō did not write "how intriguing!" just to show off his superiority like a typical tea master or haikai poet. Although Mt. Fuji could not be seen, its image was so familiar to Bashō that he felt he saw it clearly in the depths of the surrounding mist. There was an in-depth picture, so to speak, that aroused his interest. – *Komiya*

* *Tsurezuregusa* (Essays in idleness) is a collection of essays, observations, and random thoughts of the Buddhist monk Yoshida Kenkō (1283–1350). The passage quoted appears at the beginning of section 137.

On a road along the Fuji River we came upon an abandoned child,
about two years of age and crying pathetically. Apparently, its parents,
finding the waves of this floating world as uncontrollable as the turbu-
lent rapids of the river, had decided to leave it there until its life vanished
like a dewdrop. The child seemed like a tiny bush-clover blossom that
would fall at any time tonight or tomorrow, as soon as an autumn gust
blew. I tossed out some food from my sleeve pocket as I passed by.

those who have heard a monkey's cry:
how about this abandoned child
in the autumn wind?

saru l wo l kiku l hito l sutego l ni l aki l no l kaze l ikani
monkey l [acc.] l listen l person l abandoned-child l to l autumn l 's l wind l
  how

NOTE

A monkey's heart-rending shriek had been a popular theme in both Chinese and
Japanese poetry.

COMMENTARY

Poets in China and Japan have written that there is nothing more plaintive than a
monkey's cry. But they would be lost for words should they hear that child crying
in the autumn wind. By saying this the poet expressed soundless depths of pity.
— *Tosai*

Bashō here saw a deserted child crying in the autumn wind; he did not hear a
monkey's cry. Yet, during the phase of his career that immediately preceded the
present journey, he had shown a great deal of interest in Chinese poetry. It was
natural that his grief at hearing the child's cry at this time should remind him of
a shrieking monkey. And to Tu Fu, Li Po, Po Chü-i, and all the other poets who
had been so touched by a monkey's cry, he asked, almost in protest, which of the
two cries would sound more pathetic. In other words, he contrasted his genuine
pity for the deserted child with the imaginary grief that Japanese poets put into
their poems about the monkey's cry. It also meant that he became aware of a
conflict within himself, a conflict between the spirit of *fūga*, which he had hith-

erto cherished, and the humane feeling of pity aroused by the sight of an abandoned child. – *Yamamoto*

Due to social conditions, child exposure was a common practice in those days.
Bashō, a mere haikai master, could hardly do anything about it except grieve. He
tossed out some food as he passed by; that was the most he could do. In his powerlessness he was overcome with self-recrimination, which in turn made him
write this hokku. In later years Bashō said: "My *fūga* is like a fireplace in summer and a fan in winter." He was alluding, with both modesty and pride, to the
powerlessness of poetry in the practical sphere of life. The germ of that idea is already seen in this hokku. – *Imoto*

Written on horseback

by the road
a rose mallow . . . it has been
eaten by my horse!

michinobe l no l mukuge l wa l uma l ni l kuwarekeri
roadside l 's l rose-mallow l as-for l horse l by l has-been-eaten

COMMENTARY

A rose mallow will not be eaten by a horse if it is not blooming on the roadside.
It is eaten by a horse or plucked by a passerby because it grows near a road. This
hokku is a warning against forwardness. – *San'u*

According to a certain commentator, this hokku was written when Bashō was a
student of Zen under the monk Butchō. The Zen master, as anyone in his position would do, used to discourage the poet from pursuing the way of haikai. One
day, when the two were walking together on their way to a religious service at a
nearby village, Butchō brought up the subject of haikai again. Bashō thereupon
said haikai was nothing more than what happens at this place and at this moment. His Zen teacher then pointed at a rose mallow that happened to be there
and asked him to compose a poem on it. Immediately he responded with this
hokku. Butchō, after some reflection, said: "What a fine poem! I did not know a
haikai verse could have such a profound meaning." Deeply impressed, the monk
stopped trying to interfere with Bashō's poetic activities from this time on. It
must be concluded, then, that this hokku is somehow in harmony with the aims
of Zen. —That is what the commentator said, but the story is not convincing.
The hokku appears with the headnote "Written on horseback" in *Nozarashi
kikō*. Surely Bashō could not have ridden a horse when he was in Butchō's company. – *Somaru*

One source has it that a rose mallow withers in one day and is therefore a symbol for life's transitoriness. Sadly, Bashō's rose mallow was devoured by a horse
before it even had time to attain that short-lived glory. Human life is like that,
too. – *Nanimaru*

It is difficult to understand why such a pedestrian poem has come to be so famous. In my opinion, didactic poetry tends to be overpraised by people who are
not men of letters, and perhaps this poem falls into that category. That is

by the road
a rose mallow . . . it has been
eaten by my horse!

Painting and calligraphy
by Bashō. Reproduced
from Okada Rihei,
Bashō no hisseki
(Shunjūsha), by courtesy
of the publisher and the
late author's estate.

especially likely because this was the first allegorical hokku with didactic implications. In brief, this poem belongs to the lowest type of literature. —*Shiki*

The poet sketched a happening during his journey just as he saw it. I think it is an interesting depiction of a scene in a country lane. —*Meisetsu*

A transparent poem, like glasswork of the highest quality. —*Watsuji*

Surely what we have here is a quiet example of the law of nature that governs the strong and the weak, the law by which one part of nature is transferred to another part. Bashō's thought had an aspect that was religious in an animistic sense, which makes this hokku something more than a mere scenic sketch. That, however, does not mean it is a didactic poem. —*Ebara*

Before it was eaten, the white flower had been near the outer margin of the poet's consciousness. When it suddenly vanished, the flower for the first time took a clear form in his mind. That mental event resulted in this poem. —*Shūson*

Underlying Bashō's thought were a sense of life's ephemerality inherited from medieval hermits, a philosophy of intuition like that of Zen, and the nihilistic thought of Taoism. Especially in this poem, as well as in the famous frog poem, one can clearly detect elements of Zen lurking in the background. The demonstrative manner of speech in the first half of the hokku reminds us of a Zen dialogue, while the idea of freedom from discriminative thinking implied in the second half is reminiscent of the realm of momentary satori that transcends speculation. Of course, such implications are not to be found on the poem's surface but are hidden in its depths. And these multiple layers of meaning are present in the poem, regardless of what Bashō's intent might have been. It would not be enough to take this hokku for a simple descriptive poem; it would be too much to say that it is a didactic poem. The hokku stops just short of creating its own world of metaphor. —*Yamamoto*

It was sheer coincidence that brought together a horse that ate and a rose mallow that was eaten. In Buddhism, everything that happens is considered to have resulted from karma. Without a cause, there can be no result: a phenomenon that looks like a coincidental happening is thought to have sprung from a causal act, and that act is called karma. From this perspective, all things that happen in life are related to the system of karma. Here Bashō recognized that the relationship between his horse and a rose-mallow flower was one of karma. —*Utsubo*

Bashō saw a subject fit for haikai when a rose-mallow flower, which is rich in classical, elegant beauty, was devoured by a pack horse. —*Hori*

After nightfall I visited the Outer Shrine. Here and there in the dim darkness around the first torii, *lights from the holy candles were visible. The wind coming from the pine trees of the sacred mountain pierced my body and filled me with religious awe.*

last day of the month, no moon . . .
embracing a cedar tree
one thousand years old, a storm

misoka I tsuki I nashi I chitose I no I sugi I wo I daku I arashi
month's-last-day I moon I nonexistent I thousand-year I 's I cedar I [acc.] I
   embrace I storm

NOTE

Bashō wrote this hokku when he visited one of the Grand Shinto Shrines in Yamada on October 8, the last day of the lunar eighth month. A *torii* is a decorative gateway to a Shinto shrine, usually consisting of two wooden or stone columns that are connected by two horizontal crosspieces at the top.

COMMENTARY

The Inner Shrine is worshipped as a sun deity; the Outer Shrine, as a moon deity. With no moon, the invisible deity seemed even more august, and the poet looked up to the cedar tree as her holy manifestation. The phrase "embracing a cedar tree" probably refers to the poet who was so awestruck that he found himself moving rhythmically in a trance. – *Tosai*

In my reading, there was a grove of cedar trees beset by stormy winds. – *Shinpū*

I do not think it was a stormy wind besetting cedar trees. It was Bashō embracing a cedar tree. Listening to the stormy wind howling through the old tree in the dark, he embraced the tree. This is a very interesting poem. – *Rohan*

From this hokku I cannot visualize Bashō embracing the cedar tree. Of course, the poem refers to a single tree. – *Abe J.*

The word "embrace" suggests that the storm wind was not a very violent one but of the kind that blows slowly and mildly. Some commentators believe the one who was doing the embracing was the poet, but I think it was the storm. – *Higuchi*

It was the storm that was doing the embracing. Personifying the storm creates a sense of simplicity and strength reminiscent of the age of the gods. – *Ebara*

Bashō embracing a cedar tree is too theatrical. That kind of explication presumes too abrupt a pause before the word "storm" in the poem. The poet heard a storm roaring in various voices around a massive cedar tree in the dark. He used the verb "embrace" to suggest the roar of the wind blowing around a huge tree. – *Yamamoto*

"Embracing a cedar tree" refers both to the storm blowing around the ancient cedar tree and to the poet reverently embracing the tree. The tree, known as the Cedar of Five Hundred Branches, stood near a place of worship designated for priests and nuns at the Outer Shrine. The hokku has an abnormal 7-7-5 syllable pattern. – *Kon*

I stopped at a teashop. A woman named Chō, or Butterfly, asked me to
compose a verse alluding to her name and brought out a piece of white
silk. I wrote the following hokku on it.

fragrant orchid—
into a butterfly's wings
it breathes the incense

ran | no | ka | ya | chō | no | tsubasa | ni | takimono | su
orchid | 's | scent | : | butterfly | 's | wing | to | incense-burning | do

COMMENTARY

According to Master Bashō, this woman said to him, "I used to work as a courtesan at this house, but now I am married to the proprietor. I hear the previous
owner also had married a courtesan named Tsuru, and when Master Sōin of
Naniwa visited here she begged for a verse, too." Master Bashō could not decline, as she was so insistent and went so far as to bring up an interesting precedent. Using Sōin's verse

arrowroot leaves	kuzu no ha no
sadly wither and fall—	otsuru no urami
frost at night	yoru no shimo

for a headnote, he wrote this hokku and gave it to her. "Her name was Chō," he
said to me. "That explains my choice of words. I just followed Sōin's example
and dashed my poem off. Without that example, I couldn't have written it."
—Dohō

The poem compliments the woman's beauty by way of comparison. One should
note the craftsmanship it displays. —Tosai

This orchid is not of spring but of autumn. When the poet wrote the hokku, he
visualized a butterfly alighting on an orchid and imagined its wings being perfumed by the flower's scent. By analogy to a perfumed garment, the poem described the orchid's fragrance adhering to the butterfly's wings and thereby complimented the name Chō. —Mizuho

This is a charmingly colorful hokku. On a rare occasion one comes across a simi-
larly colorful poem among Tu Fu's works. The beauty of this hokku, however, is

more like that of Chinese poetry during the Six Dynasty period. Or it can be said to resemble the poetic style of that famous Chinese anthology *Wen hsüan*. — *Rohan*

Although the woman named Chō lived simply in the mountains, she had an interest in the life of *fūga*. Bashō was impressed by that fact and compared her to a butterfly whose wings are perfumed by an orchid's fragrance. — *Kobayashi*

Because the smell of an orchid is often compared to the beauty of chastity as well as of friendship, the hokku may imply a praise for the woman's virtue as a loyal, loving wife. The image of a butterfly, with its beautiful, light wings perfumed by an orchid, suggests exquisite beauty mixed with feminine sensuality. — *Higuchi*

Sōin's verse plays on the proprietress's name: Tsuru invokes the image of "falling" (*otsuru*) arrowroot leaves assailed by night frost. It was a poem written in jest, the sort of poem Sōin might have written to tease the woman while sipping a drink. Bashō's hokku is different. It depicts a butterfly motionlessly perched on a fragrant orchid flower, its wings being perfumed by the scent. The scene evokes the image of a court lady, the type who appears in a tale like *Genji monogatari*. The woman Chō is a "butterfly," and her "wings" are perfumed by the scent of an orchid. Bashō's hokku is therefore nothing like Sōin's playful poem; in a symbolic manner it portrays the woman's beauty to the full. — *Komiya*

The room of a beautiful woman smells of cosmetics, and one associates an orchid with the sort of words used to describe such a room. The poet thought of an orchid since the woman was formerly a courtesan, and he placed a butterfly on it since she was named Chō. The result evokes a novelistic world that is unusually sensual for Bashō. Perhaps he was a little embarrassed; that is probably why he spoke so apologetically to Dohō, explaining that he merely followed Sōin's example. — *Abe M.*

The butterfly, which has been flitting from one flower to another, is now resting with its wings folded and surrounded by the fragrant smell of an orchid. That butterfly, as the poem implies, is the symbol of the proprietress as she looked then. Because of its elegant dignity, an orchid is counted among the four "gentlemanly" plants (the others are plum blossom, chrysanthemum, and bamboo). The image of a butterfly's wings perfumed by an orchid's fragrance is beautiful and sensual indeed, but one should not overlook its elegant and dignified aspect. — *Yamamoto*

I arrived at my native town at the beginning of the ninth month. Nothing of my late mother remained there anymore. All had changed from what I remembered. My older brother, now with white hair in his sidelocks and wrinkles around his eyebrows, could only say, "How lucky we are to meet alive again!" Then he opened a keepsake bag and said to me, "Pay your respects to Mother's white hair. They say the legendary Urashima's hair turned white the instant he opened the souvenir box he had brought back from the Dragon Palace. Now your eyebrows look a little white, too." We wept together for some time.

should I hold it in my hand
it would melt in my hot tears—
autumn frost

te | ni | toraba | kien | namida | zo | atsuki | aki | no | shimo
hand | in | if-take | will-vanish | tear | ! | hot | autumn | 's | frost

NOTE

Written in Ueno on October 16. Urashima was the young hero of a legend who visited a Dragon Lady's palace under the sea. Returning to his native village and finding nothing there that he could remember, he disobeyed the lady's order and opened a jewel box she had given him. Instantly he turned into an old man.

COMMENTARY

The comparison here is between frost and white hair. The word "hot" connotes an infinitely deep sorrow, while the words "would melt"—*kien*—have a sonorous sound. – *Tosai*

The poet is saying he cannot take the white hair in his hand because if he were to do so his hot tears would melt it away like autumn frost. In brief, this is a hokku that depends far too much on a logical connection of ideas. In addition, it still retains something of the old style that characterized *Minashiguri*. I do not find it poetically appealing. – *Meisetsu*

An excellent poem which, without any verbal adornment, fully reveals the poet's honest, sincere personality. – *Kobayashi*

The poet just could not contain his grief. – *Ebara*

The poem's central metaphor—that of autumn frost—is a failure. In particular, the statement that the frost would melt in hot tears sounds hollow and unconvincing. We can visualize the grieving poet, but the poem does not convey the grief in a manner that moves the heart. — *Shūson*

I think it can safely be said that few other poems make us so sublimely conscious that nature and humanity are one. — *Komiya*

The underlying emotionality of the poem is manifest in the wave-like rhythm of the verse. However, if we read the hokku independently of the headnote, we get the impression that the wording of the poem does not do justice to the intensity of the poet's emotion. A poem of this kind needs to be read with its headnote to be fully appreciated. — *Iwata*

Fuwa

autumn wind—
the thickets, the fields and all
at Fuwa Barrier

akikaze l ya l yabu l mo l hatake l mo l Fuwa l no l seki
autumn-wind l : l thicket l also l field l also l Fuwa l 's l barrier

NOTE

Located near Sekigahara in Mino Province, Fuwa was well known for its government checking station in ancient times. After the capital moved away from Nara
in 784, the barrier fell into disuse. The hokku alludes to a waka by Fujiwara
Yoshitsune (1169–1206):

No one living	hito sumanu
here at Fuwa Barrier,	Fuwa no sekiya no
the shingled eaves	itabisashi
are left to decay . . .	arenishi nochi wa
Only the autumn wind blows.	tada aki no kaze

COMMENTARY

The hokku depicts the loneliness of the place, where the wind that once devastated the barrier buildings still keeps blowing over the thickets and fields that
now occupy the site. A sense of desolation clings to its concluding phrase because all previous poetic references to Fuwa Barrier have been about its desolation. – *Tosai*

Because winter arrives early in Sekigahara and its vicinity, Bashō, who visited
there toward the end of the lunar ninth month, must have flinched in the chilly
autumn wind as it came blowing down from Mt. Fuwa. As I imagine the scene,
Mt. Ibuki in the distance was already capped with snow, nearby hills were clad
in colorful autumn leaves, and shocks of rice straw lay in rows on the fields.
Standing at the site of the ancient barrier, Bashō was plunged in thoughts of days
long gone. His words "the thickets, the fields and all" enable the poem to free itself from Yoshitsune's waka-like lyricism and acquire a sense of emotional realism, thereby bringing it completely into the realm of haikai. The hokku has no
trace of the ruined barrier of which Yoshitsune sang; the thickets and fields, over

which the lonely autumn wind was blowing, had taken over the barrier site. Ba-shō stood there on his own feet, and that sense of real-life experience fills this hokku. — *Yamamoto*

When I read Yoshitsune's poem and Bashō's side by side, I find myself preferring the former to the latter. — *Seishi*

Nature does not change, but everything that is human does. This has been a mo-tif in poetry from ancient times. Bashō, too, was especially sensitive to time's passing and the process through which things traditional or historical are de-stroyed. — *Imoto*

In Taoism, which Bashō believed in, the wind is an important symbol represent-ing the basic power that stimulates everything and makes it utter the voice of heaven or of earth. The first half of *Nozarashi kikō* presents a traveler trying to listen to the voice of earth that lies hidden in everything blown in the autumn wind. This hokku is a conclusion to that section of the journal. — *Hori*

Recalling how the image of a weatherbeaten skeleton haunted my mind at the time of my departure from Musashi Plain

I am not yet dead
after many nights on the road—
end of autumn

shini | mo | senu | tabine | no | hate | yo | aki | no | kure
dying | ! | do-not | travel-sleep | 's | end | ! | autumn | 's | end

NOTE
Written at Bokuin's house in Ōgaki.

COMMENTARY

When the poet took to the road, he was afraid he might collapse somewhere in the wilderness. But now autumn is ending, and things have turned out otherwise. The emotions that suffuse this hokku are those of an aged person. – *Tosai*

The hokku's middle phrase, while not going so far as to mean the end of the journey, implies that the poet has been on the road for a considerable length of time. It also suggests that he relaxed a little at Bokuin's. He probably used such strong words as "I am not yet dead" because it was a desolate autumn evening. – *Seihō*

The poem is permeated both by the mood of late autumn and by the emotion of a person who, after starting the journey determined not to be afraid of dying, came at last to feel "I am not yet dead after many nights on the road." I therefore take the hokku's concluding phrase to denote not only the end of the autumn season but also the hazy end of an autumn day. – *Shūson*

Bashō had been emotionally drained because of his hard life on the road and the reunions he had had with his relatives. Now at an old friend's home he felt at ease for the first time. Thereupon he composed this hokku, almost muttering it to himself. – *Abe M.*

Of the verses that emerged from this journey, the ones written before this hokku tend to create a mood of desolation, and the ones following it are inclined toward a tone of *fūkyō*. Bashō's attitude during the trip with Bokuin shows something of *fūkyō* as well; perhaps Bokuin's personality was a factor. But basically the hokku suggests that, as the journey progressed, Bashō became relaxed enough to look at himself objectively. – *Yamamoto*

I went out to the beach at daybreak, when it was still dark.

twilight of dawn
a whitefish, with an inch
of whiteness

akebono I ya I shirauo I shiroki I koto I issun
dawn I : I whitefish I white I thing I one-inch

NOTE
Written on a beach near Kuwana.

COMMENTARY

As I understand, this hokku originally had "thin snow" for its beginning phrase. Master Bashō said to me, "I regret having written such a phrase." — *Dohō*

It is fascinating to imagine a beach scene where things flicker from moment to moment in the dim darkness of dawn. The poet's skill is observable in combining the expansive image of dawn with something tiny. "An inch" is an expression difficult to use in a poem. — *Tosai*

The repetition of the word "white" is artful. I have read somewhere that in Kuwana people say, "one inch in winter, two inches in spring," to describe the growth rate of an icefish. — *Abe Y.*

The poem begins on a large scale with "twilight of dawn" and gradually narrows its focus as it moves from "a whitefish" to "an inch." The technique is characteristic of Bashō, I think. It might be called a funnel-shaped rhetorical device. — *Mizuho*

The phrase "thin snow" would limit the poem's world to the beach. The juxtaposition of white snow and a whitefish would decrease the visual effect of each image, too. It was for these reasons, I think, that Bashō revised the phrase to read "twilight of dawn." — *Shūson*

The scene of a winter beach at dawn—there is still some time before sunrise— has crystallized in the image of a one-inch-long icefish. The forceful tone with which the poem ends shows the poet's attempt to express his surprise and wonderment at the sight of the icefish; it is a skillful device. — *Iwata*

Watching travelers pass by

even a horse
arrests my eyes—on this
morning of snow

uma | wo | sae | nagamuru | yuki | no | ashita | kana
horse | [acc.] | even | look | snow | 's | morning | kana

NOTE
Written at the house of Hayashi Tōyō (?–1712), an innkeeper near Nagoya and leader of a local haikai group.

COMMENTARY
There is novelty in the expression "a horse arrests my eyes." Usually people pay no attention to a horse, but because this was a snowy morning the sight of a traveler on horseback reminded the poet of things past and made a deep impression on him. — *Shōgatsudō*

After snowfall, trees and oxen and everything else look elegant. The phrase "even a horse" implicitly alludes to all those other things that were within sight. — *Donto*

A horse offers nothing elegant to the eye. Therefore the poet said "even a horse"; the phrase is striking and provides the center of interest. The word "even" implies that it was deep snow. — *Nobutane*

Clearly expressed in the poem is the childlike curiosity of the poet, who was amusing himself by sizing up each passing horse with a traveler at its reins. — *Momota*

This is a powerful poem drawing on what the poet actually felt. On a snowy morning everything is placed in a color and light different from the ordinary, and as a result we start paying attention to things to which we have been too accustomed to notice before. That is what we often experience. Horses had been a familiar sight for Bashō during the journey, but one snowy morning he noticed the beauty of a horse and watched it in fascination. As we read the poem, we feel the breathing of the poet who stood watching. — *Shūson*

Bashō's eyes caught sight of a lone traveler, and then of a horse ambling along in the snow. The pathetic sight of the horse touched his heart. Bashō, who years later wrote

departing spring—	yuku haru ya
birds weep, and fishes' eyes	tori naki uo no
are tearful	me wa namida

must have seen tears welling up in the horse's eyes. There was nothing attractive about the pack horse, yet somehow the sight gripped Bashō's heart and would not let it go. He was moved by something plain and ordinary, and that surprised him. The surprise crystallized in this hokku. – *Yamamoto*

Bashō was a traveler himself, but now, thanks to the host's kindness, he could relax inside a warm house and gaze nonchalantly at travelers on the snowy road outside. That is what this hokku implies. Tōyō's house was on the Tōkaidō highway. – *Kon*

My hat had been worn out by the rains during the long journey, and my paper coat had crumpled up because of the storms I encountered. My appearance was so extremely shabby that even I thought of myself as a pathetic roamer. It suddenly occurred to me that many years ago a talented writer of kyōka *had visited this province. Thereupon I wrote:*

comic verse
in the wintry gust
a wanderer . . . how like Chikusai
I have become!

kyōku I kogarashi I no I mi I wa I Chikusai I ni I nitaru I kana
comic-verse I wintry-gust I 's I self I as-for I Chikusai I to I resemble I kana

NOTE

Bashō used this hokku to open the first kasen in *Fuyu no hi*. As will be seen below, there are differing opinions as to whether the word *kyōku* is part of the hokku or a prefatory note. *Kyōku*, a word consisting of the characters *kyō* ("mad," "comic") and *ku* ("verse," "poem"—see the Introduction), usually refers to a seventeen-syllable verse written in a comic vein, as distinct from *kyōka*, a humorous poem written in thirty-one syllables. Chikusai is the name of a fictional quack doctor featured in a contemporary comic story, *Chikusai monogatari* (The tale of Chikusai). He has lost all his patients due to his indulgence in comic poetry; impoverished but still scribbling *kyōka*, he manages to reach Nagoya on his way to Edo.

COMMENTARY

The beginning two words, "comic verse," sound abrupt and inappropriate. Drop those words, and we will have a hokku with both a neat seventeen-syllable pattern and a deeper meaning. – *Meisetsu*

By "comic verse" Bashō meant a haikai verse. He wanted to assert this was a haikai poem. He was anxious to emphasize the element of haikai in this hokku. Of course, that element was not what Teimon and Danrin poets talked about. And yet it was something their verses contained, too—something that we can label plebeianism. Bashō had sought to give his haikai just as high a literary value as waka or renga while retaining its plebeian quality. Because of that desire he had experimented with the style of Chinese poetry during his days of *Musashi buri* and *Minashiguri*. But soon he realized that such experiments would not lead him to any new literary realm unique to haikai. It was essential that haikai be rooted in the real life of the people. It was not out of modesty that he said "comic verse" or did not say "how like Saigyō I have become!" Because it was haikai that he was writing, he focused on what was most familiar to the people. And that was Chikusai. The story of Chikusai was widely read among the people of the time, and his name was scattered through the works of kyōka and haikai, all portraying him as a whimsical, funny fellow. – *Ebara*

From the fact that Bashō compared himself to Chikusai, we can surmise that he was relaxed enough to look at himself objectively. We can see a faint smile forming on his face as he made the comparison. – *Shūson*

It goes without saying that the words at the outset, "comic verse," are not part of the poem. But by placing these words at the beginning of the hokku, Bashō showed that, in setting out on a new poetic journey, he was making great plans that would be carried out with great resolution. He was resolved, in fact, to embrace every vicissitude in a spirit of freedom and equanimity. "Comic verse" implies a humorous, plebeian, unfettered type of haikai verse. It is not a self-deprecatory term used in deference to the more elegant kyōka. Rather, Bashō here declared, while standing at the same place where the kyōka poet Chikusai stood, that he would write "comic verse." – *Yamamoto*

Bokuin, Bashō's companion at this time, wrote the following hokku when they left Ōgaki:

two wanderers	uta monogurui
gone mad with poetry	futari kogarashi
in the wintry gust	sugata kana

Bokuin's poem sheds light on the meaning of the incongruous phrase "comic verse in the wintry gust." The phrase describes a person traveling in the wintry gust while mumbling comic verses. – *Abe M.*

To the local poets whom he met for the first time, Bashō introduced himself as a person no better than Chikusai. In doing so he asserted the principle of *fūkyō*. This also shows that there were already people who were able to appreciate that principle. – *Imoto*

The hokku was Bashō's humble greeting to the poets in Nagoya who had overly high expectations of him as their teacher. At the same time, it was his way of inviting them to enter and enjoy the world of *fūkyō* with him. Chikusai is mentioned here not only because of his connection to Nagoya but because there is something that differentiates him from Tu Fu or Li Po, or from Saigyō or Sōgi, at a deeper level. Chikusai has the transparent purity that only a fictional character can have, and that quality makes sure that the spirit of *fūkyō* in this poem is pure. – *Hori*

1685

Bashō's long sojourn in the Nagoya area finally came to an end in late January. After writing a kasen with three poets in Atsuta on January 23, 1685, he took to the road and headed westward for Ueno in Iga Province, where he wanted to celebrate the lunar New Year. He arrived at his native town on January 29, five days before the year ended, and stayed there for nearly two months. A number of local poets, who had declared themselves to be Bashō's students, took this opportunity to contact their teacher and ask for his advice on their work. His letter dated March 3 shows that he taught one of them not to follow recent poetic trends in Edo and said, "Anthologies like *Minashiguri* contain many verses that are not worth discussing." Obviously he knew his poetic ideal had changed.

In mid-March Bashō resumed his journey, first stopping at Nara, where he watched a *nō* performance at Kōfuku Temple, and then at Takenouchi, where he visited Chiri once more. After spending a couple of weeks in Kyoto, he made his way to Ōtsu and found several new students waiting for him. *Fuyu no hi* had made his name well known in that whole area. More new students entered his school after he revisited Atsuta on or around April 28. He took part in several haikai gatherings in Atsuta as well as in Narumi, a town a short distance east of Atsuta. He left Narumi on May 12 and headed back to Edo, taking a mountainous northern route that passed through Kai Province. He arrived back at the Bashō Hut in Fukagawa toward the end of May.

Aside from joining a haikai gathering on July 3, Bashō seems to have spent the rest of the year in relative leisure at his hut. It was probably the period in which he tried to recollect the experiences of his past journey and discover what they meant to him and his poetry. He must have drafted *Nozarashi kikō* at this time. The final draft, however, does not seem to have been completed until the autumn of 1687.

Spending a whole day on the beach

the sea darkens—
a wild duck's call
faintly white

umi | kurete | kamo | no | koe | honokani | shiroshi
sea | grow-dark | wild-duck | 's | voice | faintly | white

NOTE

The opening verse of a kasen composed in Atsuta on January 23. A variant text has the headnote "When I was at Atsuta in Owari Province, people invited me to go boating and enjoy the year-end seascape."

COMMENTARY

A duck's call is described as being white because of the waves caused by the wind. The poem suggests the loneliness of the fishing village. It does not read smoothly as the wording is poor. – *Donto*

It was windy and noisy in the daytime, but with nightfall the waves became calm, and it was no longer possible to discern the color of the sea. As the poet faintly heard a bird's cry, he looked afar and saw the dim whiteness of a wild duck. There is an infinite amount of *yūgen* in this scene. – *Sanga*

Although the sun had set in the western mountains, the sea was not yet completely dark. There were still reflections of the lingering sunlight on the water, making that part of the sea look faintly white. One might have said, "As a wild duck called, the day came to a close and the sea looked faintly white," but the poet wrote that a duck's call was white, thereby describing the whitish color of the sea where the duck was afloat. An interesting manipulation of words. – *Meisetsu*

On a cold day our breath looks white. Didn't Bashō link that to the whitish impression of that evening and describe it as the voice being white, instead of saying that the breath was white? When he heard the duck's call, he sensed—he did not see, of course—that the bird was exhaling white breath because of the cold. – *Abe Y.*

Ordinarily one would say:

the sea darkens—	umi kurete
faintly white	honokani shiroshi
a wild duck's call	kamo no koe

But Bashō deliberately reversed the second and third phrases. He chose to continue lightly with a five-syllable second phrase and end strongly with a seven-syllable third phrase. As a result, the language of the poem does not just trail off; instead, it creates a solid sense of stability. — *Handa*

What is striking in this verse is the wording of the last two phrases, in which an auditory phenomenon is described in visual terms. The French symbolists made much of a similar device, but obviously Bashō could not have learned it from them. Rather, he gave a straightforward and honest expression to the impression he formed through his own sensibility. The result is a lively poem that has nothing artificial or unnatural about it. — *Komiya*

Faint white vapor over the sea and a wild duck's call were merged in the poet's sense perceptions. Of course, the whiteness was seen through the eye and the voice was heard through the ear, but he felt as if his eyes saw what his ears heard, and he made that delicate feeling into a poem. — *Iwata*

The reader should first recognize that the phrase "a wild duck's call" condenses frigid, nostalgic feelings of the wandering poet who was still on the road near the end of the year. Past commentators on this hokku have paid too much attention to "faintly white" and so have overlooked this point. — *Ogata*

A wild duck has a call that suits the winter season. Because the call sounds chilly, it is felt to be white. — *Imoto*

This is a poem in the "descriptive mode," a type of poem not found in Bashō's earlier hokku. It describes a scene objectively, with no imported sentiment like happiness or grief. This method, however, should not be mistaken for the *shasei* principle that became famous in early twentieth-century Japan. In Western literature, realism did not emerge until the nineteenth century. There is no way Bashō could have any idea of *shasei*, which derived from Western realism. Bashō had apparently befriended the monk Butchō in Fukagawa and begun studying Zen. And Zen monks were good at describing a landscape objectively in a few words and embodying cosmic truth in it. — *Konishi*

Removing my straw sandals here, resting my cane there, I continued to spend days and nights on the road until the year came to a close.

another year is gone—
a traveler's hat on my head,
straw sandals on my feet

toshi I kurenu I kasa I kite I waraji I hakinagara
year I have-ended I hat I wearing I straw-sandal I wearing

NOTE

Written on or around January 29, five days before the lunar New Year. Bashō was back in Ueno at around this time.

COMMENTARY

The hokku well suggests the carefree life of a man undisturbed by worldly matters. — *Meisetsu*

This poem can be said to condense Bashō's entire life. — *Higuchi*

For Bashō, even his native town was no more than a stop on his journey. The poem conveys the feeling—and even the breathing—of the itinerant poet who considered himself a homeless wanderer. He is looking at himself with a smile here. — *Abe M.*

Especially at the year's end, a person who has forsaken this world and has nothing particular to do senses his difference from other people. Bashō, being at his birthplace, was bound to feel all the more nostalgic. — *Hori*

On the road to Nara

it is spring!
a hill without a name
in thin haze

haru | nare | ya | na | mo | naki | yama | no | usugasumi
spring | is | ! | name | even | nonexistent | mountain | 's | thin-haze

COMMENTARY

This poem is haikai because it mentions a nameless hill. Singing of famous mountains is left to waka poets. *– Nobutane*

It was the kind of hill one would normally overlook, but it looked truly attractive as spring had come and a thin veil of morning haze wavered over it. The poet sought a realm of haikai in the sight of a nameless hill, but the poem embodies his deep affinity with nature. A happy traveler on a spring morning. *– Ebara*

A warm, springlike day is likely to make people happy if it arrives at a time when they are tired of winter cold. I am sure everyone has experienced that happy feeling sometime, especially if one lives in Kyoto where the winter is severe. Thus since olden times there have been many waka that express happiness at the coming of spring. But no waka has celebrated that happiness as simply, as directly, or as appealingly as this poem. Although it looks plain, the plainness is of a rare kind. *– Utsubo*

Mt. Kagu, which towers on Yamato Plain along with Mt. Miminashi and Mt. Unebi, had been regarded as both beautiful and sacred since ancient times. Generations of poets had recognized the arrival of spring when they saw haze hanging over it. That classical tradition is in the background of Bashō's poem. He was on his way to Nara, but Mt. Kagu had not yet come within sight. As he tried to recall past poets' thoughts about Mt. Kagu, his eyes fell on the haze that veiled "a hill without a name." Thereupon this hokku emerged. *– Ogata*

The soft sound of the words that make up this poem induces us to visualize the gentle contours of those hills in Yamato Province. *– Yamamoto*

A sense of ease, plus a bit of loneliness, is suggested. *– Kon*

Coming down a mountain road that leads to Ōtsu

along the mountain road
somehow it tugs at my heart—
a wild violet

yamaji | kite | naniyara | yukashi | sumiregusa
mountain-road | coming | somehow | attractive | violet-grass

COMMENTARY

The poet said exactly what he felt. This is a plain poem. – *Meisetsu*

The hokku vividly describes the emotion of the poet who felt so much tenderness toward the flower that he almost spoke to it. – *Keion*

The poem is far from profound. In its middle phrase the poet personified the violet. The flower would not have seemed so attractive if it had been a mountain rose or peony. The poet was fascinated because it was blooming inconspicuously amid the grass alongside a mountain road. – *Rohan*

The hokku's opening phrase suggests that the poet had walked a considerable distance along the mountain road. In that situation, it was natural that he should feel a great deal of attraction toward a blooming violet. Concentrating his mind, the poet gazed at it. The flower bloomed there, innocently. To the poet's eyes, it appeared to have feelings similar to his own. He could not explain why it appeared that way, but he thought it did. The hokku's middle phrase refers to that fact. – *Handa*

A violet raising its head from the forest floor is no more than a mote in the sum of existence. Yet the sun, the center of our universe, revolves around it. Bashō paid the same amount of respect to all natural phenomena, no matter how big or how small. – *Noguchi*

The reader can feel the way in which the beauty of something small and delicate, located amid quiet surroundings, gradually suffused the watcher's heart with a kind of tenderness. – *Ebara*

Buson's hokku

to the folks	hone hirou
sifting the bones, how dear	hito ni shitashiki
a violet!	sumire kana

directly expresses what Bashō suggested obliquely in the phrase "somehow it tugs at my heart." By presenting the contrasting image of people collecting a dear one's bones at a crematorium, Buson enhanced, deepened, and even added haikai-type humor to the endearing beauty of a violet. This is sufficient evidence to prove that modern haiku had its origin in Buson's time. But Bashō had a sensibility that made him say such things as "What is so good about saying everything?" and "Hokku should not spell everything out." In his poetry, what remains unexpressed is supported by something that lies behind. The loss of that "something" eventually resulted in the disintegration of sensibility, as can be seen in that romantic poem of Buson's. Bashō's sensibility enabled him to feel a thought "as immediately as the odour of a rose"—to borrow a phrase from T. S. Eliot. It also helped to prevent this poem from falling into sentimentalism.
– Yamamoto

Bashō was the type of person who was strongly attracted to things beautiful and delicate, and who was driven to seek out the source of that attraction. The source, however, turned out to lie too deep for human understanding, a quality that seems to have become an added charm to him. – Utsubo

A view of the lake

the pine tree
of Karasaki, looking hazier
than the blossoms

Karasaki | no | matsu | wa | hana | yori | oboro | nite
Karasaki | 's | pine | as-for | blossom | than | haziness | being

NOTE

The lake mentioned in the headnote is Lake Biwa, which Bashō passed on his
way from Kyoto to Ōtsu. According to one source, he wrote this hokku at the
home of Mikami Senna (1651–1723), a Buddhist priest and leader of local haikai
poets. Karasaki, located on the western shore of the lake, was famous for its scenic beauty, especially for a shapely pine tree that had inspired many a waka poet
to write poetry. Hazy cherry blossoms on Mt. Nagara, located nearby, had also
been praised for their beauty in a number of waka.

COMMENTARY

A certain poet in Kyoto criticized this hokku for ending with the particle *nite*.
Kikaku volunteered an explanation, saying "*Nite* is a word in the same category
as *kana*.* Therefore, if the opening verse of a haikai sequence ends with the particle *kana*, any verse that closely follows it, such as a third verse, should not be
concluded with the word *nite*. But this is a hokku, and Master Bashō used *nite*
in it because *kana* would close the verse in too sharp a tone." Romaru† observed,
"I can accept Kikaku's explanation about the use of *nite*. But it seems to me that
this particular verse has a style characteristic of a third verse in a haikai sequence. How could it be considered a hokku?" I responded, "Without any doubt
this is a hokku, because it expresses the author's spontaneous feeling. A third

---

* The terminal particle *kana* emphasizes the speaker's emotion without specifying its nature. *Nite* (literally "being" or "acting in connection with") is normally a connective between two clauses, but haikai poets often used it as a terminal particle in their verse when
they wanted a less emphatic ending than *kana*. In the poetics of haikai, therefore, *kana* and
nite were considered to belong to the same category of words and were not to be used in
verses close to each other.
† Kondō Romaru (?–1693) was an amateur poet who lived near Mt. Haguro in northeastern Japan. Bashō visited his house in the summer of 1689.

verse contains more speculative thinking. A hokku with speculative thinking would be a second-rate verse." Master Bashō said, "All those comments, including Kikaku's and yours, are rationalizations. I wrote this hokku simply because I thought the hazy pine tree looked more charming than the blossoms." – *Kyorai*

After rainfall, the moon was hazy at Karasaki. The marvelous effect of this hokku is beyond description. – *Sanga*

According to a certain interpreter, this hokku alludes to a waka by Emperor Gotoba [1180–1239]:

At Karasaki   Karasaki no
the green of the pine tree   matsu no midori mo
is also in the haze   oboro nite
that extends from the blossoms—   hana yori tsuzuku
dawn on a spring day.   haru no akebono
                     – *Nanimaru*

Bashō's hokku is an adaptation of Emperor Gotoba's waka, but the adaptation has been done so poorly in this instance that it is a worse crime than plagiarism. Of course, we might read the poem without reference to the waka, but even then its mediocrity is beyond dispute. For Bashō's sake, this kind of poem might best be forgotten. – *Shiki*

I have wondered whether the scene described in this poem was at night or in the daytime. My opinion is that this was a view of the lake in the daytime, and that the poet, looking over the entire landscape where the pine tree and the cherry blossoms on the shore stood enveloped in the spring haze, perceived more beauty in the pine than in the blossoms. The poem, describing the pine in the haze, well suggests its delicate shades of color. – *Mizuho*

The word "hazy" invariably refers to night. This has always been so in waka and other types of literature since ancient times. – *Keion*

The topic of this poem is haziness. That being the case, the scene cannot be in broad daylight. The time of day must be nightfall at the earliest. There are instances of the word "hazy" being used in an evening scene. – *Rohan*

Late on a hazy day, the poet saw pine needles emitting an unearthly white gleam. It may have been a mirage of a pine tree seen through eyes accustomed to the sight of cherry blossoms. In the stillness of the haze, the moon was dissolving into the lake. In the hazy moonlight the dark silhouette of the pine was brightened by gleaming ripples of lake water. – *Saisei*

"Hazy" refers to the dimness of a spring night on which the outline of everything looks blurred. Although poets since olden times have often sung of hazy cherry blossoms, no one has described a pine tree as being hazy. At the sight of the lake where the pine tree and cherry blossoms were all hazy, Bashō looked attentively and found new beauty in the haze-covered pine tree. There have been controversies as to the time of day, but I am sure it was night. — *Shūson*

The pine tree of Karasaki seemed to be in a haze, not because of the hazy spring moon, but because of vapor rising from the lake. Standing tall above the lake in the evening dusk, the tree looked as if it came from a splendid black-ink painting. The scene was incomparably more beautiful than that of hazy cherry blossoms. The poem suggests that beauty in extremely fitting, compact language. — *Komiya*

This must be a night scene if the poet was near the tree, a daytime scene if he was far away. Relying on my sensibility, I would say it was a night scene. — *Seishi*

The poet said exactly what he felt; he was not overtly comparing the beauty of the blossoms to that of the pine tree. Both the blossoms and the tree looked beautiful through the haze; the poet simply focused on the pine. — *Iwata*

Because of the distance, the pine tree of Karasaki cannot be clearly seen from Ōtsu. What Bashō's eyes caught from the distance of two and a half miles across the lake was not the real sight of the tree but an image recalled from past poetic tradition involving the pine tree of Karasaki. — *Ogata*

If what is described in *Kamakura kaidō* [Coastal road to Kamakura, 1725] is true, this hokku was followed by Senna's wakiku:

wilting cherry blossoms   yama wa sakura wo
on the hills, spring rain   shioru harusame

It goes against common poetic practice that a hokku on blossoms should be followed by a wakiku on cherry blossoms. While we have no way of knowing whether any hidden poetic principle was at work here, we can speculate as to the reason why "cherry blossoms" could follow "blossoms." Wasn't it because the word "blossoms" in the hokku referred not just to actual cherry blossoms but stressed its symbolic sense of youth and beauty? If that was the case, the pine of Karasaki is not merely a tree but a symbol of loneliness and old age. — *Imoto*

At a shop for travelers, where I stopped for lunch

azaleas in a bucket—
in their shade, a woman
tearing up a dried codfish

tsutsuji | ikete | sono | kage | ni | hidara | saku | onna
azalea | arranging | its | shade | in | dried-codfish | tearing | woman

NOTE

Composed on the way from Ōtsu to Minakuchi. In Japan azaleas are found wild and grow as tall as six feet.

COMMENTARY

Imagine a scene where, under a bucket of long azalea branches hanging from the eaves, a woman is tearing up a dried codfish on the veranda. – *Donto*

The store being so small, the woman was doing the cooking behind the azaleas. That was clever and well-mannered, the poet probably thought. The hokku vividly pictures the rustic setting where flowers, available in great abundance, had been tossed into a wooden bucket. The woman refrained from cooking in front of the guest, probably because he appeared to be no ordinary person. – *Tosai*

It should be noted that this hokku has the syllable pattern of 6-5-3-5. Around 1908 and 1909 it was fashionable among radical haiku poets to use this pattern. – *Seisensui*

The word "tear" is quite effective. It sounds rough, enhancing the wild beauty of both the azaleas and the woman. – *Mizuho*

Bashō must have been quite fascinated with the looks of the woman who was tearing up a dried codfish, which was of a brilliant white, in the shade of azalea flowers, which were as crimson as blood. The poem is not especially good or original. It is a rather strange poem for Bashō. – *Higuchi*

This might appear to be a purely descriptive poem, which is rare for Bashō. But the flowers are azaleas, and the fish is a dried codfish. These images create a rustic, *wabi*-type impression. It is likely that Bashō wanted to produce that mood of *wabi* here rather than write a merely descriptive poem. – *Ebara*

In the field of sunlight

butterflies flit . . .
that is all, amid the field
of sunlight

chō I no I tobu I bakari I nonaka I no I hikage I kana
butterfly I 's I fly I only I mid-field I 's I sunlight I kana

NOTE

The word *chō* can be singular or plural, and the word *hikage* can mean either
"sunlight" or "shadow in the sun."

COMMENTARY

The poet, wanting to thank those who had shown him hospitality, compared
himself to a butterfly soaring above the field in the sunlight. Roaming the fields
and hills all his life, he had suffered from bitter cold like a butterfly in early
spring; but, thanks to the kindness of people around him, he was now enjoying
himself like a butterfly in a sunlit field. The hokku is a fitting expression of gratitude. – *Shōgatsudō*

The grass was still short, and neither reeds nor violets had shown any color.
Only a butterfly was there, flitting as if looking for flowers. The sunlight was not
as balmy as that of a spring day. – *Donto*

The entire field was bathed in the bright spring sunshine, which felt almost a little too warm to the skin. Without even a slight breeze, all was quiet and calm.
Then, as if emerging from underground, there appeared a flitting butterfly. Because of the butterfly, the poet became more aware of the tranquillity of the surroundings as well as the brightness of the sunlight. – *Handa*

There was nothing within sight as the poet crossed the field one mid-spring day.
Only a butterfly cast its shadow in the sunlight. – *Kōseki*

The poem has something of a daydream in it, with the image of flitting butterflies
harking back to Chuang-tzu's dream. – *Hori*

To Tokoku

for the white poppy
the butterfly breaks off its wing
as a keepsake

shirageshi I ni I hane I mogu I chō I no I katami I kana
white-poppy I to I wing I break-off I butterfly I 's I keepsake I kana

NOTE

The hokku was a farewell present to Tsuboi Tokoku (?–1690), a rice dealer who
had become one of Bashō's earliest students in the Nagoya area.

COMMENTARY

A petal falling off a poppy flower resembles a wing broken off a butterfly. The
metaphor is used to suggest the sadness of parting. – *Donto*

The host's pure heart is compared to a white poppy, and the words "breaks off
its wing" show the firmness of the bond that united the two friends. – *Tosai*

The poet compared Tokoku to a white poppy and himself to a butterfly, while
suggesting the sadness of parting through the image of a butterfly breaking off its
wing. The poem expresses his deep affection toward Tokoku. – *Keion*

This hokku embodies a passion rare for Bashō. The words sound too affectionate
to say to a mere student. One wonders whether there may not have been something
more than a teacher-student relationship between Bashō and Tokoku. – *Seisensui*

In actuality a butterfly never breaks off its wing, but it looks that way when a
white petal falls at the very moment a butterfly leaves a poppy flower. The poet
may have witnessed such a scene when he wrote this poem. – *Shūson*

In my opinion, Bashō expressed his emotion symbolically in this poem. The instant a white poppy petal fell, a butterfly that had alighted on the poppy flut-
tered out, and as it did so the butterfly wished that the fallen petal be made its
keepsake. – *Komiya*

Bashō was on a journey, teaching the art of poetry to his students along the way.
He should have prepared himself for parting, allowing no room for sentimental-
ity. Regardless of what may have existed between Bashō and Tokoku, this poem
implies something extraordinarily persistent. – *Utsubo*

I think that the intensity of the poet's emotion led to an imagined scene that
could not exist in nature. One should feel the pain of Bashō's heart in that odd
expression. – *Yamamoto*

Toward the end of the fourth month, I returned to my hut and recuperated from the fatigue of the journey.

my summer robe
there are still some lice
I have not caught

natsugoromo I imada I shirami I wo I tori I tsukusazu
summer-robe I yet I louse I [acc.] I catching I complete-not

NOTE
This is the hokku that concludes *Nozarashi kikō*.

COMMENTARY
The reader should visualize a man who has been on a long journey and who, without clean clothes to change into, is tortured by lice. — *Donto*

Having just come home, the poet had not yet had time to remove all the lice from his clothes. He may still have been wearing the same clothes. I wonder if this was not a poem with which he notified his students of his arrival back home. — *Meisetsu*

The poem vividly pictures a high-minded person who recalls the pleasures of the past poetic journey while picking lice from the weatherbeaten robe he has worn. — *Kobayashi*

This poem has something humorous about it, providing a fitting conclusion to the journal. Bashō's humor around this time was much more spontaneous, markedly different from his earlier witticisms that were manufactured as the occasion arose. — *Seihō*

Echoing the poem placed at the beginning of *Nozarashi kikō*, this hokku suggests a sense of relief that permeated Bashō's mind at the time. — *Shūson*

In Bashō's time, it was common to have an infestation of lice in one's clothing. It was common, too, to sing about it in poetry. There was nothing embarrassing about saying that "there are still some lice I have not caught." In "Genjūan no ki" [The record of my life at the Genjū Hut, 1691] Bashō wrote, "On a mountain with no signs of man, I sit alone and pick lice," even though here he may have been imitating what Chinese poets had done before him. In *Sarumino* [The monkey's straw raincoat, 1691] there is also a verse:

on the palm of my hand	tenohira ni
I let a louse crawl—	shirami hawasuru
shade of the blossoms	hana no kage

Things were different, then, without DDT. – *Seishi*

A sense of relief after a long journey. A sense of weariness lingering in the body. To these, the presence of lice adds poetic humor. – *Abe M.*

Since ancient times lice had appeared in Chinese poetry as appropriate companions of a person living a carefree, reclusive life. Bashō made conscious use of that tradition. – *Kon*

clouds now and then
give rest to people
viewing the moon

kumo I oriori I hito I wo I yasumeru I tsukimi I kana
cloud I occasionally I person I [acc.] I rest I moon-viewing I kana

NOTE

Written on or around the night of the mid-autumn full moon, which was on September 13 that year.

COMMENTARY

The hokku matches Saigyō's waka:

Contrary to what	nakanaka ni
I suspected, the clouds that pass	tokidoki kumo no
from time to time	kakaru koso
are adornments of the moon	tsuki wo motenasu
that enhance its beauty.	kazashi narikeri
	– San'u

By saying he was pleased to have a chance to rest, the poet suggests how continually he had been gazing at the moon. The poem, being too highly crafted, sounds a little precious. – *Meisetsu*

How annoying it is when the harvest moon cannot be seen because of thick clouds! But it is quite a lovely sight when a cloud passes over the moon from time to time. While the moon is hidden, the viewers can carry on a conversation, pausing to look up as soon as the sky clears. This kind of moon viewing can be more stimulating. – *Kobayashi*

Bashō boldly stole sentiments from other poets' work, and yet his poems are better than theirs. This is because he was an incomparably superior poet. Mediocre poets do not even know how to imitate or steal from others. – *Saisei*

Because Bashō merely transformed Saigyō's waka into a hokku, one may wonder if this poem has any value at all as a creative work of art. In my opinion, Bashō himself gazed at the harvest moon and was overcome by the beauty of the clouds. He alluded to Saigyō's waka out of his respect and affection for the older poet, who had felt the same emotions before him. – *Shūson*

1686

During the lunar New Year season of 1686, which began on January 24, Bashō and fifteen of his students combined their efforts to write a hundred-verse sequence in honor of Kikaku, who had just declared himself to be an independent haikai master. Bashō contributed six verses. Later, in response to a request, he began annotating the sequence verse by verse but had to abandon the project at midpoint due to illness. The annotation, known as *Hatsukaishi hyōchū* (Critical notes on the New Year sequence), was not published until 1763, probably because it was unfinished. The work is noteworthy for its emphasis on *atarashimi* ("novelty"), which can be defined as newness not of diction but of perception; through the mind's eye, the poet discovers hitherto unnoticed beauty in life or nature. For instance, on the sixth verse of the sequence, which depicted a woodman building a charcoal kiln, Bashō remarked: "By writing a verse on a kiln, the poet discovered something fresh, something no one else had noticed before."

Bashō's illness was not serious, and he continued to write verses by himself or with others throughout the spring. One such verse was the frog poem that has now become the most famous of all hokku. It appears that its fame began almost as soon as it was composed, for records show that a group of poets gathered at the Bashō Hut one day that April and held a hokku contest on the subject of frogs. Bashō's verse was placed at its beginning to set the pace for the contest, which was later published under the title *Kawazu awase* (The frog contest).

Bashō hosted another poetic gathering at his hut on the night of the harvest moon, which was October 2. He and his guests got aboard a boat, rowed to a quieter part of the Sumida River, and tried to write poems on the moonlit scene around them. The person who turned in the best poem was a servant whose main job was to warm saké for the party. They stayed out on the river until midnight.

Bashō had planned to go on another westward journey later in the year but apparently changed his mind. "I have postponed the plan," he explained, "because something has come up that bothers me." What this bothersome thing was is not known. But one thing is clear: Bashō wanted to become a traveler again.

looking closely, I see
a shepherd's purse blooming
under the hedge

yoku I mireba I nazuna I hana I saku I kakine I kana
closely I when-look I shepherd's-purse I flower I bloom I hedge I kana

COMMENTARY

If one looks around in the right frame of mind on a rainy evening or a dewy morning, one will notice even the tiniest of weeds is budding or flowering in response to the coming of spring. Its beauty is in no way inferior to the widely lauded beauty of plum or cherry blossoms. — *Nobutane*

This looks like a scene where the poet, while strolling in his backyard, noticed a tiny white thing and stepped closer to see what it was. The sentiment expressed here is reminiscent of the Chinese line "Everywhere I am startled to find things renewing themselves." Idyllic life in a remote, peaceful village is vividly recreated here. — *Tosai*

Only those who have plenty of leisure can appreciate this kind of sentiment. — *Keion*

More important than leisure is a frame of mind that does not let one hurry and overlook something tiny. — *Abe Y.*

The flower of a shepherd's purse is small and offers little that attracts the eye. Yet Bashō's eyes caught it. That is the heart of this poem. — *Rohan*

In a most natural way, this poem expresses both surprise at discovering something unexpected and attachment to something small. A fine poem. — *Handa*

The poet is praising Nature in her mercy for not forgetting to whisper "It's spring" to the tiny shepherd's purse. — *Kōseki*

When he discovered a shepherd's purse blooming inconspicuously under the hedge by his hut, the poet felt a momentary release from his routine daily life. — *Yamamoto*

When Bashō discovered something, that something came to exist for him for the first time. He felt as if he had created it himself. — *Utsubo*

In his postscript to "Minomushi no setsu" [On a bagworm, 1687] Bashō wrote, "As we look calmly, we see everything is content with itself." He derived it from a poem by Ch'eng Ming-tao [1032–85]. Bashō seems to have had something like this on his mind at that time. — *Imoto*

the old pond—
a frog jumps in,
water's sound

furuike | ya | kawazu | tobikomu | mizu | no | oto
old-pond | : | frog | jump-in | water | 's | sound

COMMENTARY

Master Bashō was at his riverside hut in the north of Edo that spring. Through the soft patter of rain came the throaty cooing of doves. The wind was gentle, and the blossoms lingered. Late in the third month, he often heard the sound of a frog leaping into the water. Finally an indescribable sentiment floated into his mind and formed itself into two phrases:

a frog jumps in,   kawazu tobikomu
water's sound   mizu no oto

Kikaku, who was by his side, was forward enough to suggest the words "the mountain roses" for the poem's beginning phrase, but the Master decided on "the old pond." If I may offer an opinion, I think that although "the mountain roses" sounds poetic and lovely, "the old pond" has simplicity and substance.
— *Shikō*

This hokku is indescribably mysterious, emancipated, profound, and delicate. One can understand it only with years of experience. — *Moran*

Frogs croak a great deal in late spring, but there was none of it this day. The only sound the poet heard was that of a frog jumping into the water. That made him feel all the more lonely and put him in a poetic mood. Whereas past poets had sung of a frog's croak, he focused on the sound of its leap and thereby created his own poetic style. The unexpressed sentiment of this hokku is "I am all alone."
— *Gozan*

The Zen monk Hakuin always talked about the sound of one hand clapping. The sound of water in this hokku is also like that: it is there and it is not there.
— *Nobutane*

Many haikai poets before Bashō paid great attention to poetic craftsmanship. This hokku describes a scene exactly as the poet saw it. Not a single syllable is contrived. — *Tosai*

What we see is always complex, while what we hear is usually simple. This poem is nothing more than a report of what the poet's auditory nerves sensed. Not only did it include none of his subjective ideas or visual, moving images, but what it recorded was nothing more than a moment of time. For that reason, this poem has no breadth in time or space. That is why no poem can be simpler than this; it is why this poem is impossible to imitate. – *Shiki*

There was an old pond, a frog jumped into it, and—plop!—the sound of water was heard. That is all the poem says. The interest of the poem lies in its being purely descriptive of the scene. It goes without saying that this hokku does not rank high among Bashō's poems. I am certain Bashō and his disciples did not expect future readers to value this hokku so highly or to attach so many surprising meanings to it. – *Meisetsu*

The poem has captured a moment in which eternity manifested itself in tranquillity. Although some readers attack it for one reason or another, I still think it is a great poem. – *Abe Y.*

This is like a flash of lightning illuminating a quiet corner. – *Abe. J.*

This hokku has something of a great painting that, casually drawn as it is, shows heaven and earth. – *Rohan*

Bashō was seated in his hut, facing Kikaku. Apparently there was no one else. All was quiet. The two might have been talking, but that did not disturb the stillness. The season being the end of spring, mountain roses were blooming on the edge of a pond in the garden. The banana plant, the king of the garden, had just begun to shoot out thick, bare buds from its old stump. It was daytime. Suddenly, breaking the stillness, a frog jumped into the old pond. Next moment there was stillness again. A sudden shift from stillness (no sound) to movement (sound), and then a return from movement (sound) to stillness (no sound)—this, combined with the old pond and a frog, created an atmosphere of infinite *yūgen* and tranquillity. And that perfectly matched the sentiment that was ripening within Bashō at the time. It symbolized his innermost feelings. Deeply moved, Bashō produced this poem almost by reflex. – *Shida*

By leading many years of challenging life as a haikai poet and by devoting himself to the study of waka, Chinese poetry, Zen, Taoism, and many other subjects during that time, Bashō had cultivated a realm of tranquillity within himself to which he resorted for guidance in the conduct of his life. That realm was now stimulated by a phenomenon in nature. Therefore, this poem is neither a sketch of a frog nor a description of an old pond nor an expression of emotion in daily life. Rather, it implies that a deep layer of Bashō's mind—a layer that partook of nature itself no less than of his own flesh and blood and that, after many years, had become the very bedrock of his humanity—responded to the faint water sound caused by a frog's leap. It was as if a renowned temple bell resounded when hit by a ripe acorn falling from a tree. – *Shūson*

Although what Bashō's contemporaries aimed at in poetry was not far removed from humor of the Danrin type, no doubt their laughter was succeeded by a sense of existential melancholy. Yet they did not know how to articulate that sense. This hokku was directed precisely at that blind spot in the mentality of those poetic humorists. Because the poem presented such a clear image and because those waiting for such a presentation were so numerous, the meaning of the poem was transmitted to readers with amazing quickness. Through a device that transcended words, it appealed to the heart of people and captured their souls. The poem offers something universal that charms the reader like a smile. It has something in common with the famous Zen episode in which Buddha smiles silently while turning a flower in his fingers. In this poem the smile represents the highest attainment of intellect, completing what laughter had begun. Its secret probably lies in the extreme precision with which the poet captured the subject and passed judgment on it. His mastery admitted readers to his private circle and led them to smile like connoisseurs. By a kind of nonverbal language it built a poetic marketplace of intimate, mutual communication in people's hearts. In this sense, this is a typical haikai verse. Among Bashō's works there are any number of verses better than this, but none shows more masterfully the basic way in which a haikai verse transmits its meaning to the reader. – *Yamamoto*

In waka and renga, poems on frogs refer to their croak. For instance, twenty-nine poems that appear under the topic "frogs" in *Fubokushō* [Selected poems from the Land of the Rising Sun, 1310?], a standard waka anthology that arranges poems by topic, are all about frogs' croakings. And some 140 poems classified under the topic "ponds" include none that celebrates a frog. In this hokku Bashō wrote about a frog, yet he referred not to its croak but to the sound of its leap into the water. Clearly, therein lies its novelty as well as what makes it a haikai verse. Bashō was the first poet ever to discard traditional lyricism and instead use an extremely familiar subject—a frog jumping into the water with a plop. That sense of familiarity and plainness is what constitutes haikai humor. It is the kind of humor essential to haikai. Furthermore, when it is modified by "the old pond," the humor is submerged, internalized, and permeated by a sense of loneliness and desolation. The hokku depicts the old pond not as an old pond but through the sudden sound of a frog's jump. That is why there emerges a sentiment characteristic of haikai. It must be said that there is a delicate equilibrium between humor and loneliness, with the equilibrium deepening the poetic sentiment. – *Imoto*

the harvest moon—
I stroll round the pond
till the night is through

meigetsu | ya | ike | wo | megurite | yomosugara
harvest-moon | : | pond | [acc.] | circling | all-night

NOTE
Written on the night of October 2, when Bashō and a few of his students had a
moon-viewing party at his hut.

COMMENTARY
Because a pond has a circular shape, the walk along its rim never comes to an
end. Likewise the poet's excitement never came to an end that night. – *Nobutane*

The impression created by this hokku is extremely unclear. There are the pond
and the moon, but we do not know if the pond is located in the woods or in a
suburb or in a garden. Nor do we know the size and shape of the pond. – *Shiki*

On a beautiful moonlit night, one feels like walking on and on to the end of
time. That feeling is suggested in this poem. – *Komiya*

The hokku well expresses the feelings of an aesthetic recluse. Bashō enriched his
art by merging himself with nature. – *Handa*

This poem presents a person admiring the moon all night long. If it were written
by an ordinary poet, it would not sound true; it would appear to be an affected
or imaginarily contrived poem. But it was written by Bashō, who we know was a
recluse and a lover of nature. Accordingly, we do not hesitate to take the poem at
its face value. – *Shida*

One should not read the poem as meaning "I stroll round the pond all night
long." What actually happened was that the poet walked round and round the
pond, and the night had come to an end before he knew it. There is a profound
aftereffect. – *Shūson*

There is no need to take the poem literally and believe that the poet circled the
pond all night long. What he did was enjoy the glorious spectacle throughout the
night. – *Iwata*

Cold night

the sound of a water jar
cracking on this icy night
as I lie awake

kame | waruru | yoru | no | kōri | no | nezame | kana
jar | breaking | night | 's | ice | 's | waking | kana

COMMENTARY

The poet was thinking of his own infirmity. – *Bakusui*

The hokku implies the loneliness of a cold night. The reader should ponder over the melancholy of an old man who feels every part of his body being chilled through as he lies awake on an icy night. The water jar is in the kitchen. – *Tosai*

Water expands when it freezes, sometimes cracking the container. Apparently the poet heard the crack in the middle of night, the sound startling him and waking him up. – *Meisetsu*

The hokku's concluding phrase suggests that the time was near dawn, the coldest time of night. I do not think it was midnight. – *Rika*

During a cold night when everything seemed to freeze, the poet happened to awake from sleep and hear the sound of a jar cracking. The impression is one of intense loneliness. The hokku's first two phrases, written in tension-filled language, contain a chilly feeling of things slowly freezing. The cracking sound, erupting in this frigid, silent world, penetrates the reader's heart. – *Shūson*

1687

Bashō continued to live a leisurely life at his hut in Edo till the end of summer, jotting down his thoughts in verse or prose whenever he felt like doing so. "What an idle old man I am!" he wrote on one such occasion. "Because visitors are always bothersome, I repeatedly vow to myself that I'll never see or invite anyone. And yet, somehow I find myself longing for company on a moonlit night or a snowy morning." One visitor he did not find bothersome was Mukai Kyorai (1651–1704), a promising new student who traveled all the way from Kyoto to meet him early in the year. The delighted teacher held a kasen-writing party in Kyorai's honor, inviting Kikaku and Ransetsu to join them. On June 21 Bashō participated in another haikai gathering, this one held in commemoration of Kikaku's mother who had died five weeks earlier. Obviously he was a recluse but not a misanthrope.

As autumn approached, Bashō decided to view the harvest moon in the lake country some fifty miles northeast of Edo. He had two companions for the trip: Kawai Sora (1649–1710), a young student who often helped him with household chores, and Sōha, a Zen monk who lived near his hut. On the morning of September 20 the three boarded a boat at Fukagawa and proceeded eastward along the shore of the bay. They landed on Gyōtoku, the modern Ichikawa, and walked northward until they reached Fusa on the Tone River. As it was a bright moonlit night, they hired a boat and went down the river to their destination, Kashima, in the lake country. Unfortunately, it began to rain on the afternoon of September 21, the day of the full moon. Bashō spent the night with Butchō, his former Zen teacher who had been living a secluded life in the area. Because of bad weather, he could manage only a few fleeting glimpses of the moon toward dawn. He then visited a famous Shinto shrine in Kashima and stayed overnight at the house of a physician friend in nearby Itako before he finally started for home. The trip resulted in a short travel sketch, *Kashima mōde* (The pilgrimage to Kashima Shrine), which he completed on October 1.

The visit to the lake country marked the beginning of a busy autumn for Bashō. He compiled *Atsume ku* (Collected verses), a collection of thirty-four hokku selected from his work of the past three years. He also wrote critical comments on twelve pairs of winter poems for a hokku

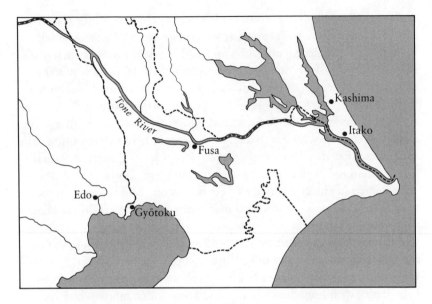

As autumn 1687 approached, Bashō decided
to view the harvest moon in the lake country.

contest entitled *Tsuzuki no hara* (The extending plain). Added to these were a number of activities arranged by his friends and disciples in antic- ipation of his renewed plans to journey to western Japan. On November 11, for example, Kikaku sponsored a haikai party in his honor, and ten poets joined him in composing a sequence of forty-four verses. There were at least four other farewell parties similar to this one, with a total of twenty-four poets writing verses for him. Those who could not take part in those events sent in poems, which were so many that Bashō later made them into a volume called *Ku senbetsu* (Farewell verses). Still oth- ers invited him to a picnic on the beach or to a banquet at a villa, or brought all kinds of farewell gifts to his home. The festivities were so nu- merous that Bashō observed, "It was like the departure of an illustrious person."

Bashō left Edo on November 29. This time his frame of mind, com- pared with what it had been on his westward journey of three years ear- lier, seemed far more relaxed and happy, not only because by now he knew the route quite well, but also because he was more confident of his ability and mission as a poet. This confidence permeates the introduc- tory passages of *Oi no kobumi* (Notes in my knapsack), the journal he kept during his travels. Taking the same route as before, Bashō trekked westward along the Pacific coastline and arrived at Narumi on December 8. He stayed there for the next seventeen days, except for an overnight visit to Atsuta and a five-day trip to Cape Irago on the tip of the Atsumi Peninsula. The latter trip, which Bashō undertook with his student Ochi Etsujin (1656–1736?), was in order to pay a visit to Tokoku, who had been exiled there on the charge of fraudulent business deals. On Decem- ber 25 he left Narumi and moved to Atsuta, where he spent the next four days. He reached Nagoya on December 29 and stayed there until mid- January 1688.

the first snow
just enough to bend
the daffodil leaves

*Painting and calligraphy by Bashō. Repro-
duced from Okada Rihei,* Bashō no hisseki
*(Shunjūsha), by courtesy of the publisher and
the late author's estate.*

the first snow
just enough to bend
the daffodil leaves

hatsuyuki I ya I suisen I no I ha I no I tawamu I made
first-snow I : I daffodil I 's I leaf I 's I bend I till

NOTE
The first snow of the winter fell on January 31.

COMMENTARY

No snow could be lighter than this. – *Donto*

The beauty of first snow consists in its being light. That lightness is skillfully suggested in the image of a bent daffodil leaf. – *Tosai*

There is something fitting about the combination of the green leaves and the snow. Daffodil leaves and first snow go well together. – *Chikurei*

The poet saw the scene of first snow with the innocent eyes of a child. – *Shūson*

The hokku is based on a small discovery the poet made in the garden. He discovered the essence of first snow when he saw the pure, elegant beauty of a daffodil. The poem makes us visualize pliant, slender, and appropriately thick daffodil leaves being bent under the slight weight of first snow. – *Yamamoto*

Being the first of the season, the snow on the ground must have quickly melted away, leaving its trace only on daffodil leaves. – *Utsubo*

The wording "just enough to bend" subtly suggests the vibrations of the mind of the poet who was delighted to see that it had snowed just as much as he had hoped for. The scene of the first snow that fell in exactly the desired amount is focused on the image of thick daffodil leaves that, looking as if they might fall to the ground, somehow manage to keep their balance under the weight of the snow. The green of daffodil leaves, standing against the pure white background of the snow-covered garden, creates a distinct impression. Bashō's own painting that accompanies the hokku shows white flowers, too. – *Kon*

Snowy night at Fukagawa

drinking saké
makes it harder to sleep . . .
snow at night

sake I nomeba I itodo I nerarene I yoru I no I yuki
saké I when-drink I exceedingly I cannot-sleep I night I 's I snow

COMMENTARY

The poet had intended to go to sleep after taking a drink, yet the snow scene was so attractive that he found it impossible to do so. He does not mean the drink kept him awake. – *Ōsha*

Unable to sleep, the poet began to drink. But that made him long for company to share the snowy evening with. He seems to be reproaching himself for harboring a desire unbecoming of a recluse. – *Tosai*

The hokku implies that the poet, who had drunk warm saké in order to go to sleep, was frustrated to find that the drink was working on him in precisely the opposite way. Bashō was not a drinker, and this must have been the way he really was. – *Rika*

Something of the loneliness that is universal to men—or should I say the wavering of a recluse's mind?—is hidden in this poem. – *Mizuho*

The hokku shows less Bashō the poet than Bashō the weak-willed man. And yet Bashō is gazing at that weak self from on high. – *Komiya*

I disagree with Komiya when he says "Bashō is gazing at that weak self from on high." The poem interests me because it makes me visualize the agonized poet writhing sleeplessly in bed. – *Abe J.*

The poem progresses in three stages, and out of that progression there emerges a portrait of the poet muttering to himself and then nodding to himself.
  – *Yamamoto*

Bashō talked of an "idle life," but this hokku suggests how his "idle life" at the Bashō Hut was fraught with continual tension. – *Utsubo*

A man named Sora has his temporary residence near my hut, so I often drop in at his place, and he at mine. When I cook something to eat, he helps to feed the fire, and when I make tea at night, he breaks ice and draws water for me. Being fond by nature of a leisurely life, he has become a most congenial friend of mine. One evening after a snowfall he dropped in for a visit, whereupon I wrote

will you start a fire?
I'll show you something nice:
a giant snowball

kimi I hi I wo I take I yoki I mono I misen I yukimaruge
you I fire I [acc.] I burn I good I thing I will-show I snowball

COMMENTARY

The poet asked his guest to start a fire while he went outdoors to make a snowball, an additional act of hospitality. He must have composed the hokku on the spot, yet the respect the host paid to the guest is manifest in its opening phrase. — *Nobutane*

Not only does the hokku suggest the relaxed way the two poet-recluses associated with each other, but it also presents a vivid picture of the two friends viewing snow in the garden by the light of a bonfire. It is an extremely pleasant picture. — *Meisetsu*

The hokku expresses the poet's childlike delight at the snow, a delight that extends to embrace his friend. The closeness of their friendship is also suggested. It is interesting indeed to know that Bashō at forty-two years of age could be so light of heart. — *Watsuji*

Hirose Tansō* wrote a poem in Chinese which reads in part:

As I open the brushwood gate, the frost looks like snow.
You draw water from the river. I'll gather firewood.

Bashō's hokku embodies a similar sentiment. The wording is probably derived from Chinese poetry. — *Seihō*

* Hirose Tansō (1782–1856), a Confucian scholar and educator, was also well known as a poet in Chinese. Cited here is part of his poem entitled "Shosei ni shimesu" (To my student, 1814).

Bashō, who at times longed for company, had probably been hoping for a visit by some congenial friend on this snowy evening. Fortunately there appeared Sora, one of his closest friends. We can imagine with what delighted looks he received the visitor. In all likelihood he did not actually make a snowball, but that does not matter. All we need to see here is Bashō's childlike heart and Sora's personality to which it responded. – *Abe M.*

As we look calmly, we see everything is content with itself.

playing in the blossoms
a horsefly . . . don't eat it,
friendly sparrows!

hana | ni | asobu | abu | na | kurai | so | tomosuzume
blossom | in | play | horsefly | not | eat | ! | friend-sparrow

NOTE

The headnote is a sentence that often appears in Taoist classics, although Bashō probably took it from a poem by the Confucian philosopher Ch'eng Ming-tao. *Tomosuzume* basically means "a flock of sparrows," but here it also seems to carry a more literal sense of "sparrows that make friends (with all things, including a horsefly)."

COMMENTARY

This hokku instructs a sparrow not to eat a horsefly since they are playmates in the blossoms. The lesson is meant for humans. — *Donto*

The older style of haikai was still popular in Bashō's time, and he probably heard of some heated controversies on poetic style that were going on among certain of his students. Deploring that fact, he stated in this hokku that all poets, whether they followed the old style or the new, were friends who played with blossoms and the moon. He taught that everyone should be content with himself, and that one poet attacking another was like a bird eating a horsefly, its playmate. This hokku is an allegorical poem through which Bashō admonished his students. — *Tosai*

I do not believe the original intent of this poem was didactic. The poet, seeing the horsefly quietly minding its own business, called out to the sparrows frolicking nearby. It was the horsefly's appearance that motivated him to write the headnote. However, the poet's call had the effect of reducing the poetic flavor of the hokku. — *Shūson*

The world of self-contentment—the world of "playing in the blossoms"—is fragile and vulnerable. From that point of view, the presence of several innocent-looking sparrows in this scene must be said to suggest, in a precise symbol, the unease inherent in that world. — *Hori*

At my grassy hut

clouds of blossoms . . .
that temple bell, is it Ueno
or Asakusa?

hana | no | kumo | kane | wa | Ueno | ka | Asakusa | ka
blossom | 's | cloud | bell | as-for | Ueno | ? | Asakusa | ?

NOTE

Ueno (not to be confused with Bashō's hometown) and Asakusa were names of
districts in Edo (they are still so named today). There was a large temple at each
place. Bashō's residence—the "grassy hut"—was located just a few miles away
from both districts.

COMMENTARY

Sugawara Michizane* wrote a poem in Chinese:

I barely make out the government tower by the color of its roof
And I know Kannon Temple only by the sound of its bell.

Bashō's hokku was probably derived from those lines. *– Moran*

There is an infinite amount of *yūgen* here. *– Tosai*

The calm, vacant mind of a man on a spring day and the infinite expanse of
spring haze and cherry blossoms seem to merge in this poem. *– Meisetsu*

The phrase "a cloud of blossoms" makes us visualize masses of blossom viewers
crowding the streets of Ueno and Asakusa in mid-spring. *– Suika*

Normally the poet could tell which temple bell it was, but in the cherry-blossom
season, when all was enwrapped in tinged haze, he *felt as though* it was impossible to tell. *– Higuchi*

At a grassy riverside hut located far away from the noisy crowd in the streets at
blossom-viewing time, the poet gazed into the distance as he indulged his leisurely mood. That mood is reflected in the elegant, calm tone of the poem. *– Iwata*

*Sugawara Michizane (845–903), one of the major Japanese poets who wrote in Chinese,
served the imperial court as a high-ranking official until 901, when he was slandered by his
political rival and exiled to Kyushu. The lines cited here are from his poem entitled "Fu-
shutsumon" (Confined within the gate).

all this long day
and yet wanting to sing more
a skylark

nagaki I hi I mo I saezuri I taranu I hibari I kana
long I day I even I singing I not-enough I skylark I kana

NOTE

In one text, this and the next hokku are introduced by the note "When I visited the grassy hut," which was apparently written by Koizumi Kooku, a student of Bashō's. It seems that Bashō wrote these two hokku on the day of Kooku's visit.

COMMENTARY

The poet must have written the hokku after listening to the lark for a considerable length of time. — *Kakei*

Here is the loneliness of a spring evening. — *Abe Y.*

We get the sense of a slow-moving spring day finally drawing to a close. — *Ebara*

Weariness surrounds the image of this skylark. Perhaps Bashō himself was tired after talking with Kooku all day long. — *Shūson*

On this spring day	uraura ni
of softly falling sunshine	tereru haruhi ni
a skylark soars high,	hibari agari
yet my heart is laden with grief	kokoro kanashi mo
as I sit alone, musing.	hitori shi omoeba

Bashō's emotions were similar to the ones embodied in this waka written by Ōtomo Yakamochi [?–785] and included in *Man'yōshū* [no. 4292]. The poem captures the mind's divagations as it strives to grasp something infinitesimal. In this type of poem, Bashō gave vent to his deepest feelings while talking of something like a skylark. — *Yamamoto*

The hokku at once captures the heaven-given nature of a skylark and takes a good look at the realm of self-contentment. There is the sense of a peaceful spring day. — *Kon*

above the moor
not attached to anything
a skylark sings

haranaka | ya | mono | ni | mo | tsukazu | naku | hibari
mid-field | : | thing | to | even | not-attach | sing | skylark

NOTE
Written on the same day as the preceding hokku.

COMMENTARY
A waka by Saigyō, with the headnote "The heart is unsettled," says:

Like a red lily	hibari tatsu
growing on the wilderness	arano ni ouru
left behind by a lark	himeyuri no
my heart remains alone,	nani ni tsuku tomo
not attached to anything.	naki kokoro kana
	– *San'u*

In a huge empty space where there is nothing visible, a skylark is singing to its heart's content. There is something lonely here; there is also something courageous. – *Abe J.*

"Not attached to anything" implies a liberated mind. It is a mind that clings to nothing, stops at nothing. It has the all-embracing tenderness of the skylark's untutored rhapsody. – *Rohan*

The hokku's middle phrase implies a mind pondering over something far, far away. It also has a mysterious quality suggesting a totally cloudless and yet unclear, soft-looking sky in spring. If I were to describe my impression of this poem in one word, it would be *yūgen*. – *Komiya*

In the image of a skylark chirping innocently and naturally, there is something cheerful, expansive, and yet infinitely lonely. The happy, unrestricted life of the skylark was at heart no less lonely than Bashō's. – *Shūson*

"Not attached to anything" refers, of course, to the singing skylark and suggests the infinite expanse of the cloudless spring sky as well as of the grassy moor. However, it is not the actual figure of the lark but its voice that is "not attached to anything." The voice flows out spontaneously and without cease, as if from wellsprings of infinity. The poem, while suggesting the peace and calm of a spring day, invites the reader to contemplate something that lasts to the end of time. – *Yamamoto*

Everything alive is conditioned by its environment, which at once helps and restricts it. For that reason, it can never have total freedom. Bashō himself was like a monk, his only desire being to write better poetry. Yet even he seems to have complained of lacking the kind of freedom he desired for himself. With that complaint in mind, he looked up at the sky above the moor and saw, with envy, a skylark singing as if "not attached to anything." The lark at that moment was in the very sphere Bashō aspired to. – *Utsubo*

A wretched man paints a self-portrait.

hair on my head
starts to show, my face has paled—
long seasonal rain

kami | haete | yōgan | aoshi | satsukiame
head-hair | growing | countenance | pale | fifth-month-rain

NOTE
Bashō had his head shaven like a monk at this time.

COMMENTARY
In early summer there are many days of fine weather during which new leaves
and grass grow luxuriantly. Then, with the fifth month, there comes the rainy
season. Trees in the garden hang their branches low, covering the windows. The
sliding screens reflect the green of the foliage, and people's faces indoors look
pale, too. One should ponder these seasonal circumstances in appreciating this
hokku. – *Nobutane*

The poet completely objectified himself, and out of that arose something poetic.
"My face has paled" is a Japanese translation of an idiom used in Chinese poetry. The device seems to be reminiscent of the way in which Bashō, in one stage
of his career, used to borrow from Chinese poetry. – *Handa*

More than any extant portrait of Bashō, the self-portrait presented in this poem
conveys his strength of character. He probed into the depths of his spiritual life
and then painted a self-portrait, never having to look into a mirror in doing so.
A life of rigorous self-discipline is suggested here. – *Saisei*

Because of the long rain there had been no visitors, and the poet had spent several days totally confined in his house. He happened to look into a mirror and
found his face pale and his hair beginning to grow. He was shocked at his own
haggard appearance and fell into even deeper melancholy. – *Ebara*

In terms of the impression it creates, a self-portrait by Van Gogh is this poem mi-
nus the sense of the season. – *Shūson*

The poet was motivated to write this hokku when, one day in his hermit's life, he
was startled to discover a change in his own appearance. The hokku is less the
poet's self-portrait than a "Portrait of a Wretched Man," done in appropriately

gloomy chiaroscuro. The poet painted the portrait using impasto, as in an oil painting, with green for the dominant tone. The poem's strongly sensory impact comes from Bashō's conscious use of Sinified words. He used those words in a deliberate attempt to underline the emotion; the use was in no way rooted in the depths of his self. The uncanny appeal of this poem derives from Bashō's neurotic sensibility, and for that reason modern readers like us find it easy to sympathize with the poem and praise it. But it cannot be said to characterize the true Bashō. – *Yamamoto*

long seasonal rain—
I'll go and see the floating nest
of a grebe

samidare | ni | nio | no | ukisu | wo | mi | ni | yukan
fifth-month-rain | in | grebe | 's | floating-nest | [acc.] | see | to | will-go

NOTE

One text has the headnote "To Lord Rosen." Naitō Rosen (1655–1733) was Fūko's son and, like his father, an ardent patron of haikai. A grebe's nest, made
from waterweeds, floats on the water.

COMMENTARY

Master Bashō said: "A willow tree in the spring rain belongs wholly to the world
of renga. A crow digging mud-snails is entirely in the realm of haikai. My grebe
poem has no haikai in its diction, but when it says 'I'll go and see the floating
nest,' there emerges something of haikai." – Dohō

This poem was sent to Rosen in place of a letter—a seasonal greeting, so to
speak. As it happened to be the rainy season, the poet said he would go and see a
grebe's nest. Here we have a glimpse of Bashō's spirit of fūkyō. – Handa

Bashō was to go on a western journey that winter and had already begun to
make plans for it. Probably Rosen had asked about it, and Bashō answered him
with this hokku. Although I have never seen a grebe's nest, I hear it is called a
"floating nest" since it appears to be floating on the water in the reeds. When Bashō said he would go and see the nest, he may have meant he would be journey-
ing in the direction of Lake Biwa, known as Grebe Lake. It is also possible that
he meant a certain pond located near Rosen's mansion, though I wonder if
grebes are likely to nest in an urban area. – Higuchi

What the poem embodies is not the lukewarm fūryū of a bystander who would
stay home and write an imaginary poem on a grebe's nest. The spirit of fūkyō—
and of haikai—lies in going out in the rain and not minding if one gets soaked.
– Imoto

Possibly the hokku implies that the poet wants to go to Lake Biwa because he'll
be able to see a floating thing there. The interest of the hokku centers on that.
The poem carries hints of what Bashō's life was to become. It was after his journey to the north that he began to use the term "floating life" formally, but his
special attachment to Lake Biwa became intense from around this time. – Andō

a tiny crab
crawls up my leg . . .
clear water

sazaregani | ashi | hainoboru | shimizu | kana
small-crab | leg | crawl-up | clear-water | kana

COMMENTARY

The small crab gives a focus to the scene in which the poet, trying to relieve the unpleasantness of a hot summer day, sits on a rock and drinks water, scooping it in his hands. The hokku creates an impression of coolness. – *Donto*

The poet's affection toward the crab permeates the hokku. We can vividly imagine both the outward appearance and the inner feelings of the poet who calmly watches a small crab crawling up his bare leg. – *Komiya*

The poem makes us imagine how it must feel to travel with straw sandals on one's feet in midsummer. The poet tried to cool his feet by dipping them in a clear stream. Just when they were beginning to feel better, he noticed a little crab, a denizen of the cold water, crawling up his leg, which was still hot. The poem presents that delicate contrast and even suggests the affection of the poet who let the crab do whatever it liked. – *Utsubo*

This is a beautifully simple poem that looks like a direct sketch of an experience the poet had one day. If that was indeed the case, this is a rare poem for the Bashō of that time. Or else we might take it for another example of those poems in which the poet found a small creature living a self-contented life and recorded its image exactly as he saw it. – *Hori*

a peasant's child
husking the rice, pauses
to look at the moon

shizu | no | ko | ya | ine | suri | kakete | tsuki | wo | miru
rustic | 's | child | : | rice | husking | leaving | moon | [acc.] | see

NOTE
Written during the trip to Kashima.

COMMENTARY

Interpreting this poem, one might talk of the moon being so beautiful that even a peasant's child had the heart to appreciate its beauty. But that would be an overly intellectualized interpretation. The poem is a purely objective work, an instantaneous sketch of a peasant's child. – *Meisetsu*

The poet had been plodding along the road in the evening, when he heard the sound of a machine used for husking rice. There were people's voices, too. Thereupon the poet, himself a seeker of beauty in nature, imagined that those peasants must also be admiring the moon, at times stopping their work to do so. – *Kōseki*

Here is a farmhouse scene of great charm, but that charm is a mere verbal invention and does not penetrate deep into the reader's heart. Beautiful as it is, the poem is too picturesque. – *Shūson*

In the spontaneous demeanor of a village child, the poet saw the spirit of *fūryū* manifesting itself naturally. – *Kon*

the moon fleets fast,
foliage atop the trees
holding the rain

tsuki | hayashi | kozue | wa | ame | wo | mochi | nagara
moon | fast | treetop | as-for | rain | [acc.] | holding | while

NOTE

Written in the early hours of September 22 at Butchō's temple in Kashima. Because of the bad weather Bashō had gone to sleep without seeing the full moon, but he was awakened toward dawn when the sky cleared a little.

COMMENTARY

A waka written by Minamoto Yorimasa and included in *Shinkokinshū* [The new collection of ancient and modern poems, 1205, no. 267] says:

Although the ground	niwa no omo wa
in the garden is not yet dry	mada kawakanu ni
there shines in the sky,	yūdachi no
looking as if it knew nothing	sora sarigenaku
of the shower, the clear moon.	sumeru tsuki kana
	— *Sanga*

The dripping trees must have sounded forlorn, and the wavering shadows, sometimes pierced by the moon's fitful gleams, must have had a harrowing effect. It was a desolate scene the poet saw. — *Tosai*

From these fast-fleeting clouds and wet treetops we can well imagine the storm-tossed yet serene image of the moon as it appeared in an interval between showers. — *Ebara*

"Holding the rain" may imply either that it is still sprinkling or that leaves are holding the glittering drops of water after rainfall. My interpretation is halfway between the two. The rain has stopped, but it looks as if it were still raining near the tops of the trees. — *Shūson*

This is a rather minor poem, I suppose; but it says something in a way a tanka cannot, and we can see from it what is characteristic of haiku. Tanka is mainly lyrical. Even a tanka that describes a scene has its core in something lyrical; it describes a scene in order to enhance the lyrical effect through concrete images.

For this reason, tanka is by nature static; few poems in this form are dynamic—such a tanka is difficult to write. As this example shows, poems in the haiku form have often described a dynamic scene just as it is, without artifice. – *Utsubo*

The hokku has captured a refreshingly beautiful scene of the autumn moon at dawn. – *Iwata*

emaciated
yet somehow the chrysanthemums
begin to bud

yase | nagara | wari | naki | kiku | no | tsubomi | kana
growing-thin | while | reason | nonexistent | chrysanthemum | 's | bud |
  kana

COMMENTARY

When plants are hurt and not growing well, they produce few buds and rarely
show open flowers since they lack the strength to do so. But a chrysanthemum is
a vigorous plant that withstands frost. Even when left neglected, it sprouts many
buds and somehow manages to have flowers open. This hokku is an example of
something in nature showing its inner will. — *Nobutane*

The poem seems to embody an indescribable feeling, something like pity.
— *Abe Y.*

This gives the impression of a skinny, sickly looking woman who has become
pregnant. — *Mizuho*

Although its shades of meaning changed over time, the expression *wari naki* ["it
is beyond reason"] had traditionally carried with it a connotation of romantic
love. I think we can see the effect of that tradition in this poem of Bashō's. *Wari
naki* here means "it is inevitable" or "it cannot be helped." It has a sense of ac-
cepting unreasonableness and hardship. For an emaciated chrysanthemum in the
garden, it is a tremendous hardship to produce flower buds, but it cannot be
helped. The chrysanthemum has accepted that hardship. — *Yamamoto*

In late autumn and early winter we often see a lean chrysanthemum, unable to
bear the weight of its buds, bent low or fallen to the ground. Bashō felt pity as he
came upon such a sight. The nature of his pity is suggested in *wari naki*. He
knew that the chrysanthemum, being a chrysanthemum, had to have buds even
though that was unreasonable in view of its leanness. This feeling can be transferred and applied to the fate of humble people who live a helpless life or of
women who have fallen into misfortune. In this sense, the poem is symbolic.
— *Utsubo*

The poet was impressed by the discovery that the dynamic force of the universe
reached even a neglected, lanky chrysanthemum and showed itself before his
eyes. Superb craftsmanship is seen in his choice of the word "buds" over "flowers." Immeasurable strength is felt in the "buds." — *Hori*

"traveler"
shall be my name—
first winter shower

tabibito | to | waga | na | yobaren | hatsushigure
traveler | so | my | name | will-be-called | first-winter-shower

NOTE

Bashō wrote this hokku on November 15 at a farewell party held for him. He reused it in *Oi no kobumi*, adding the introductory remark: "The weather was unsettled at the beginning of the tenth month, and I also felt as unsure of my future as a leaf in the wind."

COMMENTARY

Master Bashō said: "I wrote the last two phrases of this hokku in order to suggest, by the force of the words, the excitement I felt at the forthcoming travel."
– *Dohō*

We should not overlook the *fūkyō* of Bashō who was starting on a journey just when winter showers were due. This is an original poem, mixing humor with loneliness. – *Tosai*

The poet amused himself by imagining his own traveling figure and looking at it from a distance. – *Mizuho*

In my opinion, Bashō was not just excited but was deeply attracted to the word "traveler" because of his love for the solitude of traveling. The image of the first winter shower corresponds perfectly to that feeling he had. – *Watsuji*

When I meet the first winter shower on the road, I shall be called neither Bashō nor Tōsei but just a traveler. This poem expresses how Bashō felt upon starting on a journey all alone. – *Kōseki*

The juxtaposition of "traveler" and "first winter rain" was borrowed from traditional poetry, and one might think Bashō used too facile a device. Yet, in the opening passage of *Oi no kobumi*, Bashō had written: "There is one thing that permeates Saigyō's waka, Sōgi's renga, Sesshū's painting, and Rikyū's tea ceremony."* He must have attached a special set of meanings and nuances to the word "traveler." Bashō used the word in the sense that those four predecessors were "travelers." – *Yamamoto*

On the surface the hokku seems to refer to a traveler's loneliness, but underneath it is filled with the joy of traveling. Bashō's main purpose in traveling was to enrich his poetic resources by visiting new places and observing seasonal changes he had not seen before. His secondary aim was to teach his students who were waiting to welcome him at various places along the road; it was what he would love to do, too. On top of that, a winter shower was something that would deeply stir a sentiment of *mono no aware* within him, as it was supposed to do in Japan. Bashō's students, well aware of this, knew how he felt. Knowing that they did, Bashō wrote this hokku as a farewell message to them. – *Utsubo*

The tone of the hokku's first two phrases is reminiscent of a traveling monk in the nō drama who would announce himself in a powerful voice upon coming onto the stage. In that self-introduction, there is an indescribable flavor of *fūkyō*. – *Hori*

*Sesshū (1420–1506) was a Zen monk renowned for his skill in black-ink painting. Sen Rikyū (1522–91), a famed tea master, founded a school of tea ceremony that was to become the most influential in later centuries.

to Kyoto
still half the sky to go—
snowy clouds

Kyō | made | wa | mada | nakazora | ya | yuki | no | kumo
Kyoto | to | as-for | still | half-sky | : | snow | 's | cloud

NOTE

Bashō wrote this hokku in Narumi on December 9, when his host, Terashima
Bokugen (1646–1736), showed him the following waka written by Asukai Masaaki (1611–79) at the same lodging twenty-five years earlier:

Now the capital	kyō wa nao
seems farther away than ever	miyako no tōku
as I stop	Narumigata
at Narumi Bay and look back	harukeki umi wo
over a large expanse of sea.	naka ni hedatete

COMMENTARY

Masaaki had left Kyoto and was reminiscing about it from across a large area of
sea. Bashō, who had started from Edo, was halfway to Kyoto and looking toward it from across many layers of snowy clouds. We can imagine how the aged
traveler felt. – *Tosai*

In waka the word *nakazora* generally means "in the center of the sky" exclu-
sively, but that is not what is meant here. Bashō imagined a straight line extending from the sky of Edo to that of Kyoto, and he thought he was still only halfway along the line. *Nakazora* suggests that Bashō was looking up toward the
sky. – *Komiya*

The snowy clouds suggest stormy weather ahead. – *Shinpū*

Bashō, being an eternal wanderer, is not likely to have felt any special attraction
to the sky of Kyoto. Yet, when he looked at the snowy white clouds above the
desolate wintry sea, he must have been impressed by a sense of the distance
ahead and struck by the kind of loneliness travelers feel. – *Kobayashi*

In this hokku, the seasonal phrase "snowy clouds" not only suggests the season
but symbolizes the distance to be covered on the road ahead, the road that was
the poet's "way." – *Shūson*

Writing a hokku in response to Masaaki's waka was Bashō's way of thanking his host, Bokugen, who had shown the waka to him. The hokku implies, in part, that the poet was being warmly treated by the host at a place halfway between his home and his destination. — *Yamamoto*

the winter sun—
on the horse's back
my frozen shadow

fuyu | no | hi | ya | bajō | ni | kōru | kagebōshi
winter | 's | sun | : | horse-top | on | freeze | shadow

NOTE

Written at Amatsu, part of modern Toyohashi. A passage in *Oi no kobumi* explains that Bashō's horse trotted in the cold wind along a narrow road that cut across an area of rice paddies.

COMMENTARY

The hokku's first two phrases hint at the sensations of a man who was riding a horse across the rice field in the cold sea wind. Then the last phrase depicts the poet's shadow cast on the thin ice that had formed on the surface of the windy field. – *Watsuji*

In the weak rays of the winter sun, the poet's shadow cast on the horse's back looked cold. Watsuji's reading, which says that the shadow was frozen because the field was frozen, is altogether too rationalistic. – *Abe Y.*

In the feeble rays of the winter sun falling slantwise from the sky, the seemingly frozen figure of a man on horseback was a cold shadow indeed. The charm of the poem lies in the way in which the poet objectified his own figure that looked shrunken with cold. – *Ebara*

The poet first got the idea for the poem when he saw his own shadow on the surface of the rice field, but he ended up by painting a picture of himself frozen to his horse. He felt he was no more than a shadow because he was in a state of complete inanition, his senses having gone numb in the cold. – *Yamamoto*

finding a hawk
fills me with pleasure
here at Cape Irago

taka | hitotsu | mitsukete | ureshi | Iragosaki
hawk | one | finding | happy | Irago-cape

NOTE

Written during a trip to Irago, a cape that projects into the Pacific. In *Oi no ko-bumi* Bashō explained: "This was as far south as we could get into the sea, and I heard the place was the first stop for migrating hawks. The landscape looked even more beautiful as I recalled waka that featured Irago hawks."

COMMENTARY

Cape Irago was where Tokoku had his hideout. Because the place was famous for its hawks, the poet lauded Tokoku for having kept his spirits high and chosen such a place for residence. The poem is deeply moving. — *Sanga*

Having spotted one of the hawks for which the place was famous, the poet was overjoyed at his good fortune and wrote the hokku on the spot. — *Nobutane*

There were just the sea and the rocks, with nothing pleasing to the eye. What a delight it must have been when Bashō, standing before this desolate seascape, caught sight of a hawk passing across the sky! He must have felt an infinite love for that living thing. A person feels lonely when he finds himself surrounded by the immeasurable powers of nature. Consider his relief when he finds a living thing with which he can share his loneliness. Bashō described this kind of over-whelming emotion by means of a simple and straightforward expression, *ureshi* ["happy"]. — *Handa*

I agree with those who have said that the hawk obliquely refers to Tokoku. The emotion-filled middle phrase of the hokku seems to support that reading. — *Higuchi*

There is a question as to whether the hawk was flying in the sky or perched somewhere on the ground. The answer will depend on the reader, but I feel that the hawk was not flying but resting its wings on a rock or some such place at the cape. — *Shida*

I would not know what to do with the poem unless this hawk, gleaming black, was soaring in the sky off the edge of Cape Irago. — *Shūson*

What a simple, bright, transparent poem! Here is a joy similar to a young boy's.
– *Utsubo*

Since the time of Prince Ōmi who appears in the *Man'yōshū*, Irago had been known as a place where exiled criminals spent a wretched life like a fisherman's. With a hawk, Tokoku, and Prince Ōmi, the poem presents three layers of imagery. – *Yamamoto*

The words "finding a hawk" well express the *fūkyō* of the poet, who has traveled a great distance to visit a place famed in poetry. At the same time, by alluding to the legendary figure of Prince Ōmi through the lonely image of a hawk, the poem embodies its maker's delight at finding Tokoku in good health despite his life in exile. – *Hori*

Visiting Atsuta Shrine after its repair

polished anew
the holy mirror is clear, too—
blossoms of snow

togi | naosu | kagami | mo | kiyoshi | yuki | no | hana
polishing | repair | mirror | also | clean | snow | 's | blossom

NOTE

Written on December 28, when Bashō visited the famous Shinto shrine in
Atsuta. The government had completed repairing the shrine the previous summer, after some eighty years of neglect; Bashō had seen its dilapidated buildings
during his journey of three years earlier. The shrine had a mirror for its holy
icon.

COMMENTARY

The hokku's opening phrase gracefully verbalizes an impression of the repaired
shrine and reproduces its solemn atmosphere. – *Dohō*

The juxtaposition of the holy mirror and snow creates a scene of pure beauty and
leads us to visualize falling snowflakes reflected in the mirror. – *Meisetsu*

The opening phrase symbolically alludes to the repaired shrine, but it is also conceivable that the poet actually saw a clear mirror deep in the shrine's interior. It
so happened that snow was falling—snow like beautiful white blossoms. The
poet felt as though he had been cleansed both physically and mentally – *Ebara*

With the images of a spotless mirror and snow, the poet symbolized the holy atmosphere of Atsuta Shrine. The hokku may not be based on what he actually
saw. – *Kon*

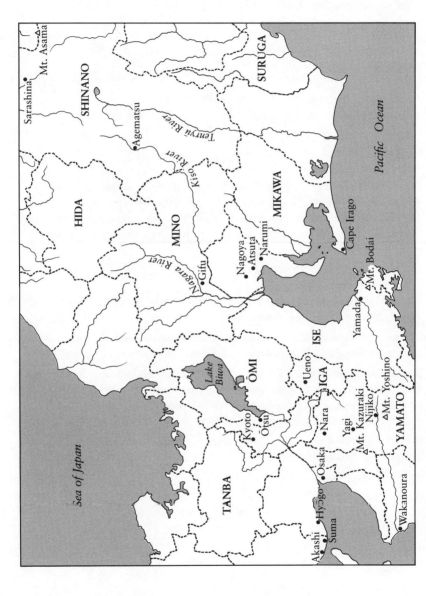

Bashō left Nagoya in mid-January 1688 to resume the western trip recorded in his journals Oi no kobumi

1688

Apparently becoming more nostalgic with the passing years, Bashō wanted to celebrate the lunar New Year with his relatives and friends in his native town. "Already four years past forty, I recall everything of the past with fond memories," he said in a prose piece he wrote at this time. Thus he left Nagoya in mid-January 1688 and arrived in Ueno toward the end of the month. He was warmly welcomed there. On February 1, which was the lunar New Year's Eve, he drank too much saké with his friends and overslept the following morning, thereby missing the traditional sunrise ceremony. Out of the same wish to see old friends, he traveled to Yamada in Ise Province on March 5 for a two-week stay, during which time he visited the Grand Shinto Shrines, Futami Coast, and other places of interest in the area. On March 19 he was back to Ueno to take part in the thirty-third anniversary of his father's death. The following day Tokoku arrived in Ueno to accompany him on the next part of his journey. The two moved into a friend's villa and spent some twenty days there, waiting for a good time to leave for Mt. Yoshino. They wanted to arrive at the mountain when the cherry blossoms, for which it was renowned, were at their best.

Bashō and Tokoku left Ueno on April 19 and headed south, reaching Mt. Yoshino after a few days. The blossoms were at their peak, and Bashō enjoyed them to his heart's content during the three days he spent there. He and his companion then trekked westward until they arrived at the coastal town of Wakanoura toward the end of the month. From there they turned back to the east and then to the north. After spending several days in Nara, they arrived in Osaka on May 12. Six days later they took a boat to Hyōgo, the modern city of Kobe. The following day they visited several famous historical sites in Suma and Akashi, both located to the west of Hyōgo. Akashi was as far west as Bashō traveled on this trip, and the journal *Oi no kobumi* ends at this point.

Bashō and Tokoku left Hyōgo on May 20 and arrived in Kyoto two days later. After some sightseeing, Tokoku parted with his teacher and went back to his hideout at Cape Irago. Bashō stayed in Kyoto until around June 7. From there he moved to Ōtsu, spending summer days on the lakeside until July 2. His next stop was Gifu, where he had a chance to see the famous cormorant fishing in the Nagara River. But his students in the Nagoya area were anxious to have him back again, and he returned there in late July. He ended up staying in Nagoya for more than a month, taking occasional short trips to Narumi and Atsuta during that time.

Part of the reason for Bashō's prolonged stay in Nagoya was his desire to pass through Sarashina at the time of the harvest moon during his return trip to Edo. Sarashina village, located in the mountainous province of Shinano, was famous for its beautiful view of the moon. The harvest moon that autumn was to be on the night of September 9. Bashō seems to have left Nagoya about five days prior to that date, accompanied by his friend Etsujin and a servant loaned to him by one of his students in Nagoya. The trip was a rugged one, as the road was often steep and they had a deadline to meet. However, they were rewarded with fine weather on the night of the full moon in Sarashina. Bashō and Etsujin then visited Zenkō Temple and passed the foot of Mt. Asama, an active volcano. *Sarashina kikō* (The journal of travel to Sarashina) is Bashō's record of this moon-viewing trip. From there the two traveled eastward along a mountainous highway and finally reached Edo in late September.

Bashō's life was filled with poetic activities for the rest of the year. On October 3 he joined other poets in writing hokku on the subject of late chrysanthemums. Three days later he hosted a party to write verses on the moon. He took an active part in many other gatherings like these. Obviously his students in Edo had missed him, and he them, during his long western journey. The presence of Etsujin, who stayed in Edo until the end of autumn, may have been another factor contributing to the increased activities. Interestingly, however, Bashō's circle seems to have shrunk. The poets with whom he associated were now limited, by and large, to those who lived in Fukagawa and its vicinity. Only rarely did he see old friends and disciples, such as Kikaku and Sanpū. Bashō was changing—again.

now then, let's go out
to enjoy the snow . . . until
I slip and fall!

iza | saraba | yukimi | ni | korobu | tokoro | made
now | then | snow-viewing | for | tumble | place | to

NOTE

Written on January 5, when Bashō was a guest at a snow-viewing party hosted
by a book dealer in Nagoya.

COMMENTARY

The hokku suggests deep love of snow. – *Donto*

The poet must have muttered this hokku while he was being helped on with his
straw raincoat. It is superbly original, mixing humor with the misgivings of advancing age. In all likelihood it was the heartfelt sentiment of a poet who would
risk death for the cause of *fūga*. – *Tosai*

Perhaps the snow was heavy and someone tried to dissuade Bashō from going
out, whereupon he jokingly retorted with this poem. – *Meisetsu*

Obviously the phrase "I slip and fall" is what gives vitality to this poem, suggesting the poet's excitement on the occasion. Sanpū's verse:

overcoming the fear   kakugo shite
of catching a cold, I go out   kaze hiki ni yuku
to view the snow   yukimi kana

may be appreciated alongside this hokku. – *Shida*

This poem is of a type that is not to my taste. Perhaps I still lack the maturity to
appreciate its underlying attitude of *fūkyō*. For the time being, however, my inability to appreciate it does not bother me. – *Shūson*

Bashō, who muttered to himself "Let's go out" and was about to brave the snow,
was full of what we call "poetic rapture." He felt he would risk anything for the
sake of *fūga*. On the other hand, he put limits on that rapture by saying "until I
slip and fall," although these limits were hypothetical rather than experiential,
belonging as they did to the realm of intellect. In Bashō's poetry intellect tends to
be inconspicuous, since it is merged with sensibility. This hokku seems all sensibility, too. But the poet could not have said "until I slip and fall" unless his intellect was at work. – *Utsubo*

town where I was born—
as I weep over my umbilical cord
the year comes to a close

furusato | ya | heso | no | o | ni | naku | toshi | no | kure
native-village | : | navel | 's | cord | on | weep | year | 's | end

NOTE

Written in Ueno. It was customary to keep one's umbilical cord as a memento.
The custom is still preserved in certain rural areas of Japan today.

COMMENTARY

When a baby is born, the parents set aside its umbilical cord and store it away
with the record of the birthdate. In this hokku the poet tearfully recollected all
those years of indebtedness to his parents. Probably he had to write something
for the year's end and then remembered about his umbilical cord. – *Donto*

The poet reflected nostalgically upon his childhood, as he was about to send off
the old year in his native town. – *Nobutane*

The hokku's middle phrase does not necessarily indicate that the poet had his
umbilical cord before his eyes at the time. The cord is a metaphor for his blood
relation to his parents. – *Handa*

The word "weep" in this hokku does not imply a sentimental, effeminate type of
emotion that makes one give free vent to one's tears. The simple, powerful style
of the poem leads us to think of a masked nō actor with eyes partly downcast in
a stylized gesture of weeping. That is an expression of sadness free from senti-
mentality, with the weeper's hands drawing close to his face in a subtle movement. The verb *naku* ["to weep"], consisting of just two hard-sounding syllables,
is there in so affirmative a way that all that was sentimental has evaporated.
 – *Yamamoto*

The year's end is the time when families do housecleaning in preparation for the
New Year. Probably Bashō discovered his umbilical cord accidentally while helping to do the cleaning. By saying "I weep," therefore, he expressed how he felt
when he made the discovery. – *Utsubo*

The image of the umbilical cord, which was a physical connection between the
poet and his mother, gives vivid expression to his longing for the dead mother. It
also provides a physical origin for all his nostalgic memories involving his
mother and his native town. – *Kon*

*An area near Iga Castle produces something known as coal. It emits a
bad smell.*

waft your fragrance!
on a hill where they mine coal
plum blossoms

ka I ni I nioe I uni I horu I oka I no I ume I no I hana
scent I with I smell I coal I dig I hill I 's I plum I 's I blossom

COMMENTARY

Coal has a very bad smell. The poet commanded the plum blossoms to over-
power it. – *Nobutane*

The poem would not be attractive if we were to think that the poet wanted the
plum blossoms to waft their fragrance because coal smelled bad. Yet what comes
to my mind through the phrase "a hill where they mine coal" is not the smell of
coal but the *scenery* of the hill. It is the color of the earth, which was probably
black. It is the squalor of an industry, something not dissimilar to what we feel
when we see a pile of coke in the corner of a factory yard today. If necessary, we
might visualize modest facilities of an old coal mine with several miners toiling
there. Toward the plum blossoms blooming in such an environment, the poet
said, "Waft your fragrance!" I think the poem becomes more interesting when
we interpret it that way. – *Abe J.*

The poet, calling out to the plum blossoms, said, "Please be as fragrant as you
can there, since I hear the coal dug out from this hill emits a bad smell when it
burns." The smell of coal is not actual but imaginary. – *Iwata*

The poem is about the merciless destruction of nature that was taking place on
"a hill where they mine coal." Because coal has a bad smell, the poet urged the
plum blossoms to rival it with their good scent. There is a contrast between a
bad smell and a good scent, between a destroyed landscape and graceful blossoms. – *Yamamoto*

The poet, making use of a subject that was unique to his home province, softly
enwrapped the evil-smelling coal in the beauty of plum blossoms. – *Kon*

dead grass—
imperceptibly, heat waves
one or two inches high

kareshiba | ya | yaya | kagerō | no | ichi | ni-sun
dead-grass | : | slightly | heat-wave | 's | one | two-inch

COMMENTARY

While there were no signs of new grass sprouting as yet, heat waves had already begun to shimmer, and spring was in the air. This hokku depicts such a scene. What is interesting is the fact that the poet referred to the height of the heat waves rather than of the grass. – *Donto*

The poet sketched exactly what he saw, and the hokku gives us a striking impression of early spring. It may seem that anyone could have written "one or two inches" here, but actually it is not easy to think of these words in this context. They are used very effectively here, too. – *Shida*

This is a fine poem that shows a close observation of nature. To use nature in this way must have been new in contemporary poetry. – *Shūson*

Here winter and spring coexist as the heat waves, which are of spring, shimmer over dead grass, which is of winter. The poet caught sight of this rare scene and gave it forceful expression, because he was deeply moved with joy at the coming of spring. – *Utsubo*

This is a fine sketch of a yard on an early spring day. It shows the poet's close observation as well as his heart anxiously waiting for spring. – *Iwata*

The poet was astute to capture a subtle sign of spring as it was about to come to the field and hills. – *Kon*

At Yamada in Ise Province

from which tree's bloom
it comes, I do not know—
this fragrance

nani | no | ki | no | hana | to | wa | shirazu | nioi | kana
what | 's | tree | 's | blossom | so | as-for | not-know | smell | kana

NOTE

Yamada is the town where the Grand Shinto Shrines are located. Bashō wrote the hokku while visiting one of them.

COMMENTARY

This hokku vaguely alludes to Saigyō's waka:

What holy being	nanigoto no
is there, I do not know	owashimasu ka wa
and yet	shirane domo
my heart feels the blessing so,	katajikenasa ni
tears flow out of my eyes.	namida koboruru
	– Dohō

Bashō based his first two phrases on Saigyō's first three phrases and his last phrase on Saigyō's last two phrases. – *Nobutane*

In order to describe how he felt as he knelt before the shrine, the poet imagined an unknown tree with an exquisite fragrance. It is not that he actually smelled a fragrance coming from a tree whose name he did not know. – *Meisetsu*

There was some kind of real fragrance confronting Bashō—blossoms, the wood, whatever. I do not think the poem resulted from his imagination working on an abstract idea. – *Mizuho*

Bashō got a hint from Saigyō's waka, but his hokku is not a translation of it. In Saigyō's poem, all we know is that he was at the shrine; there is nothing that suggests exactly where he was or how he stood in relation to his surroundings. By contrast, Bashō's poem provides us with the wood and the fragrance of blossoms, which stir a sense of holiness within us. If this poem is a translation, the translator has added something that is not in the original and made it the very life of his translation. I think Bashō's composition is far superior to Saigyō's. All that Saigyō's waka does is report an abstract emotion. Bashō's poem expresses that emotion in such a way that each reader comes without effort to feel it in a completely personal way. – *Abe J.*

While Saigyō's waka is simple, sincere, and fitting to the occasion, it is rather passive in its motif and somber in its color. By contrast, Bashō's hokku is active and concrete in a natural way, and has brightness as well as broadness of vision. This is indicative of the contrast between the times in which these poets lived: Saigyō's were torn by war and Bashō's peaceful. – *Utsubo*

Mount Bodai

on this mountain
sorrow . . . tell me about it,
digger of wild yams

kono I yama I no I kanashisa I tsugeyo I tokoro I hori
this I mountain I 's I sorrow I tell I wild-yam I digger

NOTE

Mt. Bodai, located in Ise Province, is the site of a large Buddhist temple built by
Emperor Shōmu (701–56). Damaged by fire several times, the temple was in
ruins when Bashō visited there.

COMMENTARY

The hokku expresses admiration for the loneliness and tranquillity of Mt. Bodai.
Because wild yams are dug in the woods, the poet asked the digger to tell him
how tranquil it was in the mountain. – *Nobutane*

Deep in the woods, the poet called out to a yam digger and asked him to tell
about the sorrows of the mountain temple. Sorrow is an emotion more intense
than loneliness, and Bashō always sought it out. The poem expresses that emotion well. – *Keion*

In my home province yam diggers are mostly old, decrepit, shabby-looking men
who can no longer do normal work on the farm. – *Abe J.*

I sense a bit of warmth in the "sorrow." – *Abe Y.*

At a mountain named Bodai [Buddhahood], the poet pondered over Buddha's
teachings and felt true sorrow over the ways of ordinary people indulging in the
pleasures of this world. To him, the old man silently digging a wild yam deep in
the forest appeared to be completely removed from the world in that sense.
Thereupon he asked the man to tell the people of this world about the meaning
of Buddhahood, after which the mountain had been named. – *Kobayashi*

The poet had heard of the past grandeur of the temple buildings, but saw little
trace of it before his eyes. Then, catching sight of a wild yam growing nearby, he
imagined someone digging it up and, in his heart, spoke to him: "Tell me how
sad it is to live in this degenerate age." – *Kōseki*

Near a lonely mountain temple the poet called out to a villager digging wild yams, saying, "You must know how this temple has prospered and declined with time. Please tell me about that sad history." Digging a wild yam is itself a lonely act. We think of an old man doing the digging, too. In this scene of *wabi*, Bashō longed to hear the sorrowful history of the mountain temple. – *Ebara*

The prosperity of olden times was gone, leaving no trace. That was the "sorrow on this mountain," one of the themes Bashō always had in mind. The spirit of haikai lies in his saying, "Tell me about it" to a passer-by, a yam digger carrying a hoe. – *Imoto*

The root of a yam is yellow and has many joints, with clusters of long fibrils growing from them. Because those fibrils look like an old man's beard, two Chinese ideograms meaning "field" and "old man" are used to signify a wild yam. The yam is used in New Year's decorations along with the lobster, which is written in two ideograms meaning "sea" and "old man." The poet recalled those Chinese characters, and that made him wish to hear the checkered history of the temple from a yam digger. – *Hori*

His Honor Tangan held a blossom-viewing party at his villa. There I found everything as it used to be.

many, many things
they call to mind—
those cherry blossoms!

samazamano | koto | omoidasu | sakura | kana
various | thing | recall | cherry | kana

NOTE

Tangan is the haikai name of Tōdō Yoshinaga (1676–1710), the lord of Ueno Castle at the time. He was a son of Sengin and grandson of Yoshikiyo, under whom Bashō had served in his youth.

COMMENTARY

As I understand, Tangan was only two years old when young Bashō resigned from the service. The poet wrote this hokku when he was invited by the lord and went to see him for the first time since then. We can well imagine his thoughts over the past. – *Tosai*

This hokku shows no trace of the poet's artifice. He does not seem to have asked himself such questions as to how his nostalgia was related to the cherry blossoms, or whether his feelings and the blossoms would make a poetically harmonious combination. Very likely, he was too overcome with emotion to ask such questions. As a result, the poem is a little too simple and plain in thought. Without the prefatory note, there would not be much merit in it. But, in view of the preface and the occasion for which it was written, the poem can be said to describe the scene and the emotion well enough; indeed, it can be counted among Bashō's finer poems. – *Meisetsu*

As the poet recalled this and that, thoughts of the past so flooded his mind that he did not know how to describe them except to say "many, many things." The wording suggests that it included things unknown to other people. And those things were all embodied by the cherry blossoms that bloomed there. – *Shūson*

The emotive particle *kana* indicates that the cherry blossoms stirred up all kinds of thoughts in the poet's mind. The bright beauty of the blossoms stimulated his mind and illuminated, in an instant, his past life filled with sorrow. – *Utsubo*

Tangan was in his twenty-third year when Bashō, a forty-four-year-old traveling haikai master, was invited to his villa. He was about as old as Sengin was when young Bashō knew him as a master and fellow poet. Sengin and Tangan must have resembled each other somewhat in looks, since they were father and son. The cherry tree Bashō remembered was blooming as in the old days. Momentarily for Bashō, it was as if he saw his own youth. He remembered, with nostalgia, how he and Sengin used to enjoy haikai together under the blossoms, how he had been reared as the second son of a poor musokunin before he entered the service, and how he embarked on a life of wandering after Sengin's death and finally came to make haikai his career. Many, many such sorrows and regrets springing out of this past life of his flashed through his mind like pictures on a revolving lantern. Bashō transformed all these impressions into this poem, using a language as colloquial as ordinary speech and paying proper respect to the host who had invited him. – *Ogata*

In general, memories become more beautiful the more distant they become from reality. Especially when they have been cleansed by the passage of some twenty-odd years, they gain a transparent beauty like that of pure fantasy. The first two phrases of this hokku may sound pedestrian, but actually they represent the result of the poet's assiduous effort to transmit that beauty as accurately as possible. – *Hori*

Hoso Pass
(on the way from Tafu Peak to Ryūmon)

resting higher
than a lark in the sky
a mountain pass

hibari I yori I sora I ni I yasurau I tōge I kana
skylark I than I sky I in I rest I pass I kana

NOTE

Written on the way from Ueno to Mt. Yoshino. Hoso Pass is located in the modern Yoshino County in Nara Prefecture.

COMMENTARY

Wen hsüan has a poem that says: "My thoughts go beyond the clouds in the sky." Bashō's hokku implies a similar sentiment. — *Sanga*

The chirping, which the poet had always heard high in the clouds, came from a valley down below as he was now on a mountain peak. That is how it is when one is on a summit high above the clouds. — *Nobutane*

The poem is commonplace, though it presents an appealing scene. — *Abe J.*

This is a witty poem. — *Mizuho*

But the wit is not of a very high order. — *Keion*

There is something here of surprise and childlike joy. Of course the poet composed the hokku on the spur of the moment. — *Ebara*

The poet has made an effective use of a skylark in this poem. The image of the lark well suggests not only the altitude of the mountain pass but also the weather that day. — *Shida*

A lark's song is cheerful and lively, well befitting spring. Hearing it, Bashō returned to an innocent, childlike frame of mind and called out to the lark, saying lightheartedly, "I'm higher than you!" — *Yamamoto*

When we have reached a high place, we experience a kind of elation, feeling as if we have risen higher in social status. This poem depicts such childlike elation as well as a touch of surprise. — *Iwata*

Without saying so, the hokku suggests a vast panoramic view spread out below, the entire landscape of peaceful spring in the mountains where skylarks were singing. – *Kon*

The word "rest" is just right in this context since it implies the relaxing satisfaction and pleasant fatigue felt by someone who has completed a steep climb. A felicitous choice of word. – *Hori*

During my travel through Yamato Province, I spent a night at a farm-house. Impressed by the host's warm-hearted, genial hospitality, I wrote

in the blossoms' shade
as in the nō drama
a traveler sleeps

hana | no | kage | utai | ni | nitaru | tabine | kana
blossom | 's | shade | nō | to | resembling | travel-sleep | kana

NOTE

Written at the village of Hirao in Yoshino County.

COMMENTARY

A waka by Taira Tadanori:*

Should the day end here	yuki kurete
forcing me to take a lodging	ki no shitakage wo
in the shade of the trees,	yado to seba
those blossoms will become	hana ya koyoi no
my landlord for the night.	aruji naramashi

is what Bashō had in mind when he wrote this hokku. — *Shōgatsudō*

The situation reminded the poet of a black-robed monk in a nō play sleeping under the blossoms and dreaming of an old legend. Himself traveling like a monk, he was amused to find that he was indeed an itinerent monk in the nō drama. His observation that the ultimate of *fūryū* is like the nō is at once profound and humorous. — *Nobutane*

The poet, standing under the blossoms, likened the beauty of his lodging to that described in a passage of a nō play, *Futari Shizuka.*† — *Kōseki*

The words "as in the nō drama" suggest the poet's romantic fancy. — *Ebara*

---

*Taira Tadanori (1144–84) was a general of the Heike clan who was killed in the battle of Ichinotani. The poem cited here appears in *Heike monogatari* (The tales of the Heike, 1190–1221?).
†*Futari Shizuka* (The two Shizuka) has a passage about a young general taking a lodging under cherry blossoms in the Yoshino mountains.

Having spent a night in the mountains during his blossom-viewing tour to Yoshino, Bashō must truly have felt as if he were a character in a nō play. – *Abe M.*

The fact that it was a lodging "in the blossoms' shade" drew the poet into the mood of the nō drama. But Bashō seems to have been unusually cheerful in this journey to Yoshino with Tokoku. – *Yamamoto*

Having spent a night at a farmhouse surrounded by the Yoshino cherry blossoms, Bashō painted a beautifully romantic self-portrait by likening himself to a traveler in a nō play. At the same time he implied his gratitude to the hosting farmer. The implications of the hokku come close to Tadanori's waka featured in the nō play *Tadanori*, but many other nō plays, such as *Hachinoki*,* also present a traveler receiving kind hospitalities at an overnight lodging. – *Kon*

---

*In *Hachinoki* (The dwarf trees) a couple living in a humble house give lodging to a traveler one winter night and, having no other recourse for heating, make a fire by burning their prized bonsai trees.

Nijikō

petal by petal
yellow mountain roses fall—
sound of the rapids

horohoro | to | yamabuki | chiru | ka | taki | no | oto
horohoro | with | mountain-rose | fall | ! | rapid | 's | sound

NOTE

Nijikō, located on the upper reaches of the Yoshino River, is famous for the torrential current that surges through the rocks at that point. The word *horohoro* is descriptive of thin and delicate things fluttering down one after another, but it can also be used as onomatopoeia for a pheasant's cry. *Yamabuki* is *kerria japonica*, with its yellow petals shaped like those of a wild rose.

COMMENTARY

I do not believe the poet had the flowers in sight when he wrote the hokku. On hearing the distant sound of the rapids, he imagined a scene of mountain roses falling by the stream. The poem embodies his deep sorrow over spring's departure. – *Donto*

I think the poet composed the hokku with the scene before his eyes. – *Nobutane*

Near the rapids of Nijikō, mountain roses were in full bloom. The poet, seeing a petal or two flutter down, gave play to his imagination and wondered if the sound of the rapids was not causing the flowers to fall. – *Rika*

The flowers were falling not because it was time for them to do so but because they felt the vibrations of the rapids. – *Chikurei*

What interests me is the fact that the poet, while putting something lovely and delicate in the foreground to screen a powerful, violent force of nature, has nevertheless succeeded in giving full expression to that force. – *Komiya*

A play on words is involved in the phrase *horohoro to yamabuki*, thereby creating the humorous effect characteristic of haikai. There is a flavor of old haikai poetry. The phrase echoes Gyōki's waka:*

Listening	horohoro to
to the cry of a pheasant	yamadori no naku
I wonder:	koe kikeba
Could it be my father?	chichi ka to zo omou
Could it be my mother?	haha ka to zo omou
	— Rohan

As the poet trod a shady path by the river, he saw petals of mountain roses fluttering down. That instant he awoke to the sound of the rapids, to which he had paid no attention before. In brief, I wish to interpret the poem as presenting a shift of the senses: the vision of falling petals causing the poet to shift his awareness to the sound of the rapids. *— Handa*

The sound of the rapids and the fall of the flowers cannot be said to be related to each other from a phenomenal point of view, but they are not two unrelated objects placed side by side. This is not a case of simple juxtaposition, just as it is not in the following waka attributed to Kakinomoto Hitomaro:[†]

As the rapids	ashibiki no
in the mountain river	yamagawa no se no
begin to sound,	naru nabe ni
over the Yuzuki peak	Yuzuki ga take ni
billows of cloud rise.	kumo tachi wataru

The flowers of mountain roses blooming all over the area looked so delicate and fragile that the poet thought they would fall at the sound of the rapids, which seemed to shake the whole mountain. *— Yamamoto*

This is a bright, beautiful scene. *Horohoro to* is a skillful expression suggestive of flower petals vibrating with the sound of the water. It creates the impression that the flowers were falling not because of the wind but because of the sound. *— Iwata*

---

*Gyōki (668–749) was a Buddhist monk known for traveling through various provinces and helping to build roads, bridges, and dams as well as temples. The poem cited appears, with a slightly different wording, in a book by Kenshō (1130?–1210?) entitled *Man'yōshū jidai nanji* (Problematic matters concerning the age of *Man'yōshū*).
[†]Kakinomoto Hitomaro, who is known to have lived in the late seventh century, is generally considered Japan's first lyric poet. The poem quoted is included in *Man'yōshū* (no. 1092).

Mount Kazuraki

all the more I wish to see
in those blossoms at dawn
the face of the god

nao | mitashi | hana | ni | ake | yuku | kami | no | kao
still | wish-to-see | blossom | in | dawn | go | deity | 's | face

NOTE

Mt. Kazuraki, one of the highest mountains in Yoshino, enshrines the Shinto deity Hitokotonushi, who is known for his ugly looks. To complement this hokku, Bashō drew a portrait of a mountain priest sleeping under a tree, adding the note: "This is what the priest said in his sleep."

COMMENTARY

Because an old legend had it that the deity of Mt. Kazuraki had an ugly face and did not want to show it to people, the poet here made a typical haikai joke by saying he wanted to see that face even more. – *Ryōta*

Although the legend said the deity looked ugly, the poet did not believe it and wanted to see him even more. – *Donto*

I want to see the deity all the more because he would look even uglier among the beautiful blossoms. That is what the hokku means, and it reflects the way Bashō's contemporaries felt. That, however, is only the surface meaning. The poet is really praising the beautiful scene, saying how he wished to see the blossoming mountain at dawn. – *Tosai*

A legend says that when the monk En prayed to the deities that a bridge be built between Mt. Kazuraki and Mt. Yoshino, the deity of Kazuraki, ashamed of his ugly figure, helped the work only at night. *Nao* here must mean "still." The poem means "Gossip mongers say he is an ugly deity, but still I wish to see his face." – *Abe Y.*

There may be readers who argue that the poem features a surprising contrast between beautiful blossoms and the deity's ugly face, the former looking more beautiful because of the latter. I disagree. The hokku's middle phrase creates a mysterious sense of the deity's face gradually vanishing in the blossoms at dawn.

I think the poet visualized, in the center of the blossom scene, the face of the deity who was obliged to vanish at dawn. – *Mizuho*

The middle phrase implies that the poet wanted to see the deity all the more because people had gossiped about his unsightly figure. I do not think Bashō fully believed what people said. Viewing the blossoms at dawn, he imagined that the deity might be surprisingly good-looking, or that the deity, even if he looked ugly, must have something godlike somewhere in his appearance. The scene at daybreak was so beautiful that Bashō could not bring himself to visualize the deity as an ugly figure. – *Abe J.*

When the blossoms become visible, the deity's face must become invisible. And those blossoms are part of the deity's realm. In other words the blossoms and the deity are one, and the heart that admires the blossoms is simultaneously saddened by the disappearance of the deity. The hokku's last two phrases are a beautifully poetic expression describing the mysterious moments when one face is replaced by another face of the same thing. And the opening phrase expresses the heart of the poet who wishes to see a little more of the deity's face as it fades in the dawn light. – *Yamamoto*

worn out
I seek a lodging for the night—
wisteria flowers

kutabirete | yado | karu | koro | ya | fuji | no | hana
tired | inn | rent | time | : | wisteria | 's | flower

NOTE

The first draft was written on May 10 at Yagi (now part of Kashiwara) in the province of Yamato.

COMMENTARY

The words "worn out" suggest something of a wisteria tree with its long plumes dangling and its vines asprawl. The hokku's middle phrase skillfully makes the reader visualize a scene of the setting sun. The poet's sure hand and the soul of the poem can be observed in the irreplaceable juxtaposition of tiredness and wisteria flowers. – *Kūzen*

The emotion and the scene are merged in one. This poem shows soundness and maturity in the best sense of these words. – *Abe J.*

Exhausted from walking all day, the poet finally arrived at an inn toward nightfall. Untying his laces to take off his footwear, he looked up at the wisteria plumes hanging near the eaves and admired the beauty of the evening scene. This poem is a beautiful painting. – *Kobayashi*

In "The Woodspurge" Dante Gabriel Rossetti said:

From perfect grief there need not be
Wisdom or even memory:
One thing then learnt remains to me—
The woodspurge has a cup of three.

When he reached the ultimate of grief, he discovered that the woodspurge had a cup of three. His state of mind at that moment can be said to have been similar to Bashō's when the latter, at the height of his exhaustion, discovered the beauty of wisteria. – *Noguchi*

The weary sentiment of a traveler toward the end of day. Helpless-looking wisteria flowers caught through the eyes of a tired traveler. The symbolism of wisteria has a strong appeal to the reader's heart. Certainly this is a fine poem.
— *Shida*

A plume of wisteria begins to bloom at the top, and when it becomes time for the bottom part to be in full bloom, the flowers at the top of the plume have already faded in color and started to fall. Those plumed flowers have a slovenly manner of blooming. That slovenliness perfectly matched the poet's weary feeling on the road. It symbolized the ennui of the evening of a late spring day, too.
— *Yamamoto*

It seems as though Bashō's principle of linking stanzas, known as *nioi*, was at work linking the phrases of this hokku. — *Iwata*

The feeble sunlight of a slow-ending day in late spring is falling on wisteria flowers, and a tired traveler, who happens to be passing by, stops to admire the sight. The scene emerges vividly before our eyes. — *Imoto*

The exhaustion mentioned in the poem is not just physical. Mingled with it are the loneliness of travel, sadness at spring's departure, and the nostalgia of a man who had spent the day touring through the province of Yamato, which abounded in historical sites. — *Hori*

In Suma

although the moon is there
it's like a vacant house—
summer in Suma

tsuki I wa I are I do I rusu I no I yō I nari I Suma I no I natsu
moon I as-for I there-is I but I absence I 's I like I is I Suma I 's I summer

NOTE

Suma had been known for its lonely beauty in autumn. In *Oi no kobumi* Bashō refers to a passage from *Genji monogatari* which asserted that in lonely beauty nothing can match autumn in Suma.

COMMENTARY

Although there was a hazy moon reminiscent of spring, the poet felt as if something were lacking, probably because it was the autumn moon in Suma that classical poems and tales alluded to. Fortunately the moon was there when the poet came to Suma, yet since it was summer, the true value of that famous place seemed to be absent. The value of Suma is personified in this hokku. — *Kōseki*

At the base of the poem is a longing for the autumn moon in Suma. The poet, unable to have that desire fulfilled, expressed his disappointment by saying, "It's like a vacant house," and thereby giving the poem a flavor of haikai. The expression, however, is rather commonplace. Some haikai poets of later times tried to imitate this kind of expression and ended up by producing verses that were quite soulless. — *Shūson*

Well read in classical literature, Bashō had hoped to find in Suma the kind of forlorn autumn beauty described in *Genji monogatari* and other classics. Therefore he felt a little disappointed when he saw the bright summer moon that was devoid of loneliness. — *Iwata*

a Suma fisherman
ready to shoot an arrow—
a hototogisu's cry?

Suma | no | ama | no | yasaki | ni | naku | ka | hototogisu
Suma | 's | fisherman | 's | arrow-point | to | cry | ? | hototogisu

NOTE

According to what Bashō writes in *Oi no kobumi*, the fisherman was trying to
scare off crows that had come after the fish being dried in the sunshine on the
beach. Also alluded to in the journal is the fact that Suma was the site of a fierce
battle between the Genji and Heike clans in the twelfth century. *Hototogisu* is a
bird that looks like an English cuckoo but is smaller and has a sharp, piercing cry.

COMMENTARY

The poet remembered an old battle that had been fought in Suma. — *Donto*

Kokinshū includes a waka [no. 962] by Ariwara Yukihira [818–93]:

Should anyone ever	wakuraba ni
ask about me, let him know	tou hito araba
what a wretched life I live	Suma no ura ni
on the shore of Suma, my sleeves	moshio tare tsutsu
as dripping wet as seaweeds.	wabu to kotaeyo
	— *Sekisui*

Bashō came to Suma, expecting it to be a poetic place. Yet what he found was a
fisherman scaring off crows that had come after dried fish on the beach. The
beauty of the place as sung about in old poems was nowhere to be seen. Bashō
thought the fisherman was doing a very sinful thing. The hokku, having that in
the background, focuses on the cry of a hototogisu that seems to have sounded in
the direction pointed at by an arrow. It implies uneasy feelings on the poet's part;
evidently he feared that the arrow might hit a hototogisu instead of a crow. That
uneasiness resulted in a mood that pervades this poem. — *Mizuho*

The hokku progresses in three different stages. In the first stage we see a heart
that longs for the past and thinks of nothing but the past. In the second, we see
that heart being disappointed at the unpoetic scene of fishermen chasing birds
away. And in the third, we see the heart recover its longing for the past as it hears
a hototogisu's passing cry. — *Komiya*

hototogisu—
where it disappears
a lone island

hototogisu | kie | yuku | kata | ya | shima | hitotsu
hototogisu | disappearing | go | direction | : | island | one

NOTE

Also written in Suma.

COMMENTARY

The hokku embodies the same kind of sentiment as the famous waka included in the *Kokinshū* [no. 409]:

Dimly visible	honobono to
off the coast of Akashi	Akashi no ura no
in the morning mist	asagiri ni
it vanishes behind an island . . .	shima kakure yuku
thinking of that boat, I muse.	fune wo shi zo omou

The word "disappear" suggests that the onlooker was deeply moved. He was probably looking toward Awaji Island from the Suma area. – *Donto*

The poet drew on a waka by Emperor Gomizunoo [1596–1680]:

A hototogisu	hototogisu
disappears behind an island	shima kakure yuku
with a cry,	hitokoe wo
leading me into a long muse	Akashi no ura no
like the poet on Akashi Coast.	akazu shi zo omou
	– *Nobutane*

The hokku is probably an imitation of the old waka:*

A hototogisu—	hototogisu
as I look in the direction	nakitsuru kata wo
where the cry came from,	nagamureba
I see only the moon	tada ariake no
remaining in the sky of dawn.	tsuki zo nokoreru
	– *Tosai*

*The waka, which is the poem no. 161 in *Senzaishū* (The collection of a thousand years, 1188), was written by Fujiwara Sanesada (1139–91).

This is an entirely descriptive poem, and yet underneath it alludes to the Heike refugees who embarked on a long voyage from there. — *Meisetsu*

It makes one feel as if the hototogisu gradually faded out and became an island. — *Mizuho*

I think this was a day when the sky was hazy and the atmosphere was damp. On a day like that, an island looks blurry and farther away than it is. — *Watsuji*

What disappears here is not the figure but the voice of the hototogisu. — *Komiya*

After nightfall a hototogisu flew away, crying. The poet looked in the direction of the cry and saw a black island dimly afloat on the sea. This is a large-scale poem, and yet the poet has captured what he wanted to capture. Added to that is an interesting union of the visual and aural senses. — *Handa*

Of course, this poem is concerned primarily with the hototogisu's cry; the bird's figure is secondary. When a hototogisu appears in waka and haikai, the focus is always on its cry. As the poet looked in the direction where the cry disappeared—that is, the direction in which the bird flew away—there floated an island as if it symbolized the disappearance. — *Yamamoto*

Staying overnight in Akashi

an octopus pot—
inside, a short-lived dream
under the summer moon

takotsubo | ya | hakanaki | yume | wo | natsu | no | tsuki
octopus-pot | : | short-lived | dream | [acc.] | summer | 's | moon

NOTE

An octopus pot is an unglazed earthenware vessel made for trapping an octopus, which has the habit of escaping into a dark hole when it is alarmed. Fishermen string a number of these pots on a rope, sink them in the sea, and pull them up after octopuses have entered them.

COMMENTARY

The subject had been there since olden times, but it had been overlooked by poets all that time. – *Mōen*

The shortness of the summer night is here compared to the short life of an octopus trapped in a pot. In view of the poem's headnote, I think the octopus's short dream alludes to the Heike warriors who perished after a brief stay in Akashi. – *Shōgatsudō*

An octopus that has entered the pot is content with the small world of its own and enjoys a night's dream, never suspecting that it might be pulled up in the morning. A man born into this world is like that, too, as he lives a life as brief as a dewdrop. Such a view of life is presented in this poem. In view of the site, there may be historical allusions, too. – *Kōseki*

The poet would not have been able to see an octopus pot lying at the bottom of the sea at night. We might surmise he saw a rope or something and concluded that the pots must be under the sea, but we need not go that far. He probably wrote the poem when he caught sight of an octopus pot on the beach. – *Abe Y.*

Isn't it possible to imagine that Bashō had completely entered into the mind of an octopus inside the pot? He became an octopus, so to speak. – *Watsuji*

An octopus is sleeping in a pot, ignorant of the likelihood that its life will come to an end in the morning. Shining over it is the summer moon, which is also short-lived. I am inclined to think that this poem embodies Bashō's idea of mutability. – *Mizuho*

The poet probably saw octopus pots being pulled up from the sea. Although the summer night was quickly coming to a close, the octopuses seemed to continue dreaming, not knowing that their lives were soon to end. There is humor, which then turns into pathos. This is an interesting poem, with a flavor characteristic of haikai. – *Rohan*

"A short-lived dream" was dreamed both by an octopus sleeping in a pot and by Bashō sleeping in Akashi. This is a poem that uses metaphor to make a comparison. – *Seihō*

Although this poem suggests a certain view of life, the suggestion is a very faint one. On the surface it expresses pity and sympathy toward octopuses, simultaneously describing the beauty of a moonlit summer night on the shore of Akashi. Some readers may find humor in the poem, deriving it from the octopuses' foolishness; but I do not feel that way. I feel nothing but pity and sympathy. – *Shida*

In the Japanese poetic tradition, those who complain of the shortness of the summer night are, above all, lovers who have to part in the morning. Bashō drew upon that traditional mood of romantic love and applied it to the life of an octopus dreaming a short dream in a pot, thereby turning it into humor. – *Yamamoto*

I see no humor directed toward the tricked octopus; all I see here is pity. This pity is so all-embracing that its objects can include not only trapped octopuses but all men on earth, Bashō among them. If we pursue this line of thinking, the summer moon will become Buddha's Great Law that shines over them all. It shines over them, but cannot change them. Men can be saved by learning and following the Law. That is not the case with octopuses: they cannot be saved, they can only be pitied. – *Utsubo*

in the seasonal rain
it remains unhidden—
the bridge of Seta

samidare | ni | kakurenu | mono | ya | Seta | no | hashi
fifth-month-rain | in | is-not-hidden | thing | : | Seta | 's | bridge

NOTE

The bridge of Seta was located where Lake Biwa begins to drain into the Seta River. Over 380 yards long, it was famous for its beauty as well as for its length.

COMMENTARY

As the traveling poet strained his eyes, all the famous scenes of Lake Biwa were hidden in the misty rain except this bridge, which showed itself like a sleeping dragon. We can well imagine how he felt at that sight. — *Tosai*

The poem depicts the kind of scene Andō Hiroshige [1797–1858] would have enjoyed painting. — *Higuchi*

For Bashō, this was perhaps nothing more than one stroke of his brush. Yet the image of Seta Bridge, almost but never completely invisible in the rain, is very lovely and makes us feel as if we were looking at a masterpiece of painting. — *Momota*

This is a large-scale poem presenting a magnificent scene, a scene in which everything has disappeared in the misty rain except the long and massive bridge. Such grandeur is rarely found in modern haiku. — *Shūson*

The bridge of Seta had been famous for its beauty at sunset. But this poem presents the bridge in the mist and rain, thereby creating the kind of novelty characteristic of haikai. — *Hori*

Mount Inaba

the temple bell too
seems to start ringing—
cicadas' screech

tsukigane | mo | hibiku | yō | nari | semi | no | koe
temple-bell | also | sound | like | is | cicada | 's | voice

NOTE

Mt. Inaba is located in the east of Gifu. There were several temples at the foot of
the mountain.

COMMENTARY

Imagine the sunshine at high noon on a midsummer day. *— Donto*

The cicadas' cry is loud and noisy, resembling the vibrant sound of a bell.
— Nobutane

Their chirping was so loud that the temple bell seemed to reverberate from it. A
unique thought. *— Meisetsu*

This poem can be read in two ways. It may mean that cicadas have been crying
loudly when a temple bell begins to sound and seemingly echoes the cry. Or it
may mean that the cicadas' cry resembles the sound of a bell. *— Shikei*

The cicadas' cry was so loud that the poet could hear nothing else. Then he
caught sight of a man striking a temple bell in the distance. Thereupon he wrote
this hokku, to mark his realization that the sound of the bell had formed part of
what he thought was nothing but the cicadas' cry. *— Rika*

The poet, while gazing at the bell on the one hand, listened to the sound of the
cicadas on the other and felt as if their vigorous cry would make the bell start
ringing at any moment. This is an extremely bold, powerful poem, one that
shows the poet's identification with his subject. *— Shūson*

In Mino Province I went to see fishermen manipulating a number of cormorants in the Nagara River.

so exciting
and, after a while, so sad—
cormorant fishing

omoshirōte I yagate I kanashiki I ubune I kana
exciting I presently I sad I cormorant-boat I kana

NOTE

Cormorant fishing is a unique method of catching fish used in Japan since ancient times and described in works of literature such as the nō play *Ukai* (Cormorant fishing). Today, as in Bashō's time, it is practiced only in the Nagara River, on a moonless night. In the torchlight each fisherman aboard a boat manipulates twelve cormorants by means of leashes and induces them to catch trout, which they are then forced to regurgitate. Spectators stand on the shore and watch a group of such boats slowly drift downstream.

COMMENTARY

This hokku draws on two sentences that appear in the nō play *Ukai*. One is: "The sight of cormorants catching fish one after another in rapid succession is so exciting that the thoughts of sin, retribution, and afterlife all go out of my mind." The other is: "It is so sad to see the darkness after the torchlight on the boat goes out." – *Shōgatsudō*

For a while the poet was excited to watch the fishermen working with the cormorants. The excitement was replaced by sadness when he remembered what a terrible sin it was to kill living things. He may also have been saddened by the moonrise, since cormorant fishing has to be done in the dark. – *Donto*

The poet had been watching the scene with excitement, until he saw the cormorants being forced to regurgitate the trout. Now the excitement was all gone. Struck by the sadness of the scene, he wondered if any living creature would be glad to lose its life. Readers should feel the gentle heart of the poet who pitied the sad fate of both the fishes and the cormorants. – *Nanimaru*

When the cormorant fishermen displayed their manly skills by torchlight, the scene was magnificent and exciting indeed. But soon their boats passed, the torches disappeared, and the river regained its former darkness and desolation. This poem well describes that rapid change of scene from excitement to sadness in cormorant fishing. — *Meisetsu*

This is a purely subjective poem. Instead of describing the scene's external details, it tells directly how the poet's sentiments changed with the changing scene. — *Handa*

At first the torches burn brightly, the cormorants do their work with a will, and the spectators amuse themselves by composing poems. With the passage of time, however, loneliness sets in. The effects of liquor wear off, and people are too weary to talk. The mood becomes what we might call sadness after pleasure. — *Shūson*

Beyond doubt, Bashō based his hokku on the nō play *Ukai*. Yet readers unacquainted with the play could still find themselves empathizing with his words "and, after a while, so sad." For, to use an exaggerated expression, they must have experienced the loneliness that comes after dissipation, or the emptiness that comes after release of tension, or some such feeling, any number of times in their lives. — *Imoto*

Bashō was a person capable of letting himself become completely absorbed in something. On the other hand, he was also capable of looking critically at his own self-absorption and feeling sad about it. Those two tendencies coexisted in his character. Perhaps everyone is like that to some degree, but the dualism was more pronounced in Bashō, and it showed when he saw cormorant fishing. — *Utsubo*

With remarkable craftsmanship Bashō enclosed in this hokku both the sadness that was the theme of the nō play and the sadness that he experienced after watching cormorant fishing. — *Hori*

The third day of the month

unlike anything
it has been compared to:
the third-day-moon

nanigoto I no I mitate I ni I mo I nizu I mika I no I tsuki
anything I 's I comparison I to I also I not-resemble I third-day I 's I moon

NOTE

Written on July 29, which was the third day of the lunar seventh month. Since olden times the crescent moon had been compared to a great many things, including a sickle, a bow, a comb, a boat, and a woman's eyebrow.

COMMENTARY

The poet is praising the beauty of the moon by observing that it does not truly resemble any of the many things it has been compared to by people of the past. — *Donto*

The hokku implies that all those descriptions of the moon in Chinese and Japanese literature have not yet exhausted its beauty. Note the haikai poet's pride! — *Tosai*

As the poet sauntered home in the evening, he saw a crescent moon hanging far off in the sky. Walking along a country lane, he asked himself what kind of comparison he could make in order to do justice to what he saw. He could not find a good answer. We can well see the creative process that resulted in this poem. — *Komiya*

This is a poem of admiration for the beauty of the crescent moon. The poet rejected all the traditional similes for the moon, yet could not find his own either, since he was so overwhelmed with emotion. — *Keion*

The sight of the crescent moon moved Bashō in a way that could not be expressed through any image other than the crescent moon, and he said so in this hokku. This attitude of Bashō's indicates that, while he was prepared to use everything that tradition offered him, he was not content with the traditional sentiments but tried to outdo even the most daring of them. — *Shūson*

A view of Narumi

autumn begins—
the ocean too, like the rice fields,
in one color of green

hatsuaki | ya | umi | mo | aota | no | hitomidori
early-autumn | : | sea | also | green-rice-field | 's | one-green

NOTE
Written on August 5 in Narumi.

COMMENTARY
Here is a sense of indescribably refreshing coolness. – *Tosai*

Autumn has begun. All the rice fields within sight are green, not yet showing any sign of starting to turn yellow. The ocean also looks emerald green, reflecting the lucid sky of autumn. As one gazes into the distance, ocean and rice fields appear as one. The autumn winds ravish us with their coolness. Well suggestive of the clear and cool air of autumn, the poem has a pleasant sound. – *Higuchi*

People came to see me off at the outskirts of the town, and we had several drinks together.

a morning glory
knowing nothing of the carousal
in the peak of bloom

asagao I wa I sakamori I shiranu I sakari I kana
morning-glory I as-for I saké-bout I not-know I peak I kana

NOTE
Bashō was leaving Gifu to go on the moon-viewing journey to Sarashina.

COMMENTARY
In the yard of the place where the farewell party was held, a morning glory was in bloom. It was a lovely sight. While the poet, about to set out on a long journey, enjoyed farewell drinks with his friends, the flowers bloomed there in all their beauty, looking totally unconcerned with the poet or the party. Impressed by their loveliness, the poet amused himself by describing what he saw.
— *Meisetsu*

The morning glory blooms during the fairest hours of the day. It truly deserves to be called a gentleman's flower, since it fades before becoming tainted by the filth of the world. Although the chrysanthemum is known as a recluse's flower, and the lotus as a gentleman's, there are likely to be drunkards who act boisterously where chrysanthemum or lotus flowers are in view. But hardly anyone would get drunk and misbehave himself in front of a morning glory. — *Kobayashi*

The poet started out early in the morning and exchanged toasts with his friends at a suburban teahouse as he bade them goodbye. On a nearby fence, morning glories were blooming in all kinds of colors. Looking at the flowers, he thought: "Because a drinking party is usually held in the afternoon or evening, other flowers know what one is like. Those morning glories do not, because they bloom only in the morning." The poet may be implying that unlike ordinary people he loves quiet and solitude. — *Kōseki*

The hokku's middle phrase is a humorous reference to the fact that in contrast to cherry blossoms and chrysanthemums, which had been celebrated by parties since ancient times, the morning glory had induced no one to hold a party for it.
— *Kon*

plank bridge—
clinging for their lives
ivy vines

kakehashi | ya | inochi | wo | karamu | tsutakazura
plank-bridge | : | life | [acc.] | cling | ivy-vine

NOTE

The plank bridge, located near Agematsu in Shinano Province, had been sung
about in poetry for centuries. The planks, strung together by strong vines, jutted
out from the side of the cliff without any supporting girders.

COMMENTARY

This was truly a dangerous road. That danger is implied in the image of ivy vines
clinging for their lives. —*Donto*

When the poet saw the ivy vines making a colorful display with their leaves under these hazardous circumstances, he sensed an analogy with human events and
used a word like "life" to characterize the ivy in this poem. —*Tosai*

Bashō was moved by the sight of an ivy vine single-mindedly clinging to something. As he reflected on his own lonely life, he became envious of the ivy clinging perilously to the plank bridge. —*Handa*

Bashō and Etsujin walked on tiptoe on the dangerous plank bridge, knowing
that they would plunge into the valley if they should take one wrong step. It was
the ivy vines that clung to the bridge for their lives, but that was exactly how the
two travelers felt, too. Many poems by Bashō express his own feelings through
description of nature, and this is one such instance. —*Ebara*

It was mid-autumn, and the leaves in the Kiso mountains were deeply colored.
The tinted ivy crept all over the plank bridge, entrusting its fragile life to it. The
poet, knowing how dangerous that bridge was, wondered how the ivy could en-
trust its precious life to it. Then he reflected that men were like that ivy too, since
they entrusted their lives to this perilous world. In my opinion, the ivy in this
poem symbolizes human life. —*Shida*

the Kiso acorns—
for those in the floating world
my souvenirs

Kiso | no | tochi | ukiyo | no | hito | no | miyage | kana
Kiso | 's | nut | floating-world | 's | person | 's | souvenir | kana

NOTE

Tochi, or *aesculus chinensis*, is a tree of the horse chestnut family that grows
only in remote mountains, such as those in the Kiso region in Shinano Province. Its
nuts, less tasty than ordinary chestnuts, are ground and made into cakes or gruel.

COMMENTARY

A *tochi* nut is oddly shaped, looking more like an acorn than a chestnut. Few
people have a chance to see one, so the poet plans to take some samples home
for souvenirs. – *Donto*

According to his journal, Ogyū Sorai* also brought those unappetizing nuts
back to Edo, where he showed them to young men of the upper class and
preached the importance of living modestly. Bashō, probably thinking along the
same line, planned to take those acorns home and show them to Edo residents.
– *Kobayashi*

Bashō wrote "those in the floating world" because he considered himself a traveler distant from the ordinary world. The expression is lighthearted, as it refers
to people living an urban life. The poem is pervaded by the sentiment of a man
traveling through the remote mountains of Kiso. It makes the reader recall Saigyō's waka:

Deep in the mountains	yama fukami
water dripping on the rocks—	iwa ni shitataru
I'll block its flow	mizu tomemu
and pick up the tochi nuts	katsukatsu otsuru
that fall time and time again.	tochi hirou hodo
	– *Iwata*

Tochi nuts had been considered the type of food suitable for a recluse. – *Hori*

* Ogyū Sorai (1666–1728) was a Confucian scholar and educator who also served as an
advisor for the shogun's government in Edo.

blowing the gravel
off the ground on Mount Asama,
an autumn gale

fuki | tobasu | ishi | wa | Asama | no | nowaki | kana
blowing | let-fly | stone | as-for | Asama | 's | autumn-gale | kana

NOTE

Mt. Asama is an active volcano located on the border between Shinano and Kō-
zuke provinces (the modern Nagano and Gunma prefectures). Bashō traveled
past its foot during his return trip to Edo.

COMMENTARY

No vegetation grows in this area of Mt. Asama. The poet hinted at the power of
the gale by describing pumice fragments being blown off the ground. – *Nanimaru*

The ground at the foot of Mt. Asama looked barren, with no autumn flowers
adorning the landscape. All that could be seen were pumice fragments of various
sizes that had collected there after many volcanic eruptions. As the gale blew,
some fragments fell to the right and others veered to the left, making the desolate
landscape look even more desolate. – *Kobayashi*

We can visualize Bashō and Etsujin hurrying their way across the desolate Asama
plateau on a late autumn day, looking as if they were being chased by a gale that
intermittently blasted them from behind. We can also see, beyond the two travelers pressing forward amid the blown sand and gravel, the towering shape of Mt.
Asama that turns purple each time it is shaded by ominously fast-moving clouds.
– *Imoto*

An autumn gale is usually thought of as a wind that blows at trees and grass.
Here at Mt. Asama it is going wild, blasting pumice fragments. – *Hori*

journey through Kiso
made me thin, and I still am . . .
the late harvest moon

Kiso | no | yase | mo | mada | naoranu | ni | nochi | no | tsuki
Kiso | 's | thinness | even | still | not-recover | yet | lateness | 's | moon

NOTE

Written in Edo on October 6, shortly after Bashō returned from his long western journey that had included a grueling trek through the mountainous region of Kiso. The day, which was the thirteenth of the ninth month on the lunar calendar, was traditionally known as the day of the late harvest moon. That evening Bashō hosted a moon-viewing party, inviting Sanpū, Etsujin, and six other poets to his home.

COMMENTARY

With the impression of the harvest moon in Sarashina still fresh in his memory, the poet is now admiring the late harvest moon. One can easily see how profound his love of the moon was. – *Donto*

The poet meditated on the swift flow of time. Note how the word "thin" goes with the image of the thirteenth-day moon. – *Tosai*

The poet had occasion to admire the moon of the thirteenth night while the aftertaste of his journey remained with him. That motivated him to write this poem. – *Shūson*

Although the hokku may partly refer to the swift passage of time, its focus is on the joy of the poet who was able to admire the harvest moon on two different nights. – *Iwata*

The poet held a moon-viewing party even before he had time to recover from the fatigue of his journey through Kiso. He thought of the speed with which time had passed, and inevitably that led him to meditate on the mutability of life and unpredictability of the future. – *Yamamoto*

The combination of the word "thin" and the image of Kiso with its tall mountains is especially effective. – *Kon*

chrysanthemums,
cockscombs, all are cut and gone—
the Anniversary

kiku | keitō | kiri | tsukushikeri | omeikō
chrysanthemum | cockscomb | cutting | has-exhausted | anniversary

NOTE

Written on November 5, which was the anniversary of the priest Nichiren's death. The Lotus Sect of Buddhism, founded by Nichiren (1222–82), observed the day by performing elaborate rites, at which people of all sects offered flowers of the season.

COMMENTARY

This hokku is mediocre, but here I have tried, in my own clumsy way, to use a season word no one has used in the fifty-year history of haikai. If the holy priest's soul is still around, I'd like him to take note of my name. That's the joke I tell people. — *Bashō*

Although followers of every sect observe a rite on the anniversary of its founder's death, the one celebrated by devotees of Nichiren is especially spectacular. For offerings at the rite, they always cut chrysanthemums, cockscombs, and any other flowers blooming in their yards. This poem, short as it is, well suggests the zeal characteristic of those who adhere to the Lotus Sect. — *Kobayashi*

Even the few chrysanthemum and cockscomb flowers that had managed to keep blooming were cut, so that they could be offered at the rite. By bringing in images unique to the season, the poem has skillfully captured the flavor of the time around Nichiren's anniversary. — *Ebara*

locked in for the winter . . .
again I'll be nestling close
to this post

fuyugomori | mata | yorisowan | kono | hashira
winter-confinement | again | will-nestle | this | post

COMMENTARY

It is bothersome to sit in a chair or use an arm rest. The poet just wants to sit
and meditate, with his back leaning against a post. The image of a post admira-
bly suggests what winter confinement means. — *Donto*

I am told that a poem by Po Chü-i has a line: "In my leisurely life, again I lean
against this post." As far as its literal meaning is concerned, Bashō's poem is vir-
tually the same as this line and presents no problem of interpretation. But the
charm of the poem becomes apparent when it is compared with Po Chü-i's line.
First, "locked in for the winter" carries a more specific feeling than "leisurely
life." Also, whereas the verb "lean" refers mainly to the outward appearance of
the poet leaning against a post, the expression "nestling close" is better as it implies the poet's sentimental attraction to the post. Because of that, "this post" has
come to suggest the poet's affection, an affection so tender that he almost feels
like stroking its surface with his hand — *Abe J.*

There may be that kind of affection, but there is also a feeling of loneliness, since
the modest residence offers nothing else that would divert the poet's heart.
— *Abe Y.*

The demonstrative adjective "this" may seem to be used in a casual manner here,
but that is not the case. The post had been close to Bashō's heart in his daily life.
It was the kind of post that would gently respond if Bashō opened his lonely
heart to it. Because of that, he felt like "nestling close" to it. — *Handa*

Winter is here again. I have not felt especially amicable toward this post (or,
rather, I have not paid much attention to it), but now I begin to feel an indescribable kind of affection for it. Since I'll be spending most of my time at home from
now on, I'll be always sitting close to you. . . . That's what this poem means, I
think. — *Higuchi*

Behind the hokku's last two phrases, which imply weariness and solitude, there
lie all kinds of worries and hardships the poet has undergone in his life to date.
— *Momota*

Bashō longed for a wanderer's homeless life, and yet here we see his deep affection for his old home. A man attracted to travel and yet loving his home—herein lies the true image of Bashō. — *Shūson*

We can visualize the image of the poet absorbed in quiet meditation, with his back against a post. — *Iwata*

The poet had spent many a lonely night on the road the previous winter. Now back in his old humble home, he felt an affection even for a post he used to pay no attention to. — *Hori*

On the memorial service of a certain person

don't they quench
even the banked charcoal?
those hissing tears

uzumibi | mo | kiyu | ya | namida | no | niyuru | oto
banked-fire | even | vanish | : | tear | 's | boiling | sound

NOTE

One text has the headnote "In sympathy for a person who has lost a young son."

COMMENTARY

The expression "those hissing tears" is original. – *Baigan*

I prefer to see the poet sitting by a hand-warmer, resting his elbows on its edge and letting his head droop. His eyes overflow with tears, which fall on the banked charcoal. Next moment he hears the sizzling sound. – *Komiya*

The image of banked fire leads us to visualize tears soaking into the ashes. – *Mizuho*

I would take this for a poem mourning the death of a son. In that context, the person leaning over the banked fire is not the poet but the parent of the dead youngster. By asking "Don't they quench . . . ?" the poet tried to empathize with the parent's grief. – *Abe J.*

The poet tried to imply the depth of the person's grief by imagining tears falling on the banked fire with a sizzle. We can visualize the grieving person. But his profound grief makes no heartfelt impression on the reader. In my opinion, that is because the poem is an artificial construct. – *Shūson*

In Bashō's imagination, this parent leaned over a hand-warmer one cold day and shed tears of grief over his young son who was no longer among the living. We, too, can easily stretch our imagination this far by reflecting on our own experience of life. It is not easy, however, to imagine the tears making a hissing sound and almost quenching the small charcoal fire. That is the kind of vision even the most sensitive person cannot conjure up, unless he has gone through a similar experience himself. This fact leads us to believe that Bashō always stored up grief within himself and let it issue forth at the slightest provocation, visualizing the kind of scene depicted in this poem even when he did not know the grieving person very well. – *Utsubo*

CHAPTER FOUR

The Narrow Road to the Far North

1689-1691

1689

The year 1689 was undoubtedly the most memorable in Bashō's life, as he undertook the long northern journey that resulted in his masterpiece *Oku no hosomichi* (The narrow road to the far north). The idea for such a journey seems to have entered his mind in the fall of the previous year, almost as soon as he returned to Edo from his latest western trip. Several verses he wrote that winter confirm his yearning for a traveler's life. By early February he knew where he was going on his next trip, for his letter of February 7, addressed to his older brother, states that he would soon be starting on a journey to the northern and western provinces. His friends in Edo, however, were worried about his health and persuaded him to delay his departure until it became warmer in the north.

Bashō finally left Edo on May 16. Kawai Sora, his student and neighbor, accompanied him and kept a factual record of their travel. After bidding farewell to well-wishers at Senju, the two trekked northward for three days until they arrived at Nikkō. Then they turned in a northeastern direction, reaching Shirakawa on June 7, Fukushima on June 17, and Sendai on June 20. After spending three days in Sendai, they resumed their journey and entered the coastal town of Ishinomaki on June 26. From there they walked as far north as Hiraizumi, which they reached on June 29. Then their route turned westward, cutting across mountainous areas toward the Sea of Japan. On the way they took two side trips, visiting Ryūshaku Temple near Yamagata on July 13 and Mt. Haguro near Tsurugaoka (or Tsuruoka) from July 19 to 26. On July 29 they finally entered Sakata on the coast of the Sea of Japan. The next two days were spent on a sightseeing tour of Kisagata, the northernmost point they reached on this journey. They left Sakata on August 10 and traveled southwest along the coastal road, stopping in Niigata on August 17 and in Takada (the modern Jōetsu) from August 22 to 25. They arrived at Kanazawa on August 29 and spent a week there. A local poet named Tachibana Hokushi (?–1718) became Bashō's student and served as his guide for the next three weeks. The group of three left Kanazawa on September 7 and, after stopping in Komatsu, rested at Yamanaka Hot Springs for eight days. Sora left the group here on September 18 and headed for Ise Province by himself. Hokushi, too, parted with Bashō

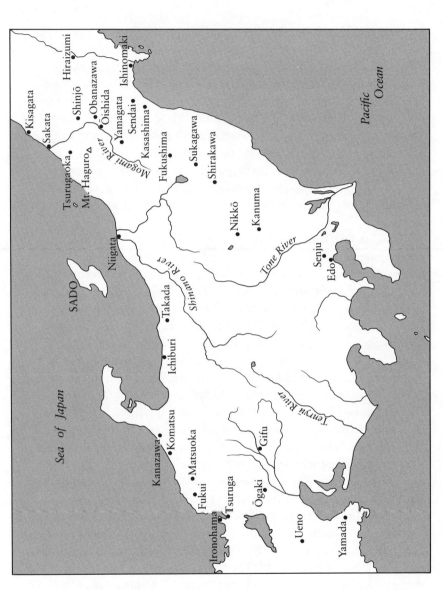

In the year 1689, Bashō undertook the long northern journey that resulted in his masterpiece

after escorting him as far as Matsuoka. Bashō's solitary journey did not last long, however. Just a couple of days later he arrived at Fukui, where an old friend named Kanbe Tōsai (?–1700) was waiting for him. Tōsai accompanied him to Tsuruga, which they reached on September 27. They were soon joined by Inbe Rotsū (1651?–1739?), a student of Bashō's. The three made an excursion to Ironohama on the coast of the Sea of Japan on September 29. Bashō and Rotsū then left Tsuruga and headed southwest, arriving at Ōgaki in early October. Ōgaki, a short distance west of Gifu, was a familiar town to Bashō, and many friends and disciples, including Etsujin and Sora, came to welcome him there. The journey described in *Oku no hosomichi* drew to a close at this point.

Bashō spent some days in Ōgaki to recuperate from the fatigue of the journey. Then on October 18, accompanied by Sora and Rotsū, he set out to visit the Grand Shinto Shrines in Yamada. Much of this journey was by boat, probably in consideration of Bashō's health. He arrived in Yamada on October 23 and stayed there for a couple of weeks, during which time he visited the Shinto shrines and other places of interest in the area. Seeing him under the good care of local poets, Sora and Rotsū parted with him here. In early November Bashō left Yamada and traveled to his native town of Ueno in Iga Province. He stayed there for the rest of the year, renewing friendships and participating in haikai gatherings.

first day of the year
I think longingly of the sun
on those paddy waters

ganjitsu I wa I tagoto I no I hi I koso I koishikere
New-Year's-Day I as-for I each-rice-field I 's I sun I ! I yearn

NOTE

Written on January 21, which was the lunar New Year's Day. The epithet *tagoto no* is generally used in connection with the famous full moon in Sarashina village, where each of the tiered rice fields is said to mirror the moon and create a picturesque sight.

COMMENTARY

Everyone admires the moon mirrored on the rice paddies in Sarashina. On New Year's Day, however, one might admire the image of the sun reflected on the same paddies. – *Donto*

The poet admired the serene beauty of the New Year's sun so much that he wished to see it reflected on each paddy in Sarashina. It is humorous and characteristic of haikai that a verse celebrating the New Year should contain an image of the sun mirrored on a rice paddy. – *Nobutane*

Because this was the New Year immediately following his trip to Sarashina, the poet, upon seeing the sunrise in Edo, was reminded of the beautiful scene of the harvest moon he saw as a traveler. – *Tosai*

We can see the poet's wanderlust still refusing to leave him. – *Yamamoto*

At Tōzan's lodging in the second month
of the second year of Genroku

heat waves shimmer
on the shoulders of my
paper robe

kagerō | no | waga | kata | ni | tatsu | kamiko | kana
heat-wave | 's | my | shoulder | on | rise | paper-robe | kana

NOTE

Written on March 27 to start a kasen. Participating in the composition were six other poets, including Tōzan, a poet from Ōgaki who was staying in Edo at that time. A paper robe is a modest kind of winter overcoat; it is so called because it is made of paper coated with persimmon juice.

COMMENTARY

Paper robes are largely worn by the aged. Here an old man whose vitality is on the decline is bathed in shimmering heat waves and feels as though he were in the springtime of his life. – *Donto*

Probably the poet's paper robe was wet with rain. By the time he arrived at the inn, it had begun to dry. Thereupon he imagined heat waves shimmering on his robe—that is, on his own body—but, in the poem, he asserted they actually were. – *Meisetsu*

Heat waves were faintly rising on the garden ground, on the fence, and on everything else in sight. The poet felt as if they were shimmering on his robed shoulders, too, as he enjoyed bathing in the glorious spring sunshine. – *Seisensui*

Probably the sunlight was falling on the windows of the inn. The poet suddenly noticed heat waves shimmering around the shoulders of his paper robe. As he gazed at them, his heart was filled with a feeling of spring. The hokku's middle phrase hints at the poet's surprise. The paper robe must have looked old from many years of use; it gave the impression of *wabi*, too. The poet was surprised to find heat waves rising on the shoulders of that robe; a sense of unexpectedness shimmers in that middle phrase. The expression is calm, but in that calm one senses the observant eyes of the poet who would not overlook the signs of even the most minute phenomenon. – *Shūson*

This poem, too, shows winter coexisting with spring. One often becomes keenly aware of the season at a time of seasonal transition. — *Seishi*

Heat waves must have been rising in abundance everywhere on the ground, if they were shimmering on the poet's paper robe. And the paper robe in the poem can be taken to refer to the poet himself, who was wearing it. Bashō's mind was hypersensitive. It would not be unreasonable to imagine that he felt both the great earth and himself were merged in the rising heat waves. — *Utsubo*

The poem, dealing with a minor surprise on the surface, embodies a springtime mood in its depths. What appeals to me even more strongly, however, is the desire for travel that shimmers like the heat waves in the poet's heart. — *Konishi*

a skylark sings—
marking time through the song
the cry of a pheasant

hibari | naku | naka | no | hyōshi | ya | kiji | no | koe
skylark | cry | inside | 's | beat | : | pheasant | 's | voice

COMMENTARY

Master Bashō tried to capture the peaceful atmosphere by describing the singing of a skylark interrupted from time to time by a pheasant's cry. He settled on this version after a number of attempts at different wording. – *Dohō*

A lark played a flute in the sky, and a pheasant beat a drum in the bush. The poet was fascinated by the music of nature. – *Tosai*

I feel this hokku is a little too contrived. – *Mizuho*

There is a subtle difference between

a skylark sings—   hibari naku

marking time through the song   naka no hyōshi ya
the cry of a pheasant   kiji no koe

and

a skylark sings—   hibari naku
marking time through the song   naka no hyōshi ya

the cry of a pheasant   kiji no koe

In the latter reading [with a longer break before the last phrase], the poet who was listening to the monotonous voice of a skylark wished for one or more beats that would accentuate it, and that wish led him to take note of "the cry of a pheasant." Or, to put it in another way, that wish made him discover how charming a pheasant's cry was. – *Andō*

departing spring—
birds weep, and fishes' eyes
are tearful

yuku | haru | ya | tori | naki | uo | no | me | wa | namida
go | spring | : | bird | crying | fish | 's | eye | as-for | tear

NOTE

Oku no hosomichi says that the poet wrote this hokku on May 16, when he set out on his northern journey and bade farewell to his friends and disciples who came to see him off at Senju, a northern suburb of Edo.

COMMENTARY

Tu Fu's poem "Spring View" says:

In grief for the times, I shed tears at the sight of flowers.
Resentful of parting, I brood over the cries of birds.
    — *Yasuyoshi*

The hokku has succeeded splendidly in expressing through metaphor the sorrows of those who are leaving as well as of those who are staying behind. The reference to fishes' tears is ingenious. Examples that pair birds and fishes are too numerous to cite. — *Tosai*

"Returning to Live in the Country" by T'ao Ch'ien [365–427] says:

A migrant bird longs for its native woods.
A fish in the pond recalls the mountain pond it came from.
    — *Sekisui*

The poet compared himself to departing spring, and his friends to birds and fishes. He was pleased and thankful to see them worrying about his journey and shedding tears over his departure. — *Chikurei*

Because of the opening phrase, it is clear that the hokku uses the image of birds and fishes to express sorrow over the passing of spring. But the core of the poem lies in the sorrow of parting. Its last two phrases imply that even insensitive birds and fishes are tearful over departing spring, and that implication has been transferred, by the poet's consummate skill, to the emotion of the people who find it difficult to part with each other. — *Mizuho*

As I imagine, Bashō got off the boat in Senju and saw some fishes being displayed at a store. A fish's eyes, as we see them at a fishmonger's today, have the kind of gleam, moisture, and size that remind us of tearful eyes. I therefore feel that the expression "fishes' eyes are tearful" is both the motif and focus of this hokku. — Komiya

The poem makes us feel as though everything the eyes could see was drenched in the sorrow of parting. — Abe J.

It is probably reasonable to assume that birds, which fly away, stand for the poet embarking on a long journey, and that fishes, which usually continue to live in the water where they were born, represent his friends remaining behind. — Higuchi

A picture of Gautama Buddha's death traditionally portrays birds and beasts gathered around his body in tearful mourning. This poem also has something of that mythical world, as it depicts birds and fish mourning the departure of spring. Reading the poem in a symbolic way like this appeals to me. I even fantasize flowers falling from heaven. — Seisensui

The motif of the poem is the sorrow of parting, but the surface meaning is sorrow over the end of spring. The rhetoric of the poem was perfected when the sorrow of parting was expressed in words that mourn spring's departure. A haiku, being seasonal poetry, does not directly vent the poet's emotion but expresses it through some seasonal touch. It has to have the characteristics of a highly metaphorical poem. — Yamamoto

The theme of this poem is spring's departure. It would be farfetched to read too much of the sorrow of parting into it. I disagree, therefore, with some past commentators who identified the bird with the poet and the fish with people who were sending him off. My reading is also related to the fact that Bashō did not actually write the poem at the beginning of his journey. This was a farewell poem not in fact but in his travel journal. It does not appear in Sora's travel journal nor in any haikai book published during Bashō's lifetime. He probably composed it between 1692 and 1694, when he was writing *Oku no hosomichi*. — Imoto

village where they ring
no bells—how do they live?
nightfall in spring

kane | tsukanu | sato | wa | nani | wo | ka | haru | no | kure
bell | not-ring | village | as-for | what | [acc.] | ? | spring | 's | evening

NOTE

Written in the vicinity of Kanuma in Shimotsuke Province (Tochigi Prefecture) on
or around May 18.

COMMENTARY

In a village where they ring no bells—that is, where no sound of bell is heard—
how, or by what means, do they know the spring day is coming to a close? Without the sound of a temple bell, one does not feel as if it is a spring evening. That
is what the poet wanted to say, and he said it skillfully in this hokku. Yet the
twisted wording "village where they ring no bells" sounds a little too contrived.
There is a little intellectualization, too, when the poet asks how they know the
spring day is ending. In brief, this is not a very good poem. – *Bōtō*

Spring nightfall somehow makes people feel weary and sorrowful, inducing them
to seek some spiritual support. Bashō wished to hear the sound of a temple bell
and use it for solace during his time of grief. That led him to wonder what spiritual support people had in the village where they rang no bells. – *Shūson*

The hokku alludes to the monk Nōin's waka in *Shinkokinshū* [no. 116]:

Spring nightfall   yamazato no
in a mountain village   haru no yūgure
where, at the sound of a bell   kite mireba
tolling the close of a day,   iriai no kane ni
cherry blossoms keep falling.   hana zo chirikeru
                              – *Abe K.*

how solemn!
green leaves, young leaves, and through them
the rays of the sun

ara | tōto | aoba | wakaba | no | hi | no | hikari
ah | solemn | green-leaf | young-leaf | 's | sun | 's | light

NOTE
Written on May 19, when Bashō visited Tōshō Shrine in Nikkō. The name
Nikkō literally means "sunlight."

COMMENTARY
The hokku describes the solemnity of the scene by alluding to the name of the
place. It also suggests the sun shining in the heavens and extending its blessings
in all directions. – *Tosai*

On the surface the poem describes the scene objectively, but underneath it implies the praise of the deity enshrined in Nikkō. The reference to the sunlight is
too obvious. This is not a good poem. – *Meisetsu*

The mountain was covered with verdant leaves, on which the sunlight was falling. Perhaps it was a windy day: all the trees were shaking, and the entire mountain seemed to quiver in the abundant sunlight of an early summer day. At such a
sight, the words "How solemn!" automatically escaped the poet's lips. To put it
in another way, the poet was inspired directly by nature, and not by admiration
for the local deity. – *Komiya*

I disagree with Komiya. I think the solemn feeling the poet had toward the deity
on Mt. Nikkō led him to the image of the sunlight. – *Mizuho*

The grandeur and renown of Tōshō Shrine echo in this poem. It is beautiful to
see the gilded structure standing against the background of young green foliage.
The sunlight is falling on it, too. The poet's virtuosity here is almost intimidat-
ing. – *Rohan*

Everyone feels something akin to the joy of living when he sees the glossy sheen
of rich, luxuriant foliage bathed in sunlight. It may be going too far to describe
that feeling as a religious sentiment, but, if it is to be described in terms border-
ing on that state, one will have to say, "How solemn!" – *Handa*

As is often the case in hokku, the poem pays respect to the locale. – *Imoto*

for a while I sit
meditating by the falls—
start of a summer retreat

shibaraku | wa | taki | ni | komoru | ya | ge | no | hajime
short-time | as-for | waterfall | at | is-secluded | : | summer-retreat | 's |
  beginning

NOTE

Written on May 20 at Urami Falls, some four miles west of Nikkō. *Ge* refers to
the ninety-day period of ascetic seclusion prescribed for Buddhist monks each
summer. In 1689, the period started on June 3.

COMMENTARY

The poet spoke out in this manner because a waterfall was often the place where
monks engaged in an ascetic exercise or purification rite. – *Nobutane*

The falling water could be seen from behind at Urami Falls. It was early summer,
too. So the poet felt as if he were there to do the usual religious exercise. He had
a good sense of humor. – *Meisetsu*

Bashō regarded this northern journey as a form of ascetic exercise. Accordingly,
here he said he began it by secluding himself in a cave behind Urami Falls for a
while. – *Kōseki*

The mood of a traveler is well expressed in the words "for a while." – *Iwata*

According to Sora's journal, Bashō went to see the falls on the morning of May
20. It was still some time before the beginning of the summer seclusion. That is a
valuable clue to the reading of this hokku. The seasonal phrase "start of a summer retreat" signifies that the period of seclusion has begun, not that the period
is forthcoming. Bashō seems to have wanted to say he tasted something of the religious exercise unexpectedly. – *Andō*

On a painting showing a crane and a banana plant

a crane screeches,
its voice ripping the leaves
of a banana plant

tsuru I naku I ya I sono I koe I ni I bashō I yarenubeshi
crane I cry I : I its I voice I with I banana-plant I will-be-torn

NOTE
Written in Kurobane, a town located northeast of Nikkō, sometime between
May 22 and June 2.

COMMENTARY
There are lines of a Chinese poem that say:

As the crane screeches in a deep valley
Its voice reaches as high as heaven.

Or the hokku may allude to the unbearably pathetic sound of a crane crying for
its child at night. In either case, the image of a banana plant is irreplaceable here.
— *Tosai*

The poem well describes the strong, high-pitched cry of a crane. — *Sokotsu*

As the poet gazed at the painting, he was fired with creative energy and gave free
rein to his imagination. — *Shūson*

Capturing the essence of the crane's piercing cry and the soft, delicate banana
leaf, the poem well harmonizes with the painting. — *Kon*

*The chief councilor in charge of the mansion lent me a horse as I left
there. The groom asked if he could have a poetry card from me. Moved
by his elegant request, I wrote*

road across a plain—
turn my horse sideways
toward that hototogisu!

no I wo I yoko I ni I uma I hiki I muke I yo I hototogisu
plain I [acc.] I sideway I to I horse I pulling I turn I ! I hototogisu

NOTE

Written on June 3, when Bashō was traveling across Nasu Plain in Shimotsuke
Province. A poetry card is a thick, rectangular sheet of paper on which one
writes a poem and gives it to someone as a gift.

COMMENTARY

This is a powerful poem that suggests the vastness of the plain. – *Keion*

The poet was lightly amused at the groom, and that feeling is indirectly reflected
in this hokku. We can tell this is a poem composed on the spur of the moment.
Words of command often make a poem sound pompous and conceited, but in
this instance we do not feel that way because the language is so spontaneous and
natural. – *Shida*

There is no way here that Bashō could have failed to recall the famous waka by
Minamoto Sanetomo [1192–1219]:

On the bracers	mononofu no
of a samurai	yanami tsukurou
readying arrows	kote no ue ni
hailstones spatter and roll—	arare tabashiru
a bamboo field at Nasu.	Nasu no shinohara

As he rode across Nasu Plain, there emerged in his mind a panoramic view of
various past samurai performing heroic deeds in the field now overgrown with
bamboo grass. The impression of that view was transmitted to this poem and became part of its force. – *Yamamoto*

Bashō responded to the groom's "elegant" heart—*fūryū*—by asking him to turn
the horse in the direction of the hototogisu, the most poetic subject in summer.
There is a sense of pleasant surprise at suddenly encountering a hototogisu's cry
on a vast plain. – *Kon*

The Killer Stone

the stone's smell
summer grasses look red,
dewdrops warm

ishi | no | ka | ya | natsugusa | akaku | tsuyu | atsushi
stone | 's | smell | : | summer-grass | red | dew | hot

NOTE

The Killer Stone is a large rock (7 feet square, 4 feet high) located in Nasu Hot Springs. It is so called because poisonous gas rises from the ground around it, killing any creature that comes near. According to a legend, a fox with nine tails transformed itself into a beautiful woman and succeeded in seducing Emperor Toba (1103–56), but finally its true identity was exposed by an exorcist. The fox fled to Nasu Plain, where it was slain by pursuers. It has been said that the Killer Stone is the manifestation of that fox's vengeful spirit.

COMMENTARY

An intense, forceful poem. – *Bakusui*

The scene is superbly described, making the reader shudder. – *Tosai*

The poet depicted the scene with the legendary fox's burning hatred in mind. – *Meisetsu*

The poisonous gas is probably arsenious acid. Because of it, the summer grasses growing in the area had become reddish and the dew on their leaves conveyed a sense of oppressive warmth. The hokku's opening phrase presents an olfactory sensation accompanied by a visual impression. The middle phrase is purely visual. The last phrase implies a tactile sensation induced by the sight. This process of moving from one sense to another is extremely skillful. – *Handa*

The image order suggests that the poet first looked at the stone from a distance and then examined it closely from nearby. We can even guess the hour of the day, too. – *Utsubo*

A stone is normally scentless, but here it has a smell. Grass, which is normally green, is here described as red. Dew, considered to emit a cool feeling, is here said to be warm. By describing everything in sight as abnormal, the poem has captured the eerie atmosphere surrounding the Killer Stone. It has done so with no artifice, too. – *Iwata*

The willow tree about which Saigyō wrote the famous waka still stood by a rice field in Ashino village. Because Mr. Kohō, who governed this county, always wanted to show the tree to me, I had been anxious to discover its location. I was happy to stop by the tree today.

over an entire field
they have planted rice—before
I part with the willow

ta | ichimai | uete | tachisaru | yanagi | kana
rice-field | one | planting | leave | willow | kana

NOTE

Saigyō's waka referred to in the headnote is included in *Shinkokinshū* (no. 262). It is also a focal poem in the nō play *Yugyō yanagi* (Yugyō and the willow). It reads:

Alongside the road	michi no be ni
a stream of clear water	shimizu nagaruru
shaded by a willow—	yanagi kage
wanting to take a short rest	shibashi to te koso
I stopped—and am still here.	tachidomaritsure

Kohō is Ashino Suketoshi (1637–92), governor of the district, whose Edo residence was located near Bashō's house and who was therefore acquainted with him. Bashō visited this willow tree on June 7, but composition of the hokku may have come three or four years later, when he wrote *Oku no hosomichi*.

COMMENTARY

The hokku, drawing on Saigyō's waka, implies that the traveling poet had intended to rest only for a short while, but ended up by staying there for so long that, to his surprise, rice planting of an entire field had been done before his departure. — *Ryōta*

Having finished planting the entire field, men and women stopped singing rice-planting songs and began to chat with each other. That change awakened the poet from his reverie, giving him a chance to leave. — *Watsuji*

Since his departure from Edo, Bashō had yearned to see the famous willow tree. Now that his longtime wish was fulfilled, he allowed himself to bask in happiness—for so long that when he came to he found that the planting of an entire rice field was over. He had intended to rest only for a short time, but he did not, and that feeling was given concrete poetic form when he described what he actually saw. He wrote the introductory note to express how he felt up to the time when he stopped by the tree, and he wrote a hokku to describe how he felt during the time he was there. The hokku follows the prose in the same way two verses are linked in haikai. – *Shūson*

Bashō went there to see the willow tree, but when he stood under the tree his mind became almost vacant and his eyes just followed the actions of the girls planting rice. That "brief" time of rest allowed the girls to finish planting an entire field. To put it from another viewpoint, it was Bashō who made it possible for rice planting to be completed over the whole field. Of course, the actual planting was done by the peasant girls, but it was what might be called the passage of Bashō's "inner time" that allowed it. The inner and outer landscapes merged together during that time. – *Yamamoto*

Bashō mentioned Kohō's name in his headnote. If that was not just a form of name-dropping, we must assume he intended to mourn Kohō's death by writing the headnote and the hokku. Here he wrote a requiem for Kohō, disguising himself as an itinerant monk in the nō play *Yugyō yanagi*. The rice planting was a ritual Bashō performed as a requiem for the dead. The ritual was dedicated to the spirit of the willow, but it was also for Saigyō, whose poetic spirit had lingered around the tree, and for Kohō, who used to display so much *fūga*. – *Ogata*

Here is a contrast between the literary world of Saigyō's waka as well as the nō drama *Yugyō yanagi*, on the one hand, and, on the other, the actual world of peasants who, totally unconcerned with such literary interests, went on to finish planting a rice field. The charm of the poem lies in that contrast, and in the position of the poet who placed himself halfway between those two worlds. – *Imoto*

On crossing the Barrier at Shirakawa

the beginning
of fūryū—a rice-planting song
in the far north

fūryū | no | hajime | ya | oku | no | taueuta
fūryū | 's | beginning | : | depth | 's | rice-planting-song

NOTE
Written on June 9 at Sukagawa. Bashō stayed at the house of his friend Sagara
Tōkyū (1638–1715) and participated in a kasen composition. This poem was its
opening verse. Shirakawa Barrier was the entrance to the northern provinces for
those who traveled from the south.

COMMENTARY
In a rustic region where nothing looked elegant, the poet heard a traditional rice-
planting song and speculated that it must be the origin of all art. According to
another interpretation, the poet, who had just crossed Shirakawa Barrier and entered the northern region, felt he encountered the first poetic event when he
heard a rice-planting song. The reader may choose whichever of the two interpretations he likes. – *Shōgatsudō*

This poem contains nothing in particular that calls for adverse criticism, but it
offers nothing especially praiseworthy either. – *Shiki*

Nature lies, above all, in the soil. It lies in the life of the people who make their
living from the soil. Isn't a rice-planting song the spontaneous voice of the soil?
Doesn't the joy of a traveler lie precisely in listening to the simple beauty of such
a song? What an auspicious start for my poetic journey! I can see Bashō smiling
as these thoughts occur to him. – *Seisensui*

People at Tōkyū's house were engaged in rice planting, too. Bashō saw that and
wrote this poem, at once complimenting Tōkyū and expressing his admiration
for the simple, rustic arts of the north. – *Yamamoto*

According to a study by Ōmori Shirō [b. 1905],* ritual rice planting in which
girls would sing songs was no longer practiced in Japan at that time except in the
northern provinces. Witnessing such rice planting and its accompanying songs
for the first time, Bashō must have found the event attractive and poetic. – *Imoto*

*The study is entitled *Nihon bunkashi ronkō* (Essays on the history of Japanese culture, 1975).

Because the ideogram Chestnut is written by combining two letters that signify West and Tree respectively, a chestnut tree is associated with the Western Paradise. Hence Bodhisattva Gyōki is said to have used chestnut both for his cane and for the pillars of his house.

few in this world
notice those blossoms—
chestnut by the eaves

yo | no | hito | no | mitsukenu | hana | ya | noki | no | kuri
world | 's | person | 's | not-find | blossom | : | eave | 's | chestnut

NOTE

Written on June 11, when Bashō participated in composing a kasen at the monk Kashin's residence in Sukagawa.

COMMENTARY

The poet praised the monk's anchoritic life by comparing it to inconspicuous chestnut blossoms. – *Tosai*

Chestnut blossoms are noticed only after they fall to the ground; they are inconspicuous on the tree. Because of that, the poet compared them to a monk who has left the world behind. – *Rohan*

In the relationship between chestnut blossoms and the anchoritic monk we can sense something like *nioi*, which Bashō used for linking two haikai stanzas. – *Shūson*

whereabouts is
Kasashima? this rainy month,
this muddy road

Kasashima | wa | izuko | satsuki | no | nukarimichi
Kasashima | as-for | where | fifth-month | 's | muddy-road

NOTE

Written on June 20, when Bashō passed by Kasashima village where the grave of
Fujiwara Sanekata (?–998) was located. A legend has it that Sanekata, a reputed
waka poet in Kyoto, was exiled to a northern province because of his misbehavior at the imperial court. It is said that he fell from a horse and was killed in Kasashima the following year, when he dared to pass before a local shrine without
getting off the horse. Saigyō visited his grave in the twelfth century and wrote the
waka:

He has left nothing	kuchi mo senu
but an undying name	sono na bakari wo
in this world . . .	todome okite
On his grave in the withered moor	kareno no susuki
pampas grass is all I see.	katami ni zo miru

The name Kasashima literally means "hat island," the hat referring to the kind
that was often worn on a rainy day.

COMMENTARY

The name Kasashima is also related to rain. The road was so muddy that the
poet could not visit the place but only looked in that direction from a distance as
he passed by. – *Donto*

We have to say this is an extremely mediocre poem, as it merely works on the humorous association of a hat and the rainy season. Why did a poet of Bashō's caliber write such a mediocre poem? It is because that association was not concocted in the poet's brain but emerged spontaneously at that time and place. The
humor was spontaneous, the kind that Bashō liked. – *Seisensui*

Wherever Bashō traveled, he was always confronted with long rain and a muddy
road. He always had miles to go, under an overcast sky. – *Hagiwara*

This was a spontaneous poem, which Bashō wrote in an effort to soothe his disappointment at not being able to visit the place. It is amusing to imagine a visibly despondent Bashō speaking to Sora in this way. — *Ebara*

In traditional tales of heroes in exile, a high-ranking nobleman like Narihira or Sanekata always leaves the capital and goes down to the eastern provinces. Such stories of exile formed the main current in the tragic literature of ancient Japan. The same stories, which in *Genji monogatari* were more of an undercurrent, appealed to Bashō the wanderer. Bashō, himself on a journey now, could not be unconcerned with the fate of the tragic hero Sanekata, or of Saigyō, who had written a poem before Sanekata's grave. When Bashō, rained on and exhausted, was frustrated in his quest and thus reduced to asking, "Whereabouts is Kasashima?" he had an irresistible urge to invoke Sanekata, who had become the guardian spirit of the place. — *Yamamoto*

The hardship of travel on a muddy road tinged the poet's nostalgic thoughts of Sanekata, the noble hero of a tragic tale of exile, thereby adding a delicate shade to the poem's emotion. — *Kon*

At Takadachi in Mutsu Province

summer grasses
where stalwart soldiers
once dreamed a dream

natsugusa | ya | tsuwamono-domo | ga | yume | no | ato
summer-grass | : | warrior | 's | dream | 's | site

NOTE

Takadachi was a castle that Fujiwara Hidehira (?–1187), the lord of Mutsu Province (Aomori and Iwate prefectures), had built in Hiraizumi for Minamoto Yoshitsune (1159–89), younger brother of Shogun Yoritomo (1147–99), in the twelfth
century. When Hidehira died, his son sent a troop to attack Yoshitsune and, after
a fierce battle, killed him and his retainers. Bashō visited Takadachi on June 29.

COMMENTARY

Here is a great deal of wordless pity. – *Shōgatsudō*

Dead bodies were heaped in hills, surrounded by rivers of human blood. That
battle, however, was long past and now seemed like a dream. The hokku makes
good use of the image of summer grass, whose leaves are scorched at their tips
under the flaming sun. – *Nobutane*

The poem, casually written in seventeen syllables, implies the rise and fall of a
clan as well as of human life, filling the reader with deep emotion. Some may say
it is too plain a poem. Yet its greatness lies precisely in its plain look. It looks
plain because it is that much farther removed from artifice and closer to nature.
– *Shiki*

I like the plural suffix *domo* following *tsuwamono*. It is as though each soldier's
dream were lingering on each blade of grass. – *Mizuho*

If the poem had consisted of just the last two phrases, it would be nothing more
than a plain expression of sentimental nostalgia. But the simple presentation of
the actual scene in the opening phrase gives a strong sense of reality to that nostalgic sentiment. The transitoriness of glory, the emptiness of prosperity, all are
seen in the luxuriant summer grass. – *Ebara*

The summer grass in this poem is not picturesque like the gale in Buson's hokku:

to Toba Palace   Toba-dono e
five or six horsemen hurry—   gorokki isogu
an autumn gale   nowaki kana

This is the grass that grows green with the luxuriance of summer in the actual world, at the same time cradling the warriors' dreams. This is the grass that connects the dream world of the former days to the real world from which those dreams have vanished without trace. Bashō created his own poetic realm by merging his emotions (contained in the last two phrases) with the summer grass. Whereas the autumn gale in Buson's poem is "cold," Bashō's summer grass is "warm" with blood. – *Shūson*

An ancient battlefield is a sacred place where mythology, history, and literature originate. It is a kind of purgatory, a place where the souls of the slain soldiers, still retaining their anger and resentment, utter war cries day and night. The nō drama, which often stages the sufferings of ancient warriors in beautiful poetic form, can be considered the end product of an artistic tradition that originated in the literature intended to soothe the souls that haunted the locale. It is conceivable that that tradition survives in this hokku of Bashō's. – *Yamamoto*

I am inclined to think that "stalwart soldiers" refers not only to Yoshitsune and his retainers but also to the Fujiwara clan and its warriors who created a unique culture in Hiraizumi. Nostalgia for past glory, as expressed in *Oku no hosomichi*, and a contrast between insentient nature and fragile human existence are condensed into this poem. – *Imoto*

The warriors' dreams, juxtaposed with the image of summer grasses, represent the futility of courageous men's endeavors, endeavors that have left no trace on the present landscape. To use a Buddhist expression, what we have here is the idea of "impermanence" contrasted with "permanence." For the first time in the history of haikai, an idea has become the subject of a poem. – *Konishi*

did all the seasonal rains
come and go, leaving out
this Shining Hall?

samidare | no | furi | nokoshite | ya | hikaridō
fifth-month-rain | 's | falling | leaving | ? | Shining-Hall

NOTE

Hikaridō, or the Shining Hall, is part of Chūson Temple in Hiraizumi. Built by
the Fujiwara clan in 1124, the pavilion was famous for its gilded walls. A protective structure covering the hall was built in 1288. Bashō visited here on June 29.

COMMENTARY

All the ancient buildings, adorned with gold and silver, had been devastated by
the rains and the winds, with the exception of the Shining Hall, which had managed to survive the years. Although there was no sun (it was the rainy season),
the hall alone was shining brightly. We should visualize the poet standing there
and pondering bygone days. – *Donto*

The poet visited the Shining Hall on a rainy day. Because the hall was the only
thing still shining, the poet said it had been "left out" by the seasonal rain and
shone alone in a rain-shrouded world. – *Meisetsu*

The poet, after walking in the gloomy rain, suddenly stepped inside the Shining
Hall where gilt still remained on the walls. The poem describes how he felt at
that instant. – *Abe J.*

The rains have not fallen on the Shining Hall because of its protective outer
structure. The hall, as a result, is shining even more brightly than before. Surely
we can read the poem in this way. It is the kind of emotion Bashō was likely to
have felt. – *Seisensui*

There is no need to assume it was raining when Bashō was there. The Shining
Hall itself was covered by an outer structure; the hall in the poem, therefore, is a
building that shone radiantly in Bashō's imagination alone. Thus the seasonal
rain in the poem has to be the rain in his mind, too—the rain that came and
went for many generations. – *Shūson*

What the poem depicts is a rainy scene. It presents a contrast between the
gloomy seasonal rain and the radiantly shining hall. In actuality one could not
have seen the hall standing radiantly in the rain, because it was covered by an

outer building. But Bashō, using a poet's prerogative, removed the image of the outer building and joined the images of the rain and the hall directly. – *Yamamoto*

The thematic emotion of this poem is the poet's fellow feeling for humanity's bold defiance of nature's hegemony in time and in space. It is admiration for the permanence of art. Bashō felt a strong—almost painful—empathy for the artistic masterpiece fighting for survival with all its might. – *Imoto*

From Narugo Hot Springs we tried to enter the province of Dewa through Shitomae Barrier. Because there were few travelers along this road, the officials at the barrier interrogated us at length before finally letting us pass. As the sun set when we reached the summit of a large mountain, we asked for lodging at a barrier-keeper's house we spotted. A storm raged for the next three days, during which time we were confined to this boring place.

fleas, lice—
a horse piddles
near my pillow

nomi | shirami | uma | no | shitosuru | makuramoto
flea | louse | horse | 's | piddle | near-pillow

NOTE

Shitosuru is a verb referring to a child's urination. The ideogram used for *shito* is the same as *shito* in Shitomae. Bashō spent the nights of July 1 and 2 at this "barrier-keeper's house," which was actually the house of a village headman. Dewa Province covered the modern prefectures of Akita and Yamagata.

COMMENTARY

The poet was on a mountain road leading to Shitomae Barrier. The hokku plays on the place name. – *Tosai*

Bitten by fleas and lice, the poet was tossing this way and that on his pallet when he heard the sound of a horse urinating near his pillow. The situation was disgusting—so much so that he could not help smiling a little. It was the forced smile of a man who wandered into a blind alley. Perhaps Bashō had been wondering why the place had such an inelegant name as Shitomae, when he heard a horse urinating. At that instant, I believe, this poem sprang into his mind. – *Seisensui*

The charm of this poem lies in the way it gives extremely cheerful, unrestrained expression to wretched circumstances. Under attack from fleas and lice in the darkness of night, the poet had been unable to sleep. Suddenly, he was startled by a nearby sound that was all too familiar to him. Confronted with something totally unexpected, he distanced himself from it through laughter. – *Yamamoto*

Here, too, I see the spirit of *wabi* according to which something ugly is not considered ugly, or something insufficient is not considered insufficient. – *Seishi*

This hokku makes me think of the power of a fixed verse form. If the fact presented here were to be described in prose, the results would be a composition not very pleasant to read. But here the poet was bold enough to toss out three nouns and then link himself to them by the words "near my pillow," whereupon there emerged a world that arouses nothing unpleasant in the reader's mind. To be sure, the writer was Bashō; but the technique is not something that requires the touch of a great poet. It has more to do, I think, with the magic of the seventeen-syllable form. – *Utsubo*

The humor and haikai spirit of this poem lie in the word "piddle," which compares a horse urinating to a little child. Without that word, the image of a horse urinating near one's pillow would create a filthy impression and nothing else. – *Imoto*

The poet's irritation, loneliness, and other feelings at being forced to take these unlikely lodgings because of a storm are here given concrete form by reference to the actual situation in the modest mountain hut, where he suffered not only the attack of fleas and lice but also the sound of a horse urinating by his pillow. – *Kon*

come crawling out!
under the silkworm nursery
a toad's croak

hai | ide | yo | kaiya | ga | shita | no | hiki | no | koe
crawling | exit | ! | silkworm-nursery | 's | underside | 's | toad | 's | voice

NOTE
Written in Obanazawa, where Bashō stayed from July 3 to July 12.

COMMENTARY
Toads are attracted to silkworms. A poem in the *Man'yōshū* [no. 2269] says:

In the morning mist	asagasumi
under the silkworm nursery	kaiya ga shita ni
a toad croaks . . .	naku kawazu
If only I could hear your voice,	koe da ni kikaba
none of this yearning for you!	ware koime ya mo

Bashō, staying in modest quarters near a silkworm nursery, felt so lonely that when he heard a toad croak, he asked the creature to crawl out and keep him company. Here is another display of *sabi*. – *Donto*

The poet wrote this playful poem on the spur of the moment. There is hardly any substantive content. It is a very commonplace poem. – *Bōtō*

Under the silkworm nursery a toad was croaking in a low voice. Bashō, who had been sitting there absentmindedly with nothing particular to look at, felt a kinship with the toad and hollered, "Come crawling out!" Picture the poet who, while everyone else was busy tending to the silkworms, alone had time on his hands and so called out to the sluggish toad, "Won't you come out and keep me company?" It is a charming picture. – *Ebara*

Somewhere a toad is croaking in a low, blunt voice. It seems to be under the floor of the silkworm nursery. Toad, stop crying and come out of that dark, lonely place! That is what the poem says. The lonely heart of the traveling poet is attracted to the forlorn voice of a toad. – *Imoto*

There is a humorous tone in the poet's address to a slow-moving, ugly toad, and that tone suggests he was enjoying some moments of relaxation at his lodging. The allusion to the *Man'yōshū* poem adds patina to the hokku, well matching the simple, old-fashioned way in which silkworm farming was practiced in the northern provinces. – *Kon*

the stillness—
seeping into the rocks
cicadas' screech

shizukasa | ya | iwa | ni | shimiiru | semi | no | koe
stillness | : | rock | to | permeate | cicada | 's | voice

NOTE

Written at Ryūshaku Temple. Bashō arrived here for an overnight stay on July 13.

COMMENTARY

A poem by Tu Fu says, "Cicadas' voices merge together at an old temple." Bashō further enhanced the poetic beauty of the scene by introducing the image of rocks absorbing the voices. – *Moran*

Not a single sound was heard at this quiet place, except the voice of the cicadas that was so forceful that it seemed to seep into the rocks. As the poet listened to it, his thoughts became collected and his mind attained tranquillity. The poem's meaning goes beyond its words and points toward the profound secrets of Zen. – *Sanga*

Cicadas' cries are a metaphor for men's earthly desires. The poem suggests how such desires disappear in the court of Buddha's Law. – *Nobutane*

If my sensibility is reliable, there should not be many cicadas here. – *Mizuho*

I disagree. The whole mountain is filled with the cicadas' screech. – *Watsuji*

I'd rather have many cicadas in this scene. It is a little dark and cool out there, and the cicadas' cries are sounding in unison. – *Komiya*

In the word *shimiiru* we sense motion in stillness, and stillness in motion. Bashō, with his consummate art, captured this oneness of motion and stillness in a short poem. – *Ebara*

What Bashō felt on hearing the cicadas' cries "seeping into the rocks" was probably a mysterious kind of loneliness emanating from his absorption into the unified, serene chirping of the cicadas. It was not the type of sad, empty feeling that we experience when we cannot obtain what we seek in our daily lives. Nor was it the kind of helpless feeling we have when, all alone, we ponder over life's frightening aspects. This was the type of loneliness we feel when we encounter nature at its fullest moment and touch on its motionless motion—when we sense the movement of the Prime Mover that does not move. It is at once "loneliness" and "stillness." Or, more precisely, it is a pure "apprehension of nature" before it branches into those two emotions. *– Shūson*

"Cicadas' screech" is a symbol. Through it, Bashō listened to the stillness of nature, to the rhythm of nature. *– Seisensui*

gathering the rains
of the wet season, how swiftly flows
the Mogami River!

samidare I wo I atsumete I hayashi I Mogami-gawa
fifth-month-rain I [acc.] I gathering I swift I Mogami-River

NOTE

Written in Ōishida on the eastern shore of the Mogami River. Bashō stayed here for three days, beginning on July 14.

COMMENTARY

This river goes through many rapids and falls as its abundant water flows turbulently through the valley. Because it is the largest river in the province, the poet suggested it had gathered all the province's rains. We get a lively picture of the current as it swirls and gushes. This is a powerful, sublime poem. – *Nobutane*

The swift, torrential flow must have been frightening to look at. The poem is magnificent in the way it suggests the river's force, but the phrase "gathering the rains" is overly rhetorical and constitutes the one small flaw. – *Rika*

The hokku creates the impression that the poet was not looking at the river from a distance but was immersed in the *swiftness* of the Mogami. – *Watsuji*

Doesn't a stream look swifter when looked at from the shore rather than from a boat? – *Komiya*

The poem gives the impression of the water in the river rising and falling as it flows downstream on a fine day after a long period of rain. – *Mizuho*

Normally (grammatically, that is), one would say, "Rains have gathered." But Bashō wrote "gathering the rains" because he was not describing the scene as it presented itself but rather was merging himself with it. He saw the torrential current not from a materialistic point of view but as something alive, as something gigantic that was breathing like himself. – *Handa*

It does not matter whether Bashō was on the shore or aboard a boat. All that matters is that he was at one with the stream and was flowing with it himself. – *Seishi*

This poem hints at the mighty powers of nature. Mountain lay piled upon mountain, all covered in green leaves. Over the greenery hung black clouds from which the rain descended in torrents. Amidst all, there was something like a big vein or artery that, fed by all the smaller veins, was carrying the flow of blood with a pulsing beat. That was the Mogami River. Here is the soul of nature in all its majesty—no, that is not the right word, because a soul is formless. Here is nature manifesting itself in a giant, breathing body. — *Seisensui*

At Seishin's house

scent in the wind
also suggests the south—
the Mogami River

kaze I no I ka I mo I minami I ni I chikashi I Mogami-gawa
wind I 's I scent I also I south I to I close I Mogami-River

NOTE
Written on July 17, when Bashō visited Shibuya Kurōbei, a prosperous merchant
in Shinjō. Seishin was Shibuya's haikai name.

COMMENTARY
This was probably how Bashō felt when the seasonal rain stopped and a cool
wind began to blow. The "scent in the wind" is not the kind of scent that assaults
the nose but a sense of warmth in the wind that was experienced as a scent. By a
similar poetic convention, southerly winds are often described as "fragrant."
— *Meisetsu*

A wind came from the south, and there seemed something special about its
smell. That was because it had come across the Mogami River, which flowed in
the south. This "something special" combined with the poet's visualization of the
big river flowing in the vicinity to produce the wording of the poem. — *Ebara*

By referring to the great river that was the pride of the locality, Bashō complimented his host on the coolness of his residence. The poem alludes to Po Chü-i's
line, "The fragrant wind comes from the south." — *Kon*

the coolness—
faintly the crescent moon
above Mount Haguro

suzushisa | ya | hono | mikazuki | no | Haguro-yama
coolness | : | vague | third-day-moon | 's | Haguro-Mountain

NOTE
Written during Bashō's week-long stay on Mt. Haguro, which began on July 19.
The name Haguro literally means "feather-black."

COMMENTARY
This describes the scene just as the poet saw it. – *Abe J.*

This is a highly nuanced poem that can be compared to a black-ink painting.
– *Handa*

Haguro is not just a proper noun here. Through its semantic and phonetic effect,
it creates the image of a black, massive mountain looming in the evening dusk.
– *Shūson*

By describing the refreshing sight of Mt. Haguro under the crescent moon, the
poet tried to give form to the experience of the sacred that he received from this
Buddhist mountain. – *Abe K.*

The hokku's opening phrase is in praise of the mountain. This is probably an evening scene. – *Yamamoto*

where peaks of the clouds
have crumbled one after another
the moon's mountain

kumo | no | mine | ikutsu | kuzurete | tsuki | no | yama
cloud | 's | peak | how-many | crumbling | moon | 's | mountain

NOTE

The hokku's concluding phrase means at once "a moonlit mountain" and Mt. Gassan (literally "moon-mountain"), a tall mountain located near Mt. Haguro. Bashō climbed this mountain on July 24.

COMMENTARY

Cloud peaks appear in the daytime and crumble toward evening. The poet wondered how many such peaks had been demolished to build that mountain. — *Nanimaru*

The poem has two meanings. (1) During the day there were cumulus clouds, but as the night approached they disappeared, giving way to the moon—they turned into the moon's mountain. (2) The mountain called "moon-mountain" really became a moonlit mountain, and that fact impressed the poet. Bashō must have worked hard to weave this complexity into the poem, but I don't much care for the result. — *Seisensui*

If we take this for a descriptive poem, we must assume Mt. Gassan was being looked at from afar. But if we believe Bashō wrote the hokku on top of the mountain, we can imagine he was at one with Gassan, and the poem is given life by that experience. — *Shūson*

How many of those towering clouds, which reigned in the daytime sky, have crumbled down to build this divine-looking mountain that now stands high among the clouds in the moonlight? The poet praised the magnificent appearance of Mt. Gassan by fancying that part of heaven might have come falling down to form the mountain on earth. — *Ogata*

The text of *Oku no hosomichi* says, "The moon of enlightenment was clear," the sentence implying a state of mind in which wisdom has appeared like a bright moon after all sinful thoughts are gone. Probably such a meaning is suggested by the poem's statement that the "moon's mountain" has appeared after the cloud's peaks have crumbled away. But the tone of the poem is all innocence, its last two phrases sounding like part of a children's song. — *Yamamoto*

the scorching day—
dipping it into the ocean
the Mogami River

atsuki I hi I wo I umi I ni I iretari I Mogami-gawa
hot I day I [acc.] I sea I into I have-put I Mogami-River

NOTE

Bashō wrote the first draft of this hokku to open a haikai sequence in Sakata on July 30. The word *hi* can mean either "day" or "sun."

COMMENTARY

This is a description of a cool evening by the estuary, where the water extends into an infinite distance. – *Tosai*

This is a scene in which the blazing sun is just about to set so deeply in the sea that only one-tenth of it will show above the water. That sun was located where the Mogami River flowed out to the sea, and the poet skillfully described the scene by saying that the river had pushed the sun into the ocean. The crucial word is "dipping," which suggests the force of the river. – *Rohan*

It was an uncomfortably hot summer day, but toward evening it somehow began to get cooler. In the area where the Mogami River flowed into the ocean there was a cool evening breeze. At that the poet fancied the hot day had been carried into the sea by the large river. – *Ebara*

This is a grand sunset scene, with the poet's feeling of refreshment lurking somewhere in the subtext. Magnificently beautiful, it shows two great forces of nature, the river and the sun, in rivalry with each other. – *Yamamoto*

Sora's diary says this was an especially hot day. Also, the first draft of the poem had "the coolness" for its first line. For these reasons, it seems more natural to take the word *hi* as meaning not "sun" but "day," a hot day as against "the coolness." – *Imoto*

In view of its syntax, I think the hokku implies at once that the river is carrying the hot day into the sea and that the river is pouring itself into the sea. By personifying the Mogami and making it into an active agent, the poet dynamically portrayed a sunset scene on the Sea of Japan. The hokku's opening phrase also carries the image of the sun sinking into the ocean. – *Kon*

Kisagata—
in the rain, like Hsi Shih,
flowers of a silk tree

Kisagata | ya | ame | ni | Seishi | ga | nebu | no | hana
Kisagata | : | rain | in | Hsi-Shih | 's | silk-tree | 's | flower

NOTE

Bashō visited Kisagata on August 2. The hokku includes a play on words, as
nebu means both "silk tree" and "to sleep." Hsi Shih (Seishi in Japanese) was a
Chinese woman of ancient times who was noted for her beauty. The defeated
king of Yüeh offered her to his conqueror, the king of Wu, who subsequently became so infatuated with her that he came to neglect affairs of state. It was said
that she looked most charming when she was in grief.

COMMENTARY

A poem by Su Tung-p'o says:

With ripples sparkling, it is beautiful on a fine day.
With mountains in a haze, the rainy scene is marvelous, too.
Compare this Lake Hsi to Hsi Shih—
She will be lovely with either heavy or light make-up.

Bashō likened Kisagata to Lake Hsi and brought out the association of Hsi Shih.
— *Moran*

The image of misty rain falling on those delicate silk-tree flowers evokes a feeling
of profound tranquillity. — *Shinpū*

To suggest the misty, forlorn landscape of Kisagata, the poet described the forlorn, rain-wet silk flower and compared it to Hsi Shih's sad looks. — *Abe Y.*

Here is a symphony of images. — *Watsuji*

A silk tree looks feminine and graceful, and even its name suggests a woman
with her head bowed in sorrow. — *Higuchi*

Light pink silk flowers are blooming in the rain. . . . How sad—and how beautiful! Those slender, hairlike stamens look as if they would get entangled at the
first drop of rain. They make us think of a woman in grief who, her eyelashes
laden with tears, is trying not to break down completely. And those flowers are

blooming on the rugged seashore in the desolate north, where sand is swirling in the wind. – *Seisensui*

This is a mosaic poem artificially assembled by stringing four images—Kisagata, the rain, Hsi Shih, and the flower of a silk tree—through the magical use of grammatical particles. Each of the images is different in the degree of clarity as it is different in its distance from reality. – *Yamamoto*

in the shallows
a crane, with its legs splashed—
coolness by the sea

shiogoshi | ya | tsuru | hagi | nurete | umi | suzushi
shallow | : | crane | thigh | being-wet | sea | cool

NOTE

Written in Kisagata. *Shiogoshi* originally was a common noun referring to the shallows located at the entrance of a bay but later, probably by Bashō's time, became a proper noun designating such a place in Kisagata.

COMMENTARY

The hokku's concluding phrase is superfluous. It would have been better if the coolness were suggested without being mentioned. — *Seisensui*

This is a scene of a crane frolicking in the shallows of the Shiogoshi River, with its legs splashed by the water. The blue waters of the northern sea provide the background. One who reads this poem will immediately feel the coolness. As a poem, Buson's hokku

the evening breeze—	yūkaze ya
water splashes at the legs	mizu aosagi no
of a blue heron	hagi wo utsu

is perhaps neater and more charming, but Bashō's poem has a more primitive, artless beauty. — *Ebara*

This describes the monk-like figures of Bashō and Sora standing at the mouth of the river with their robes tucked up as they tried to cool themselves off. — *Andō*

Looking toward Sado Island from a post town called Izumozaki in the province of Echigo

the rough sea—
flowing toward Sado Isle
the River of Heaven

araumi | ya | Sado | ni | yokotau | amanogawa
rough-sea | : | Sado | on | lie | Heaven's-River

NOTE

Bashō spent the night of August 18 at Izumozaki in Echigo Province (Niigata Prefecture). Sado, an island in the Sea of Japan, was known for its production of gold on the one hand and for many sad stories of prisoners exiled there on the other. *Amanogawa*, literally meaning "Heaven's River," is the Milky Way.

COMMENTARY

As we recite this hokku, the limpid sky of autumn strikes our eyes and the turbulent waves of the sea startle our ears. We feel the loneliness of travel without taking to the road. – *Tosai*

Even among Bashō's works, few poems have the kind of grandeur this one has. It provides evidence that hokku, despite its brevity, is capable of encompassing a vast scene. – *Abe Y.*

The hokku's opening phrase is not merely a broad depiction of rough waves on the northern sea. It embodies sad thoughts of Sado Island, a name forever burdened by the pathetic accounts of those who had been exiled there. We should not overlook the sorrow that underlies the grandeur. – *Ebara*

Bashō mentioned the name Sado in order to invoke all its historical associations. And those associations induce awareness of man's everlasting sadness.
   Yamamoto

The gloomy scenery characteristic of the Sea of Japan has here been captured with the words "the rough sea" and "Sado." By juxtaposing these with the Milky Way, the poet represented the grandeur of the universe as well as the insignificance and solitude of man. – *Kon*

under the same roof
courtesans, too, are asleep—
bush clover and the moon

hitotsuya | ni | yūjo | mo | netari | hagi | to | tsuki
one-house | in | courtesan | also | is-asleep | bush-clover | and | moon

NOTE
Written at an inn in Ichiburi, where Bashō spent the night of August 26.

COMMENTARY
Unexpectedly a traveling monk and traveling courtesans were to sleep in the
same house; hence the concluding phrase "bush clover and the moon."
— *Nobutane*

To Bashō, the thought of lodging in the same house with courtesans seemed to
have something in common with the impression made by the phrase "bush clover
and the moon." This hokku provides a good example of what Bashō called *nioi*.
— *Mizuho*

The bush clover stands for the courtesans, the moon for Bashō. The bright moon
in the sky and the delicate, lovely bush clover are friendly with, yet keep a certain
distance from, each other. Bashō and the courtesans associated with each other
in a similar way as they shared the same lodging. — *Kōseki*

Although the clover and the moon were no doubt there, they are more metaphors
than part of the actual scene in the poem. Yet if we were merely to take the clover
as a metaphor for the courtesans and the moon as one for Bashō, we would be
finding in the poem a device not far from the type of surprise comparison favored by the Danrin school. What we have here, however, is not a simple or intellectual comparison. The clover and the moon are what we might call the
"nioi" of the courtesans and Bashō, respectively. The delicate, lovely bush clover
and the serene, unworldly moon—in Bashō's mind, they were not only what he
saw with his own eyes but what represented the courtesans and himself. — *Ebara*

An unexpected encounter in human life is here viewed from far above and is
placed side by side with a similar contrast in nature. — *Imoto*

One day the monk Saigyō, having encountered a sudden shower in the village of
Eguchi, asked for shelter at a nearby house but was denied by its mistress, a
courtesan. Thereupon he sang out:

You'd never bring yourself   yo no naka wo
to hate and forsake this world   itou made koso
no matter how I plead . . .   katakarame
Yet, how can you begrudge   kari no yadori wo
to lend a temporary shelter?   oshimu kimi kana

The mistress responded with the waka:

Knowing you are someone   yo wo itou
who has forsaken this world,   hito to shi kikeba
I naturally thought   kari no yado ni
you would not be concerned   kokoro tomuna to
with this temporary shelter.   omou bakari zo

This legend was recorded in *Senjūshō* [Selected tales, 13th c.] and was also made into a nō play, *Eguchi*. Bashō drew upon the legend in writing this hokku.
— *Yamamoto*

A man named Isshō had gradually become known to a wide circle of people for his devotion to poetry. He died last winter, however, and now his brother held a haikai gathering in his memory.

move the gravemound!
my wailing voice,
the autumn wind

tsuka | mo | ugoke | waga | naku | koe | wa | aki | no | kaze
mound | also | move | my | weep | voice | as-for | autumn | 's | wind

NOTE

This memorial verse was offered on September 5 at the haikai gathering mentioned in the headnote. Kosugi Isshō (1653–88), a tea dealer and haikai poet in Kanazawa, had died on November 28 of the previous year, but Bashō did not know of this until his arrival in Kanazawa on August 29.

COMMENTARY

The preface to the *Kokinshū* says poetry can move heaven and earth without exerting force. — *Donto*

So much emotion is embodied in the poem that, in view of the fact that Bashō had never met the deceased in person, we feel the manner of expression is exaggerated. — *Rika*

The tone of the hokku is dignified indeed—too grand for a poem mourning Isshō's death. I think the poem expresses Bashō's feelings about human life in general, Isshō's death merely providing an occasion to give vent to them. — *Watsuji*

I don't think there is exaggeration. If we feel the manner of expression is exaggerated, that is because we cannot get to the bottom of what Bashō was feeling. I think Bashō did feel he wanted the gravemound to move. Bashō's emotions were always so intense. — *Komiya*

Here we see Bashō's persistent determination to make nature serve his own emotions rather than to let himself be absorbed into nature. — *Abe Y.*

Isshō and Bashō had never met. Bashō had been looking forward to meeting Isshō, until he received the shocking news of the latter's death. That shock led to the strong expression "move the gravemound!" — *Shinpū*

In the hokku's concluding phrase the poet at once compared his wailing voice to the wind and described the wind that happened to be blowing there. The opening phrase is very forceful in suggesting the poet's grief, but as a sequel to that emotional beginning, the remainder of the poem seems a little lacking in force. It may be that there is something wrong with the ordering of the phrases, but we should also keep in mind that the hokku is not an appropriate verse form for giving vent to such an intense emotion. – *Seihō*

Bashō's grief is related to the infinite size of the universe. The desolate sound of the autumn wind is the voice of his soul, a shriek that, as it pierces through his helpless solitude, is close to the voice of nihilism. Because of the same nihilistic attitude, the young Buddha left the world for the woods and eventually gained enlightenment with which to save mankind. Likewise, Bashō also grieved with his neighbor and wailed over the death of his friend. Yet, being the poet he was, he did not proclaim himself a savior. Instead, he obscurely suffered the griefs of humankind in his heart and wandered endlessly in quest of poetic beauty amidst grief. – *Hagiwara*

Bashō traveled in order to discipline himself as a poet, and he was willing to risk his life for that. In his mind, to write poetry was life itself. Isn't it possible, then, that when Bashō heard a promising poet like Isshō had died still in his thirties, he felt as though the late poet illustrated the unhappy fate he himself could have suffered? – *Utsubo*

Although some say that the emotion is exaggerated for a poem mourning the death of someone the poet had never met, we have no choice but to accept it as expressive of his true grief. Ever since he had left Sakata, Bashō's main aim had been to reach Kanazawa—that is to say, to meet Isshō. Then, on arrival at his destination, he discovered that the image of Isshō which he had cherished in his mind for the past twenty days had disappeared without trace from the land of the living. His fondness for Isshō had grown increasingly intense for the past few years, and at last it found a powerful expression here. – *Yamamoto*

how piteous!
under the helmet
a cricket

muzan I ya I na I kabuto I no I shita I no I kirigirisu
piteous I ! I ! I helmet I 's I underside I 's I cricket

NOTE

Bashō conceived this hokku when he visited Tada Shrine in Komatsu on September 8 and saw the helmet of Saitō Sanemori, an aged warrior killed in a battle fought at nearby Shinohara. Lest his enemies would know he was an old man, Sanemori had gone to war with his hair dyed. After the battle, his severed head was examined by an enemy general named Higuchi Jirō (?–1184), who cried out, "How piteous!" The incident is described in several works of Japanese literature, including *Heiki monogatari*, *Genpei seisuiki* (The rise and fall of the two clans, 13th c.), and the nō play *Sanemori*.

COMMENTARY

The poet paid a tribute to Sanemori as he looked at the old warrior's arms on display. He compared Sanemori, who despite his old age had fought his last battle with the courage of a young man, to a late autumn cricket vigorously chirping. The poet prefaced the comparison by the words of mourning, "How piteous!" – *Shōgatsudō*

The image of a cricket suggests the figure of an old samurai with his hair and whiskers dyed. – *Nobutane*

Ages ago the helmet was on a war hero's head. Today, a cricket is singing underneath it. The poet wrote the hokku as he felt life was like a dream. – *Tosai*

The cricket trapped under the helmet and crying in a pathetic voice must be Sanemori's soul. After so many years, his resentment still lingered on and had found this piteous outlet. – *Higuchi*

As the poet gazed at the helmet of Sanemori, who had chosen to wear it for his last battle, he must have formed a vivid picture of the heroic way in which the aged warrior had died in that remote area of the north. To him, the voice of a cricket crying nearby seemed to be recounting the brave soldier's last battle. It reminded Bashō of the words of Higuchi Jirō, who cried out, "Oh, how piteous!" – *Ebara*

In all likelihood, the helmet at once reminded Bashō of Sanemori's head, with its hair dyed black. The pond where the head is said to have been washed is located close to Komatsu. This hokku, like the one at Takadachi, was a dirge composed at an old battlefield. – *Yamamoto*

There have been three different readings. (1) A cricket was actually chirping under the helmet. (2) The poet did not actually hear the cricket but imagined it was chirping when Sanemori was killed. (3) It does not matter whether the cricket was actually chirping at the time. Each reading has its merit, but I can most readily accept the first one. – *Iwata*

I visited a Kannon temple at Nata.

whiter than
the rocks of Ishiyama
autumnal wind

Ishiyama | no | ishi | yori | shiroshi | aki | no | kaze
Ishiyama | 's | stone | than | white | autumn | 's | wind

NOTE

Bashō visited Nata Temple in Komatsu on September 18. The temple was dedicated to the bodhisattva Kannon and situated on top of a hill, which was composed of quartz trachyte, a whitish rock. Ishiyama, literally meaning "stone-
mountain," may refer either to this hill or to Ishiyama in Ōmi Province, which
was renowned for its white rocks.

COMMENTARY

At Ishiyama Temple in Ōmi Province, the entire hill is formed of white rocks.
The poet suggested the fresh, clean feeling of the autumn wind by saying it was
whiter than those white rocks. – *Gosodō*

The poem presents the clean air of autumn. Needless to say, the poet wrote
"whiter than the rocks" here because traditionally spring is associated with
green, summer with red, autumn with white, and winter with black. – *Chikurei*

Some say that Ishiyama refers to a place in Ōmi Province, but it seems more natural to read it as meaning the rocky hill where the poet was at that time. He felt
the autumn wind was whiter and more desolate than the white rocks lying before
his eyes. – *Higuchi*

Bashō felt the autumn wind as being white at that time, all the more because in
the depth of his mind there still remained the pain of parting with Sora, which
plunged him into still greater depths of solitude. – *Yamamoto*

In view of the contemporary belief that the rocks at Nata Temple were whiter
than those at Ishiyama Temple in Ōmi, we cannot say the comparison between
the rocks at those two sites was not in Bashō's mind when he wrote the poem.
But the main point of the hokku lies in the poet's discovery that the autumn wind
was even whiter to his mind's eye than the rocks he saw with his real eyes.
– *Imoto*

Just as the landlord had predicted, it rained on the night of the full moon.

the harvest moon—
weather in the north
unpredictable indeed!

meigetsu | ya | hokkoku | biyori | sadame | naki
harvest-moon | : | northland | weather | certainty | nonexistent

NOTE

Written in Tsuruga on September 28, which was the day of the full moon. According to *Oku no hosomichi*, the sky was very clear the night before, but the landlord warned Bashō, "In this northern province, tomorrow night's weather can't be predicted."

COMMENTARY

Only a few minutes ago it was a clear, beautiful night, but now it has begun to cloud over. On the other hand, those clouds look as if they would go away in no time. The poem describes especially well the unpredictable way in which the weather changes on the coastal area in the north. *– Higuchi*

The hokku begins with high hopes ("the harvest moon"), which are then (after the cutting word *ya*) completely crushed. That flow of words is directly expressive of the poet's feelings. Also, one can recognize humor in the poet's being unable to complain about the situation (because the northern climate is in truth unstable) and turning the complaint into a poem. *– Seisensui*

While deploring the bad weather that robbed him of moon viewing, the poet showed his haikai humor by stealing the landlord's words and utilizing them in the poem. Also, the hokku has summed up in the fewest words possible the characteristic climate of the region facing the Sea of Japan. *– Kon*

The same night the landlord told us a story. "A temple bell is lying deep under this sea," he said. "Once the governor of the province had divers search for it. They found it, but because it lay in an upside-down position, there was no way to pull it up."

where is the moon?
the temple bell is sunk
at the bottom of the sea

tsuki | izuku | kane | wa | shizumeru | umi | no | soko
moon | where | bell | as-for | is-sunken | sea | 's | bottom

NOTE
Written in Tsuruga on the same day as the previous hokku.

COMMENTARY
Amid the misty rain and the surging waves the poet thought he heard the sound of a bell coming from under the sea. He must have felt as if he were at the bottom of the sea himself. — *Sanga*

The hokku is descriptive of the dark seascape, with the moon behind the clouds. — *Tosai*

The legend of a sunken bell exists not only in Japan but in many other countries as well. It is not clear whether the legend had been handed down in Tsuruga because a temple bell was actually lying under the sea there, but in Japan it had been believed that because dragons love a temple bell they overturn a boat carrying one aboard. In this hokku, the opening phrase is very effective and harmonizes perfectly with the image of a bell hidden deep under the sea. — *Higuchi*

There is no way to hear the bell since it is under the sea, but where is the moon hiding its serene rays? The poem, drawing on the legend of a bell, expresses how much the poet missed the harvest moon. — *Ebara*

In his mind Bashō saw the light of the full moon and heard the faint sound of the bell. Although there was no moon in actuality, its absence led him to fly on wings of fancy to a mysterious but concrete world in his imagination. The dark mood that resents the bad weather corresponds to the darkness at the bottom of the sea where the bell lies. The poem fascinates us with its consummate craftsmanship. — *Shūson*

between the waves
mingling small seashells
bush-clover debris

nami I no I ma I ya I kogai I ni I majiru I hagi I no I chiri
wave I 's I interval I : I small-seashell I in I mix I bush-clover I 's I debris

NOTE
Written on September 29 at Ironohama, a beach near Tsuruga. The beach was
famous for a special kind of clam with a tiny, pink-colored shell.

COMMENTARY
The surf was pounding the shore. During the short interval between two breaking waves, the poet saw scattered on the beach tiny seashells and, mingled with
them, fallen petals of bush clover that looked like debris. The lovely scene is before our eyes. – *Meisetsu*

It would have been beautiful indeed if bush-clover petals had actually fallen
there, but the poet is here probably describing tiny fragments of seashells through
the metaphor of bush clover. – *Higuchi*

Bush clover could be considered a metaphor if the hokku's closing phrase were
"bush-clover petals." Yet the poet wrote "bush-clover debris" here. There is no
way he could have used the word "debris" to describe colorful seashells washed
in the waves and shining bright. Because he actually saw those fallen, withered
petals amidst the glossy seashells, he got the sense of "debris." – *Ebara*

The poet had probably seen fallen bush-clover petals in the yard of a Buddhist
temple, where he had stopped to rest earlier in the day. Accordingly, there is no
way in which seashells scattered on the beach could have mingled with flower
petals in the temple yard; it was Bashō's art of poetic fiction that brought the two
together. – *Yamamoto*

not grown to a butterfly
this late in autumn
a caterpillar

kochō I ni I mo I narade I aki I furu I namushi I kana
butterfly I to I even I without-turning I autumn I deepen I vegetable-worm I
   kana

NOTE
Written shortly after arrival in Ōgaki on or around October 4.

COMMENTARY
It may seem that the poet is reflecting on his life and deploring the fact that he
has put on years in vain. Implicit in his reflection, however, is the nobility of
mind that has brought him peace in his nonutilitarian pursuit. The poem faintly
echoes the story of Chuang-tzu's butterfly. — *Tosai*

The poet saw a caterpillar on a late autumn day and pitied it for not having become a butterfly. Permeating the hokku, however, are his thoughts on the attachment to poetry that has made him refuse to live like an ordinary man and forced
him to struggle in poverty and loneliness throughout his life. — *Shūson*

There is an undercurrent of self-debasement in this poem. — *Kon*

A man named Sogyū, who lives in Seki, came to visit me at my lodging in Ōgaki. White wisteria flowers were blooming there just as beautifully as in those days when Sōgi wrote about them.

wisteria beans
will be my haikai,
flowers being gone

fuji I no I mi I wa I haikai I ni I sen I hana I no I ato
wisteria I 's I seed I as-for I haikai I to I make I flower I 's I subsequence

NOTE
The renga poet Sōgi once passed through Ōsaka Barrier and saw white wisteria flowers blooming on the slope nearby. Thereupon he remembered White Wisteria Slope, a famous place in Kii Province, and wrote the verse:

I cross the barrier—   seki koete
here is another White   koko mo fujishiro
Wisteria Slope!   misaka kana

The Japanese word for "barrier" is *seki*; hence Bashō's allusion to Sōgi's renga. Sogyū was the haikai name of Hirose Gennojō (?–1711), who later came to be known by the name Izen.

COMMENTARY
Indeed, the wisteria's beautiful flowers provide proper material for renga, but its strange-shaped beans for haikai. The hokku's last phrase is a complimentary reference to Sōgi. – *Nobutane*

Wisteria flowers have the kind of beauty fitting for renga. Their beans, while not very beautiful, show something of *wabi* and in that respect have a quality common to haikai. Through this poem Bashō taught Sogyū what the essence of haikai is. It is not about the beans. – *Shinpū*

Wisteria beans have neither practical use nor poetic elegance, yet they dangle down in a way that suggests detachment from worldly things, and are therefore a fitting subject for haikai. The poem is intended to teach the true purpose of haikai to Sogyū, who had become Bashō's student only a short time earlier. – *Yamamoto*

At Bokuin's house

a hermitage—
the moon, chrysanthemums,
one acre of rice field

kakurega | ya | tsuki | to | kiku | to | ni | ta | san-tan
hideout | : | moon | and | chrysanthemum | and | to | rice-field | three-tan

NOTE

Bashō wrote the hokku when he was invited to Bokuin's villa in Ōgaki. One *tan*
is about a quarter of an acre.

COMMENTARY

The Zen monk Ikkyū [1394–1461] wrote the waka:

If I retire,	sankyo seba
one acre of fertile land	jōden san-tan
with forty gallons	miso hatto
of miso, a servant, and	komono hitori ni
a supply of good water.	mizu no yoki tokoro
	– *Ryōta*

By saying that the hermitage was well located for viewing the moon and chrysanthemums and had a rice field in addition, Bashō complimented Bokuin for his
love of *fūryū* as well as for his comfortable life. – *Ebara*

The chrysanthemum, which is the season word here, implies the life of a hermit
(compare Chou Mao-shu's line, "The chrysanthemum is a hermit's flower").*
Three tan of land is small for a farm and helps to suggest a simple life of retirement. – *Kon*

* Chou Mao-shu (1017–73) was an influential philosopher of the early Sung dynasty, who
tried to synthesize various concepts he took from Confucianism, Taoism, and the science of
divination. Among his disciples was Ch'eng Ming-tao, mentioned earlier.

At a place called Nakamura in Ise Province

autumn wind—
a graveyard in Ise
even more lonely

aki | no | kaze | Ise | no | hakahara | nao | sugoshi
autumn | 's | wind | Ise | 's | graveyard | more | lonely

COMMENTARY

The poet happened to pass by a graveyard when the autumn wind was blowing.
Wind and the graveyard both create an impression of loneliness and desolation.
But he was even more deeply affected when he reminded himself that he was in
Ise, a province under the powerful influence of Shintoism, which has strong ta-
boos against pollution by human corpses. Bashō probably used the word
"lonely" here in the same sense that Saigyō often used it in his waka.* – *Iwata*

*One of the most notable uses of the word "lonely" by Saigyō occurs in the waka already
cited on p. 57.

first winter shower—
the monkey also seems to want
a small raincoat

hatsushigure | saru | mo | komino | wo | hoshigenari
first-winter-shower | monkey | also | small-straw-raincoat | [acc.] |
   look-wanting

NOTE

Written in early November, when Bashō was on his way from Ise Province to his
hometown of Ueno. The hokku was later placed at the beginning of *Sarumino*.

COMMENTARY

The reader can easily visualize a scene in which, all the leaves having fallen, a
monkey on a tree has nowhere to hide. The juxtaposition of a monkey and a
raincoat is elegant. Who else could have used such images? – *Donto*

The traveling poet, feeling unbearably lonely, felt pity toward a monkey that
crouched there and was shrieking in the winter shower. People say monkeys don't
like rain. – *Sanga*

This is a good poem, but does not seem especially profound—rather tame, in
fact. This is the kind of poem that, while not everyone can write it himself, every
reader can appreciate. – *Abe J.*

In Bashō's mind at that moment, there was no distinction between a monkey and
a human being. There was only a feeling of kinship shared by two living things.
   – *Kōseki*

Renga poets living in the war years often used the image of winter rain to suggest
a sense of life's transience and mutability, which they derived from Buddhist concepts. But this poem of Bashō's is not one of renga convention's seasonal homi-
lies. It goes beyond the usual stereotyped implications of winter showers and
touches on the very roots of human existence. There is "a direct sensuous apprehension of thought" (in T. S. Eliot's words) that refuses to let itself be confined by
such clichés as joy at the first winter shower or pity toward the monkey.
   – *Yamamoto*

The first winter shower was a theme that had been worked over continuously in
traditional Japanese literature, resulting in many waka and renga verses. Bashō,
on encountering a winter shower toward the end of a long journey, made it into

a fascinating poetic experience. He was not distressed at being rained on. However, he knew he would not be creating anything new in haikai if he were to follow the traditional concept of the first winter shower and sing of it as something sad and lonely. He rather chose to surprise the reader by saying that a monkey, too, seems to be enjoying the shower and looks as though it wants to wear a small raincoat and frolic in the shower. That was the reason why this poem became famous among contemporary readers. — *Imoto*

the winter garden—
thinning to a thread, the moon
and an insect's singing

fuyuniwa I ya I tsuki I mo I ito I naru I mushi I no I gin
winter-garden I : I moon I also I thread I being I insect I 's I recitation

NOTE
Written in Ueno to start an eighteen-verse sequence of haikai.

COMMENTARY
An indescribably quiet, lonely feeling. – *Tosai*

As the poet listened intently, the cry of an insect that was barely surviving the winter nights sounded as thin as a thread. As if that singing crystallized into a visual image, a thin moon hung in the sky. – *Shūson*

For a kasen written at Ryōbon's house on the first day of the eleventh month in the second year of Genroku

come, children,
let's go out and run
in the hail!

iza | kodomo | hashiri | arikan | tamaarare
now | child | running | will-walk | hail

NOTE

Written on December 12, which is the date mentioned in the headnote. Ryōbon was the haikai name of Tomoda Kakuzaemon (1666–1730), a samurai serving at Iga Castle.

COMMENTARY

This is a plain poem that records exactly what the poet said. It shows how effortlessly Bashō wrote poetry. – Ōsha

It had begun to hail. As the poet watched hailstones rolling on the ground, he felt an urge to run like a child. It is one of those impulses we occasionally experience ourselves. It was also natural for the poet to call out to children for company. – Abe J.

It would be more natural to assume, from the hokku's opening phrase, that there were children close by. I think, however, that it also makes sense even if children were not there. The middle phrase is very suggestive of the poet's *fūkyō* spirit. – Handa

Bashō seems to have had a moody, rather gloomy personality, and yet he could also be more impulsive than a child and would sometimes make merry like one as on this occasion. And he made merry here, not because he was charmed by the beauty of hail, but because his heart overflowed with the true spirit of lyric poetry. – Utsubo

Surrounded by young students of poetry in his native town, Bashō felt as if he had returned to his own childhood, and that happy mood enabled him to take delight in the hail that had begun to fall. Participating with him in the haikai composition that day were Chishū (Ryōbon's wife and 18 or 19 years of age), Dohō (32 or 33), Hanzan (35 or 36), and San'en (age unknown), in addition to the host Ryōbon (22 or 23). Bashō playfully addressed those young poets as "children." – Kon

1690

The two-month sojourn in his native town apparently allowed Bashō
sufficient time to recover from the fatigue of the rugged journey to the
far north. Accompanied by Rotsū, he took to the road again in early January. First he visited Nara to see the famous festival of Kasuga Shrine on
January 7. It is not clear where he went from there, but on February 3 he
is known to have been at Kyorai's house in Kyoto. Several days later he
moved to Zeze, a town near Ōtsu, where a group of students were waiting for him. It was there that he welcomed in the lunar New Year's Day,
which was February 9.

Leaving Rotsū in Zeze, Bashō traveled back to Ueno on February 11
and stayed there for a large part of the next three months. Again he was
warmly treated by the people of his native town, including Lord Tangan
who invited him to his castle almost as soon as he arrived there. Bashō
took part in at least eight haikai gatherings during his stay in Ueno.
Among them, the one held on April 10 is especially significant because it
was here that he first made mention of what was later to become his new
poetic principle, *karumi*.

Bashō went back to Zeze in late April or early May. His students in
that lakeside town were better prepared for his visit this time, for they
had repaired a small mountain cottage, named the Genjū ("unreal dwell-
ing") Hut, for his use. Located halfway up a hill, the secluded cottage
commanded a panoramic view of the entire area, overlooking Lake Biwa
with the Seta River in the distance. Bashō moved into the cottage on
May 14 and was so delighted with the place that he lived there for the
next four months. The leisurely life he enjoyed at the cottage is described
in his famous haibun, "Genjūan no ki" (The record of my life at the
Genjū Hut), which he drafted toward the end of his stay there. He did,
however, go down the hill for short visits from time to time. On one
such occasion he visited Kyorai in Kyoto for some ten days in July, during which time they discussed compiling a haikai anthology to be entitled *Sarumino*.

Bashō finally left the Genjū Hut on August 23. He spent much of the
following two months at another cottage his students rented for him.
This one stood in the precincts of a Buddhist temple named Gichū, which
was located on the lakeshore between Zeze and Ōtsu. Unfortunately his

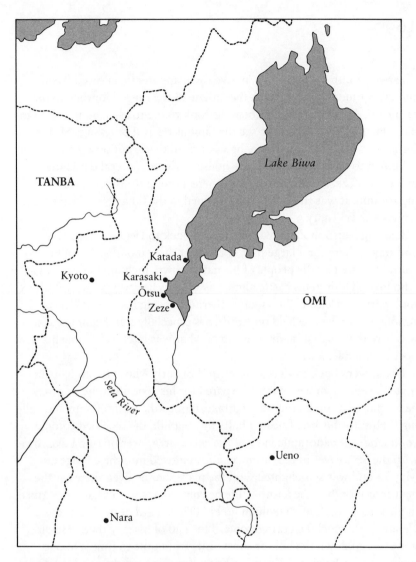

Bashō moved into the Genjū Hut in Zeze on
May 14, 1690, where he lived for the next four
months; during this time he often visited
friends in nearby towns.

life there was hampered by ill health, but that was not enough to dampen his spirit or curtail his poetic activities. He hosted a moon-viewing party on September 17, though he had to entertain the guests from his bed. When he felt strong enough, he took short trips to such places as Kyoto and Katada, a scenic town on the western shore of Lake Biwa. Finally, at the end of October, he left Gichū Temple and went back to his native Ueno, where he spent the rest of the year.

what makes this bird
hurry to the year-end fair?
a crow

nani I ni I kono I shiwasu I no I ichi I ni I yuku I karasu
what I for I this I year's-last-month I 's I market I to I go I crow

COMMENTARY

Master Bashō said, "This hokku derives its life from the force of the opening phrase." — *Dohō*

This poem carries a message of self-deprecation. — *Bakusui*

A crow, too, is hurrying to the bustling town. What on earth brings it there? This is a lighthearted, playful poem. — *Bōtō*

Why is that lone crow flying into the midst of people who are frantically struggling to get ready for the New Year? Although the poet may be caricaturing himself here, he took the theme of this poem from the kind of emotion he experienced when he looked up and saw a crow hurrying to town. — *Momota*

When he watched crows noisily flying toward town in the snowy winter sky, Bashō the eternal wanderer must have felt the kind of anguish that almost made him groan aloud. That sorrowful poet Nietzsche who, like Bashō, lacked a spiritual home, also sang:

The cawing crows
    Townwards on whirring pinions roam;
Soon come the snows—
    Thrice happy now who hath a home!*

Ultimately all poets, Eastern or Western, sing of the same anguish, and all lyrics deal with the same theme. — *Hagiwara*

Looking up to the sky, the poet saw a crow flying hurriedly toward town and wondered why it was leaving such a quiet place for the noisy town at the year's end. The poem epitomizes Bashō's own longing to be left alone in some quiet, unspoiled place. — *Ebara*

---

*The English translation is by Herman Scheffaur in Oscar Levy, ed., *The Complete Works of Friedrich Nietzsche* (London: J. N. Foulis, 1909–13), vol. 17, p. 163.

Bashō was not opposed by temperament to lively places. This poem, too, indicates his heart was attracted to the bustle of Zeze, where he had never welcomed the New Year but was about to do so. The tone of accusation at the poem's beginning is directed less at the crow than at himself. There is even a hint of envy toward the crow which has no hesitation in going to the year-end fair "as the crow flies." Bashō was aware of something within himself urging him to fly to town like that greedy crow, whereupon he asked his own heart, "Why? For what good reason?" – *Yamamoto*

Welcoming the New Year near the capital

man who wears a straw mat—
what sage could he possibly be?
blossoming spring

komo I wo I kite I tarebito I imasu I hana I no I haru
straw-mat I [acc.] I wearing I what-person I is I blossom I 's I spring

NOTE

Written for the lunar New Year's Day, which was February 9. *Imasu* is an honor-
ific verb implying that its subject is a person to be revered.

COMMENTARY

Five hundred years ago Saigyō, in *Senjūshō*, cited many examples of sages living
beggarly lives. With my uninitiated eyes, I am not able to distinguish a sage from
a beggar. Sadly remembering Saigyō, I wrote this hokku. I hear, however, people
in Kyoto are saying what an abominable poet I am to refer to a beggar in a verse
celebrating the New Year. How silly of them! – *Bashō*

The poet imagined a man of noble birth living a hermit's life on the roadside,
with a straw mat for clothes. He contrasted that with the showy image of "blossoming spring." – *Keion*

In my opinion, Bashō actually saw beggars and thought that among them was
likely to be the kind of virtuous man cited in *Senjūshō*. – *Mizuho*

The hokku's concluding phrase seems to allude at once to the New Year's season
and to Kyoto, the nation's capital. "Blossoming spring" and "a straw mat" make
a contrast, yet they share a common quality in that both create a Kyoto-like
mood. – *Abe J.*

I do not think Bashō wrote the poem actually with a beggar in sight. He surmised that there would be some men with outstanding qualities living humble
lives among beggars, while he and his students indulged in blossom viewing and
drinking. When he thought of that, his current frivolous life began to seem despicable. – *Higuchi*

Because a beggar owns nothing, he has no fear of losing anything or of falling any farther down the social ladder. He is blessed with the same ease of mind as a plant that is rooted in the ground. Bashō himself had that ease of mind.
– *Seisensui*

In the New Year season, when all was color and gaiety, Bashō fixed his eyes on a person wearing a straw mat and crouched in a shady place. He felt no contempt for that person; rather, he wondered whether the beggar might not be a sage. The hokku, which discloses the poet's complete lack of pretension, appeals to us warmly. – *Iwata*

Hana is a season word that can mean either cherry blossoms specifically or spring flowers in general. Here, in the New Year season, it was too early for cherry blossoms, yet the word still evokes their colorful image in the reader's mind. Then there appears the image of a tattered beggar, which adds a touch of *sabi*. In a beggar under the blossoms, Bashō momentarily saw concealed nobility or past glory. – *Yamamoto*

Even when he was in his thirties, Bashō had called himself "an old beggar." He believed there were some wise men among those who had been forced out of society and were living beggarly lives. – *Imoto*

Blossom viewing

under the tree
soup, fish salad, and all—
cherry blossoms

ki | no | moto | ni | shiru | mo | namasu | mo | sakura | kana
tree | 's | base | at | soup | also | fish-salad | also | cherry | kana

NOTE
Written to start a kasen at a blossom-viewing party in Ueno on April 10.

COMMENTARY
When he wrote this hokku, Master Bashō said: "Having learned something about writing a verse on blossom viewing, I gave a tone of *karumi* to this hokku." – *Dohō*

During a blossom-viewing party under a cherry tree, petals from the fading blossoms sprinkled the soup, fish salad, and other refreshments, covering them all in white. Using the poetic exaggeration characteristic of a short verse form, Bashō said soup and fish salad turned into cherry blossoms. When the exaggeration is this extreme, it is delightful. – *Handa*

A popular diversion like blossom viewing, which one shares with a big crowd, is difficult to make into a good tanka or haiku. In view of that, we have to say this is an exceptionally fine poem, a poem rich in the mood of blossom viewing. – *Utsubo*

The middle phrase of this poem suggests a realm of haikai that is alien to waka. Where such mundane words as "soup" and "fish salad" are used to describe the beautiful poetic mood of spring, we encounter a concrete manifestation of Bashō's tendency to seek poetry in things familiar. – *Iwata*

butterfly's wings—
how many times do they flit
over the roofed wall?

chō | no | ha | no | ikutabi | koyuru | hei | no | yane
butterfly | 's | wing | 's | how-many-times | cross-over | fence | 's | roof

COMMENTARY

Seated in a room, Bashō was looking across a large, beautiful garden in the direction of its roofed wall. A flitting butterfly crossed and recrossed the wall, enhancing the quietness. – *Komiya*

This hokku has two features: it implies passage of a long period of time, and it focuses on the butterfly's wings. If it had said merely that a butterfly crossed over a wall, it would have been a trite poem. But, because it directs our attention specifically to the wings, we can clearly visualize the way in which the butterfly, with its large (in proportion to its body) and delicate wings, flitted over the roofed wall. This is a fine poem that has captured the atmosphere of a lazy day in spring. – *Handa*

The poem well describes the quietness of an affluent residential district on a spring day. Its middle phrase suggests that the poet has been watching for a long time, while its concluding phrase makes us think of a large samurai house, its premises enclosed by roofed walls. – *Iwata*

I lamented the end of spring on the lakeside.

spring goes away—
with the people of Ōmi
I share the sorrow

yuku | haru | wo | Ōmi | no | hito | to | oshimikeru
go | spring | [acc.] | Ōmi | 's | person | with | have-lamented

NOTE

A note introducing an earlier draft of this hokku specifies "the lakeside" as the
town of Karasaki on the western shore of Lake Biwa. After writing the hokku,
Bashō apparently had it discussed among his students, including Kyorai and Esa
Shōhaku (1650–1722).

COMMENTARY

Master Bashō asked me, "Shōhaku criticized this hokku and said that 'Ōmi'
could be replaced by 'Tanba,'* and 'spring' by 'year.' What do you think?" I answered, "Shōhaku's criticism misses the point. The image of Ōmi Province, with
mist spreading over the large lake, helps to enhance sorrow over spring's departure. Besides, the hokku expresses how the poet actually felt at that time." The
Master replied, "You're right. People in the old days felt just as much regret at
spring's departure in this province as they did in Kyoto." I said, "I'm deeply
moved by what you have said. If you were in Ōmi at the end of the year, how
could you feel as truly sad as you did? If you were in the mountainous province
of Tanba when spring ended, you wouldn't have felt that way either. How true an
emotion is when it arises from the heart of someone moved by an actual scene
from nature!" The Master was very pleased and said, "Kyorai, you are someone I
can talk poetry with." – *Kyorai*

The previous year the poet had mourned the end of springtime with the people of
Musashi Province. This year he was in Ōmi Province and did the same with the
people of Ōmi. – *Shōgatsudō*

We should read the poem as though it were prefaced by Bashō's words, "People
in the old days felt just as much regret at spring's departure in this province as

*Tanba was a province covering the northern parts of the modern prefectures of Kyoto and
Hyōgo.

先師曰尚白が難に近江は丹波にも近江の雑に

湖水朦朧として春を

一とし江いてへ聞侍るや去来曰尚白が雑

うへ侍るとや先師曰志や古人も此国の春を愛す

もとし古人も此国ま春を愛す

近江は居たまに江ぞ此歳のまへをんり春丹波に

ぬはさん也よりは情うふま風光の人と感動せ

す春なくふとや先師曰汝や去来とも素風雅をなくへ

春ぎまみなりとよろこひ給へり

りち春成ふと狂人をを上げる　　芭蕉

上

二

A page from Kyorai shō (Kyorai's essays) that records the conversation between Bashō and his disciple Mukai Kyorai (1651–1704) on the hokku:

spring goes away—
with the people of Ōmi
I share the sorrow

Reproduced from Nakamura Shunjō and Yamashita Tokiko, Kyorai shō (Kasama Shoin), by courtesy of the publisher.

they did in Kyoto." The poem implies that, like the poets of old days, who looked over the misty lake and lamented spring's departure, Bashō too shared this sorrow with the people of Ōmi. – *Kōseki*

Those who like the condensed language of haiku seem to have reservations about this poem, saying that its tempo is too slow and too much like that of waka. I see nothing unnatural in it, since it is a poem expressing a lament over the end of spring. – *Shūson*

Bashō had kept in poetic storage many old waka that sang of spring at Lake Biwa, and there was always a path of poetic communication open between him and them. Spatially Bashō belonged to the same community as the haikai poets of Ōmi, and temporally he belonged to the same community as past waka poets. He wrote poems always from this kind of perspective, and that is why they always transcend his individuality and link themselves to something larger and deeper. – *Yamamoto*

Bashō made the comment to Kyorai probably because he felt that there was no sense in mourning spring's end in Tanba, where people were like monkeys and did not understand *furyū*. They would not lament spring's passing, anyway. Bashō must have felt he could share such disappointment only with those who read literature and understood *furyū*. – *Imoto*

*On entering the Genjū Hut in the mountains
behind Ishiyama*

my temporary shelter—
a pasania tree is here, too,
in the summer grove

mazu I tanomu I shii I no I ki I mo I ari I natsu I kodachi
first I rely I pasania I 's I tree I also I exist I summer I grove

NOTE

Bashō moved into the Genjū Hut on May 14. This hokku appears at the end of
"Genjūan no ki." *Shii* is *pasania cuspidata*, a tall evergreen tree that belongs to
the beech family.

COMMENTARY

Old waka often mention someone picking pasania nuts for livelihood or relying
on a pasania tree for shelter. Such examples are too numerous to cite. – *Tosai*

Of many trees growing in summer, a pasania is most dependable because it produces nuts in autumn and holds on to its leaves in winter. But perhaps we need
not keep that in mind. Perhaps the poet just felt it was pleasant to see a pasania
among the many trees that were there. The image of a pasania tree and its nuts
has a rustic flavor of haikai and harmonizes well with the locale, the Genjū Hut.
– *Chikurei*

This hokku embodies the loneliness of Bashō who, like a bird, sought shelter in
the shade of a pasania tree. No person living in the mundane world would look
for protection in a tree's shade. Because Bashō had forsaken the world, that was
where he sought shelter. The charm of the poem lies in the comparison of himself
to a bird. It is a simple, plain poem which, however, hides many intricate threads
of emotion beneath its rough surface texture. – *Rohan*

Bashō, on moving into the hut as the dog days started, thought how unbearable
it would be if the residence were in the open and exposed to all that hot sun. Fortunately there was a big pasania tree shading the hut almost completely. The
hokku expresses the poet's delight when he learned he could above all rely on
that big tree providing shade for his hut. – *Shida*

The hokku conveys the relief felt by the poet who, after a long period of wandering in the far north, finally found a small hut to settle in. Phrases such as "shade for shelter" or "tree shade for shelter" had already come to carry a symbolic meaning at this time, after having been used repeatedly in old waka. The shade beneath the pasania tree was not only a shelter from heat and rain but also a personal refuge during a life that passed like a dream. The pasania tree represented, among all things that change, one thing that did not change—and therefore could be relied on as shelter—for the time being. – *Yamamoto*

A pasania tree looks stout and dependable; with its dense foliage, it makes a good shade in summer. As Saigyō said in his waka

A titmouse, always	narabi ite
perched with its friends, has	tomo wo hanarenu
a dependable roost	kogarame no
in the lower branches	negura ni tanomu
of a pasania tree.	shii no shitaeda

it is also a tree where birds roost. Bashō may have had this waka in mind. The hokku artlessly expresses the sentiment of the poet who arrived at a temporary place of rest in the midst of a wandering life. – *Imoto*

toward the sun's path
hollyhock flowers turning
in the seasonal rain

hi | no | michi | ya | aui | katamuku | satsuki-ame
sun | 's | road | : | hollyhock | lean | fifth-month-rain

COMMENTARY

The hokku is about the subtle force of nature that makes a plant lean toward the
sun's path even when the sky is covered with thick rain clouds. – *Tosai*

What motivated the poet to write this poem was the sight of hollyhocks, but its
theme has more to do with "the sun's path." Here is a subjective image that represents the poet's desires as one confined to his hut for many days because of
rain. – *Yamamoto*

even in Kyoto
I long for Kyoto—
a hototogisu

Kyō | nite | mo | Kyō | natsukashi | ya | hototogisu
Kyoto | in | even | Kyoto | long-for | ! | hototogisu

COMMENTARY

Somehow we tend to feel nostalgic in early summer, when hototogisu cry. At times we get homesick, too, while in our own home. – *Keion*

The first Kyoto in the poem is the real city; the second is the city that lives yet in ancient poetry and fiction. – *Shūson*

As in the monk Sosei's waka:*

A hototogisu	iso no kami
in the ancient capital—	furuki miyako no
its crying voice,	hototogisu
the only thing that remains	koe bakari koso
unchanged from the years past.	mukashi narikere

a hototogisu's cry makes one think of the past in the old capital. With the cry, to-day's Kyoto is instantly transformed into the Kyoto of the past. – *Yamamoto*

*Sosei was a poet and Buddhist monk who lived in the late ninth century. The waka cited appears as the poem no. 131 in *Shinsen waka* (Newly selected poems, 929?).

A hermit named Tōko came from the Naniwa
area to see an untalented teacher like me.

don't resemble me—
cut in half
a musk melon

ware | ni | niru | na | futatsu | ni | wareshi | makuwauri
I | to | resemble | not | two | in | is-split | musk-melon

NOTE

Bashō gave this hokku to Emoto Tōko (also known as Shidō, 1659–1712), a young merchant in Naniwa who wanted to become his student in haikai. "A melon cut in half" is an idiomatic phrase in Japanese describing two persons who look almost identical.

COMMENTARY

Although you and I have a similar disposition, don't try to model your life after mine because you are living the life of a normal man. This, in my opinion, was the lesson Bashō meant to convey in this poem. – *Tosai*

Probably Tōko was such an ardent admirer of Bashō that he had done nothing but imitate his poetry. Accordingly, alluding to a melon that happened to be there, Bashō advised that Tōko should not be like one half of a melon, that he should become aware of his own individuality. Or it may be that Bashō was warning Tōko against becoming a wanderer like him. – *Kōseki*

Death strikes quickly.

soon they will die—
yet, showing no sign of it,
cicadas screech

yagate | shinu | keshiki | wa | miezu | semi | no | koe
soon | die | appearance | as-for | not-show | cicada | 's | voice

COMMENTARY

This seems to be based on a passage in *Tsurezuregusa* that says: "Of things that have life, none lives longer than man. A mayfly dies before the day is over, and a summer cicada knows no spring or autumn." – *Donto*

Although men laugh at a cicada for not knowing of its impending death, they are unaware that their own death is drawing near. Bashō imagined that if Buddha noticed this he would think men were no wiser than cicadas. – *Kūzen*

Because of its theme, this poem appeals mainly to the intellect. Inevitably, its beauty as poetry has been reduced almost to nothing. – *Meisetsu*

I don't think Bashō wrote this poem from such a didactic motive as critics attribute to him. Listening to the loud cry of cicadas, he became interested in the fact that they were chirping to their heart's content, quite heedless of their imminent death in early autumn. – *Kobayashi*

Undeniably this is a philosophical poem on the mutability of life, but I think it also contains the poet's irritation at the noisy screech of the cicadas, tempting him to cry out to them, "You're going to die soon!" – *Imoto*

a dragonfly
vainly trying to settle
onto a blade of grass

tonbō | ya | toritsuki | kaneshi | kusa | no | ue
dragonfly | : | holding | is-unable | grass | 's | upside

COMMENTARY

In general a short verse form, as it evolves with time, tends to focus more and more on things minute and delicate. This hokku shows the beginning of that tendency. – *Handa*

This looks like a simple descriptive poem, and yet it makes us wonder whether Bashō's eyes were not observing something important in the very heart of nature. – *Momota*

Unchiku, a monk living in Kyoto, had painted what appeared to be a self-portrait. It was a picture of a monk with his face turned away. Unchiku showed me the portrait and asked me for a verse to go with it. Thereupon I wrote as follows—

You are over sixty years of age, and I am nearing fifty. We are both in a world of dreams, and this portrait depicts a man in a dream, too. Here I add the words of another such man talking in his sleep:

will you turn toward me?
I am lonely too,
this autumn nightfall

kochira | muke | ware | mo | sabishiki | aki | no | kure
this-way | turn | I | also | lonely | autumn | 's | evening

COMMENTARY

This is an interesting hokku as a companion to the portrait. It is equally interesting, though, to read it as a poem expressing the sentiments of Bashō himself, who somehow felt lonely one autumn evening at the Genjū Hut and wanted company. Of course, I would not want to ignore the fact that the hokku was written to accompany the portrait, but I think the poem clearly reveals the ambivalence of Bashō, who loved loneliness and yet could not completely suppress the more human side of himself. The latter reading, I believe, adds more depth to the poem. – *Abe Y.*

To the portrait of a monk looking the other way, Bashō called out, "Turn around!" There is tasteful humor in that. But the poem has a deeper meaning, because Bashō's words sound as if he were calling out to humanity in general. – *Watsuji*

Moon viewing at an old temple

in this group of people
admiring the full moon
not one beautiful face

tsukimi | suru | za | ni | utsukushiki | kao | mo | nashi
moon-viewing | do | gathering | at | beautiful | face | even | nonexistent

NOTE

Written on the night of the autumn full moon, which was September 17. Bashō
held a moon-viewing party in his hut at Gichū Temple.

COMMENTARY

Even the most beautiful woman cannot rival the beauty of the moon. Here the
moon is compared to a lady. – *Donto*

An old temple has an atmosphere of *sabi*. There, people who are not beautiful
are viewing the moon. This is a scene well suited to haikai. – *Chikurei*

The people at the party were all monks or poets, and they had serene looks on
their faces suggestive of their peaceful life away from the earthly mire. – *Mizuho*

The hokku presents the beauty of the moon without describing it. – *Rohan*

It is far-fetched to assume that the hokku suggests the beauty of the moon by
contrasting it with the ugly faces of people who were there. I think the poem is
based on the spontaneous impression of the poet, who looked around and found
no pretty face at the party. Bashō discovered poetic beauty everywhere. – *Shūson*

In addition to admiration for the beautiful moonlight, the poem's language contains hidden touches of loneliness and humor. – *Iwata*

In Katada

a wild duck, ill
on a cold night, falls from the sky
and sleeps a while

byōgan | no | yosamu | ni | ochite | tabine | kana
ill-wild-duck | 's | night-cold | with | falling | travel-sleep | kana

NOTE

Katada, located on the northwestern shore of Lake Biwa, was famous as a scenic place where wild ducks often flew down from the sky. At the invitation of some haikai poets in that area, such as Kōno Riyū (1662–1705), Bashō visited there from October 14 to 26, during which time he caught a severe cold. This hokku is included in *Sarumino*, compiled by Kyorai and Nozawa Bonchō (?–1714).

COMMENTARY

When we were compiling *Sarumino*, Master Bashō asked us to select either this verse or

the fisherman's hut—   ama no ya wa
mingled with little shrimps   koebi ni majiru
a cricket   itodo kana

for the anthology. Bonchō observed, "The hokku on the ailing duck is a good poem, but the one about shrimps is truly superb in terms of the use of words as well as freshness of material." He wanted to select the latter. I argued, "Although the hokku on shrimps does draw on novel material, I could have written it if I had come upon the scene. The one on the duck is a poem of high order, with profound implications. It is the kind of verse far beyond my capabilities." In the end we pleaded with the Master and included both verses in the anthology. Afterwards the Master said, laughing, "Did you discuss the duck poem on the same level as you discussed verses like the one about shrimps?" – *Kyorai*

The hokku alludes to the wild ducks for which Katada is famous, and yet it reflects the poet's life as well. – *Kūzen*

It does not matter whether a sick duck actually fell from the sky. Bashō heard a wild duck's cry and imagined that it was ill and resting somewhere on the lake in the cold of the night. He speculated how lonely it must be feeling, and he gave lyrical expression to that sentiment in his poem. — *Watsuji*

Because of the night cold, an ailing duck could not keep flying; it fell to the lake and spent the night there. In my opinion, Bashō stayed overnight with Riyū at Honpuku Temple in Katada (famous for wild ducks) where, attacked by some kind of illness, he composed the poem in pain. — *Higuchi*

Lying on his sickbed, Bashō heard a wild duck's cry. Or, perhaps, he did not. Perhaps in his fever he may have merely imagined a duck dropping out of formation and flying down to Katada. The image of that duck became linked to the loneliness of Bashō, who was ill on the road. Reflecting on his own life, he fancied that the lone duck must be ill. Like the ailing duck, he was suffering the night cold in Katada. It is more proper to say that he symbolized himself through the duck than to say that he likened himself to the duck. — *Yamamoto*

Here is beautiful symbolism. Tu Fu in his last years wrote many poems expressing deep grief and solitude. In this hokku I see the shadow of that great Chinese poet who, like Bashō, roamed the country despite his frail health. — *Konishi*

At Shōzui Temple in Katada

a monk sips
his morning tea, and it is quiet—
chrysanthemum flowers

asa | cha | nomu | sō | shizukanari | kiku | no | hana
morning | tea | drink | monk | is-quiet | chrysanthemum | 's | flower

COMMENTARY

Tea is said to clear the mind. It is often used in Zen. A monk is making tea at a quiet Zen temple, where there is a chrysanthemum blooming inconspicuously. The scene is infinitely beautiful. – *Sanga*

The hokku's middle phrase sounds typical of Bashō, but on the whole the phrases are too neatly packaged. – *Mizuho*

I don't like "it is quiet." – *Rohan*

The images of the monk and morning tea create an impression of stillness and serenity. The chrysanthemum is probably wild. This is an artless poem that well suggests the refreshing feeling of an autumn morning. – *Saisei*

Here is a serene state of mind. Yet the impression of a flowering chrysanthemum goes too well with the image of a monk, and as a result the poem is lacking in the kind of profundity that would be derived from a more ambiguous comparison. – *Shūson*

a wintry gust—
cheeks painfully swollen,
the face of a man

kogarashi | ya | hohobare | itamu | hito | no | kao
winter-gust | : | cheek-swell | hurt | person | 's | face

COMMENTARY

The reader can vividly picture a person suffering the pangs of toothache in a gust
of winter wind. – *Kūzen*

I visualize the swollen face of a man who is holding his cheeks with both hands
so that they will be exposed to the chilly wind as little as possible. – *Abe Y.*

When I try to determine the location of that face, what comes to my mind is the
face of a man seated opposite the poet across a handwarmer inside a house.
– *Komiya*

In Tokyo the wind is dusty on a day like this. So, trying to prevent the dust from
getting into their eyes, people twist their eyebrows and make their faces look
very unpleasant. But the man in this hokku has not twisted his eyebrows; the focus of his facial look is on the cheeks. In view of that fact, I assume this gust was
that in Kyoto. In any case, the man's face was ugly. Yet the poet, great as he was,
did not see that ugliness but described it as "painfully swollen." – *Watsuji*

There is an impressionistic similarity between a swollen-cheeked man with
mumps and a chilly winter gust. The piercing chill in the gust was linked to the
pain of a man with swollen cheeks; then the poet felt the pain as if it were his
own. – *Mizuho*

The nonchalant tone of the concluding phrase suggests the weight of human reality and creates a faint, humorless humor. – *Shūson*

At each blow of the wintry gust, the face with a smileless smile is contorted in
pain, thereby giving concrete form to the impression of the gusty wind. The poet,
having sensed the season in the gust, gave it artistic expression through his sickly,
morbid sensibility. – *Ogata*

1691

Bashō continued to use his native town of Ueno as a base from which to take trips to the neighboring provinces. In early January 1691 he traveled to Kyoto and participated in several haikai compositions hosted by local poets. One such composition was a kasen known as "Tobi no ha" (The kite's feathers), which later came to be considered one of the finest examples of the genre. Late in the month Bashō moved to Ōtsu and celebrated the coming of the lunar New Year there with his students. For the first time in years, he did not write a verse for the New Year's Day, which arrived on January 29. Shortly after, however, he did take part in a haikai gathering held in honor of a student leaving for Edo. He returned to Ueno during the first week of February and enjoyed the spring season with his old friends and relatives.

In late spring Bashō again traveled to Kyoto and moved into an old house which his student Kyorai had bought and repaired. Called the Rakushi ("fallen persimmons") Villa, it was located in a northwestern suburb of Kyoto named Saga. Bashō stayed there from May 15 to June 1 and authored the last of his major prose works, *Saga nikki* (Saga diary). Although he liked the quiet, rustic surroundings, he was quite busy receiving visitors. During the two-week period he stayed there, he was alone for only four or five days. Two of the most frequent visitors were Kyorai and Bonchō, who were compiling *Sarumino* and wanted as much guidance as possible from their teacher. Bashō, too, was eager to help make the anthology meet the high standard he had set for it. He continued to give editorial advice after he moved from the Rakushi Villa to Bonchō's house, where he stayed until July 16. He did have a day of relaxation from time to time, now going to see a kabuki play, now visiting students on the shores of Lake Biwa.

Bashō left Kyoto for Ōtsu on July 20, one week before the publication of *Sarumino*. This time his students in that area had a new cottage built for him in the precincts of Gichū Temple, where he had stayed the previous year. The cottage was called the Mumyō ("nameless") Hut. Bashō loved the cottage, so much so that he was later to will that his body be buried there when he died. His health at this time, however, was considerably better than the year before, and he engaged himself in a number of activities. He went to a party in Ōtsu on September 6, the day before the harvest moon. The following evening he hosted a moon-viewing party at his cottage. The next day he and his students went on an excursion to Katada by boat. On October 9, and again on November 2, he visited Ishiyama Temple with his students. It is quite likely he made several trips to Kyoto and many other nearby places, although no clear evidence survives today.

In the meantime, Bashō's students in Edo were becoming anxious to have their teacher back. Bashō, who had kept postponing his return trip mainly for health reasons, finally decided he was strong enough to travel back to Edo. Thus he left the Mumyō Hut on November 17, taking his cousin Tōrin with him. The route was a familiar one for him, and he had a number of students welcoming him along the way. One of them, Kagami Shikō (1665–1731), joined him in Atsuta and kept him and Tōrin company for the rest of the trip. The three arrived in Edo on December 18. Because Bashō had given up his residence in Fukagawa when he left for the northern journey, he had to move temporarily into a rented house in Nihonbashi. In a letter dated January 1, 1692, he wrote he had no idea where his permanent address was going to be. On the other hand, he must have felt happy that he was able to return to Edo safely after spending so many days on the road. He had been away for more than two years and seven months.

*During my sojourn in Kyoto, I heard the lonely voice of a Kūya pilgrim
making his round every night.*

a dried salmon
and a Kūya pilgrim's gauntness
in midwinter cold

karazake I mo I Kūya I no I yase I mo I kan I no I uchi
dried-salmon I also I Kūya I 's I gauntness I also I midwinter I 's I inside

NOTE

A Kūya pilgrim is a lay monk who goes around town in midwinter reciting su-
tras for forty-eight consecutive nights to commemorate the anniversary of the
holy priest Kūya's (903–72) death. The pilgrim usually carries a small bell or a
hollowed gourd, which he strikes to punctuate his recitation.

COMMENTARY

Of this hokku, Master Bashō said: "I sweated for several days to capture the flavor of the impression produced by the subject." – *Dohō*

This hokku skillfully combines two images in order to suggest intense cold.
– *Nobutane*

When the poet saw a dried salmon become even drier in midwinter, he recalled
how Kūya had done ascetic exercises during the coldest season of the year.
– *Nanimaru*

As those who are familiar with the ascetic life of a Kūya pilgrim will know, there
is something spiritual in the pilgrim's gauntness. Midwinter cold minimizes the
sensual, physical aspects of human life. Those two things, then, have a similar
"flavor." And a dried salmon is an excellent visual representation of the flesh that
has been overcome. – *Watsuji*

Followers of Kūya attained a realm of ecstatic joy when they recited his prayers.
They ate dried salmon meat to maintain good health during their ascetic exercises; some even bore a dried salmon at the waist like a sword. When we read
this hokku with these things in mind, we can see the three images it presents
share a common impressionistic quality. – *Rohan*

The "flavor" Bashō spoke of is something similar to *kotan*, *hie*, and *sabi*; it is
the most profound type of beauty cultivated in medieval Japanese art. It has been

said that this type of beauty can be attained only by a great master whose art had matured in old age, after many years of arduous training and effort; it is far beyond the reach of a young, beginning artist. Bashō probably did not write this hokku with a salmon or a pilgrim actually in sight. Through his poetic sensibility he had grasped the essence of each of these things in the past; now he brought them together and juxtaposed them with the same structural method he used in linking haikai stanzas. – *Nose*

Both a dried salmon and a Kūya pilgrim belong to postmedieval, plebeian life, and here they merge into "midwinter cold," a natural phenomenon. The poem illustrates how a medieval literary ideal could manifest itself even in the characteristic haikai style. – *Yamamoto*

The arctic internal landscape of the poet, who was painfully aware of his aging body as well as of his destiny as a wanderer, was made here into an abstract painting that suggests the coldest season through the images of a dried salmon and a Kūya pilgrim. Probably this hokku shows the highest point reached by Bashō in his art of poetry during the *Sarumino* period, a period when he tried to body forth the colors of his mind through objects and scenes in nature. – *Ogata*

always hateful—
those crows, except in this
morning's snow scene

higoro I nikuki I karasu I mo I yuki I no I ashita I kana
ordinarily I hateful I crow I even I snow I 's I morning I kana

COMMENTARY

A very amateurish motif. *– Meisetsu*

If I were to rewrite this poem in the style of Jules Renard, it would come out
something like: "Crows—moles on the snow." *– Seishi*

Early spring in the mountains of Iga Province

in the mountain village
Manzai dancers are late—
plum blossoms

yamazato I wa I Manzai I ososhi I ume I no I hana
mountain-village I as-for I Manzai I late I plum I 's I blossom

NOTE
Manzai dancers are a troupe of itinerant players who go from house to house in
the New Year season and perform good-luck dances for a small amount of rice
or money.

COMMENTARY
A hokku involves a movement of the mind that advances and then returns. It can
be illustrated by this verse on Manzai dancers. The poet first proceeded to assert
that the dancers were late in coming to the mountain village, and then he came
back to observe that the plum blossoms were in bloom. Such "advancing" and
"returning" of the mind is what makes a hokku. If the poet's mind goes only in
one direction, resulting in such phrases as

in the mountain village   yamazato wa
Manzai dancers are late—   Manzai ososhi

that would make only a *hiraku*. According to a certain haikai book, Master Bashō also said, "One should know that a hokku is made by combining things."
— *Dohō*

Manzai dancers are expected to come in the New Year season. But in a remote
mountain village they make their appearance so late that plum blossoms are already blooming. This is a poem based on accurate observation and can be said
to be a good one. — *Shikei*

The dancers did not come to the village even though it was well past the New
Year season. The poet could recognize spring's arrival only by the sight of plum
blossoms. — *Kobayashi*

Manzai dancers make their rounds early in the New Year, but plum blossoms do
not bloom at that time, unless they are of a very early kind. Especially in a

mountain village, plum trees blossom a little later. It is only after the dancers finish their rounds in town and the New Year mood is gone from the busy life of townsmen that they begin their tour through the countryside. Plum blossoms are in full bloom at that time. This is a fine poem that well suggests the peaceful, leisurely mood of an early spring day. – *Higuchi*

This hokku presents two problems, each of which has divided critics' opinions. The first is the question of whether the poet actually saw the dancers and thought they came late, or he was complaining at the lateness of the dancers who had not yet arrived. My opinion is that the hokku expresses the feeling of the poet when he saw the troupe. The second is the question of what is late. Is it the dancers who are late, or is it both the dancers and the plum blossoms? I think the former is the more reasonable assumption. – *Iwata*

It is past the New Year season, yet the dancers are not here. Hidden in the mind of the poet who noted this fact was his wish for the arrival of spring as well as his love of the simple life in a mountain village where civilization had arrived late. – *Ogata*

If the poem were to be interpreted, as it has been by many commentators, to represent the emotion of a person looking forward to the dancers' arrival, then it would be seen as nothing more than a socially inept collage put together to satisfy a passing whim. The true intent of the poem has to do with its suggestion that the plum blossoms are waiting for the dancers. – *Andō*

lingering a while
above the blossoms, the moon
in the night sky

shibaraku | wa | hana | no | ue | naru | tsukiyo | kana
short-time | as-for | blossom | 's | top | is | moonlit-night | kana

COMMENTARY

The poet was delighted to have a chance to see cherry blossoms wide open by moonlight. Not stated but implied is the idea that a man's prosperity is as fleeting as that scene. – *Tosai*

This hokku, though favored by amateur poets, has no profound appeal. That is because the poet did not sketch an actual scene but relied on his imagination. – *Shiki*

The theme is rather intellectualized. This flaw, however, will seem less conspicuous if we assume that the poet was looking at the scene from a high place or from a short distance away. – *Handa*

The night is still young. In the moonlight, the cherry blossoms look like billowing clouds. Nothing else attracts the poet's attention. The phrase "lingering a while" refers to the poet's mind as well as to the peaceful moonlit night. – *Momota*

The opening phrase implies that the poet, while enjoying the sight of the blossoms and the moon, speculated how lonely everything would become when the moon declined in the sky. While intoxicated by enjoyment of beauty, he was already aware of the sadness that was bound to follow. – *Ebara*

Instead of picking on small details, the poet decided to work on a grand scale and depict both the blossoms and the moon. This approach enabled him to capture the essence of a spring night, a feat that only a poet of Bashō's ability could have accomplished. – *Shūson*

ebbing strength—
my teeth detect a grain of sand
in the dried seaweed

otoroi I ya I ha I ni I kui I ateshi I nori I no I suna
decline I : I tooth I in I eating I has-hit I dried-seaweed I 's I sand

COMMENTARY

A young man does not savor the food he eats. He is so full of vigor that he does
not chew it well enough to discern its true taste. With age, a person becomes
more particular about the shape, color, freshness, and taste of the food he eats.
He becomes so attentive to it that his teeth can even find a grain of sand in dried
seaweed. When this happens, he realizes, sadly, that his strength is on the decline.
—Nobutane

The sense of spring implied in the season word "seaweed" enhances an old man's
melancholy feelings. —Ebara

Old age, which the poet had forgotten about in his daily routine, suddenly re-
vealed itself the moment his teeth hit on the sand in the seaweed. This is an unadorned poem written with no excess of sentiment. —Shūson

In the hokku's opening phrase the poet makes the gesture of a frontal attack, like
a swordsman brandishing his sword high above his head. With the phrases that
follow, the sword comes down and the poem is concluded. We rarely see this
kind of frontal attack in modern haiku. I cannot bring myself either to begin a
haiku with a phrase like "ebbing strength—." In another text, this hokku appears as:

my teeth detect   kami atsuru
ebbing strength—a grain of sand   mi no otoroi ya
in the dried seaweed   nori no suna

This version is more like a modern haiku, but it is weaker as a poem. The hokku
raises a difficult problem for a modern poet. —Seishi

It was a trivial incident in ordinary life, the kind of incident that even an old man
would pay little attention to. But Bashō was aroused by it, so much so that he
began the poem with a lament: "ebbing strength—." At the time he was in his
forty-eighth year—still the prime of life. The poem shows what a delicate constitution he had and, more importantly, how sensitive he was to the pulse of life
within himself. —Utsubo

many sad junctures—
in the end, everyone turns into
a bamboo shoot

uki | fushi | ya | take | no | ko | to | naru | hito | no | hate
sorrowful | node | : | bamboo | 's | child | to | turn | person | 's | end

NOTE

Written on May 16, when Bashō was taking a walk in Saga and came upon Ko-gō's grave in a bamboo grove. Kogō, a favorite concubine of Emperor Takakura (1161–81), drew the ire of a tyrannical politician and eventually committed suicide by throwing herself into a river. The word *fushi* originally meant a node on a stem, but later came to be used figuratively for designating any distinctive point in time or space.

COMMENTARY

The hokku implies that no one born into this world can escape living a life or dying a death as sorrowful as Kogō's. Some may wear fine array while others live in tatters, yet all their lives are but a dream. – *Nobutane*

In my opinion, the flaw of this hokku lies in its opening phrase. The poem seems to say that human life has many sad junctures, and even after the person is re-born as a bamboo, many nodes will appear on its stem and continue to haunt the person. I do not care for that karmic implication. – *Keion*

The hokku is based on what Bashō felt when he visited the site of Kogō's house and saw bamboos growing in the ruins. But in describing his feeling he depended on the device of wordplay, using the word "nodes" as he saw them on the bamboos in front of him. The result is a gap between emotion and expression; the rhetorical device becomes too conspicuous. – *Shūson*

With deep emotion Bashō had been looking around Kogō's grave, when he noted a bamboo sprouting out of the ground and wondered if it might not be Kogō's reincarnation. Humor is mixed with sadness. – *Iwata*

hototogisu—
through a vast bamboo forest
moonlight seeping

hototogisu I ōtakeyabu I wo I moru I tsukiyo
hototogisu I large-bamboo-grove I [acc.] I seep I moonlit-night

NOTE
Written on May 17 in Saga, where there were many bamboo groves.

COMMENTARY

The verb "seep" is here used from a spectator's viewpoint. The moon is not yet high in the sky. It is not a case of moonlight falling on the floor of the bamboo grove. – *Keion*

I like having the moonlight fall on the grove's floor rather than seeing it seep through sideways. When the grove is large and dense, the moonbeams make intricate patterns of shadow on its floor, creating a mystic mood. – *Abe J.*

In Saga, one can really see the moonlight seeping sideways through a large bamboo forest. Since bamboos grow in dense clusters there, the forest is dark, and, at first glance, one surmises no light would seep through it, but it actually does. The word "seep" is therefore very fitting. There is a mystic feeling here. – *Watsuji*

Waka poets commonly sing of a hototogisu in combination with saxifrage flowers or the shade of green leaves. The juxtaposition of a hototogisu and a large bamboo forest is original, with no precedent in the waka tradition. It sounds exquisite, too, because the originality is not a contrived one but is based on the poet's actual experience. – *Kobayashi*

Surprisingly large forests of bamboos still exist today in the vicinity of Mt. Arashi in Kyoto. In summer the moonlit night is veiled in purple. Suddenly a hototogisu's cry falls from the sky like a shooting star. Receiving the blessing, the night earth trembles. What a mysteriously beautiful poem! – *Noguchi*

The moonlight seeping through the thicket creates an infinite stillness. – *Seihō*

As a hototogisu flew over a large bamboo forest with a cry, the poet looked around and saw the moonlight seeping through the thicket and casting shadows on the ground. The moon, being of the twentieth night, was more than half full. The combination of the moonbeams slanting through the grove and the hototogisu calling as it flies straight for the horizon creates a world so mysterious that it is almost frightening. – *Yamamoto*

I'm filled with sorrow—
make me feel more lonely,
cuckoo!

uki | ware | wo | sabishi | garese | yo | kankodori
sorrowful | I | [acc.] | lonely | cause-to-feel | ! | cuckoo

NOTE

Cited in a haibun dated May 19 and included in *Saga nikki*. It was a revision of
a hokku Bashō had written on October 19, 1689:

I'm filled with sorrow—	uki ware wo
make me feel more lonely,	sabishi garese yo
temple in autumn	aki no tera

COMMENTARY

Even a recluse has to face a number of things that cause him pain. Whenever
something painful happens, his mind becomes agitated and lacking in serenity.
Serenity is the ideal state toward which an agitated mind strives. Therefore the
poet here asked a cuckoo to grant him solitude and help his mind attain serenity.
This is a poem of high order. – *Gozan*

I feel sorrow whenever there is no solitude. Let me hear your lonely voice! That is
what this hokku means. In *Sankashū* [no. 937], Saigyō wrote:

Folks no longer	tou hito mo
think of coming to visit	omoi taetaru
this mountain village—	yamazato ni
if I had no loneliness to live with	sabishisa nakuba
it would be sorrowful indeed!	sumi ukaramashi

If the reader contemplates this waka, he will be able to understand the pleasure
those two old masters enjoyed. – *Tosai*

A sorrowful mind becomes enlivened by tension when it is stimulated by loneliness. – *Abe Y.*

Sorrow is a passive, heavy, melancholy emotion, whereas loneliness implies an
active heart that can soar—aspiring to infinity, for instance. – *Watsuji*

It is more poetic to say "A bird has cried, and the forest is even more silent" than to say "There is not a single bird's cry, and the forest is silent." In this hokku, too, a cuckoo's cry intensifies the loneliness. — *Rohan*

On the surface of the poem, the poet is calling out to a cuckoo. It is more proper, however, to assume that Bashō was muttering to "the unknown" within himself. He had a nameless sorrow in his heart, and he wished to question it and find out what it was. That wish made itself known through the medium of a cuckoo. — *Handa*

We can see Bashō's desire to be immersed in the world of *sabi*. The hokku's beginning phrase implies his dissatisfaction with his own self, which is not yet merged with that world of solitude. — *Ebara*

as I clap my hands
with the echoes, it begins to dawn—
the summer moon

te | wo | uteba | kodama | ni | akuru | natsu | no | tsuki
hand | [acc.] | when-clap | echo | with | dawn | summer | 's | moon

NOTE

Written on May 20 at the Rakushi Villa.

COMMENTARY

With the clapping, echoes. With the echoes, the summer dawn. At dawn, the summer moon. Through a skillful use of words, the poet has linked these three things in such a way that one flows into another. The technique has enabled the poet to condense the language of the poem on the one hand and to create a harmonious interrelationship among the images on the other. In my opinion, the way in which the poetic material is given form here illustrates the ultimate art of haiku. — *Watsuji*

Past midnight, the poet awoke and went out to the veranda. In the pale moonlight, all was quiet. He was so lonely that he clapped his hands. The clapping caused echoes, and with them the moonlight seemed to become even more pale. Before he knew it, the eastern sky had whitened and the night was over.
— *Kobayashi*

In the dusky twilight of summer dawn, Bashō got up and took a stroll in the neighborhood. He was in a cheerful mood as one often is early in the morning, so he clapped his hands for no particular reason. The sound faded into the distance, with its echoes and re-echoes. Suddenly he realized that the night had ended, leaving only a wan moon in the sky. In the fading echoes we can sense the transitory nature of the short summer night as it ends. — *Ebara*

The poet probably clapped his hands in prayer to Shinto gods or to the rising sun in the east. — *Ōtani*

The essence of that refreshing feeling one has at dawn on a summer's day. — *Kon*

Saddened by the prospect of leaving the Rakushi Villa the following day, I toured all the rooms in the house.

long seasonal rain—
where a poetry card was peeled off,
traces on the wall

samidare | ya | shikishi | hegitaru | kabe | no | ato
fifth-month-rain | : | poetry-card | has-peeled | wall | 's | trace

NOTE

Written on May 31.

COMMENTARY

As it is humid at this time of the year, a wall becomes soggy and something pasted on it is apt to come off. This is even more so in a dilapidated house. There are implications of nostalgia in this poem. – *Donto*

Hearing the lonely sound of seasonal rain outside, the poet walked through one room after another, until he discovered the traces of a poetry card on the wall and wondered what poem had been there in former days. The emotion makes a deeper impression this way than if he had actually seen the card on the wall. It fits well with the reclusive life of the poet. – *Kobayashi*

There is a subtle correspondence between the impression of dismal seasonal rain and that of the old traces of a poetry card on the wall. – *Iwata*

though the autumn wind
has begun to blow, it is green—
a chestnut bur

akikaze | no | fuke | domo | aoshi | kuri | no | iga
autumn-wind | 's | blow | although | green | chestnut | 's | bur

COMMENTARY

Because of its appearance, a chestnut bur gives a strong impression of what
might be called unsociability. The embittered poet must have felt a degree of empathy for it when he said it resisted the autumn wind and remained green.
—*Handa*

The poet took an interest in the appearance of a chestnut bur, which looks rugged and, one might say, honest to a fault. I detect humor here. The hokku makes
us picture the image of the poet sunk in thought with his eyes fixed on a chestnut
bur. —*Iwata*

in a cowshed
mosquito buzz sounds dusky . . .
lingering summer heat

ushibeya | ni | ka | no | koe | kuraki | zansho | kana
cow-room | in | mosquito | 's | voice | dark | lingering-heat | kana

COMMENTARY

The sweaty smell of an animal, scatterings of hay, the faint buzz of still surviving mosquitoes—all these were in the dusky interior of the cowshed. In that faint darkness the poet sensed an unmistakable trace of summer heat. The expression "mosquito buzz sounds dusky" hits the mark precisely; it is irreplaceable.
— *Ebara*

When hot days continue into autumn, our bodies, which have been weakened during summer, begin to protest. We let out a sigh and wonder how long the heat will continue. Oppressive thoughts of that nature are among the contents of this hokku. — *Imoto*

The harvest moon

shall we go and knock
on the gate of Mii Temple?
the moon of tonight

Miidera | no | mon | tataka | baya | kyō | no | tsuki
Mii-Temple | 's | gate | knock | wish | today | 's | moon

NOTE

Written on September 7, when Bashō hosted a moon-viewing party in his hut at
Gichū Temple on the shore of Lake Biwa. Mii Temple, founded in the seventh
century, was located just a few miles to the northwest. The name Mii literally
means "three wells."

COMMENTARY

This hokku drew on Chia Tao's [779–843] lines:

Birds are asleep on a tree in the pond.
A monk knocks on the gate in the moonlight.

Bashō, trying to enjoy the full moon in every way possible, wanted to knock on
the gate of Mii Temple. *– Shōgatsudō*

Anyone enjoying the beauty of the harvest moon would wish to walk along the
beach from Gichū Temple to Mii Temple and look over the lake from the hill
where the latter temple is located. From there, one can see all of the eight famous
views of Lake Biwa. *– Nobutane*

This poem may be based on a thought that occurred to Bashō while he enjoyed
the view of the moon aboard a boat. From the lake, he could tell whereabouts
Mii Temple was located. The boating under the moon was so enjoyable that he
did not want to go straight home. He wondered if monks at Mii Temple too were
not viewing the moon and reciting poetry, and he felt like stopping by the temple
and chatting with them over a cup of tea. *– Shida*

I can visualize the poet admiring the moon. Yet I feel as if the poem were made
to order. Though I think it is skillfully made, it does not stir my emotions with
irresistible force. *– Shūson*

The last two phrases add depth of meaning to the poem by alluding to Chia Tao's famous lines. Also, it was ingenious of the poet to refer to Mii Temple, whose name evokes the image of wells and leads to the association of water. Thus, through the poet's masterful art, the hokku offers a flavor of Chinese poetry on the one hand and the beauty of the lake on the other. Its profundity is further increased by its peripheral allusion to the nō plays *Miidera* [Mii Temple] and *Tōru*.
— *Iwata*

mushroom—
from some unknown tree, a leaf
sticking on it

matsudake | ya | shiranu | ki | no | ha | no | hebaritsuku
mushroom | : | unknown | tree | 's | leaf | 's | stick

COMMENTARY

It is a joy to seek out a mushroom that has come up with an unknown leaf on its
head. The poet was in an unfamiliar forest for mushroom hunting. – *Donto*

As we trace the evolution of Bashō's poetic style, we notice that it gradually
moved from a style that sought novelty and dexterity to one that tried to discover a deep meaning in a common object or scene—the so-called *karumi* style.
This poem is one of the best illustrations of the later style. – *Kobayashi*

This is not a large-scale poem, but it reveals something highly characteristic of
the poet who loved life and paid attention to even the most trivial things around
him. – *Shūson*

deep-rooted leeks
washed spotlessly white—
how cold!

nebuka I shiroku I arai I agetaru I samusa I kana
leek I white I washing I has-completed I cold I kana

NOTE

Written on or around November 29 at Tarui in Mino Province. The area was famous for its production of *nebuka* (literally "deep-root"), a special kind of leek
whose white underground stem is sometimes as much as a foot long. Bashō's
own drawing that accompanies this hokku depicts three such leeks lying on a
cutting board.

COMMENTARY

A girl with her clothes tucked up to the knees, washing leeks in a mountain
stream—what a chilly sight! – *Donto*

The poet saw a great number of leeks that farmers had washed white in preparation for shipment. In that whiteness he felt an intense cold that he made the subject of this poem. – *Kōseki*

This hokku is very simple: the poet found a visual correlative of coldness in the
bright, pure white of freshly washed leeks. – *Yamamoto*

daffodils,
white paper screens, reflecting
one another's color

suisen | ya | shiroki | shōji | no | tomoutsuri
daffodil | : | white | shōji | 's | mutual-reflection

NOTE
Written on or around December 9 at the house of Baijin, a poet living in Atsuta.

COMMENTARY

By suggesting an impression of the utmost purity, the poet paid respect to the host and his residence. – *Tosai*

The words "reflecting one another's color" may imply the kindred spirit shared by the host and the guest. – *Meisetsu*

This poem well illustrates the simple beauty of a Japanese room as praised by Pierre Loti. – *Abe Y.*

I am attracted to this poem especially because it gives a clear sense of light. The beauty of a simple life far removed from the mundane world is suggested here in an impressionistic way. – *Komiya*

It seems that a pot of daffodils was on a desk near some white paper screens. The white of the flowers and that of the screens reflected one another, creating an atmosphere of extreme purity. It may be that Bashō also intended to suggest the congenial friendship between Baijin and himself, but I prefer not to strain the interpretation. – *Handa*

At Kōgetsu's house

the faces of those
who love to drink—
a flash of lightning

yuki I wo I matsu I jōgo I no I kao I ya I inabikari
snow I [acc.] I await I drinker I 's I face I : I lightning

NOTE

Kōgetsu was the haikai name of Suganuma Gon'emon, a samurai serving the lord
of Shinshiro in Mikawa Province (Aichi Prefecture). Bashō stayed at his house
during his return trip to Edo.

COMMENTARY

In my opinion, here are people who have gathered to wait for snow. Their faces
are flushed because of drinks they have had, and that glow is humorously compared to lightning. – *Mukō*

Winter lightning often signals the coming of snow flurries. Perhaps there were
some wine lovers at the gathering who looked forward to it, and Bashō took
note of that. The tone of the poem suggests he was amused at the kind of atmosphere that existed at that gathering. – *Shūson*

Being wine lovers, people at the party were all enjoying drinks. Being men of
fūga also, they had kept all the windows open and were eagerly waiting to see
snow begin to fall outside. All of a sudden there was a flash of lightning, momentarily illuminating everyone's face. Some readers speculate the lightning in this
poem is descriptive of the face of a person drinking saké, but that kind of comparison was rarely used by Bashō at this phase of his career. – *Iwata*

the winter gust
sharpening a rock with its blow
through the cedars

kogarashi | ni | iwa | fuki | togaru | sugima | kana
winter-gust | with | rock | blowing | become-sharp | cedar-gap | kana

NOTE
Written at Hōrai Temple, some ten miles northeast of Shinshiro.

COMMENTARY
Needless to say, the poet used the winter gust to communicate his impression of
a pointed rock he saw among the cedars. The description vividly conveys the appearance of massive cedar trees and the precipitous rock as well as the force of
the gust. — *Shida*

Finding it hard to live a settled life, I spent most of my last six or seven years on the road. I survived a number of painful illnesses, and, not being able to forget my friends and disciples of many years, I finally came back to Edo again. Soon they began to visit me at this grassy hut every day, so I addressed them with this hokku:

somehow, in some way,
it has managed to survive—
pampas grass in the snow

tomokakumo | narade | ya | yuki | no | kareobana
somehow | not-become | ! | snow | 's | dead-pampas-grass

COMMENTARY

Sei Shōnagon [966?–1025?] in her *Makura no sōshi* [The pillow book] wrote: "Unaware that its head has become gray and haggard, a stalk of pampas grass continues to stand until the end of winter, meekly tottering in the wind and looking as if it would reminisce about the past. It is very much like an aged man." *– Sanga*

By way of metaphor the poet expressed his thought on aging. *– Tosai*

I cannot help recalling the unconquerable spirit of Bashō, who squarely faced death all alone. He played with death despite his fear of it, gaining a spirit of freedom that emerges in his haikai. *– Shūson*

Whenever Bashō took to the road, he would envision his skeleton lying in the wilderness, and in that imaginary picture there always seems to have been a cluster of pampas grass near the skeleton. But now he is still alive, and the pampas grass, familiar from that picture, is actually in front of him. "The pampas grass in the snow" is an ironic statement of the poet who has not died. It is his sigh of relief. What used to be associated with his death has now turned into a proof of his being alive. *– Yamamoto*

CHAPTER FIVE

Last Years

1692-1694

1692

Bashō was unusually inactive as a haikai poet for the first seven months of 1692. As far as we can tell from the surviving records, he participated in only three haikai compositions during that period, despite the fact that he was now back in Edo where he had a great many people to write poetry with. Although it is possible that he was still tired from his recent wanderings, a more likely reason is the change that had taken place in the Edo poetic scene during his prolonged absence. In a letter dated April 4 and addressed to a student in Zeze, he stated: "Everywhere in this city I see people writing poetry in order to win prizes, thereby making contest judges extremely busy. You can well imagine what kind of verses they write. Whatever I say about them is bound to end in harsh words, so I pretend not to hear what they say and not to see what they write." In brief, haikai had become a game people would play for honor or money, and Bashō did not like that. It made him especially sad to see some of his former students, such as Kikaku and Ransetsu, joining the popular trend and working as contest judges. That spring he did not go out for blossom viewing, saying that "places famous for cherry blossoms are filled with fame-seekers who know nothing better than screaming and making noise." He even thought of abandoning haikai altogether. In a haibun written in late March or early April, he said: "I tried to give up the way of *fūga* and stop writing verses. But each time I did so, a poetic sentiment would tug at my heart and something would flicker in my mind. Such is the magic spell of *fūga*." Bashō had found himself alienated from most haikai circles in Edo, and that "magic spell" was the only thing that made him continue being a poet.

Bashō did have a small group of poets, such as Sanpū and Sora, to whom he could relate. They in their turn continued to be loyal to Bashō, combining forces to build a new hut for him at a site not far from his previous residence in Fukagawa. He moved into the three-room hut in late June or early July. A couple of months later his banana plant, which had been kept by his friends during his absence from Edo, was transplanted to the yard of the new hut. Thus he became the master of the third Bashō Hut.

Settled in the new hut, Bashō gradually began to resume poetic and social activities. On August 18, for example, he took part in a haikai composition held in honor of Sodō's mother. He attended another such event on September 25, this one to admire the harvest moon. Two haikai gatherings were held, with his participation, during the month of October; three more, during November. He also began to receive visitors from far-off provinces, whom he had met in his past journeys. Some of them stayed with him at the Bashō Hut for a number of days. He was also often invited out. In a letter dated December 20 and written in reply to a student who had visited his residence at least twice during his absence, he said his schedule was full through December 26 and unsettled after December 28; would the student or his messenger please come and see him on December 27, the only day he was certain to be home? The leisurely life he had led at the beginning of the year was indeed over.

how fish and birds
feel at heart, I do not know—
the year-end party

uo | tori | no | kokoro | wa | shirazu | toshiwasure
fish | bird | 's | heart | as-for | not-know | year-end-party

NOTE

Written at a year-end haikai party hosted by Sodō.

COMMENTARY

It appears that the poet, realizing that no creature is as noisy as man, pondered over the mundane sentiments stirred up in the human heart in daily life. – *Donto*

This is a philosophical poem in which the poet, lamenting the passing of the year, felt envious of fish and birds that have no such feelings. – *Nobutane*

The poet, while not knowing exactly how fish and birds feel at heart, wished he could swim or fly as freely as they did. The hokku expresses his desire for the life of a hermit. It has *yūgen* as well as a sublime tone. – *Tosai*

Hōjōki [Account of my ten-foot-square hut, 1212] says: "Look how fish and birds live. Fish are never tired of living in the water, and no one except a fish can know why. Birds want to be in the woods, and no one except a bird can know why. A recluse's life is like that, too: no one who does not live it can know what it is like." – *Nanimaru*

Looking back over the passing year, Bashō had been liable to depression and regret. But now he was at a party intended to make everyone forget the passing year. He was relaxing himself with other people, whether by drinking saké or writing haikai verses. In the midst of that, a thought about the year's end sneaked into his mind. In spite of the occasion, he could no longer maintain a leisurely, relaxed mood. Although he knew he was at a party intended to make him forget the mundane world, he felt he was no longer in a mood to enjoy nature with the heart of a fish in the water or a bird in the woods. That is what he meant by the first two phrases of this hokku. The concluding phrase, therefore, refers not to a heart that has forgotten the passing year but a heart that is vainly trying to forget. In such a wretched emotional state, the poet longed to possess the heart of a fish or a bird. – *Watsuji*

Bashō, having a good time with other poets at the party, thought that what they felt could not be understood by anyone outside his group. He thought they alone knew how they felt. This is a philosophical poem pointing at the difference between Bashō and his fellow poets on the one hand and fish and birds on the other, between those trying to forget the worries of the past year and those having no such worries. – *Yamamoto*

spring that people
do not notice—plum blossoms
on the back of a mirror

hito | mo | minu | haru | ya | kagami | no | ura | no | ume
person | even | not-see | spring | : | mirror | 's | backside | 's | plum

NOTE
A flower design was often carved or cast on the back of a mirror in premodern
Japan.

COMMENTARY
I think the poet was moved to write this hokku when he smelled the fragrance of
plum blossoms that had begun to bloom by his rustic hut. He thought those
blossoms blooming in the small yard were as unnoticed as a design on the back
of a mirror. – *Gozan*

On the surface the hokku expresses the poet's sympathy for plum blossoms on
the back of a mirror, but underneath it suggests how a recluse like him, who had
a mind of *fūga* as beautiful as plum blossoms, was enjoying a life of retirement
at a place far away from the world and unnoticed by ordinary people. – *Meisetsu*

I wonder if there is not sympathy—and envy as well—for plum blossoms on the
back of a mirror. – *Mizuho*

Bashō was always attracted to inconspicuous beauty, to something that showed
pure and noble beauty at a place hidden from people's eyes. – *Ebara*

bush warbler—
a dropping on the rice cake
at the veranda's edge!

uguisu | ya | mochi | ni | funsuru | en | no | saki
bush-warbler | : | rice-cake | on | excrete | veranda | 's | edge

COMMENTARY

This hokku shows the kind of innovation I am trying to achieve nowadays.
— *Bashō*

Here is a scene of birds and butterflies, unafraid of men, coming to a hermitage deep in the woods. It is a most peaceful scene that suggests the leisurely life of the person who lives there. — *Tosai*

In waka and other traditional forms of Japanese poetry, a bush warbler has always been depicted as an elegant bird that sings among the blossoms. In haikai, however, a poet tries to discover new beauty in things familiar and mundane, such as rice cakes and bird droppings. This hokku presents a scene of moldy rice cakes placed in the sunlight on the veranda several weeks after the New Year. Suddenly a bush warbler flew in from the garden and let a dropping fall. This is an idyllic scene filled with spring sunshine. — *Yamamoto*

A crystallization of *karumi*. — *Kon*

cats' love—
when it is over, hazy
moonlight in the bedroom

neko | no | koi | yamu | toki | neya | no | oborozuki
cat | 's | love | stop | whereupon | bed | 's | hazy-moon

COMMENTARY

This must be a poem written on the spot, but the image of hazy moonlight in the bedroom makes the reader think of human love as well. Somehow, it is an appealing poem. — *Meisetsu*

There is a clear contrast between the din of the caterwauling and the peace of the hazy moonlight in the bedroom. And yet the two are related to each other by the mood of eroticism. Where two such contrasting things merge, a delicate beauty is born. — *Utsubo*

The caesura in the middle of the hokku's second phrase accentuates the tone of the poem and emphasizes the abruptness with which cats in heat stop meowing. The stillness after the caterwauling enhances the beauty of the hazy moonlight in the bedroom. Through the images of cats in love and the bedroom, the poem captures the atmosphere of a spring night which is somehow erotic. — *Kon*

hototogisu
cries—a blade of iris
five feet tall

hototogisu | naku | ya | goshaku | no | ayamegusa
hototogisu | cry | : | five-shaku | 's | iris

NOTE

The hokku draws on an anonymous waka included in *Kokinshū* (no. 469):

In the fifth month	hototogisu
when a hototogisu cries	naku ya satsuki no
and an iris blooms	ayamegusa
I am utterly lost	ayame mo shiranu
in the darkness of love.	koi mo suru kana

as well as on Emperor Gotoba's teaching: "One should write a waka in the same way that one pours water over a five-foot-tall iris." One *shaku* is slightly less than a foot.

COMMENTARY

An iris blade and a hototogisu's cry: think of the force suggested by these images. The length of five feet indicates healthy growth. – *Donto*

On hearing a hototogisu's cry, the poet made a straightforward statement of what he felt. The poem creates a refreshing mood. Over a burgeoning iris, a hototogisu flew with a cry. The poet caught that moment and opened his eyes on a new cosmos. – *Rohan*

With a hototogisu crying in the sky and a tall iris growing straight up from the earth, the poet suggested the refreshing atmosphere of a day in early summer. – *Kōseki*

The scene described is probably at dawn or in the evening, when the seasonal rain has stopped and the sky has cleared for a time. We should note the craftsmanship of the poet who cleverly changed one word of the famous waka and utilized a common phrase in Japanese poetics to suit his own purpose. – *Ōtani*

under the crescent moon
the earth looms hazily—
buckwheat flowers

mikazuki | ni | chi | wa | oboronari | soba | no | hana
third-day-moon | with | earth | as-for | is-hazy | buckwheat | 's | flower

COMMENTARY

The hokku's last two phrases are effective in suggesting the faint rays of the crescent moon. When the pale white flowers of buckwheat bloom all over the field, they look indistinct and can be described as the "light" of the crescent moon. *—Nobutane*

In general the crescent moon is difficult to depict in poetry, but the last two phrases of this hokku have well succeeded in suggesting the mysterious impression it creates. *— Watsuji*

Because buckwheat flowers were blooming, it must have been in the lunar eighth month. The haze mentioned in the poem, therefore, is evening haze that gives a rather chilly impression; unlike spring haze, it has no warmth. Above the hazy, cold whiteness of the buckwheat field there hangs the crescent moon. The scene offers no glittering beauty; its beauty is clear but without luster. *— Shūson*

The scene here is unspectacular yet has something too attractive to overlook. Its beauty belongs to the realm of *karumi*. It was characteristic of Bashō to pay attention to such a common, familiar subject as buckwheat flowers and find something in it that comes close to elegance. *— Utsubo*

the harvest moon—
crawling up to my gate
the rising tide

meigetsu I ya I mon I ni I sashi I kuru I shiogashira
harvest-moon I : I gate I to I rising I come I tide-head

NOTE
Written on the night of the mid-autumn full moon, which was September 25.
The Bashō Hut was located near the estuary of the Sumida River.

COMMENTARY
The tide always rises high on a full-moon night, especially on the night of the
harvest moon. This hokku is quite convincing when we read it with that in mind.
The tide, which would usually fall well short of the gate, came surging up on this
night. With the full moon hanging in the sky and the tide closing in toward the
gate, there is action in this poem. – *Rohan*

We can visualize the poet absorbed in verse writing on the night of the harvest
moon while leaning against a pillar of his hut that seemed as if it were drifting in
the rising tidewater. This is a likable poem. – *Higuchi*

Through the image of the tide waves crawling toward the gate, the poem has
captured the great movement of nature on a night of full moon. The profundity
of the poem's theme is suggested in the way in which a familiar phenomenon like
the rising tide has been conceived as a manifestation of something that has life.
– *Yamamoto*

At an evening party in Fukagawa

as green as ever
it should have remained—
the pepper pod

aokute | mo | aru | beki | mono | wo | tōgarashi
green | also | is | should | thing | yet | pepper

NOTE
This was the opening verse of a kasen composed at the Bashō Hut, with Taka-
miya Shadō (?–1737) as the honored guest.

COMMENTARY

A pepper pod grows red in color and hot in taste as it ripens. Therefore the poet playfully asked why it does not remain green, why it has to become hot. Further-more, a red pepper looks as if it were angry. The poet wished that it would not become agitated and angry but remain composed and gentle. – *Meisetsu*

I would read this as a remark on how to live. It expresses the idea that one would do better to live an inconspicuous life. – *Keion*

The true color of a pepper pod is green, yet it is too eager to turn red. Isn't this poem in praise of a green pod, saying that it looks more like a pepper when it is green? A green pepper pod looks quite attractive. – *Shinpū*

The true color of a pepper pod is red. – *Mizuho*

This poem is in praise of a colored pepper pod, with the implication that al-though a green pod is attractive it becomes even more attractive when it turns red. That is as far as the written poem goes. Each reader should take over from that point on and interpret the poem according to what he feels. – *Rohan*

What the poet saw in his mind's eye was a red pepper pod. And that redness led to the sentiment he expressed here. This hokku can therefore be said to be a poem that has captured the essence of a pepper pod. The substance of that senti-ment is complex, mixing sympathy, apprehension, and sorrow toward something with a force in it that is too strong to contain, something that has to turn red even if it wants to remain green. – *Abe J.*

Implied in this poem is a philosophical comment on life, namely, that people adorn themselves needlessly. – *Kōseki*

Bashō wanted to confine himself within his gate and refuse to see visitors, and yet he could not help going on to enjoy himself composing haikai with others. In this hokku, he compared such display of his *fūga* spirit to a pepper pod that naturally turns red. — *Ebara*

Because of the wording in its first two phrases, we cannot help feeling there is some kind of allegorical meaning in this hokku. But, with what we have, we cannot determine exactly what that meaning is. That is all right; as long as we sense this is an allegorical poem, it is enough. — *Shūson*

I wonder if Bashō were not trying to teach Shadō by way of this hokku. Shadō, along with Kyokusui, Otokuni, and Masahide,* belonged to a group of poets who lived on the southern shore of Lake Biwa and who looked up to Bashō as their teacher. Bashō loved them for their amiable personalities and for their manner of composition, which avoided the pitfalls that beset the professional poet. Perhaps Shadō had decided to become a professional at this time. Bashō felt apprehensive about it and warned him implicitly in the first two phrases of this hokku. — *Yamamoto*

The poet wrote this hokku while gazing fondly at a red pepper pod in the front yard. It indicates that he was pleased with the enthusiasm of Shadō who had come a long way to study haikai with him, while he also wanted to admonish the young student for his excessive enthusiasm. — *Kon*

---

*Suganuma Kyokusui (1647?–1704), a samurai living in Zeze, was especially close to Bashō and arranged the use of Genjū Hut for his teacher. Kawai Otokuni, a wealthy merchant in Ōtsu, did even more for Bashō: in 1691 he bought a house so that his teacher could celebrate the New Year there. Mizuta Masahide (1657–1723), who practiced medicine in Zeze, was a leader of the group of poets who built the Mumyō Hut for Bashō.

at autumn's end
still with hope for the future
green tangerines

yuku | aki | no | nao | tanomoshi | ya | aomikan
go | autumn | 's | still | promising | ! | green-tangerine

COMMENTARY

In a desolate scene where everything is withering, only some tangerines, being green, give reason for hope. – *Meisetsu*

The poet saw some unripe tangerines in late autumn and imagined how frost would turn them into a rich golden color before long. Looking forward to that promising future, he wrote the poem. – *Kōseki*

*For a haikai sequence written at Kyoriku's lodging on the third day of
the tenth month in the fifth year of Genroku*

just for today
let us all be aged men—
first winter shower

kyō | bakari | hito | mo | toshiyore | hatsushigure
today | alone | person | also | grow-aged | first-winter-shower

NOTE

The date mentioned in the headnote is November 10. Morikawa Kyoriku (1656–
1715), a samurai at the service of a lord in Ōmi Province, had become Bashō's
student that autumn while he was in Edo.

COMMENTARY

Young people, being full of energy, rarely feel *mono no aware*. When they become old and lose their vitality, they are easily bothered by little things. That is
the difference between youth and old age. The poet therefore asked everyone to
grow aged that particular day before looking up at the showery sky. Here is a
display of superb art. – *Nobutane*

This poem takes another view of the same sentiment as expressed in Bashō's
hokku:

life in this world   yo ni furu mo
just like a temporary shelter   sara ni Sōgi no
of Sōgi's   yadori kana

The poem well suggests the fascination and admiration a haikai poet feels toward the beauty of the first winter shower. – *Momota*

salted sea breams—
their gums, too, look cold
at the fish shop

shiodai | no | haguki | mo | samushi | uo | no | tana
salted-sea-bream | 's | gum | also | cold | fish | 's | shop

COMMENTARY

Master Bashō said: "The hokku

in a hoarse voice	koe karete
a monkey shrieks, its teeth white—	saru no ha shiroshi
above a peak, the moon	mine no tsuki

is typical of Kikaku. The hokku about salted sea breams is typical of the style in my old age. The plain ending, 'at the fish shop,' is typical of me, too." – *Dohō*

Because of the stormy winter weather, shelves at the fish shop had become almost empty. Only two or three salted sea breams lay there, with their white teeth exposed. It must have been a cold, desolate sight. – *Tosai*

Kikaku's poem on the monkey is the product of his romantic imagination, and the reader needs a knowledge of Chinese poetry to appreciate it. Bashō's poem on breams is based on his actual experience, and that experience has been given verbal expression not through a forced comparison but through the word "too," which makes the breams symbolize the cold pervading the entire scene. That is why Bashō's poem is superior to Kikaku's. – *Kōseki*

Kikaku's poem, too, shows his extraordinarily refined sensibility, but it seeks to shock the reader through what Shikō called "the sound of a golden bell." The nature of his sensibility was entirely different from Bashō's. Buson's highly developed power of perception also has much in common with Kikaku's. Kikaku, however, tended to parade his sensibility, whereas Bashō kept it hidden beneath the surface. As a result, Bashō's poem came to have a subdued beauty like that of oxidized silver. In this particular instance, there is no doubt that that beauty has been created through the concluding phrase. – *Yamamoto*

while sweeping the yard
it forgets about the snow—
a broom

niwa I hakite I yuki I wo I wasururu I hahaki I kana
garden I sweeping I snow I [acc.] I forget I broom I kana

NOTE

This hokku accompanies a portrait of Han Shan drawn by Bashō. Han Shan,
along with Shih Te, was a famous Zen monk of the T'ang Dynasty and has been
a popular subject in Zen painting. Most painters have portrayed Han Shan with
a sutra and Shih Te with a broom, but this portrait by Bashō shows a rear view
of Han Shan holding a broom.

COMMENTARY

While sweeping the snow, he has forgotten about the snow. The poem has succeeded in portraying Han Shan. — *Watsuji*

In our own life we sometimes do forget about the snow while sweeping it. In this
respect, the poem is solidly based on actual experience. And yet it has something
that implies the realm of Zen. Therein lies the charm of this hokku. — *Shūson*

*while sweeping the yard
it forgets about the snow—
a broom*

*Painting and calligraphy
by Bashō. Reproduced
from Okada Rihei,
Bashō no hisseki
(Shunjūsha), by courtesy
of the publisher and the
late author's estate.*

1693

Bashō's busy life continued into the new year. "Disturbed by others, I have no peace of mind," he confessed to a friend in a letter dated January 8, 1693. He became even more disturbed when he took poor Tōin into his home. This nephew of his, whom he had brought to Edo seventeen years earlier, was dying of tuberculosis. Bashō tried everything he could to save the young man, even borrowing a considerable amount of money from a student. He had also begun to look after a woman named Jutei and her three children, although, except for one of the children, they lived separately from him. Surviving records are vague on Jutei's identity, but they suggest Bashō had had some kind of close relationship with her in his young days. Her children, however, do not seem to have been fathered by Bashō. At all events, he let one of the children, named Jirōbei, live in the Bashō Hut and help with the care of the sick man and with household chores in general.

Tōin died around the end of April. Bashō, who had loved him as a son, was heartbroken. He became so despondent that he did not feel like writing poetry or going out to see cherry blossoms. Yet, partly in order to earn a living, he continued to attend haikai parties and try composing verses. When these sources of mental stress were combined with summer heat, the whole became too much for him to bear. In mid-August he closed the gate of his residence and refused to see people altogether. "Whenever people come, there is useless talk," he explained in a haibun. "Whenever I go for a visit, I have the uneasy feeling of interfering with other men's business. Now I can do nothing better than follow the examples of Sun Ching and Tu Wu-lang, who confined themselves within locked doors." This reference to two Chinese hermits suggests how valiantly he tried to rationalize his despondency, but the depths it had reached are also evident.

Perhaps the cooler weather helped him on his way to recovery. About a month later Bashō reopened his gate and gradually resumed his normal activities. On October 2 he visited the grave of a disciple who had died a week earlier. Ten days later he joined Sanpū, Sora, and four other poets to compose a kasen. He wrote another kasen with another group around the end of the month. On November 6, he went to Sodō's house and joined a party to admire late-blooming chrysanthemums. He continued to take part in these and similar activities for the rest of the year. Physically he was not yet completely recovered, but mentally he seems to have reached some kind of compromise with his current life. According to Dohō, Bashō in his last years is said to have taught: "Keep your mind in a high realm of enlightenment, and then return to the realm of the mundane." He transcended the world of social obligations while continuing to live in it—or, at least, he was trying to do so.

sting the fool
given to the moon and blossoms!
the coldest season starts

tsuki I hana I no I gu I ni I hari I taten I kan I no I iri
moon I blossom I 's I foolishness I on I needle I will-prick I cold I 's I entrance

NOTE

Kan ("cold") refers to a month-long period designated as the coldest time of the year. In 1693, it began on January 5.

COMMENTARY

The poet was shocked to find how fast the year had gone while he was wasting time on spring blossoms and the autumn moon. The ancients had talked of teaching someone a lesson by stinging his skin with a needle. Because intense cold feels like the sting of a needle, the poet used the metaphor to meditate on the foolishness of his life. – *Donto*

Even today, people in rural areas receive acupuncture treatment when they have stiff shoulders. In this hokku, the poet is thinking of himself as someone whose body has stiffened because of his foolish devotion to the moon and blossoms. If we read the poem in this way, the word "sting" will take on more reality. – *Komiya*

When the year's coldest season was about to start, the popular custom was to prepare for it by receiving acupuncture or some such treatment. This hokku contains a mixture of self-derision, self-admonishment, and self-confidence. – *Imoto*

New Year's Day

year after year
on the monkey's face
a monkey's mask

toshidoshi I ya I saru I ni I kisetaru I saru I no I men
each-year I : I monkey I on I let-wear I monkey I 's I mask

NOTE

Written for the lunar New Year's Day, which was February 5.

COMMENTARY

Master Bashō said, "People in general want to be safe in writing a poem. Experts, however, venture into dangerous territory. Therefore, experts always produce many bungled poems. My New Year's hokku on the monkey is a completely bungled poem." – *Kyoriku*

On this New Year's hokku Master Bashō said, "I scrawled this poem because I felt sorry to see people remain on the same spot and tumble into the same pitfalls year after year." – *Dohō*

It serves no purpose for a monkey to wear a monkey mask. Yet this monkey looked very proud, and the poet compared that to a man who looked smug despite the fact he had been repeating the same foolish acts year after year. – *Shinpū*

I think that "a monkey's mask" means "a mask worn by a monkey," and that it displays a human face, not a monkey's. – *Mizuho*

The poem presents a monkey who has become deluded into believing he has undergone a complete transformation by wearing a monkey's mask. Therefore, the mask has to be monkey-faced; no other mask will do. – *Abe Y.*

A person does not change as visibly as a caterpillar changes into a butterfly. This poem expresses the feelings of a man who believes he is growing old without making any visible progress. – *Rohan*

If the mask is worn by a real monkey, the poem must be interpreted as presenting a monkey mime in which the monkey is wearing the mask of a person it is impersonating. "A monkey's mask," then, is a mask made for a monkey, and not a monkey-faced mask. In this interpretation, the poet is contemplating human life at the beginning of the year and feeling that what man does each year is nothing better than a monkey mime. On the other hand, if the mask is worn by a man in a monkey's role, the poem must be read as describing a person like an actor in the *kyōgen* play *Utsubozaru* [The quiver monkey]. In this case, "a monkey's mask" comes to mean a mask showing a monkey face. The poet would then be saying that what man does each year is like wearing a monkey-faced mask and dancing a monkey dance. I do not know which reading is correct, but I am inclined not to accept the first interpretation, since I am not sure if there is any instance of a mask being used in a monkey mime that comes around during the New Year season. —*Nose*

Bashō told Kyoriku this was a botched poem, probably because he regretted that the material had not been given sufficient poetic transformation, so that his abstract idea still remained on the poem's surface. —*Imoto*

On the portrait of Master Shrimp

whitefish
opening their black eyes
in the net of the Law

shirauo I ya I kuroki I me I wo I aku I nori I no I ami
whitefish I : I black I eye I [acc.] I open I Law I 's I net

NOTE

Master Shrimp was a Chinese Zen monk of the Five Dynasties period, who was so nicknamed because he lived on shrimps he caught in a nearby river. Zen artists have portrayed him standing in a stream and catching shrimps with a net.

COMMENTARY

An ordinary Buddhist monk would never catch a fish or any other living creature. But Master Shrimp's viewpoint was that it did not matter whether or not one caught a fish. The net that catches and kills life can be thought of as the net of Buddha's Law as well. Here, lovely whitefish are caught in the monk's net and have opened their black eyes. They are not outside the Law that saves all lives. Conveying such a meaning, the poem complements the portrait well. – *Abe Y.*

I think the whitefish refers to Master Shrimp himself. – *Mizuho*

What the monk caught in his net were shrimps. But Bashō changed them to whitefish, and therein lies his haikai art. He said "opening their black eyes" because black eyes are such a distinctive feature of a whitefish. The phrase has implications of Buddhist enlightenment. – *Rohan*

The poet might have used shrimps in place of whitefish, but then this was a poem accompanying a portrait of Master Shrimp, and in that context the use of shrimps would have been redundant. Also, for a creature to be netted and saved, a tiny, clean-looking, and lovable whitefish is preferable to a shrimp. The hokku's middle phrase, referring to the opening of the whitefish's lovely black eyes, must imply the joy of entering Buddhahood through the help of a wise monk. By being caught and eaten, the whitefish gained a chance to enter Buddhahood. – *Higuchi*

hototogisu—
the shriek lies stretched
across the water

hototogisu | koe | yokotau | ya | mizu | no | ue
hototogisu | voice | lie | : | water | 's | topside

COMMENTARY

I was so deeply grieved over my nephew's death, which occurred in my hut, that
I decided not to write verses on hototogisu. Then Sanpū and Sora came for a
visit and urged me to try relieving my sorrow by writing a verse on the theme
"hototogisu by the water." So I came up with this hokku:

hototogisu—	hototogisu
the shriek lies stretched	koe yokotau ya
across the water	mizu no ue

To convey the same meaning, I also wrote:

a shriek, and it lies	hitokoe no
stretched across the river—	e ni yokotau ya
hototogisu	hototogisu

I drew on Su Tung-p'o's line, "The gleaming water extends to heaven, and the
white mist lies stretched across the river." The wording, "lies stretched," is in the
center of both verses. I was having a hard time in deciding which of the verses
was better, when a man named Mizunuma Sentoku* came for a visit, so I asked
him to be the judge. He responded that the second verse followed Su's line so
closely that it had become too heavy in tone, and that the first verse, without the
word "river," looked more relaxed and sounded better. In the meantime other
lovers of poetry, such as Yamaguchi Sodō and Hara Anteki,† had arrived, and we
all concluded that the first verse was the better of the two. It is by no means a re-

---

*Sentoku (1662–1726) was an influential haikai master of the Danrin school. He and Ba-
shō knew each other, probably because both belonged to Rosen's circle in their early ca-
reers. His family name was Mizuma; apparently Bashō remembered it wrong.
†Hara Anteki (?–1716) was a physician who lived near Bashō's residence in Edo. A talented writer of both waka and haikai, he wrote farewell verses for Bashō when the latter
took to the road in 1687 and 1689.

markable poem, but I hope people will read it with Su's excellent line, "the white mist lies stretched across the river," in mind. – *Bashō*

The hokku's middle phrase amply suggests the spaciousness of the water that spreads out there. – *Mizuho*

It creates an impression of the bird's cry tailing off like a comet. – *Abe J.*

The form of the poem makes me think of smoke from a steam engine trailing off over the railway tracks on a balmy spring day. – *Komiya*

At night, a hototogisu flew over a large river or lake, uttering a sharp cry. That is all that happened, but Bashō thought of the cry (through which he knew the bird was a hototogisu) as part of the bird's appearance and gave it physical length (which also suggests the characteristics of a hototogisu's cry). The phrase "the shriek lies stretched" emerged at the same time. This is a form of "magic" (the word is used by Kikaku in his preface to *Sarumino*) through which an aural perception is transformed into a visual one. – *Handa*

A little earlier Bashō had grieved over Tōin's death by comparing him to Emperor Wang of Shu, whose lamenting soul, according to legend, became a cuckoo when he died far away from his homeland. Am I reading too much into the poem when I imagine that Bashō heard the voice of Tōin's soul in this cry of a hototogisu? – *Miyamoto*

The wording "lies stretched" not only provides a link to Su Tung-p'o's lines that describe a nocturnal landscape lying in dim darkness but shows a new way to view a hototogisu, for it presents a poet searching for the echo of its cry still lingering vaguely in the white mist. Furthermore, the phrase conveys how Bashō sought in that echo the image of his late nephew, who faded away as ephemerally as white mist. In this sense, the expression "lies stretched" plays an important role as the "core" of the poem. – *Ogata*

When Kyoriku set out on the Kiso road

try to emulate
a traveler's heart,
pasania blossoms!

tabibito | no | kokoro | ni | mo | niyo | shii | no | hana
traveler | 's | heart | to | also | resemble | pasania | 's | blossom

NOTE

Kyoriku, who had been serving his lord in Edo, was transferred back to his home province of Ōmi and set out on the journey along the Kiso road on June 9. The first draft of this hokku had a long headnote describing how dignified Kyoriku looked in his formal costume, attended by a spearman and riding on a horse. A pasania tree opens its small, yellow blossoms in or around June.

COMMENTARY

A waka in the *Man'yōshū* [no. 142] says:

The rice I eat	ie ni areba
out of a bowl at home—	ke ni moru ii wo
because I am	kusamakura
now on the road, I place it	tabi ni shi areba
on a pasania leaf.	shii no ha ni moru*

The hokku is in praise of the traveler who, while riding a horse and attended by a spearman, still continued to seek out *fūga*. – Ryōta

The pasania blossoms in the last line are a metaphor for Kyoriku. And the traveler mentioned before that is a weary wanderer, who is often used as a metaphor. The hokku, therefore, admonishes Kyoriku to emulate the heart of a wayworn wanderer and behave himself in the spirit of *fūga*. – Somaru

The hokku pretends to call out to the pasania trees, asking them to open their inconspicuous blossoms and please Kyoriku, who delights in knowing the truth of

*The poem was written by Prince Arima (?–658) during the last journey of his life. He had been sentenced to death for conspiring against the government.

things. But in reality the poet was calling out to Kyoriku. "A traveler's heart" is the spirit of *karumi* that refuses to stop at one place or attach itself to one thing. — *Yamamoto*

This is a farewell poem which, while praising Kyoriku for his eager pursuit of *wabi* as a poet, implicitly teaches that he should continue the pursuit even further. — *Kon*

the moonflower—
I stick my drunken face
out of the window

yūgao | ya | yōte | kao | dasu | mado | no | ana
moonflower | : | being-drunken | face | thrust-out | window | 's | hole

COMMENTARY

Toward the end of the day the drunken poet is sticking his head out of a shabby window and letting the evening breeze blow over it when he catches sight of a moonflower blooming all white before his very eyes. There is a humorous contrast between the red of the drunken face and the white of the flowers. — *Donto*

Bashō wrote this hokku probably when he visited a hermitage covered by moonflower vines. The poem sounds humorous as usual; it sounds lonely as usual. — *Tosai*

We can vividly envision a hermit who thinks nothing of poverty. In the waka tradition, moonflowers always bloom on the fence of a humble hut. It is charming indeed to see them blooming on a fence in the twilight. — *Kobayashi*

This is not a profound poem, but it shows a vignette of the poet's life at his hut and makes the reader smile. — *Iwata*

children!
bindweed flowers have opened,
I'll peel a melon

kodomo-ra | yo | hirugao | sakinu | uri | mukan
children | ! | bindweed | have-bloomed | melon | will-peel

NOTE

As against the morning glory, which is called *asagao* or "morning face" in Japanese, the bindweed is called *hirugao* or "noontime face" because its flower, shaped like a morning glory, opens at high noon.

COMMENTARY

This is a simple poem as it is written for children. *– Sanga*

The loving eyes of the old poet seated in the center of the room and about to begin peeling a melon. Innocent faces of children happily gathered around him. Here is a picture of peace. *– Ebara*

In the autumn of the sixth year of Genroku, I grew weary of people and closed my gate.

the morning glory—
all day long, a bolt
fastened on my gate

asagao | ya | hiru | wa | jō | orosu | mon | no | kaki
morning-glory | : | daytime | as-for | bolt | fasten | gate | 's | fence

COMMENTARY

The hokku is about the flowers of the morning glory that have opened on the fence, even though the gate is locked throughout the day. It describes the gate of a recluse's residence without saying so. – *Shōgatsudō*

The expression "a bolt fastened" suggests Bashō's firm resolve. He is resolved to live a life with just the morning glory for his friend. – *Ebara*

Around the time when I closed the gate of my residence in Fukagawa

the morning glory—
that, too, now turns out to be
no friend of mine

asagao | ya | kore | mo | mata | waga | tomo | narazu
morning-glory | : | this | also | again | my | friend | is-not

COMMENTARY

Because the morning glory blooms so very early in the morning, the poet, now aged and weary, found it difficult to get up early enough to befriend the beautiful flowers. This is a playful poem. Needless to say, it has the further implication that the poet has no friend in the world of men. – *Meisetsu*

Bashō must have written the poem when he was lonely and depressed—for instance, after the end of a visit by someone like Kikaku. At a loss, he looked at the morning glory in the garden. He warmed to the flowers at first, but then came to think they were not his friends either. – *Abe J.*

It is as if the poet spat out those words. – *Komiya*

Bashō at first thought the morning glory was his friend because it was short-lived. Yet on further reflection he came to feel that it too was not his friend because its ephemerality is no different from that of any other flower. Although the morning glory is short-lived, human life is even more unpredictable. – *Rohan*

On the fence the morning glories were blooming in blue, indigo, red, and white, as if to compete in brightness of color. The poet, disappointed at their competitiveness, said they were not friends of someone like him who loved the beauty of *wabi*. – *Kōseki*

Why couldn't Bashō think of the morning glory as his friend? Many reasons are conceivable and have actually been pointed out by commentators over the years. In brief, it was a time when Bashō was deeply depressed, and even the beautiful flowers of the morning glory could not lift up his heavy heart; he sank into still more intense grief and loneliness. – *Iwata*

how fishy they smell!
on a waterweed
dace entrails

namagusashi | konagi | ga | ue | no | hae | no | wata
fishy | konagi | 's | topside | 's | dace | 's | intestine

Konagi is a common waterweed that is also sometimes called *mizuaoi* or "water hollyhock" because of the shape of its leaf. It opens small purple flowers in late summer or early autumn.

COMMENTARY
The image of dace entrails suggests lingering summer heat. — *Shikō*

I think this describes a dace lying on a waterweed pulled up onto the roadside from a moat or small stream. The fish was trampled and showing its entrails. — *Komiya*

There is no *sabi* here. This is a rather modernistic poem. — *Mizuho*

The fish's entrails lay on the luxuriant leaves of waterweed that covered the surface of the water almost completely. There was a fishy smell, as the summer sun beat down on them. — *Rohan*

Because a dace is small and not highly valued, probably a child who caught it threw it away, and it lodged on the leaves of a waterweed. The poet, who noticed the dace emitting a fishy smell, made the little scene into this hokku. I visualize a muddy stream of not much depth. I can also see strong sunlight beating on the glossy leaves of the waterweed. — *Seihō*

Probably a fisherman who caught many dace cleaned them and threw away the entrails because they would quickly begin to rot on a hot day, which it was. We can well get the sense of the season, a time when summer heat continues into autumn. — *Imoto*

Mourning the death of Matsukura Ranran

in the autumn wind
it lies, sadly broken—
a mulberry stick

akikaze | ni | orete | kanashiki | kuwa | no | tsue
autumn-wind | in | being-broken | sad | mulberry | 's | stick

NOTE

Ranran (1647–93) was one of Bashō's oldest students in Edo, who three years earlier had resigned his position as a samurai in order to devote his entire time to verse writing. He died suddenly on September 26.

COMMENTARY

Ranran was a talented man, and Bashō had depended upon him, more than upon any other disciple, as his supporting "stick." The poem contains the poet's dejection and grief. — *Meisetsu*

The image of a hard mulberry stick being broken creates a chilling impression. — *Watsuji*

"A mulberry bow" would have been too stereotyped an expression.* The originality lies in the phrase "a mulberry stick." It suggests Ranran's disciplined, samurai-like character. — *Rohan*

Bashō had written some excellent hokku mourning other people's deaths. In this poem, however, he does not give vent to his grief but seals it deep within himself. The result penetrates the reader's heart even more poignantly. — *Shūson*

"A mulberry stick" is a staff made from mulberry wood. The word is used here because Ranran's death occurred roughly in his forty-eighth year, which is known as *sōnen* or "mulberry age." — *Iwata*

* "A mulberry bow" is part of an old Chinese phrase wishing future success for a boy. It has its origin in an ancient Chinese ritual, in which the father of a newborn boy would shoot an arrow with a mulberry bow as a token of his good wishes.

chrysanthemums
flowering amid the stones
in a stonemason's yard

kiku I no I hana I saku I ya I ishiya I no I ishi I no I ai
chrysanthemum I 's I flower I bloom I : I stonemason I 's I stone I 's I gap

COMMENTARY

A poem like this, which is plain and yet has *yojō*, can be written only by a total amateur or a great master. – *Chikurei*

Amongst the stones a wild chrysanthemum was seen blooming yellow or white. Because it bloomed there every year, the stonemason had made sure that no stone would be placed on that spot. The subject is interesting, but I think this is a rather mediocre poem for Bashō – *Saisei*

At first glance the poem may seem to offer nothing attractive, but its very plainness suggests Bashō's surprise. He was surprised, for he discovered a chrysanthemum blooming amidst ordinary-looking stones in a stonemason's yard. – *Shūson*

At a haikai party with Yaba and three others

how old the pine
appears on the gold screen!
locked in for the winter . . .

kinbyō | no | matsu | no | furusa | yo | fuyugomori
gold-screen | 's | pine | 's | oldness | ! | winter-confinement

NOTE

Shida Yaba (1663–1740), one of Bashō's later disciples, edited *Sumidawara* (A
sack of charcoal, 1694), a haikai book that became well known for its *karumi*
style. He worked as a clerk at an exchange house.

COMMENTARY

Originally this hokku read:

on the screen	byōbu ni wa
a painted mountain—	yama wo egakite
locked in for the winter	fuyugomori

Master Bashō revised it later. — *Dohō*

A gold screen is warm; a silver screen is cold. This is the way each screen makes
its true nature felt. — *Shikō*

The person was in winter seclusion, gazing at a gold screen and thinking of ages
long past. The poem has *yojō*. — *Sanga*

Looking at an old screen on which the gold color had faded and the pine tree had
become indistinct, the poet and others were earnestly discussing poetry around a
handwarmer. The poem presents the charms of a secluded life in winter.
— *Kobayashi*

The pine drawn in black ink on a gold screen combines the warmth of the gold
and the beauty of age emanating from the old tree. Furthermore, since the screen
is old, there is an additional effect of *sabi*. All these things led the poet to find the
tranquillity, warmth, idleness, and loneliness of secluded life in winter. Perhaps
the poet was staying at a wealthy house and wanted to express his gratitude, too.
— *Higuchi*

Yaba and the three others who were there were said to be clerks or executives of an exchange house, Echigoya (predecessor of the present Mitsui Bank). I am inclined to believe they were executives, judging from Yaba's biography as well as from the fact that they were selected as editors of *Sumidawara*. This poem, which has a theme taken from human society, makes the reader visualize someone leading an affluent life; it is the kind of poem that would have been likely to please Yaba and his associates. If Bashō wanted to write a poem for Yaba to learn from, it is likely that he would have come up with one like this. – *Shida*

We had a chrysanthemum-viewing party at Sodō's house on the ninth day of the tenth month. We did so because the flower buds had still been hard on the ninth day of the ninth month, the normal day for such an event. There is a Chinese poem that says, "It is a chrysanthemum festival whenever chrysanthemum flowers open." Postponement of a chrysanthemum festival is not without precedent, either. For those reasons, we decided to have a party and write verses on autumn chrysanthemums.

chrysanthemums' scent—
in the garden, a worn-out sandal
upside down

kiku I no I ka I ya I niwa I ni I kiretaru I kutsu I no I soko
chrysanthemum I 's I scent I : I garden I in I broken I sandal I 's I bottom

NOTE
Written on November 6, which is the date mentioned in the introductory note. The Chinese poem cited is by Su Tung-p'o.

COMMENTARY
Sodō was famous for his love of chrysanthemums. Bashō went to his chrysanthemum garden and was enjoying the flowers in full bloom, when he caught sight of a worn-out sandal lying on the ground. The host must have worn it out as he frequented the garden so much and, man of *fūryū* as he was, he did not mind the sandal lying there. Bashō praised Sodō's character through this poem. – *Chikurei*

winter chrysanthemums
covered with rice bran
near the hand mill

kangiku | ya | konuka | no | kakaru | usu | no | hata
winter-chrysanthemum | : | bran | 's | fall | mortar | 's | edge

COMMENTARY

The juxtaposition of winter chrysanthemums and a hand mill covered with rice bran is very attractive. I am tempted to turn the scene into a painting. – *Meisetsu*

The poem is a vignette of peaceful life in the countryside in wintertime. – *Handa*

I visualize the yard of a farmhouse. The scene is rustic and lonely, well harmonizing with the impression of winter chrysanthemums. – *Seihō*

The pounding of rice in a hand mill was one of the commonest scenes in the domestic life of those times. But no one had ever written a verse about rice bran from the mill falling on winter chrysanthemums nearby. – *Imoto*

I ate vegetable roots and talked with samurai all day long.

samurai's gathering—
their chat has the pungent taste
of daikon radish

mononofu | no | daikon | nigaki | hanashi | kana
samurai | 's | daikon | pungent | chat | kana

NOTE

This was the opening verse of a haikai sequence Bashō wrote with two samurai. "I ate vegetable roots" in the headnote alludes to Wang Hsin-min's words: "A person who can get along just by chewing vegetable roots all the time will be able to achieve hundreds of things." Daikon is a large white radish commonly grown in Japan.

COMMENTARY

Because the headnote says "I ate vegetable roots," Bashō must have eaten daikon there, and its pungent taste on the tongue was felt to have something in common with the serious conversation that went on among the samurai that day. That became the theme of this hokku. – *Shūson*

The word "pungent" is not derogatory here. Their conversation was so serious that Bashō was amused as well as impressed. This poem must have softened the atmosphere of the party. The allusion to Wang's words also implies Bashō's respect for the people present. – *Iwata*

1694

Early in 1694, Bashō began planning for another westward journey. His frequent illnesses in the recent past had caused him to lose confidence in his health, and he wanted to see his relatives and friends in Ueno for one last time. In a letter dated February 13, he told a hometown friend that he would like to see him soon since "I feel my end is drawing near." He had also been disturbed at news of friction among his students in such western cities as Nagoya and Osaka, and he knew he was the only person capable of serving as a mediator. A third reason was more literary: having traveled to the far north, he now wanted to undertake a similar poetic journey to the far west, possibly as far as Shikoku and Kyushu, which he had never seen. It is not known, however, how serious he was about this intent, because he knew only too well that his health was failing. As a matter of fact, he had to postpone the start of the journey for health reasons. At first he had planned to set out in late April. For more than a month, however, he had to keep canceling the departure because of his physical condition.

Bashō was still healthy enough to go to haikai gatherings, and his disciples in Edo wanted to take advantage of his presence as long as he remained there. During that spring, he attended at least eight such parties and contributed verses on each occasion. All of these verses show the last phase of Bashō's poetic style, which he called *karumi*. At the last of those gatherings, which took place in late May, Bashō tried to explain what *karumi* meant. "The style I have in mind these days," he said, "is a light one both in form and in the method of linking verses, one that gives the impression of looking at a shallow river with a sandy bed." A number of students in Edo had gathered there to bid farewell to Bashō, and those words turned out to be the last direct guidance they were to receive from their teacher.

Bashō left Edo on June 3, carried on a litter. His hut was left to the care of the ailing Jutei and her two daughters. Jutei's only son, Jirōbei, accompanied Bashō to help him along the road. Anxious about his health, Sora traveled with him as far as Hakone even though he had not planned to do so at first. Unfortunately it was the rainy season, and the road was difficult even for young Jirōbei, but they arrived safely at Nagoya on June 14. Delighted friends and disciples in that area held a kasen party in Bashō's honor. Three days later he was on the road again, reaching Ueno on June 20. Poets in his hometown welcomed him, too, but he was too exhausted for poetic or social activities. He attended a verse-writing party only once during his two-week stay in Ueno. He had declined to participate even in that event at first, saying that "I do not feel ready to write poetry yet."

Tired or not, Bashō eventually had to go and meet with students in other areas, who he knew had been eagerly waiting for him. Leaving Ueno with Jirōbei on July 8, he traveled north and visited the Ōtsu area for four days. Then he moved to Kyoto and settled down at a familiar place, the Rakushi Villa. A number of friends and students visited him during the twenty-three days he was there. In a letter dated July 24, Bashō wrote: "Penniless students of mine in Kyoto and Osaka rush here one after another these days; they eat all the food available and spend their time in loud laughter." Of course, there were days without merry-making, too. Bashō and his students talked poetry and wrote haikai together, completing at least five kasen during his stay at the villa. He also received the shocking news, probably on July 28 or 29, that Jutei had died in the Bashō Hut. He was grief-stricken. In a letter dated July 29, he wrote: "Jutei was an unfortunate woman. So are her daughters, Masa and Ofū. I do not know what to say." At once, he sent Jirōbei back to Edo to help take care of the family matters.

Bashō left the Rakushi Villa on August 5 and went back to the area south of Lake Biwa, where he spent the next twenty days. His main residence during that period was another familiar place, the Mumyō Hut. He went out to participate in haikai gatherings in Ōtsu and Zeze from time to time; records of three such gatherings survive today. He was also pleased to hear that a new haikai collection of the Bashō school, entitled *Betsuzashiki* (The detached room) and published in Edo several months earlier, had been well received in the Kyoto area. Another anthology, *Sumidawara*, was published by his students in Edo on August 18. "The reputation of *Betsuzashiki* and *Sumidawara* has been remarkable," he jubilantly told Sora in a letter a short time later.

Bashō moved out of the Mumyō Hut on August 25 and, after spending a few days in Kyoto, returned to Ueno and settled down in a new cottage that local students had built for him in back of his brother's house. He thanked them by hosting a moon-viewing party on the night of the harvest moon, which was October 3. Unlike the last time he spent in Ueno, he was quite active during this two-month period. Thirteen hai-kai sequences he participated in during that period have survived. It may be that he was eager to teach *karumi* to the local poets, whose style seemed too old-fashioned to him. In a letter to Kyorai, he reported: "Recently there have been a number of haikai parties, but poets here have not yet been able to accept the *karumi* style, and their halfhearted efforts have resulted in nothing but mediocre verses. I am worried."

The same wish to propagate *karumi* must have been one of the main motives for his trip to Osaka, which he began on October 26. Probably because of his frail health, four people traveled with him: two students, his nephew Mataemon, and Jirōbei, who had returned from Edo by that time. They stopped in Nara that evening and enjoyed themselves observing the chrysanthemum festival there the following day. But almost as soon as they reached Osaka later that same day, Bashō fell ill. In order not to disappoint the local poets who had invited him, he forced himself to attend their haikai parties despite persistent headaches, fever, and chill.

He recovered a little on November 7, but the recovery was only temporary. Severe diarrhea started on November 15, and his already weakened body could not withstand it. According to one of his students, his emaciated figure looked like "a bare tree standing by a rock in winter." On November 26, Bashō knew his end was near. He stopped eating, washed himself, and had incense burnt. He called for a disciple and dictated three wills addressed to his relatives and friends. Then he managed to sit up and himself wrote a short letter to his older brother. It said, in part: "I am sure you will feel sorry that I go before you. I hope you will reach a ripe old age under Mataemon's care and complete your full life in peace and calm. There is nothing more I have to say." The following day he asked each of the attending students to write a verse for him, adding, "From this moment, assume that your teacher is gone. Don't ask me for advice even on one word." He was mostly asleep on November 28, but did wake up briefly around noon. As it was a balmy day, many flies had gathered around the sliding screens, and the students were trying to catch them with a lime stick. Bashō, amused that some were more skillful than others in handling the stick, laughed and said, "Those flies seem delighted to have a sick man around unexpectedly." He spoke no more. He breathed his last at around four that afternoon.

still alive
they are frozen in one lump
sea slugs

iki | nagara | hitotsu | ni | kōru | namako | kana
living | while | one | in | freeze | sea-slug | kana

COMMENTARY

This hokku reminds one of the scenes in Dante's *Divine Comedy* where traitors are frozen in the ice of the eight cold hells and greedy people of uncertain identity are writhing in the hell reserved for gluttons and misers. – *Abe J.*

I think the poet identified with the sea slugs and expressed his sympathy for them in this poem. – *Komiya*

I wonder if one doesn't find this hokku humorous when one thinks of a sea slug's dumb, slow-witted nature. – *Mizuho*

In this poem Bashō did not express his emotion overtly, but underneath the surface we recognize his love for little creatures. An inconsolable sorrow toward all living things passed through his mind at that time, like a cloud drifting across the sky. – *Handa*

The poem reads smoothly, with no striking or emotive word in it. Yet I seem to hear the poet's sigh in its depths. – *Iwata*

The hokku has captured the impression of intense winter cold through the image of sea slugs. – *Kon*

housecleaning day—
hanging a shelf at his own home
a carpenter

susuhaki I wa I ono I ga I tana I tsuru I daiku I kana
year-end-cleaning I as-for I self I 's I shelf I hang I carpenter I kana

NOTE

In preparation for the New Year, the Japanese traditionally cleaned their houses
on the thirteenth of the lunar twelfth month. Translated into the Gregorian calendar, that day in 1694 was January 8.

COMMENTARY

Normally a carpenter is so busy in working at other people's houses that he
would do nothing at his own home. But on the day of the year-end cleaning, he
cannot keep his eyes closed: he is repairing a broken shelf in his house. Bashō
took note of a happening unnoticed by other poets. — Donto

By describing a relaxed carpenter performing the rare role of a family man on the
annual housecleaning day, the poem creates the congenial atmosphere of a common household during the busy year-end period. The poet, drawing on a happening in ordinary life, has produced an exemplary poem that displays *karumi*.
— Kon

This carpenter had always wanted to improve and beautify his house. He had
been simply too busy, too tired, and consequently too lazy to do so. But this day
he was able to stay at home all day long, and that is why he began to work on
the shelf. The scene has humor, yet it also shows an ordinary man trying hard to
get on with his life. For that reason, we cannot regard the situation as only a
laughing matter. There is something human and warm, something redolent of
the common man, that underlies the poem and adds a touch of pathos. This is
another of the *karumi* poems Bashō wrote in his last years. — Imoto

there too was a night
when a robber visited my home—
the year's end

nusubito | ni | ōta | yo | mo | ari | toshi | no | kure
robber | with | have-met | night | also | is | year | 's | end

COMMENTARY

Whether in ancient or modern times, men tend to become more reckless and un-principled toward the end of the year, when all debts have to be paid off. Bashō was victimized by one such desperate man. —*Kōseki*

The poet calmly reflected on the past year and recalled the times when the rough waves of earthly life had closed in on his quiet residence. He felt neither anger nor sorrow. All there was in his mind was loneliness that quietly enwrapped the world with its shadow. —*Shūson*

in the scent of plums
suddenly the sun peeps out—
the mountain path

ume I ga I ka I ni I notto I hi I no I deru I yamaji I kana
plum I 's I scent I in I suddenly I sun I 's I rise I mountain-road I kana

COMMENTARY

There was still unmelted snow in the shade, and the lingering cold penetrated the skin. The poet had seen no sign of spring while climbing up the mountain road. But as he reached the peak he found the morning sun shining on a very peaceful landscape. Plum blossoms bloomed fragrantly, too, adding to the beauty of the scene. – *Donto*

The phrase "in the scent of blossoms" shows Bashō's characteristic elegance. Buson would have said "in the white plum blossoms" or "in the pink plum blossoms." The merging of the two sensations, one smelled through the nose and the other seen through the eye, is attractive too. This is a pleasant poem that makes the reader see a refreshingly beautiful scene alongside a mountain road at dawn on a February day. – *Mizuho*

All blossoms, including the plum, emit a stronger smell when they begin to bloom in the morning sun. – *Rohan*

This hokku can be said to be one of the most representative verses that show Bashō's idea of *karumi*. It has a plain theme as well as a lighthearted tone, and yet it makes us sense the presence of something rich. – *Shida*

on some boil
it seems to touch—the supple
branch of a willow

haremono | ni | sawaru | yanagi | no | shinae | kana
boil | on | touch | willow | 's | bend | kana

COMMENTARY

The poet suggested the suppleness of a willow branch by saying that whenever it touches anything it does so in such a manner as if it were touching on a boil. Observe the art of haikai that utilizes something as inelegant as a boil. – *Tosai*

This hokku should be read as an allegorical poem meaning, "In living this life, one should act with the flexibility of a willow branch touching on a boil." – *Kōseki*

While advocating *karumi* in his last years, Bashō also exercised his abnormally sharpened sensibility, in this instance by capturing the delicate suppleness of a drooping willow branch. – *Ogata*

spring rain—
down along a wasps' nest, water
leaking through the roof

harusame | ya | hachi | no | su | tsutau | yane | no | mori
spring-rain | : | wasp | 's | nest | go-along | roof | 's | leak

COMMENTARY

The image of a wasps' nest invites the reader to imagine an uninhabited hut that is left to fall into ruin. – *Shōgatsudō*

I think this describes a lonely residence rather than an uninhabited hut or temple. The scene focuses on a wasps' nest. The sooty ceiling, the timeworn tatami, even the soft sound of spring rain, can easily be imagined. – *Abe Y.*

Of course, the wasps' nest was from the summer of the previous year or earlier; it, too, looked very old. The leak through the roof attracted the poet's attention to the old nest, and it is interesting to imagine how he must have felt at that moment. The poem well suggests the mood created by spring rain. – *Watsuji*

Of course, the setting is not a palace shining like gold, but one need not go so far as to make it a dilapidated hut. In my reading, the poet was seated on the veranda of a large country house and looking vacantly at the rainwater running down the roof to the eaves and then to the wasps' nest, finally dripping down on the ground. – *Ebara*

There is no evidence in the hokku to prove that the nest is of the previous year. Quite possibly it was a new one. If wasps were still living in it, and if the leaking rain was running down alongside it, that creates a pitiful impression, an impression distinctly different from that created by the image of an old, empty nest. This reading of the poem makes it seem attractive enough. – *Shida*

What is original in this hokku lies in the poet's discovery of leaking water running down a wasps' nest. The hokku has captured the essence of spring rain. It is plain and yet has *yojō*—a fine poem written in the *karumi* style. – *Imoto*

green willow branches
hanging down on the mud
at low tide

aoyagi | no | doro | ni | shidaruru | shiohi | kana
green-willow | 's | mud | on | hang | low-tide | kana

NOTE

One text has the headnote "The third day of the third month," a day that was
believed to cause the lowest tide in the entire lunar year. Translated into the Gregorian calendar, the day was March 28, 1694.

COMMENTARY

A willow tree by the riverside, which usually dipped its branches in the abundant
water, presented a rare sight that day because of the low tide: it hung down on
the mud. The haikai humor lies in this image of tree branches touching on the
mud. — *Somaru*

I wonder if the hokku does not hint at the figure of a courtesan who, having enjoyed a little drink, came out to the beach to pick seashells. — *Tosai*

Black mud is dripping from the green branches of a willow tree. That is a rather
unusual choice of scene, and I think this is an interesting poem. — *Meisetsu*

Verdant branches of a willow and slimy mud on the seashore at low tide. Certainly the scene stirs a poet's creative urge. — *Seishi*

The poem simply describes nature as it is, and yet there is something serene and
reposeful in it. It shows the ripeness of Bashō's art. — *Iwata*

hydrangea and a wild
thicket, providing a little garden
for this cottage

ajisai | ya | yabu | wo | koniwa | no | betsuzashiki
hydrangea | : | thicket | [acc.] | small-garden | 's | detached-room

NOTE
Written as the opening verse for a kasen at a farewell party held in Bashō's honor
at the house of his student Shisan (?–1699).

COMMENTARY

As Master Bashō was soon to start on a journey, I invited him to my cottage and,
after urging him to come home next spring, asked him to talk about haikai. He
responded: "The style I have in mind these days is a light one both in form and in
the method of linking verses, one that gives the impression of looking at a shallow river with a sandy bed. Verses become especially meaningful when their style
reaches that point." All those who were present were deeply impressed and
vowed to try writing in that style. Then we begged him to compose a hokku on a
thicket in the garden and, unskilled poets though we were, we participated in
writing verses that followed his until a kasen was completed. – Shisan

A cottage that utilizes the edge of a wild thicket for its garden is often seen in a
rustic area. A hydrangea is often found in such a thicket because it is a plant that
loves shade and coolness. – Nobutane

The poet lauded the host's simple taste by a simple description of what he saw. It
seems that he wrote this artless verse to show Shisan and others how to practice
the principle of karumi. – Yamamoto

I left Edo in the fifth month of the seventh year of Genroku. For those who came to see me off, I wrote

clutching wheat ears
to support myself, I bid
farewell

mugi | no | ho | wo | chikara | ni | tsukamu | wakare | kana
wheat | 's | ear | [acc.] | strength | for | clutch | parting | kana

NOTE
Written on June 3, when Bashō set out on his last westward journey.

COMMENTARY
About to part with his friends, the poet felt so weak that he staggered and had to get hold of wheat ears to support himself. The hokku expresses the sadness of parting by referring to some ears of wheat that happened to be nearby. Also implied is his feeling that although he was growing old and more helpless than ever on the road, he could no longer depend on their assistance. Grabbing ears of wheat for support is uniquely imaginative. The hokku beautifully articulates the sadness of parting. – *Meisetsu*

In China, people who part pluck branches of a willow tree. Here the poet used wheat instead, and therein lies the spirit of haikai. – *Rohan*

The ears of wheat were actually in front of the poet's eyes. Yet he did not actually grab them; he just felt like grabbing them. – *Ebara*

This hokku is not as fine a farewell poem as the one Bashō wrote on his previous journey:

departing spring—   yuku haru ya
birds weep, and fishes' eyes   tori naki uo no
are tearful   me wa namida

That is because the poet's emotion is more manifest on the surface of the poem. – *Yamamoto*

The image of wheat ears came to Bashō's mind because this poem was a response to some farewell verses written by his students, several of whom had used the same image. It was the climax of his poetic exchange with them. If that was the

case, I wonder whether "clutching wheat ears to support myself" does not suggest the poet's wish to lean on their hearts (represented by the image of wheat ears) for his spiritual support. The hokku contains a reconfirmation of his bond with them, as well as his reflection, sympathy, gratitude, and sadness at parting.
—*Ogata*

A helpless, lonely feeling at parting is well expressed in the poet's attempt to use wheat ears for supporting himself, for wheat stems are not strong enough to bear his weight. Indeed, Bashō was never again to see those who parted with him here. He may have had some premonition. The poem resounds with sorrow.
—*Iwata*

In fully grown wheat ears reside the forces of health and life. The goodwill of my friends, who have come to see me off, is as encouraging to me as those wheat ears. It is on the strength of that encouragement that I start on this long journey. . . . This is an occasional poem addressed to the well-wishers; but, filled with the poet's sincerity, it is far more than an ordinary poem of courtesy.
—*Konishi*

Emerging from this poem is a portrait of Bashō enfeebled by old age and chronic illnesses. —*Kon*

long seasonal rain—
a silkworm ailing
in the mulberry field

samidare | ya | kaiko | wazurau | kuwa | no | hata
fifth-month-rain | : | silkworm | ail | mulberry | 's | field

COMMENTARY

In my area, diseased silkworms are buried in the mulberry field. But some silkworms escape from the hole and climb up mulberry trees. Also, ailing silkworms
that have been dumped out with the garbage are often seen later perching on
mulberry trees. I think Bashō wrote this poem when he saw such silkworms.
— *Mizuho*

In my opinion, there is only one silkworm involved here. If we were to visualize
ten or twenty of them, that would completely change the tone of the poem.
— *Komiya*

This poem revives in me the kind of sympathy I used to feel toward discarded,
ailing silkworms when I was a child. – *Abe J.*

It was the rainy season and the sky was dark. Some silkworms thrown away at a
corner of the mulberry field were writhing in the rain, looking as though they
would not live much longer. That lonely, sad sight tugged at the poet's heart.
— *Ebara*

The poet saw his own image in the lone silkworm ailing in the mulberry field.
— *Yamamoto*

Silkworms are prone to illness, not when they are very young, but when they
have grown to the point where they are almost ready to begin weaving cocoons.
Here a number of grown-up silkworms are eating mulberry leaves without
knowing that they have become ill and been dumped. It is a pitiful sight. Bashō
described it skillfully by a simple but emotion-laden middle phrase. – *Utsubo*

The poet gave form to the gloom of the rainy season by focusing on an ailing
silkworm. – *Kon*

On entering Suruga Province

the Suruga road—
orange blossoms also
smell like tea

Surugaji l ya l hanatachibana l mo l cha l no l nioi
Suruga-road l : l blossoming-orange l also l tea l 's l smell

COMMENTARY

This province is noted for its tea. The poet therefore praised the famous product as he reached there. Facing an ocean in the south, Suruga is also a warm province where many orange trees grow. The hokku says that even the scent of orange blossoms is overwhelmed by the smell of tea. It implies that other things, too, are surrounded by the same smell. – *Nobutane*

Whenever Bashō included a place name in his poem, he infused it with an extraordinary amount of emotion. One might say he had a kind of religious faith in place names. Suruga, in particular, was a familiar province for him, a province he passed through a number of times as he traveled along the Pacific coast. He complimented that province by referring to its two famous products, the tea and the orange. – *Yamamoto*

On the surface the poem implies that the smell of new tea has overmatched that of orange blossoms, but the poet's intent probably lay in presenting two objects with exquisite fragrances and thereby suggesting the bright, pleasant, refreshing feeling of traveling along the Suruga road. – *Iwata*

long seasonal rain—
blast down that sky,
Ōi River!

samidare | no | sora | fuki | otose | Ōigawa
fifth-month-rain | 's | sky | blowing | let-fall | Ōi-River

NOTE
Written at Shimada, a town located by the Ōi River. Bashō arrived there on June
7 but could not cross the river for the next three days because of a rainstorm.

COMMENTARY
Because of the continuing rain, the Ōi River was flowing with torrential force.
The poet commanded the river to use that force and blast down the dark rain-
clouds that covered the sky. — *Abe Y.*

I think his command was directed toward the wind, and not toward the water.
— *Mizuho*

Of course the poet was calling to the wind, but he made no mention of the wind
in the poem. He made it sound as if he were speaking to the river. Therein lies
Bashō's craftsmanship. — *Rohan*

Bashō had become extremely impatient, as the storm kept raging and the water
did not recede. That impatience exploded, resulting in this hokku. In essence the
poem expresses the poet's wish for a clear day, but the phrase "blast down that
sky" is fully suggestive of his intense emotion. He called out to the furious gale,
"Blow down that rainy sky into the flooded river and let it be carried away in the
torrent!" Here is a bold, magnificent fancy. — *Shida*

I do not share the view that Bashō's irritated state of mind resulted in the strong
tone of this poem. Like

gathering the rains   samidare wo
of the wet season, how swiftly flows   atsumete hayashi
the Mogami River!   Mogamigawa

this hokku also expresses the poet's amazement at the force of the torrential
flow. The amazement led him to use the expression in the poem that makes him
sound as if he were calling out to the Ōi River. — *Yamamoto*

the coolness—
growing straight, the branches
of a wild pine

suzushisa | ya | suguni | nomatsu | no | eda | no | nari
coolness | : | straight | wild-pine | 's | branch | 's | form

NOTE

Written on the night of July 3, when Bashō visited the house of Hirooka Sesshi (1670–1711), an amateur poet in Ueno.

COMMENTARY

The poet was refreshing himself in the shade of a towering old pine tree. The hokku implies that no pine tree grown under men's care would produce such coolness. — *Donto*

The pine tree, because it grew straight up, gave an impression of coolness. The poem is an objective sketch of a refreshing scene, but there is also a covert suggestion that the master of the house is as pleasant as the scene is. — *Meisetsu*

This is purely a landscape painting. — *Akutagawa*

the sixth month—
with clouds laid on its summit
Mount Arashi

rokugatsu | ya | mine | ni | kumo | oku | Arashiyama
sixth-month | : | peak | on | cloud | lay | Mount-Arashi

NOTE
Written at the Rakushi Villa. Mt. Arashi (literally "storm mountain"), renowned since ancient times for its cherry blossoms and autumn leaves, could be seen from there. In 1694 the lunar sixth month lasted from July 22 through August 20.

COMMENTARY
I heard that Master Bashō had taken a great many pains in composing the last two phrases. – *Dohō*

One might expect Mt. Storm to blow the clouds away. Yet the clouds stayed immobile, and the poet felt this was typical of the sixth month. The hokku hints at the unbearable heat of the day without saying so. – *Tosai*

In spring, fully opened cherry blossoms look like clouds. Now the poet looked at clouds hanging over the peak and was reminded of those blossoms. – *Kobayashi*

Mt. Arashi immediately makes us visualize an elegant scene with cherry blossoms or crimson leaves, but this poem describes the mountain under the sweltering sky in midsummer. The mountain is covered with dense green foliage, and cumulus clouds are billowing from behind its summit. Unlike the feminine scenes of spring and autumn, here is a masculine, strongly colored landscape. – *Ebara*

This poem, written at the Rakushi Villa, implicitly complimented the owner of the cottage by praising the scenery around it. The hokku's last two phrases are in praise of Mt. Arashi in midsummer, but Bashō did so in order to praise the villa. – *Yamamoto*

At first glance one might think the clouds on the peak could be of any shape or kind. But as long as midsummer is implied in the first phrase and a storm in the last, they must be thunderclouds. – *Andō*

in the morning dew
spotted with mud, and how cool—
melons on the soil

asatsuyu I ni I yogorete I suzushi I uri I no I tsuchi
morning-dew I in I smudged I cool I melon I 's I soil

COMMENTARY

This hokku refers to a person whose appearance is like a melon smeared with mud in the morning dew, but whose heart is so spotless that his effect on other people is like that of a cool breeze. – *Shōgatsudō*

Some may say muddy melons are dirty and give no impression of coolness. Exercise some poetic imagination, though, and you will see that melons look appealing precisely because they are spotted with mud. Clean melons are a common sight, with no appeal to the imagination. – *Meisetsu*

The poem makes me want to get up early in the morning. – *Mizuho*

The poem shows Bashō's art in its maturity. But, as far as this type of poetry is concerned, Buson seems to have been his superior. – *Higuchi*

plates and bowls
dim in the twilight—
the evening cool

sarabachi | mo | honokani | yami | no | yoisuzumi
plate-bowl | also | faintly | darkness | 's | evening-cool

COMMENTARY

The poet, while cooling off outdoors, looked back toward the room where he
had just finished supper. In the dusk nothing was distinguishable, except plates
and bowls that loomed white. — *Shinpū*

A poem that uses commonplace material like tableware and still creates such an
exquisite scene could have been written only by a poet of extraordinarily refined
sensibility. — *Handa*

The fact that people went out to get cool without doing the dishes suggests intol-
erable heat continuing indoors. The scene does not seem to be that of a rural village; it was probably somewhere on a back street or at the edge of downtown.
— *Utsubo*

In order to let the cool air in no lamp had been lit, although the room was dark.
The breeze finally began to feel cooler. In the dark, plates and bowls loomed
dimly white, faintly showing the designs on them. The poet found some coolness
in the tactile sensation he imagined being emitted by the chinaware. — *Yamamoto*

The poem, taking its material from daily life, has skillfully captured coolness
through visual images. — *Kon*

At Bokusetsu's hut in Ōtsu on the twenty-first day of the sixth month in the seventh year of Genroku

sensing autumn's approach
four hearts draw together
in a small tea room

aki I chikaki I kokoro I no I yoru I ya I yojōhan
autumn I nearing I heart I 's I draw I : I four-mat-half

NOTE

Mochizuki Bokusetsu, a physician, was an amateur poet belonging to the Bashō school. The date mentioned in the headnote is August 11. *Yojōhan* refers to a tea room that is usually four-and-a-half mats wide.

COMMENTARY

The hokku's beginning phrase suggests loneliness, whereas the concluding one hints at warmth. In my opinion, this poem describes autumn loneliness being dispelled by the warmth of friendship. – *Watsuji*

As we read this poem closely, we feel as if Bashō, when he sensed autumn's approach, also heard the faint footsteps of death coming closer. – *Shūson*

Three students and their teacher sat close together in a tea room, which was only four-and-a-half mats wide. Bashō, grief-stricken at the news of Jutei's death, found something heartwarming in the atmosphere of that gathering in the tiny room. – *Yamamoto*

On the wall of a stage at Honma Shume's house, there hung a picture of skeletons playing music and performing a nō play. Is anything people do in their lifetime different from this picture? Chuang-tzu, who once used a skeleton for his pillow when he slept, said he could not distinguish reality from dream. His purpose in doing so was to suggest the insubstantiality of human life.

a flash of lightning—
where there were faces
plumes of pampas grass

inazuma | ya | kao | no | tokoro | ga | susuki | no | ho
lightning | : | face | 's | place | [nom.] | pampas-grass | 's | plume

NOTE
Honma Shume, who wrote haikai under the name Tan'ya, was a nō actor living in Ōtsu. In an episode referred to in the headnote, Chuang-tzu was told in a dream by a skeleton that man is happier after death because he is free of the worries he must face in the present life. The last two phrases of the hokku allude to a legend about a famous poetess, Ono no Komachi. According to the legend, when Komachi died and was reduced to a skeleton, plumes of pampas grass grew where her eyes had been.

COMMENTARY
After establishing his own style, Bashō almost completely stopped writing on ghostly themes. But his verses on the impermanence of life still continued to show something eerie in mood, if not in theme. – *Akutagawa*

From the viewpoint of an enlightened man, the pleasure derived from playing music is nothing more than a dance of death, and everything else in life is like that, too. – *Kōseki*

This is a philosophical poem that conveys life's mutability through a vision of dancing skeletons, but its macabre beauty also has a certain sensuous appeal. – *Kon*

it feels cool
to put the feet against the wall . . .
a midday nap

hiyahiya I to I kabe I wo I fumaete I hirune I kana
cool I so I wall I [acc.] I planting-feet-on I midday-nap I kana

COMMENTARY

"How do you read this hokku?" Master Bashō asked me. "I think it is about lingering summer heat," I answered. "The person in this hokku is sunk in thought, perhaps with the cord of a mosquito net coiled around his hand." The master laughed and said, "You've solved the riddle!" – *Shikō*

The poem well depicts the carefree, relaxed life of a recluse. Because it was so hot, he had raised his feet and put them against the wall while lying on his back. The wall, having somehow absorbed autumn's coolness from the air, felt cool to his feet. The poem is also a good depiction of lingering heat. – *Meisetsu*

Product of a townsman's life and written in a lighthearted tone, the poem nevertheless has something in it that makes everyone nod in agreement. – *Shūson*

The poet was not asleep, since he could feel the coolness. Lying on his back, he was thinking of things. Yet if he had said

it feels cool	hiyahiya to
to put the feet against the wall . . .	kabe wo fumaete
I think of things	mono omou

it would not only have been an inferior poem but would have reduced the spirit of haikai. The strength of this hokku is that, through the word "a midday nap," it makes the reader visualize a person sunk in thought. Of the things Bashō thought of, one must surely have been the late Jutei. – *Imoto*

At the news of the nun Jutei's death

never think of yourself
as someone who did not count—
festival of the souls

kazu | naranu | mi | to | na | omoiso | tamamatsuri
number | is-not | person | so | not | think | soul-festival

NOTE

Tamamatsuri, more commonly known as *urabon* (the *bon* festival), is an annual
Buddhist rite at which each family offers prayers to the souls of its ancestors. In
Bashō's time it was held for four days, beginning on the thirteenth of the lunar
seventh month. In 1694, that day was September 2.

COMMENTARY

In this world there are the noble and the humble, but after death there are no
such social distinctions. The poet wrote this hokku on the festival of souls to imply how far-reaching Buddha's teaching is. – *Ōsha*

Do not consider yourself too humble a person to accept the prayers I am offering
at this rite today. That is what this hokku means, I think. – *Tosai*

The tone of the poem is so touching, it is as though the poet were calling to the
woman right in front of him, with no one else allowed to come near them. It is as
though the poet thought that he must tell the woman how important she had
been in his life, that unless he did so she would think poorly of herself and disappear from his sight, so that he wanted to call her back and encourage her.
– *Shūson*

Bashō attended the annual service for the dead at his native home in Ueno. But
the service was for the Matsuo clan, and the family shrine had no memorial tab-
let for Jutei. Kneeling before the shrine, Bashō recited Jutei's name and offered
his sincerest prayers. As he thought of Jutei's status, which precluded her from
the family shrine, he could not help saying "never think of yourself as someone
who did not count." – *Imoto*

a flash of lightning—
passing through the darkness
a night heron's scream

inazuma | ya | yami | no | kata | yuku | goi | no | koe
lightning | : | darkness | 's | direction | go | night-heron | 's | voice

COMMENTARY

This is a charming scene, with a night heron crying in a lonely voice as it passes over dusky pine trees lining the road, and with a flash of lightning momentarily illuminating the field that looms vague in the evening twilight. – *Donto*

Lightning flashed. The next moment a night heron, flying in the opposite direction, passed through the darkness with a scream. I have often heard a night heron's cry near my former residence, and I can tell you that it is weird and ghastly. The scream harmonizes well with the lightning in this fine poem, creating an eerie beauty. – *Keion*

Noteworthy is the mental process through which visual awareness of the lightning is transformed, suddenly and yet naturally, into aural awareness of a heron's cry passing through the darkness. – *Handa*

Because a night heron has not only a terrifying voice but lustrous wings that show up in the dark, it has often appeared in ghost stories since ancient times. The flash of lightning that cuts through the dark and the uncanny cry of such a bird create an eerie atmosphere, making the reader feel as if a ghost were close by. – *Ebara*

village has grown old—
not a single house without
persimmon trees

sato I furite I kaki I no I ki I motanu I ie I mo I nashi
village I aging I persimmon I 's I tree I have-not I house I even I nonexistent

NOTE
Written on September 25, when there was a haikai gathering at the house of Katano Bōsui (?–1705), a merchant in Ueno.

COMMENTARY
The hokku makes us visualize a peaceful, affluent village. — *Tosai*

In Ueno there were many persimmon trees, with at least two or three of them to be seen around every house. When the poet looked at a persimmon tree growing tall in Bōsui's yard, he was struck with the poignant reflection that this area had been settled for a long time. In artless, plain wording, the poem expresses how the poet felt. The vermilion of the fruit is a very effective touch, contributing to the atmosphere of an old village. — *Shūson*

Through the poem Bashō paid respect to Bōsui, yet that implication is so subtle and so hidden in its artless means of expression that the reader has to detect it spontaneously. — *Iwata*

winter melons—
what changes there have been
on each other's faces!

tōgan | ya | tagai | ni | kawaru | kao | no | nari
winter-melon | : | each-other | to | change | face | 's | appearance

COMMENTARY

The poet met someone after many years, and they found each other's faces had greatly changed because of gray hair, wrinkles on the forehead, etc. The hokku begins with the image of a winter melon because it is not shapely like a watermelon or cucumber but has a kind of primitive beauty with its white-powdered surface and angular shape. — *Kōseki*

Flowing underneath is sadness over the passage of time, accompanied by a bit of humor. — *Shūson*

looking as though
the harvest moon had blossomed,
a cotton field

meigetsu | no | hana | ka | to | miete | watabatake
harvest-moon | 's | flower | ? | so | looking | cotton-field

NOTE
Written in Ueno on the night of the harvest moon, which was October 3.

COMMENTARY
Everything within the poet's sight was white, looking as if the moonbeams had fallen to earth as flowers. – *Tosai*

The poet, seeing opened cotton bolls displaying their white fibers in the moonlight, wondered if they were not flowers in bloom. – *Ōtani*

departing autumn—
with their hands opened wide
chestnut burs

yuku | aki | ya | te | wo | hirogetaru | kuri | no | iga
go | autumn | : | hand | [acc.] | spread | chestnut | 's | bur

NOTE
Written in Ueno on October 23, three days before Bashō's scheduled departure.

COMMENTARY
Near the end of autumn all chestnuts fall from the trees, leaving only empty burs
on the branches. The leaves are all gone, too, in the gusty wind that blows for
days, and the trees look lonely in the faint rays of the setting sun. In this kind of
setting, the chestnut burs that still remain here and there on the trees with their
"hands" open look forlorn indeed. To suggest the sadness of autumn, poets commonly used a broken-down subject like dead pampas grass. Bashō's uncommon
talent can be seen in his choice of tough-looking chestnut burs for that purpose.
– *Kobayashi*

The chestnut burs were not lying on the ground but were still attached to the
bare branches. To the poet, they looked as if they were trying to stop autumn,
which was preparing to depart. – *Ebara*

The hokku's middle phrase can be read as referring to either open arms or open
palms. My choice is for arms, spreading left and right. – *Shūson*

The middle phrase, which depicts chestnut burs split open, is the focus of this
hokku and, unlike Shūson, I think it refers to open palms. Palms that have been
tightly closed are now open; they suggest the gesture of people who, lovers of autumn as they are, try to prevent its departure. That image also hints at the sentiment of Bashō's students who did not want to see him go. He on his part made
his departure feeling as if his heart were being left behind, and that is what this
poem expresses. – *Yamamoto*

With quick steps autumn makes its way through a grove of tinted leaves, the
dark world of winter its destination. As autumn hurries forward, a chestnut
blocks the way with its arms fully open, even spreading its fingers as wide as it
can. When autumn moves one step forward, the next tree opens its hands; then
another, and still another. The chestnuts, though looking full of fun, are laden

with the sad awareness that, in the end, they cannot stop the march of the seasons. Such was the imaginary scene created by the sad thoughts of Bashō, who wanted to block the way of autumn as it hurried toward the season of death.
— *Ogata*

Most chestnuts fall during the night, when no one is watching. People often notice burs on the branches only after they have become empty. Those burs—especially the ones "with their hands open"—are the most noticeable sign of departing autumn for those who live in a mountainous area. Not all such burs show their insides; a good number of them are open only halfway. It was observant of Bashō to notice those burs. He wanted to convey to his students that he would be leaving them without notice (one record says that "he set out in the morning fog, saying he found it difficult to handle friends' farewells"). More important, he wanted to transmit the mood of departing autumn, which looked contented and without remorse, through the image of chestnut burs. Many readers think this poem describes chestnut burs (people of Ueno) trying to prevent the departure of autumn (Bashō). Their sentimental reading is precisely the opposite of what the poet is trying to say. — *Andō*

chrysanthemums' scent—
in Nara, many ancient
Buddhas

kiku I no I ka I ya I Nara I ni I wa I furuki I hotoketachi
chrysanthemum I 's I scent I : I Nara I in I as-for I old I Buddhas

NOTE
Written in Nara on October 27, the day of the chrysanthemum festival. Nara
was the capital of Japan from 710 to 784, a period that saw Buddhism flourish
as a state religion.

COMMENTARY
The elegant and noble fragrance of chrysanthemums is presented through the image of ancient Buddhist statues. The fragrance represents the statues and vice
versa. – *Mizuho*

This poem exemplifies the ultimate in *yūgen* style. – *Komiya*

The chrysanthemum's scent, which is not sensual and yet is pure and strong, fits
in well here. – *Abe Y.*

This is abstract verse. I do not think it makes a good poem. – *Rohan*

The pure, exquisite fragrance of chrysanthemums and the solemn, lonely appearance of old Buddhist images are united through poetic association and thereby
given a new life. This poem, therefore, is not a sketch of what he actually saw.
His mind's eye had turned toward the realm of *sabi* that extended infinitely beyond the chrysanthemums and the ancient Buddhas. – *Handa*

Both "chrysanthemums' scent" and "many ancient Buddhas" were actually before the poet's eyes. Those two things, however, were not directly related to each
other; they were brought together by the poet's feeling for them. We all know the
smell of orange blossoms reminds us of our old friends and bygone days. In the
same way, all other scents evoke characteristic associations. Especially the chrysanthemum, which is featured in many old legends, awakens nostalgic sentiments in us with its scent. This, then, could be the connecting link between the
chrysanthemums and the ancient Buddhas. – *Shida*

Because it was the day of the chrysanthemum festival, Bashō must have seen any
number of chrysanthemums in Nara. Yet even without them the mind of the
poet, who had chosen that particular day to come to Nara, was filled with the

chrysanthemums' scent—
in Nara, many ancient
Buddhas

*Painting and calligraphy by Bashō. Repro-
duced from* Zusetsu Nihon no koten: Bashō
Buson *(Shūeisha), by permission of Idemitsu
Art Museum.*

scent of chrysanthemums. That imaginary scent became a medium for recollecting the past glory of Nara. It came to provide the basic tone for the poet's reminiscences as well as for this poem, eventually leading to the image of ancient Buddhas. – *Yamamoto*

Of all the flowers the chrysanthemum has the noblest fragrance and reminds us of the smell of incense offered to Buddha. – *Utsubo*

This poem includes what Bashō called *nioi*. In connecting two haikai verses he advocated "linking through *nioi*," some delicate, almost imperceptible flow of air moving from one verse to the next. Here is that *nioi* within a single verse. – *Iwata*

While visiting the Sumiyoshi Fair on the thirteenth

a measuring box I bought
made me change my mind
about moon viewing

masu I kōte I funbetsu I kawaru I tsukimi I kana
measuring-box I buying I reasoning I change I moon-viewing I kana

NOTE

The opening verse for a kasen to be composed at the house of Hasegawa Keishi
(?–1695?), an Osaka poet, on November 1. Bashō had been invited by Keishi to
a moon-viewing party the previous night, but he had fallen ill earlier that day
and could only send this hokku through a messenger. *Masu* refers to boxes of
various sizes with which to measure the volume of grain or liquid. These boxes
were frequently found at a merchant's, but a housewife also used one regularly
for measuring the amount of rice to cook for each meal. The Sumiyoshi Fair was
famous for selling those boxes and other household utensils.

COMMENTARY

A measuring box is a household utensil. Once a person had bought such a box,
he would feel like buying a pan and a bucket, too. A hermit who started doing
this would be taking the first steps in the wrong direction. This hokku, then, provides a moral lesson. – *Shikō*

The poet is saying that, now he has bought a measure, he would like to stop
being a haikai master and become a merchant. That is a joke. In actuality he is
describing the fair, which was so crowded and lively as to destroy any inclination
for moon viewing. One should appreciate the humor of the poem. – *Tosai*

Bashō had been dissatisfied with himself because he could not completely drive
out all the worldly desires lurking in his heart. This poem is a hyperbolic expression of that dissatisfaction, an expression Bashō created with the kind of pain
one feels when one opens up an old wound. – *Komiya*

The poet forgot about the moon and went out to buy a measuring box, which is
said to bring in a good fortune. After buying the box, he chanced to look up at

the sky and discovered the moon of the thirteenth night. At that his frame of mind completely changed: he now wanted to enjoy the view of the moon.
– *Abe J.*

In actuality Bashō had to go home without stopping at Keishi's house because he felt a chill, so he said, "A measuring box I bought changed my mind," as a way of apologizing for not attending the party. – *Ōtani*

At Shioe Shayō's house on the twenty-first day of the ninth month

autumn night—
striking and making it crumble
this jovial chat

aki I no I yo I wo I uchi I kuzushitaru I hanashi I kana
autumn I 's I night I [acc.] I striking I demolish I chat I kana

NOTE

Written on November 8, the day mentioned in the headnote. Shayō, an Osaka
merchant, was a student in the Bashō school of haikai.

COMMENTARY

The conversation at the party reached a climax. Someone said something amusing, and the entire group burst out laughing. The laughter demolished the loneliness of the autumn night, making the atmosphere totally unseasonal. – *Meisetsu*

It is as if they shattered the autumn night and established a world of their own.
– *Abe Y.*

They erupted in laughter, which enhanced the stillness of the surroundings. I
think the contrast is attractive. – *Mizuho*

At this gathering Bashō helped to make peace between two factions of his students that had been at odds with each other. He deliberately used a rather exaggerated expression in the hokku's middle phrase to celebrate the reconciliation.
– *Iwata*

It was a rainy night in autumn. Hence, although the party was lively and the
people were relaxed and even laughing, all was surrounded by the lonely night.
Everywhere it was dark and lonely, with the exception of where the party was
being held. This poem, then, is about the autumn night, and the loneliness of
such a night courses through it. – *Imoto*

Bashō paid respect to his host by describing a congenial gathering, and yet his
words implicitly suggest the loneliness of autumn night. The hokku has complex
connotations. – *Kon*

Expressing how I feel

on this road
where nobody else travels
autumn nightfall

kono | michi | ya | yuku | hito | nashi | ni | aki | no | kure
this | road | : | go | person | nonexistent | with | autumn | 's | evening

NOTE

The opening verse of a half-kasen composed at an Osaka restaurant on November 13.

COMMENTARY

While singing of the loneliness of autumn, the poet deplored the scarcity of people following the way of haikai. — *Shōgatsudō*

This poem is more symbolic than allegorical. The instant we visualize the scene presented in it, we are struck by what Bashō had in mind. — *Komiya*

"This road" is a conceptual road that is all-inclusive. It is real, and yet ultimately it transcends reality. It is not as limited or identifiable as the road of haikai to which Bashō dedicated his entire life. — *Handa*

Sometimes we see a road without any passers-by, and that sight makes us realize how utterly lonely our life is. This hokku seems to embody loneliness of that kind, only more refined in quality by going through Bashō's mind. — *Saisei*

"This road" is not a road leading to a bright future. Standing at the "autumn nightfall" of his life, Bashō looked back to the road he had trodden. Thereupon it occurred to him that he had always been alone, that he would also be alone in the future, and that that was the fate given him. — *Yamamoto*

An artist's road is ultimately a lonely one. The greater the artist, the farther the distance between himself and the mass. — *Imoto*

For the aged and ailing poet, the road led straight to the nether world. Surely this poem pictures Bashō walking away all alone into that twilight. — *Miyamoto*

A wanderer's thought

this autumn
why am I aging so?
to the clouds, a bird

kono | aki | wa | nande | toshiyoru | kumo | ni | tori
this | autumn | as-for | why | grow-old | cloud | to | bird

NOTE
Written on the same day and at the same place as the previous hokku.

COMMENTARY
Master Bashō concentrated on composing this hokku from the morning onward.
He underwent a great deal of pain to write the concluding phrase. – *Shikō*

That autumn the poet felt especially tired and helpless, as if age had caught up
with him all of a sudden. I do not think the ending phrase describes what he actually saw. He used the expression to suggest how he felt as a wanderer. – *Mizuho*

The poet saw a bird flying near the clouds in actuality or in his mind, and that
prompted him to think of himself. – *Abe Y.*

The poet wrote "to the clouds, a bird" to express his lonely heart that longed to
be far away. – *Komiya*

The core of this poem lies in "to the clouds, a bird," which supports the two
phrases of monologue that precede it. The force of the last phrase is beyond
words. The deep solitude that has been given form here is not one that derives
from a particular cause. It is a more basic, existential solitude, the kind of solitude so profound that nothing can alleviate it. – *Shūson*

The concluding phrase presents a bird disappearing into the clouds, a solitary
bird that looks like a fading speck. In relation to the rest of the poem, the phrase
creates a kind of shock effect. The effect is more forceful than that of juxtaposition, so forceful, indeed, that it seems to make sparks fly. The poem succeeds in
conveying a deep allegorical message about human life. – *Yamamoto*

This is one of the poet's finest poems, as it beautifully symbolizes his life of wandering, his sad awareness of old age, and, above all, his loneliness. – *Kon*

white chrysanthemum
without a speck of dust
the eyes can catch

shiragiku | no | me | ni | tatete | miru | chiri | mo | nashi
white-chrysanthemum | 's | eye | in | catching | see | dust | even | nonexistent

NOTE

The opening verse of a kasen composed at Shiba Sono's house on November 14. Sono (1664–1726), one of Bashō's few women students, was living in Osaka at that time with her husband Ichiyū, a physician.

COMMENTARY

There is a waka written by Saigyō and included in *Sankashū* [no. 717]:

A clear mirror	kumori naki
with just a speck of dust—	kagami no ue ni
yet the eyes	iru chiri wo
have caught it, the world	me ni tatete miru
having become what it is.	yo to omowabaya
	– *San'u*

The poet implicitly praised Sono's pure heart and elegant taste. – *Rika*

I would prefer to read this strictly as a poem on white chrysanthemums.
– *Komiya*

As is customary in haikai, this hokku pays respect to the hostess. But it is wrong to assume that the poet created the image of a white chrysanthemum just to compliment Sono. He described the white, pure beauty of the flower because it happened to be there. That description came to imply the poet's respect for the hostess, with no deliberate intent on his part. – *Shūson*

All the hokku says is that the chrysanthemum is of a pure, shining white; it has no reference to anything else. It is the simplest kind of praise. Yet the poem emits the beauty of *yūgen*, helped by its melodiously flowing rhythm. The reader feels as if there were nothing between heaven and earth except a white chrysanthemum. – *Utsubo*

The haikai gathering was held in the morning. This hokku hints at the cold, nippy morning air. – *Yamamoto*

Written at Keishi's house on the topic
"Accompanying a lovely boy in the moonlight"

the moon is clear—
I escort a lovely boy
frightened by a fox

tsuki | sumu | ya | kitsune | kowagaru | chigo | no | tomo
moon | be-clear | : | fox | fear | boy-lover | 's | attendance

NOTE

Written on November 15 at a verse-writing party where poets were asked to
write a hokku on various topics related to love. In the haikai tradition the theme
of love covered a wide range of subtopics and included homosexual love, which
was prevalent in Bashō's day. Bashō himself, recalling his youth, once wrote:
"There was a time when I was fascinated with the ways of homosexual love." In
Japanese folklore, a fox has supernatural powers and often works mischief on
unsuspecting men.

COMMENTARY

With the image of a fox we can visualize the scene of a country lane at night,
where dead pampas grass and wild chrysanthemums are quivering in the wind;
the glint of dew under a clear moon further intensifies the loneliness of the scene.
The hokku has a touch of humor, too. – *Tosai*

Because all the hokku written at that party were on the theme of love, the boy in
this poem must be the younger partner in a homosexual liaison. He has parted
with his older partner and is now returning home with an attendant, but the attendant himself is more frightened at the prospect of encountering a fox. This
charming poem well describes the serene beauty of the moon and the loneliness
of the road they are walking along. – *Bakujin*

In my reading, the older lover himself is escorting the boy, who is afraid of walking alone at night. This reading enhances the warmth and intensity of the love
between the two lovers in the poem, and we know the poem was written on the
theme of love. – *Hyōroku*

Bashō's craftsmanship can be seen in his ability to work on such a topic as homosexual love and create a fairy-tale atmosphere out of it. I do not think this is

an especially good poem, but I cannot help smiling to think that Bashō retained his spirit of *fūryū* to the last. — *Handa*

The boy is afraid that a fox might jump onto the road ahead of him. A moonlit night is frightening in a way different from a dark night. The poem describes less the boy's pale face in the moonlight than night air that chills to the bone. — *Seihō*

On a clear moonlit night, the poet kept company with a lovely boy and walked along a country road. A fox's howl came from a distance. The boy was frightened, and in the way he looked then the poet saw something sensually beautiful. — *Ebara*

Bashō had written this type of verse in haikai sequences before. But he had written few hokku like this because, unlike hiraku, which were mostly composed out of pure imagination, hokku allowed him to express how he felt at that point in his life. The kind of aestheticism seen in this hokku was explored at length by Buson in later years. — *Shūson*

On a beautiful moonlit night, a man walks along a lonely road across the field, escorting his boy lover. Suddenly a fox's howl comes from somewhere in the vicinity. Frightened, the boy rushes into the man's arms. The poem creates a romantic, picturesque scene; it is written in what Bashō called "a narrative style." To his last days, Bashō did not reject this type of playful fancy in poetic composition. — *Yamamoto*

autumn deepens—
the man next door, what does he do
for a living?

aki | fukaki | tonari | wa | nani | wo | suru | hito | zo
autumn | deep | neighbor | as-for | what | [acc.] | do | person | ?

NOTE

Bashō had been invited to a verse-writing party on November 16, but because he
had not been feeling well he declined the invitation and had this hokku sent to
the host, Negoro Shihaku (?–1713). He seems to have written the hokku on November 15.

COMMENTARY

The loneliness of late autumn was too much for the poet to bear. He called out
to his neighbor, saying he would join him if there was some diversion they could
share. The hokku suggests the poet's life growing lonelier with deepening autumn. – *Donto*

During that long span of three hundred years, Bashō alone was capable of creating such solemn verbal music. – *Akutagawa*

The quiet house next door seemed eerie on a late autumn day. It looked haunted.
– *Mizuho*

Something in this poem makes me think of death. – *Watsuji*

It is like the sound of a temple bell trailing across an immense valley. – *Rohan*

I am against romantic interpretations that find eerie or ghostly qualities in this
poem. What I find is the opposite type of stillness, the type that touches the
heart. It is something peaceful and mysterious found at high noon, with nothing
ghostly about it. – *Abe J.*

Bashō was not able to attend the verse-writing party held at Shihaku's house.
This hokku expresses both his irritation at not being able to go and his envy at
the imagined success of the gathering. – *Handa*

The quiet way in which his neighbor lived, making not a single sound, was the
poet's own lifestyle, too. Awareness of his lonely existence led to his sympathy
for the neighbor, who was living a lonely life also. That sympathy has been given
a specific form through the seasonal sentiment contained in the first phrase of the
hokku. – *Yamamoto*

This poem conveys something more than loneliness. It does not just preach on the sadness of life or the loneliness of man. Its last two phrases may even contain something of a warm sentiment, something like a longing for human companionship. The poet had not concluded that life is lonely. He implies that life is lonely, yet it is also sweet and warm. A poem, a haikai verse, presents the complexity of life as it is. — *Imoto*

The time seems to be high noon rather than during the night. The solitude of the poet who, confronted with death, has freed himself from the bounds of body and mind pervades this poem and expands beyond it into the uncharted vastness of eternity. — *Miyamoto*

During illness

on a journey, ailing—
my dreams roam about
on a withered moor

tabi | ni | yande | yume | wa | kareno | wo | kake | meguru
travel | on | ailing | dream | as-for | withered-field | [acc.] | running | go-round

NOTE
Bashō, who was near death, dictated this hokku to his student Donshū in the small hours of November 25.

COMMENTARY
Late that night I heard Master Bashō calling Donshū, who had been tending him. Then there was the sound of ink being prepared, and I wondered what message he had for us. It turned out to be this hokku. Later he called me and cited another hokku he had just composed:

. . . .
continuing to roam about   nao kake meguru
my dreaming mind   yumegokoro

He then asked, "Which of the two hokku do you think is better?" I wanted to ask him to repeat the opening phrase of the second one, but I did not do so because he seemed too sick to speak. Instead I said, "How could your first hokku be inferior to any verse?" Regrettably, we now have no way of finding out whatever splendid phrase the second hokku began with. He then reflected, "I know this is no occasion for writing a hokku, as I am faced with death. Yet poetry has been on my mind all through my life, which is now more than fifty years long. Whenever I sleep I dream of hurrying along the road under the morning clouds or in the evening haze, and whenever I awaken I am startled at the sound of a mountain stream or the cry of a wild bird. Buddha taught that all this was sinful attachment, and now I realize I am guilty of it. I wish I could forget all the haikai that I was involved with during my lifetime." He said this regretfully again and again. – *Shikō*

The poem well describes the lonely, helpless feeling of a man who has fallen ill during a journey. – *Meisetsu*

The style of this poem suggests not so much fear as the distressed or deranged mind of a person taken ill during a journey. – *Mizuho*

The poet's mind may have been liberated, but, because his body is tormented by illness, the poem does not show his usual calm. – *Watsuji*

It is as if the poet felt he were being chased by something. He was assailed by all kinds of strange illusions. But he also kept sufficient calm of mind to reflect on them. – *Abe Y.*

Looking back on his past life, all of which had been spent in traveling and writing verses, the poet simultaneously pitied, consoled, and calmed himself. This poem conveys a complex mixture of such feelings. Mother-of-pearl is precious because it shines simultaneously in blue, yellow, and red. This is one aspect of nature, and also of a good poem, as we can see here. – *Rohan*

This poem is a most fitting conclusion to the career of Bashō, who had pursued *sabi* throughout his life. It is a very good poem indeed. Compare it with Buson's death poem:

winter's warbler	fuyu uguisu
ages ago, on the hedge of	mukashi Ō I ga
Wang Wei's house*	kakine kana

Each poem clearly reveals the talent characteristic of each poet. – *Higuchi*

Bashō, who spent his entire life in traveling, had wanted to go as far as Nagasaki on this journey. While his body lay on the sickbed, his soul flew to the sky above that area. – *Kōseki*

Even in dreams Bashō saw himself walking around in search of something, and he recognized in this the tenacity of his sinful attachment. He dreamed of himself as an obsessed man running around on a frenzied quest. His entire life flashed through his fevered mind like a panorama. Aware that death was near, he singled out from that vision the image of a traveler on a withered moor and made it symbolize his entire life. He presented the image through the hokku's last two phrases, using simple and powerful language. – *Yamamoto*

This is not a poem that expresses an enlightened mind. There is a dash of bitter sorrow as well as a sound of one gasping for breath. This is an unadorned, honest, truthful poem. – *Imoto*

Illness imposes restrictions on both the body and the mind; dreams alone are free. Perhaps that is what this haikai master who advocated *karumi* came to realize. – *Andō*

---

*Wang Wei (Ō I in Japanese, 699–759) was a Chinese poet-painter who loved living a peaceful, meditative life in the heart of nature. Buson was a life-long admirer of his art.

Reference Matter

Notes on the Commentators

Abe J. Abe Jirō (1883–1959), professor of philosophy at Tōhoku University, who specialized in ethics and aesthetics. He was a member of the distinguished group of scholars who regularly met to discuss Bashō's hokku. The records of these discussions were published as Abe Yoshishige et al., *Bashō haiku kenkyū* (Studies in Bashō's hokku, 3 vols., 1922–26).

Abe K. Abe Kimio (1909–70), professor of Japanese at Meiji University. He is the author of many books on haikai and haiku, including a concise biography of Bashō entitled *Matsuo Bashō* (1961). His annotations on Bashō's early hokku appear in the first volume of Komiya Toyotaka, gen. ed., *Kōhon Bashō zenshū* (Complete works of Bashō, 10 vols., 1962–69).

Abe M. Abe Masami (b. 1932), lecturer in Japanese at Kokugakuin University. He is especially well known for his biographical studies of Bashō. His comments are found in Asō Isoji et al., eds., *Haiku taikan* (Hokku and haiku, a comprehensive view, 1971).

Abe Y. Abe Yoshishige (1883–1966), an eminent scholar and educator who taught German philosophy at Keiō University, Hōsei University, and elsewhere. For a brief time in 1946 he served as Minister of Education. He was also a leading member of the Bashō study group whose discussions resulted in Abe Yoshishige et al., *Bashō haiku kenkyū* (1922–26).

Akahane. Akahane Manabu (b. 1928), professor of Japanese at Okayama University and author of several studies in haikai, including the recent book on Bashō's hokku, *Bashō haiku kanshō* (Appreciation of Bashō's hokku, 1987).

Akutagawa. Akutagawa Ryūnosuke (1892–1927), a major novelist of modern Japan who also wrote haiku under the name Gaki. His comments are from a series of short essays on Bashō published between 1923 and 1927, "Bashō zakki" (Miscellaneous notes on Bashō) and "Zoku Bashō zakki" (Miscellaneous notes on Bashō, a second series).

Andō. Andō Tsuguo (b. 1919), professor of comparative literature at Tokyo University of Foreign Languages and a well-known free-verse poet. He has long had an active interest in Bashō's poetry and has published several books on it. His comments are from *Bashō hyakugojikku* (One hundred and fifty hokku by Bashō, 1989).

Baigan. Ishibashi Baigan (?–1785), a Buddhist priest, literary scholar, and haikai poet. He annotated some eighty hokku by Bashō but was able to publish only a small part of the work during his lifetime as *Akanebori* (Digging madder-root, 1782).

Bakujin. Hoshino Bakujin (1877–1965), a poet and editor of several haiku magazines. He was a member of a poets' group whose discussions on Bashō's hokku are recorded in Kakuta Chikurei, ed., *Bashō kushū kōgi* (Collected hokku of Bashō, with critical commentary, 4 vols., 1908–15).

Bakusui. Hori Bakusui (1718–83), a prominent haikai poet of the eighteenth century. A romantic by temperament, he tried to emulate Bashō's youthful style shown in *Minashiguri*. His cryptic comments on Bashō's hokku are contained in his book *Jōkyō shōfū kukai densho* (Orthodox style of the Jōkyō era: Verses with critical commentary, 1770).

Bashō. Aside from those that appear in *Kai ōi* (1672), most of Bashō's written comments on his own poetry are casual remarks made in his letters. These letters are included in several modern collections, such as Hagiwara Yasuo, ed., *Bashō shokanshū* (Bashō's letters, 1976) and the eighth volume of Komiya Toyotaka, gen. ed., *Kōhon Bashō zenshū.*

Bōtō. Makino Bōtō (1876–1913), a librarian and newspaper editor who studied haiku composition under Chikurei. His comments on Bashō's hokku are published in *Bashō kushū kōgi* (1908–15), edited by his teacher.

Chikurei. Kakuta Chikurei (1856–1919), an attorney and politician who served in a number of public offices, eventually becoming a member of the National Diet. A haiku poet in private life, he was a leading member of a Bashō study group and served as the editor of *Bashō kushū kōgi* (1908–15) when the group decided to publish the records of its discussions in book form.

Dohō. Hattori Dohō (or Tohō, 1657–1730), a haikai poet who lived in Bashō's hometown of Ueno. Apparently having known Bashō from childhood, he became the master's student in 1684 and associated with him closely. Dohō's book, known as *Sanzōshi* (The three notebooks, 1709), is considered to be one of the most reliable records preserving Bashō's teachings on the art of haikai.

Donto. Tōkai Donto (1704–?), a haikai poet and author of a book commenting on 654 of Bashō's hokku, *Bashō kukai* (Notes on Bashō's hokku, 1769). Little is known about his life, but it has been surmised that he was born in Shinano Province and later moved to the Izu Peninsula.

Ebara. Ebara Taizō (1894–1948), professor of Japanese at Kyoto University, who published many works in the renga and haikai genres. His critical remarks on Bashō's hokku are taken from *Haikai meisakushū* (Masterpieces of haikai, 1935), *Bashō tokuhon* (A Bashō primer, 1939), and *Bashō haiku shinkō* (New notes on Bashō's hokku, 1951).

Gosodō. Raisetsuan Gosodō, who completed a book of textual commentary on Bashō's *Oku no hosomichi* in 1830, *Oku no hosomichi kai*. Nothing else is known about his life, though his name suggests that he was in some way related to Sodō, a longtime friend of Bashō's.

Gozan. Aida Gozan (1716–88), a scholar who wrote a number of studies on language and literature, including the first dictionary of Japanese dialects. His *Akemurasaki* (Red and purple, 1784), includes his readings of fifty hokku by Bashō.

Hagiwara. Hagiwara Sakutarō (1886–1942), one of the most respected symbolist poets in modern Japanese literature. Although he wrote most of his poems in free verse, he had a deep interest in haikai and attempted a brilliantly new interpretation of Buson's poetry. His thoughts on Bashō's hokku can be glimpsed in his essay entitled "Bashō shiken" (Bashō: A personal view, 1935).

Handa. Handa Ryōhei (1887–1945), a tanka poet whose posthumous book of poetry *Kōboku* (The tree of happiness) won an Academy of Arts prize in 1949. His *Bashō haiku shinshaku* (New commentary on Bashō's hokku, 1925) contains explications of 305 hokku by Bashō.

Higuchi. Higuchi Isao (1883–1943), a scholar specializing in haikai in general and Bashō in particular. His interpretations of some 300 hokku by Bashō are presented in his *Senpyō Bashō kushū* (Notes on selected hokku of Bashō, 1925).

Hori. Hori Nobuo (b. 1933), professor of Japanese at Kobe University and a specialist in the early history of haikai. His critical comments on Bashō's hokku appear in several books he has co-authored; those included in this book are from Imoto Nōichi et al., eds., *Bashō kushū* (Collected hokku of Bashō, 1984; rev. ed., 1989), published by Shōgakukan.

Hyōroku. Asai Hyōroku (1870–1909), a haiku poet, scholar, and member of the Bashō study group that jointly produced Kakuta Chikurei, ed., *Bashō kushū kōgi* (1908–15).

Imoto. Imoto Nōichi (b. 1913), professor of Japanese at Ochanomizu Women's University and later president of Jissen Women's University. An expert in renga and haikai, he edited or co-edited several annotated editions of Bashō's writings. His comments are taken from his *Bashō* (1958; rev. ed., 1977) and *Bashō kushū* cited under Hori above.

Iwata. Iwata Kurō (1891–1969), professor of Japanese at Gakushūin University. Among his many works on Bashō and the history of haikai is *Shochū hyōshaku Bashō haiku taisei* (Variorum commentary on Bashō's hokku, 1967), an exhaustive collection of critical comments made on Bashō's hokku by readers in the past. The book also includes his own explication of each poem.

Kakei. Nakajima Kakei, a member of the Bashō study group whose discussions resulted in Kakuta Chikurei, ed., *Bashō kushū kōgi* (1908–15).

Keion. Nunami Keion (1877–1927), a scholar in the history of haikai who taught at Tokyo University and elsewhere. His comments on Bashō's hokku are contained in Abe Yoshishige et al., *Bashō haiku kenkyū* (1922–26).

Kobayashi. Kobayashi Ichirō (1876–1944), an authority on the Nichiren sect of Buddhism who taught at Tokyo University, Tōyō University, and elsewhere. In addition to many scholarly works on Buddhism, he published a book of critical commentary on Bashō's hokku, *Bashō kushū hyōshaku* (Collected hokku of Bashō, with critical commentary, 1924).

Komiya. Komiya Toyotaka (1884–1966), professor of German at Tōhoku University. A scholar of broad literary interests, he published books on haikai and the nō drama as well as on the novels of his mentor, Natsume Sōseki. His comments on Bashō's hokku appear in Abe Yoshishige et al., *Bashō haiku kenkyū* (1922–26), and in his own book, *Bashō kushō* (Selected hokku of Bashō, 1961).

Kon. Kon Eizō (b. 1924), professor of Japanese at Chūō University. Among his many works on Bashō are *Matsuo Bashō* (with Miyamoto Saburō, 1967) and *Bashō kushū* (Collected hokku of Bashō, 1982, 1989), published by Shinchōsha. The former is an informative introduction to Bashō, while the latter presents one of the most reliable texts of Bashō's hokku available today with commentary by Kon.

Konishi. Konishi Jin'ichi (b. 1915), professor of Japanese at Tsukuba University, who later became its vice president. His numerous publications cover a wide area of Japanese literature, including hokku and haiku. At present he is writing a multi-volume history of Japanese literature to be published in both Japanese and English. His comments on Bashō are found in his *Haiku no sekai* (The world of hokku and haiku, 1981).

Kōseki. Hattori Kōseki (1877–1927), an artist specializing in seal engraving. He also wrote poetry and founded a haiku magazine. His two-volume *Bashō kushū shinkō* (Collected hokku of Bashō, with new critical commentary, 1932) has all the surviving hokku by Bashō arranged in chronological order, each followed by his critical comment.

Kūzen. Matsumoto Kūzen (or Saika, 1785–1840), a physician and haikai poet. In 1828 he published *Sarumino sagashi* (Exploring *Sarumino*), one of the earliest studies of *Sarumino*, the famed haikai book of the Bashō school.

Kyorai. Mukai Kyorai (1651–1704), a samurai and haikai poet who later became one of Bashō's most trusted students. He co-edited *Sarumino* under his teacher's guidance. His book known as *Kyorai shō* (Kyorai's essays, 1775) is a valuable record of comments made by Bashō and his students on the art of haikai.

Kyoriku. Morikawa Kyoriku (or Kyoroku, 1656–1715), a samurai from Ōmi Province who became Bashō's student in or around 1689. A gifted artist, he was Bashō's teacher of painting for a time. *Haikai mondō* (Dialogues on haikai, 1698) includes records of his debates with Kyorai on the art of haikai, touching on Bashō's work.

Meisetsu. Naitō Meisetsu (1847–1926), a scholar and educator who began writing haiku when Shiki moved into a dormitory of which he was the superintendent. Besides several collections of haiku, he published *Bashō haiku hyōshaku* (Critical commentary on Bashō's hokku, 1904).

Miyamoto. Miyamoto Saburō (1911–81), professor of Japanese at Gakushūin University. His book of essays on the Bashō school of haikai won an Education Minister's prize in 1974. His comments on Bashō's hokku are taken from Miyamoto Saburō and Kon Eizō, *Matsuo Bashō* (1967).

Mizuho. Ōta Mizuho (1876–1955), a tanka poet and classical scholar. An admirer of Bashō throughout his life, he helped to organize a Bashō study group and published the records of its discussions in his tanka magazine, *Chōon* (The sound of the tide). These were later published in book form as Abe Yoshishige et al., *Bashō haiku kenkyū* (1922–26).

Mōen. Yamamoto Mōen (1669–1729), a samurai from Ōmi Province who studied haikai under Kyoriku. He later became a monk and spent much of his life in traveling. His comments on Bashō's work are from his *Shōfū Bashō ōgiden hiunshū* (Secrets of the orthodox style transmitted by Bashō, 1724).

Momota. Momota Sōji (1893–1955), a free-verse poet and writer of juvenile literature. While attracted to European modernist poetry, he was also interested in haikai and published a book of commentary on Bashō's hokku, *Kanshō Bashō kushū* (Appreciation of Bashō's hokku, 1928).

Moran. The haikai name of Nichijū (1713–79), chief priest of Myōhō Temple in Shimousa Province. In 1765 he completed a book presenting his critical notes on Bashō's hokku, *Hizamoto sarazu* (Close by the knees).

Mukō. Mori Mukō (1864–1942), a journalist and haiku poet who took part in the group discussions that resulted in Kakuta Chikurei, ed., *Bashō kushū kōgi* (1908–15).

Nanimaru. Moro Nanimaru (1761–1837), a physician, haikai master, and literary scholar who wrote a number of books on Bashō's poetry. Well versed in Chinese and Japanese literature, he tried—sometimes too eagerly—to find classical allusions in Bashō's hokku. His comments are from his *Bashō-ō kukai taisei* (The collection of comments on Master Bashō's hokku, 1827).

Ninkō. Saiganji Ninkō (1602–82), chief priest of Saigan Temple in Kyoto. Well known as a poet, he associated with many eminent literary figures of the time. He served as a referee in *Roppyakuban haikai hokku awase* (The hokku contest in six hundred rounds, 1677), in which the young Bashō was a participant. Bashō visited him at his temple in the spring of 1685.

Nobutane. Shinten-ō Nobutane, the author of *Oi no soko* (At the bottom of a knapsack, 1795). This eight-volume book contains his critical notes on some 530 hokku by Bashō. The notes focus on literary sources as well as on the animals and plants alluded to in the poems. Nothing is known about his life, except that he was living in Edo when he worked on the notes.

Noguchi. Noguchi Yonejirō (1875–1947), a bilingual poet known as Yone Noguchi outside Japan. He lived in the United States and England from 1893 to 1904, during which time he published several volumes of poems in English. The poems of his later years are largely in Japanese. His comments on Bashō's hokku are collected in his *Bashō haiku senpyō* (Selected hokku of Bashō, with critical commentary, 1929).

Nose. Nose Tomoji, also known as Asaji (1894–1955), professor of Japanese at Tokyo University of Education and later president of Nara Gakugei University. He was famous for his studies of the nō drama, but he also had some interesting comments to make on the poetics of haikai in his *Sanzōshi hyōshaku* (Critical commentary on *Sanzōshi*, 1954).

Ogata. Ogata Tsutomu (b. 1920), professor of Japanese at Tokyo University of Education, Seijō University, and elsewhere, who has published a number of books on Bashō, Buson, and the history of haikai. His *Matsuo Bashō* (1971) contains detailed critical comments on forty-one hokku by Bashō.

Ōsha. Imura Ōsha (?–1796), a haikai poet and calligrapher who lived in Nagoya. In 1776 he completed *Shō-ō kukai kakodane* (Classical sources of Master Bashō's hokku), which attempts to read Bashō's hokku in the light of past literary tradition.

Ōtani. Ōtani Tokuzō (b. 1912), a haikai scholar and professor of Japanese at Osaka Women's College. He has served as an editor and annotator for several collections of Bashō's poetry, including *Bashō kushū* (Collected verses of Bashō, 1962), published by Iwanami Shoten and the second volume of Komiya Toyotaka, gen. ed., *Kōhon Bashō zenshū.*

Rika. Fun'ya Rika, a member of the Bashō study group that produced Kakuta Chikurei, ed., *Bashō kushū kōgi* (1908–15). He is in no way related to Bashō's disciple named Rika.

Ritō. Sakurai Ritō (1681–1755), a haikai master who studied under Ransetsu, an early disciple of Bashō's. He wrote several books on the art of haikai, and his comments on Bashō's work are included in his *Wakumonchin* (Strange dialogues, 1732).

Rohan. Kōda Rohan (1867–1947), an eminent novelist and scholar who devoted much of his later life to studying the Bashō school of haikai. He contributed written comments to Abe Yoshishige et al., *Bashō haiku kenkyū* (1922–26), although he did not attend the discussion sessions in person.

Ryōta. Oshima Ryōta (1718–87), one of the most influential of eighteenth-century haikai masters, who reportedly had some three thousand students all over Japan. In 1759 he published *Bashō kukai* (Notes on Bashō's hokku), containing his critical remarks on eighty-six hokku by Bashō.

Saisei. Murō Saisei (1889–1962), a free-verse poet in his early career who later became more famous as a novelist. He also wrote haiku as well as a number of essays on Bashō. His comments are taken from his *Bashō zakki* (Miscellaneous notes on Bashō, 1942).

Sanga. Horoan Sanga, a haikai poet who studied under Yasuyoshi. His book *Bashō aramaki* (The new collection of Bashō's works, 1793) contains his notes on 278 hokku by Bashō; the emphasis is on classical allusions.

San'u. Shoshian San'u, who in 1758 published *Bashō hokku hyōrin* (Critical commentary on Bashō's hokku), containing critical notes on eighty-seven hokku by Bashō. Although nothing is known about his life, his name suggests that he may have studied under Sanpū, a lifelong friend and disciple of Bashō's.

Seihō. Shimada Seihō (1882–1944), a journalist and haiku poet who taught at Waseda University for a time. His critical commentary on Bashō's hokku appeared in book form as *Bashō meiku hyōshaku* (Critical notes on Bashō's major hokku, 1934).

Seisensui. Ogiwara Seisensui (1884–1976), one of the pioneers and most energetic proponents of free-style haiku. Despite his general aversion to fixed verse forms, he was a lifelong admirer of Bashō and wrote a number of books and essays on that haikai poet. His comments are taken from his *Bashō kusen ryakkai* (Brief notes on selected hokku of Bashō, 2 vols., 1922), *Bashō tokuhon* (A Bashō primer, 1924), and *Bashō kanshō* (Bashō: an appreciation, 1966).

Seishi. Yamaguchi Seishi (b. 1901), one of the most prominent haiku poets in the twentieth century. Famous for his daring use of images that characterize modern industrialized Japan, he has nevertheless shown a profound interest in Bashō's poems and recorded his thoughts on them in *Bashō shūku* (Superior hokku of Bashō, 1963).

Sekisui. Ishiko Sekisui (1738–1803), a samurai from Edo who retired early and spent the rest of his life in writing and studying haikai. His book *Bashō kusen nenkō* (Selected hokku of Bashō: A study of their dates of composition), completed in the last years of the eighteenth century, is a conscientious attempt to date and authenticate some 670 hokku by the master poet and incorporates Sekisui's own critical notes.

Shida. Shida Gishū (1876–1946), a haiku poet and haikai scholar who taught at Tokyo University and several other schools. His two-volume *Bashō haiku no kaishaku to kanshō* (Interpretation and appreciation of Bashō's hokku, 1940, 1946) contains detailed analyses of 107 hokku by Bashō.

Shikei. Nozaki Shikei, a member of the Bashō study group whose discussions were published in Kakuta Chikurei, ed., *Bashō kushū kōgi* (1908–15).

Shiki. Masaoka Shiki (1867–1902), a major poet of early modern Japan who initiated a successful reform movement in both waka and haikai. Unhappy with the idolatry of Bashō that persisted in his time, he proposed a radical re-evaluation of the famed master's work in several of his essays. His comments are taken from "Bashō zatsudan" (Chats on Bashō, 1893).

Shikō. Kagami Shikō (1665–1731), one of Bashō's later students. A theorist by temperament, he wrote several books to elucidate Bashō's idea of haikai, but his arguments became increasingly dogmatic after his teacher's death. His comments are taken from his *Kuzu no matsubara* (Pine forest of Kuzu, 1692) and *Oi nikki* (Records in a knapsack, 1695).

Shinpū. Katsumine Shinpū (1887–1954), a poet, scholar, and editor of a haiku magazine. He helped to introduce the works of past haikai poets like Bashō, Kikaku, and Issa to modern readers by publishing them in readable editions. His comments on Bashō are included in volumes 2 and 3 of Abe Yoshishige et al., *Bashō haiku kenkyū* (1922–26).

Shisan. Shisan (?–1699), Bashō's student who lived in the Fukagawa district of Edo and who edited *Betsuzashiki* (The detached room), a haikai anthology of the Bashō school published in 1694 shortly before Bashō's death. His comments on Bashō's hokku appear in his preface to *Betsuzashiki.*

Shōgatsudō. Author of *Shiwasubukuro* (Year-end bag), presenting critical commentary on some 150 of Bashō's hokku. The book seems to have been published in 1764 or 1765. Nothing more is known about him, except that he was from Osaka.

Shūson. Katō Shūson (b. 1905), a leading modern haiku poet who is also well known for his scholarly work on Bashō. He has published critical commentaries on Bashō's hokku in several books, most notably in the first three volumes (1943–48) of *Bashō kōza* (Bashō study series, 9 vols., 1943–51), *Bashō shūku* (Superior hokku of Bashō, 2 vols., 1952, 1964), and *Matsuo Bashō shū* (The collection of Matsuo Bashō's works, 2 vols., 1960, 1961).

Sokotsu. Samukawa Sokotsu (1875–1954), a journalist, haiku poet, and one of the most loyal students of Shiki. When his late teacher's house was destroyed during the Second World War, he rebuilt it and lived there himself. His book of commentary on Bashō's hokku, *Zoku Bashō haiku hyōshaku* (Critical commentary on Bashō's hokku, a second series, 1913), was intended to be a sequel to Meisetsu's similar work that had appeared nine years earlier.

Somaru. Mizoguchi Somaru (1713–95), a government official who, after his retirement in 1772, devoted himself full-time to the writing and study of haikai. In 1773 he published *Bashō-ō hokku-kai sessō taizen* (Variorum commentary on Master Bashō's hokku), in which he presented his own interpretations as well.

Suika. Masumoto Suika, a member of the workshop that produced Kakuta Chikurei, ed., *Bashō kushū kōgi* (1908–15).

Takamasa. Suganoya Takamasa, a haikai poet of the Danrin school. He pub-

lished a number of haikai books between 1675 and 1696. His comment on Bashō's crow poem appears in his preface to an untitled haikai book he compiled
in 1681.

Tosai. Chijitsuan Tosai (1750–?), a poet who lived in Dewa Province and who
apparently belonged to the Shikō school of haikai. His critical comments on
some 750 hokku by Bashō are found in his *Bashō-ō hokku-shū mōin* (Master
Bashō's hokku: A guide, 1815).

Utsubo. Kubota Utsubo (1877–1967), a distinguished tanka poet and professor
of Japanese at Waseda University. He was one of the few scholars who had
both the scholarship and the energy to write critical comments on all the waka
included in the *Man'yōshū, Kokinshū,* and *Shinkokinshū.* His book on Bashō's hokku, *Bashō no haiku* (Bashō's hokku, 1964), was written when he was
eighty-six.

Watsuji. Watsuji Tetsurō (1889–1960), an intellectual leader of his generation
who taught at both Tokyo and Kyoto universities. Primarily a scholar in philosophy and ethics, he nevertheless published brilliant studies in Japanese history and comparative culture, such as *Fūdo* (Climate and culture, 1935) and
Sakoku (National Seclusion, 1950). He was a member of the team that produced Abe Yoshishige et al., *Bashō haiku kenkyū* (1922–26).

Yakumu. Roppeisai Yakumu, the author of *Haikai ikkanshō* (The lineage of haikai), which appeared in 1830. The book purports to be a study of renga and
haikai styles, but it also includes the author's comments on some 320 hokku
by Bashō.

Yamamoto. Yamamoto Kenkichi (1907–88), a critic noted for his insightful essays on both classical and modern Japanese literature. His *Bashō: sono kanshō to hihyō* (Bashō: Appreciation and criticism of his work, 3 vols., 1955–
56), an intensive study of 147 hokku by Bashō, won a Shinchō Literary Prize.
He later published *Bashō zen hokku* (Complete hokku of Bashō, 2 vols.,
1974), increasing the number of annotated poems to 973 but shortening the
comment on each poem.

Yasuyoshi. Ozaki Yasuyoshi (1701–79), a painter and haikai poet who lived in
Kanazawa. In *Haikai Kinkaden* (Notes on the golden treasury of haikai, 1773)
he set forth his views on Bashō's hokku after citing interpretations by others.

Glossary

Italicized words are defined elsewhere in the Glossary.

fūga. The spirit of elegance and refinement that is thought to permeate art in general and, in Bashō's time, *haikai* in particular. It may also imply the attitude of the artist who works in that spirit. In this latter sense, its implications approach *fūryū.*

fūkyō. "Madness" characteristic of the mind of a poet or artist. A man dedicated to poetry or art is considered "mad" in the sense that he is undisturbed by the worldly concerns of an ordinary—"sane"—person. Often used by the poet himself, the term carries implications of both pride and self-derision. The origin of the concept probably goes back to Zen Buddhism.

fūryū. The refined taste of a poet or artist that is manifested in his work and lifestyle. In *haikai,* it usually presumes freedom from the conflict-ridden activities of ordinary life.

haibun. Prose written in the spirit of *haikai.* Poetic in both theme and style, it is usually interspersed with *hokku* or *haiku.*

haikai. Abbreviation of "haikai no renga," a variety of *renga* that is more inclusive in language and subject matter. As against the elegant, courtly norm of renga, it draws more on common people's emotions and uses a more plebeian vocabulary, at times even evoking laughter through the use of colloquial expressions. In a more general sense, the term haikai may refer to all types of literature derived from haikai no renga, including *hokku, haiku,* and *haibun.*

haiku. An independent verse form normally having a 5-7-5 syllable pattern and containing "kigo" ("season word"), a word suggestive of the season. In this book, only such verses written in the modern period (1868–present) are called haiku.

hie. Cold, icy beauty cherished by some medieval artists. The *nō* actor-playwright Zeami (1363–1443), for instance, admired the beauty of snow piled in a silver bowl and used the image to describe one of the three best styles of nō performance. The poet Shinkei (1406–75), the foremost proponent of hie in *waka* and *renga,* went so far as to say "Nothing is more beautiful than ice."

hiraku. Any verse of a *renga* sequence, except the first three and the last.

hokku. The opening verse of a *renga* sequence, consisting of seventeen syllables and including a season word. Sometimes, especially in the late Edo period (1600–1868), it was singled out and appreciated independently of the rest of the sequence. When *renga* became almost extinct in the late nineteenth century, hokku attained complete independence and came to be known as *haiku.*

karabi. An aesthetic ideal pursued by some medieval poets. Literally meaning "dryness," it denotes the austere, monochrome beauty suggested by the image of a dried flower.

karumi. A poetic ideal advocated by Bashō in the last years of his life. Literally meaning "lightness," it points toward a simple, plain beauty that emerges when the poet finds his theme in familiar things and expresses it in artless language. Bashō tried to teach the concept to his students by giving such directives as "Simply observe what children do" and "Eat vegetable soup rather than duck stew."

kasen. A *renga* sequence of thirty-six verses. Bashō favored the form and helped to make it the most popular type of *haikai* in the generations that followed.

kotan. Simple beauty created by an aged artist who has mastered all the intricacies of his art. Made up of two ideograms, "ko" ("death of a plant") and "tan" ("plainness"), the word suggests the image of a dead tree that has completed the full cycle of its lifespan.

kyōgen. A short comic interlude performed between two *nō* plays.

kyōka. Comic *waka*. Written in the same form as *waka*, it induces laughter by such means as wit, parody, satire, wordplay, and vulgar language. Its popularity reached a peak in the Edo period.

mono no awaré. A literary and aesthetic ideal cultivated in the Heian period. Literally meaning "pathos of things," it usually refers to sadness or melancholy arising from a deep, empathic appreciation of the ephemeral beauty manifested in nature, human life, or a work of art.

nioi. A term used in the Bashō school of *haikai* to indicate the subtle way in which two sequential verses are linked. Literally meaning "fragrance," it refers to the sentiment or mood of one verse imperceptibly drifting into that of the next verse, like the fragrance of a flower drifting in the wind.

nō. A major dramatic form that flourished especially in the fourteenth and fifteenth centuries. Having evolved from religious rituals, the nō drama often presents a scheme of salvation for its central theme, using highly poetic language laden with symbols.

renga. Linked poetry of various types, usually with two or more poets participating in its creation. The most common type, which flourished in the fourteenth and fifteenth centuries, consisted of one hundred verses that alternately had seventeen and fourteen syllables each. Derived from courtly *waka*, renga at first aimed at producing an elegant, graceful mood through its subject matter and style, until a more plebeian variety, haikai no renga (or *haikai*), emerged in the sixteenth century.

sabi. Lonely beauty cherished in the Bashō school of *haikai*. Elements of sadness, old age, resignation, tranquillity, and even happiness can also be found in it. Underlying this aesthetic is a cosmic view typical of medieval Buddhists, who recognized man's existential loneliness and tried to accept it with calm resignation.

shasei. "Sketch from life," a poetic principle first advocated by Masaoka Shiki (1867–1902). It recommends that the poet observe life or nature closely and record his impressions in simple, precise language. Because of Shiki's literary fame, the principle found a number of followers in succeeding generations.

shibumi. Subtle, unobtrusive beauty cherished by artists and connoisseurs since medieval times. Originally designating a sour taste, the word has come to be used as an antonym not only of sweet taste but of decorative, ostentatious beauty. The subdued voice of a master singer, the disciplined performance of a seasoned actor, or the simple pattern designed by an expert ceramic artist has a beauty of understatement, and as such it is praised as showing shibumi. Its adjectival form is "shibui," a term better known in the West.

tanka. *Waka* written in the modern period.

wabi. An aesthetic and moral principle advocating the enjoyment of leisurely life free from worldly concerns. It prescribes that one find spiritual wealth in material poverty and luxuriate in the beauty of things modest and simple. Etymologically derived from "wabu" ("to languish") and "wabishi" ("lonely"), it has much in common with the connotations of *karabi, sabi,* and *yase.* The principle is especially valued in the tea ceremony.

waka. A traditional verse form consisting of five phrases with a 5-7-5-7-7 syllable pattern. *Man'yōshū* (The collection of ten thousand leaves, 8th c.), *Kokinshū* (The collection of ancient and modern poems, 905), and *Shinkokinshū* (The new collection of ancient and modern poems, 1205) are the three anthologies containing the best samples of waka, each showing a different poetic style characteristic of the age. Waka written in the modern period is usually called *tanka.*

wakiku. The second verse in a *renga* sequence. Normally written by the host poet, it consists of two phrases with seven syllables in each.

yase. Consumptive beauty, spare and slender, especially valued by medieval poets. The image often cited to suggest it is an old plum tree blossoming on a cold day. The term is often used as equivalent to or in association with *hie* and *karabi.*

yojō. A sentiment or sentiments evoked but not overtly expressed in a poem. It also refers to a poetic style that especially aims to produce such a sentiment. The style was favored by a number of medieval poets.

yūgen. Beauty of mystery and depth, often combined with other effects such as elegance, refinement, ambiguity, darkness, calm, ephemerality, and sadness. The relative proportions of these ingredients differed among the different poets and artists who cultivated this aesthetic ideal, roughly from the twelfth to the fifteenth centuries. The term is still used today, with all its broad range of meaning.

Selected Bibliography for
Further Reading

ON HOKKU AND HAIKU

Blyth, R. H. *Haiku.* 4 vols. Tokyo: Hokuseidō, 1949–52. Presents a large number of hokku and haiku in English translation, most of them followed by the author's enlivening comments. Historical origins and poetic characteristics of the seventeen-syllable form are discussed in the first volume.

————. *A History of Haiku.* 2 vols. Tokyo: Hokuseidō, 1963–64. Traces the evolution of the genre from its beginning to the twentieth century. More an annotated anthology than a book of history.

Brower, Gary L. *Haiku in Western Languages.* Metuchen, N.J.: Scarecrow Press, 1972. An exhaustive bibliography of books and articles on hokku and haiku written in English, French, German, Italian, Spanish, and Portuguese. Each item is briefly annotated by the author.

Henderson, Harold G. *An Introduction to Haiku.* Garden City, N.Y.: Doubleday, 1958. A good introductory survey describing the characteristics of the verse form and sampling the works of major poets who wrote in it.

Higginson, William J. *The Haiku Handbook.* New York: McGraw-Hill, 1985. Subtitled "How to Write, Share, and Teach Haiku." A handy compendium that gives much useful information related to hokku and haiku.

Japanese Classics Translation Committee, trans. *Haikai and Haiku.* Tokyo: Nippon Gakujutsu Shinkōkai, 1957. A scholarly yet readable introduction to haikai and hokku, written by a team of experts representing the best Japanese scholarship on the subject at that time.

Yasuda, Kenneth. *The Japanese Haiku.* Rutland, N.J.: Charles E. Tuttle, 1957. Based on a doctoral dissertation submitted to Tokyo University, the book attempts to elucidate the aim and method of haiku in the light of Western literary aesthetics.

ON BASHŌ

Aitken, Robert. *A Zen Wave.* New York: Weatherhill, 1978. A study of Bashō's hokku from a Zen point of view. The author is one of the first Americans who have gained the title of *rōshi* (venerable Zen master).

Britton, Dorothy, trans. *A Haiku Journey.* Tokyo: Kōdansha International, 1974. Translates Bashō's *Oku no hosomichi* in a style of English that is a good compromise between the two earlier translations by Corman and Kamaike and by Yuasa. Some hokku are accompanied by Dennis Stock's color photographs.

Chamberlain, Basil Hall. "Bashō and the Japanese Poetical Epigram," *Transactions of the Asiatic Society of Japan*, vol. 30 (1902), pp. 241–362. Reprinted in his *Japanese Poetry* (London: John Murray, 1910), pp. 145–260. A pioneering work by an erudite scholar of Victorian England. Now dated in both scholarship and literary taste, it nevertheless offers a number of unique insights into individual poems.

Corman, Cid, and Kamaike Susumu, trans. *Back Roads to Far Towns*. New York: Grossman, 1968. An English rendering of *Oku no hosomichi* that aims to reproduce Bashō's "sometimes unusual syntax, the flow and economy of his language" by translating the text as literally as possible.

Keene, Donald. *Travelers of a Hundred Ages*. New York: Henry Holt, 1989. A collection of essays on Japanese diaries, including all of Bashō's. The Japanese version of the book won two literary prizes.

———. *World Within Walls: Japanese Literature of the Pre-Modern Era, 1600–1867*. New York: Grove Press, 1976. In addition to a chapter on Bashō, several other chapters, such as "The Transition to Bashō" and "Bashō's Disciples," help to place his poetry in its historical context.

McCullough, Helen Craig, ed. *Classical Japanese Prose: An Anthology*. Stanford, Calif.: Stanford University Press, 1990. Includes a complete translation of *Nozarashi kikō* and *Oku no hosomichi* done by one of the most reliable translators of Japanese literature.

Miner, Earl, and Hiroko Odagiri, trans. *The Monkey's Straw Raincoat*. Princeton, N.J.: Princeton University Press, 1981. Includes a complete translation of *Sarumino* and four other haikai sequences of the Bashō school. The verses are accompanied by the translators' helpful notes.

Stryk, Lucien, trans. *On Love and Barley: Haiku of Bashō*. Harmondsworth, England: Penguin Books, 1985. Contains 253 hokku by Bashō. The style of translation reflects Stryk's deep interest in Zen.

Ueda, Makoto. *Matsuo Bashō*. New York: Twayne, 1970, and Tokyo: Kōdansha International, 1982. Originally published in Twayne's World Authors Series, the book gives a compact survey of Bashō's life and works as well as his influence on later literature.

Yuasa, Nobuyuki, trans. *Bashō: The Narrow Road to the Deep North and Other Travel Sketches*. Harmondsworth, England: Penguin Books, 1966. A smooth, readable translation of Bashō's travel journals. Hokku are rendered into four lines of English, which tends to reduce the sense of compactness and tension inherent in the Japanese verse form.

Indexes

Index of Bashō's Hokku in English

children! / bindweed flowers have opened, / I'll peel a melon, 359
chrysanthemums, / cockscombs, all are cut and gone— / the Anniversary, 214
chrysanthemums / flowering amid the stones / in a stonemason's yard, 364
chrysanthemums' scent— / in Nara, many ancient / Buddhas, 400
chrysanthemums' scent— / in the garden, a worn-out sandal / upside down, 367
clouds now and then / give rest to people / viewing the moon, 137
clouds of blossoms . . . / that temple bell, is it Ueno / or Asakusa?, 154
clutching wheat ears / to support myself, I bid / farewell, 381
come and look! / put on a Jinbei robe / and admire the blossoms, 30
come, children, / let's go out and run / in the hail!, 278
come crawling out! / under the silkworm nursery / a toad's croak, 248
comic verse / in the wintry gust / a wanderer . . . how like Chikusai / I have be-
    come!, 120
the coolness— / faintly the crescent moon / above Mount Haguro, 254
the coolness— / growing straight, the branches / of a wild pine, 386
a crane screeches, / its voice ripping the leaves / of a banana plant, 233
the crescent moon— / a bud on the morning glory / swelling at night, 82

daffodils, / white paper screens, reflecting / one another's color, 325
dead grass— / imperceptibly, heat waves / one or two inches high, 180
deep-rooted leeks / washed spotlessly white— / how cold!, 324
departing autumn— / with their hands opened wide / chestnut burs, 398
departing spring— / birds weep, and fishes' eyes / are tearful, 119, 228, 381
did all the seasonal rains / come and go, leaving out / this Shining Hall?, 244
don't resemble me— / cut in half / a musk melon, 295
don't they quench / even the banked charcoal? / those hissing tears, 217
do those blossoming faces / make you feel bashful? / hazy moon, 27
a dragonfly / vainly trying to settle / onto a blade of grass, 297
a dried salmon / and a Kūya pilgrim's gauntness / in midwinter cold, 306
drinking saké / makes it harder to sleep . . . / snow at night, 150
the Dutch consul too / is prostrate before His Lordship—spring under His reign,
    46

ebbing strength— / my teeth detect a grain of sand / in the dried seaweed, 312
emaciated / yet somehow the chrysanthemums / begin to bud, 165
even a horse / arrests my eyes—on this / morning of snow, 118
even in Kyoto / I long for Kyoto— / a hototogisu, 294

the faces of those / who love to drink— / a flash of lightning, 326
felling a tree / and gazing at the cut end— / tonight's moon, 41
few in this world / notice those blossoms— / chestnut by the eves, 239

finding a hawk / fills me with pleasure / here at Cape Irago, 171
first day of the year—/ as I ponder, a lonely / nightfall in autumn, 87
first day of the year / I think longingly of the sun / on those paddy waters, 224
the first snow / just enough to bend / the daffodil leaves, 148
first winter shower—/ the monkey also seems to want / a small raincoat, 275
the fisherman's hut—/ mingled with little shrimps / a cricket, 300
a flash of lightning—/ passing through the darkness / a night heron's scream,
    394
a flash of lightning—/ where there were faces / plumes of pampas grass, 391
fleas, lice—/ a horse piddles / near my pillow, 246
a fool in the dark / grabs a bramble—/ firefly hunt, 74
for a town doctor / the mansion sends a horse—/ a royal reception!, 33
for a while I sit / meditating by the falls—/ start of a summer retreat, 232
for the white poppy / the butterfly breaks off its wing / as a keepsake, 134
fragrant orchid—/ into a butterfly's wings / it breathes the incense, 110
from which tree's bloom / it comes, I do not know—/ this fragrance, 181

gathering the rains / of the wet season, how swiftly flows / the Mogami River!,
    251, 385
green willow branches / hanging down on the mud / at low tide, 379

hair on my head / starts to show, my face has paled—/ long seasonal rain, 158
the harvest moon—/ crawling up to my gate / the rising tide, 340
the harvest moon—/ I stroll round the pond / till the night is through, 143
the harvest moon—/ weather in the north / unpredictable indeed!, 268
heat waves shimmer / on the shoulders of my / paper robe, 225
here in Kyoto / ninety-nine thousand people / out to see the blossoms, 24
a hermitage—/ the moon, chrysanthemums, / one acre of rice field, 273
Hollanders too / have come for the blossoms—/ saddle a horse!, 50
hototogisu / cries—a blade of iris / five feet tall, 338
hototogisu—/ the shriek lies stretched / across the water, 354
hototogisu—/ through a vast bamboo forest / moonlight seeping, 314
hototogisu—/ where it disappears / a lone island, 199
housecleaning day—/ hanging a shelf at his own home / a carpenter, 374
how fish and birds / feel at heart, I do not know—/ the year-end party, 333
how fishy they smell! / on a waterweed / dace entrails, 362
how old the pine / appears on the gold screen! / locked in for the winter . . . , 365
how piteous! / under the helmet / a cricket, 265
how solemn! / green leaves, young leaves, and through them / the rays of the sun,
    231
hydrangea and a wild / thicket, providing a little garden / for this cottage, 380

I am not yet dead / after many nights on the road—/ end of autumn, 116
ice, tasting bitter / in the mouth of a sewer rat, / quenches his thirst, 78
I'm filled with sorrow—/ make me feel more lonely, / cuckoo!, 315
in a cowshed / mosquito buzz sounds dusky . . ./ lingering summer heat, 320
in the autumn wind / it lies, sadly broken—/ a mulberry stick, 363
in the blossoms' shade / as in the nō drama / a traveler sleeps, 189
in the misty rain / Mount Fuji is veiled all day—/ how intriguing!, 102
in the morning dew / spotted with mud, and how cool—/ melons on the soil, 388
in the mountain village / Manzai dancers are late—/ plum blossoms, 309
in the scent of plums / suddenly the sun peeps out—/ the mountain path, 376
in the seasonal rain / a crane's legs / have become short, 73
in the seasonal rain / it remains unhidden—/ the bridge of Seta, 203
in the shallows / a crane, with its legs splashed—/ coolness by the sea, 259
in this group of people / admiring the full moon / not one beautiful face, 299
is that warbler / her soul? there sleeps / a graceful willow, 88
it feels cool / to put the feet against the wall . . ./ a midday nap, 392
it is spring! / a hill without a name / in thin haze, 126

journey through Kiso / made me thin, and I still am . . ./ the late harvest moon,
    213
just for today / let us all be aged men—/ first winter shower, 344

Kisagata—/ in the rain, like Hsi Shih, / flowers of a silk tree, 257
the Kiso acorns—/ for those in the floating world / my souvenirs, 211

last day of the month, no moon . . ./ embracing a cedar tree / one thousand years
    old, a storm, 108
life in this world / just like a temporary shelter / of Sōgi's, 83
lingering a while / above the blossoms, the moon / in the night sky, 311
locked in for the winter . . ./ again I'll be nestling close / to this post, 215
long seasonal rain—/ a silkworm ailing / in the mulberry field, 383
long seasonal rain—/ blast down that sky, / Ōi River!, 385
long seasonal rain—/ I'll go and see the floating nest / of a grebe, 160
long seasonal rain—/ lighting dragon candles / a municipal guard, 40
long seasonal rain—/ where a poetry card was peeled off, / traces on the wall, 318
looking as though / the harvest moon had blossomed / a cotton field, 397
looking closely, I see / a shepherd's purse blooming / under the hedge, 139
the lover cat / over a crumbled stove / comes and goes, 39

man who wears a straw mat—/ what sage could he possibly be? / blossoming
    spring, 284

many, many things / they call to mind—/ those cherry blossoms!, 185
many sad junctures—/ in the end, everyone turns into / a bamboo shoot, 313
a measuring box I bought / made me change my mind / about moon viewing, 403
a monk sips / his morning tea, and it is quiet—/ chrysanthemum flowers, 302
the moon fleets fast, / foliage atop the trees / holding the rain, 163
the moonflower—/ I stick my drunken face / out of the window, 358
moonflowers so white / at night, alongside the outhouse / in the light of a torch,
    75
the moon is clear—/ I escort a lovely boy / frightened by a fox, 409
the moon will guide you . . . / this way, traveler; please come / into the inn here,
    21
the morning glory—/ all day long, a bolt / fastened on my gate, 360
a morning glory / knowing nothing of the carousal / in the peak of bloom, 209
the morning glory—/ that, too, now turns out to be / no friend of mine, 361
the morning of snow—/ all alone, I chew / dried salmon meat, 65
move the gravemound! / my wailing voice, / the autumn wind, 263
Musashi Plain—/ no more than one inch, / a deer's call, 34
mushroom—/ from some unknown tree, a leaf / sticking on it, 323
my horse ambles along . . . / I see myself in a painting / of this summer moor, 90
my summer robe / there are still some lice / I have not caught, 135
my temporary shelter—/ a pasania tree is here, too, / in the summer grove, 291

never think of yourself / as someone who did not count—/ festival of the souls,
    393
night . . . silently / in the moonlight, a worm / digs into a chestnut, 56
not grown to a butterfly / this late in autumn / a caterpillar, 271
now then, let's go out / to enjoy the snow . . . until / I slip and fall!, 177

an octopus pot—/ inside, a short-lived dream / under the summer moon, 201
oh, nothing's happened to me! / yesterday has passed—/ fugu soup, 42
the old-lady cherry / is blossoming—in her old age / an event to remember, 22
the old pond—/ a frog jumps in, / water's sound, 140
on a bare branch / a crow has alighted . . . / autumn nightfall, 57
on a journey, ailing—/ my dreams roam about / on a withered moor, 413
on some boil / it seems to touch—the supple / branch of a willow, 377
on the blue ocean / waves smell of rice wine—/ tonight's moon, 52
on the scales / Kyoto and Edo in balance / this everlasting spring, 36
on this mountain / sorrow . . . tell me about it, / digger of wild yams, 183
on this road / where nobody else travels / autumn nightfall, 406
over an entire field / they have planted rice—before / I part with the willow,
    236

a peasant's child / husking the rice, pauses / to look at the moon, 162
petal by petal / yellow mountain roses fall— / sound of the rapids, 191
the pine tree / of Karasaki, looking hazier / than the blossoms, 129
plank bridge— / clinging for their lives / ivy vines, 210
plates and bowls / dim in the twilight— / the evening cool, 389
playing in the blossoms / a horsefly . . . don't eat it, / friendly sparrows!, 153
polished anew / the holy mirror is clear, too— / blossoms of snow, 173

rainy day— / bounding the world's autumn / Boundary Town, 47
resting higher / than a lark in the sky / a mountain pass, 187
road across a plain— / turn my horse sideways / toward that hototogisu!, 234
the rough sea— / flowing toward Sado Isle / the River of Heaven, 260

salted sea breams— / their gums, too, look cold / at the fish shop, 345
samurai's gathering— / their chat has the pungent taste / of daikon radish, 369
scent in the wind / also suggests the south— / the Mogami River, 253
the scorching day— / dipping it into the ocean / the Mogami River, 256
the sea darkens— / a wild duck's call / faintly white, 123
sensing autumn's approach / four hearts draw together / in a small tea room, 390
shall we go and knock / on the gate of Mii Temple? / the moon of tonight, 321
should I hold it in my hand / it would melt in my hot tears— / autumn frost, 112
the sixth month— / with clouds laid on its summit / Mount Arashi, 387
a skylark sings— / marking time through the song / the cry of a pheasant, 227
so exciting / and, after a while, so sad— / cormorant fishing, 205
somehow, in some way, / it has managed to survive— / pampas grass in the snow,
     328
soon they will die— / yet, showing no sign of it, / cicadas screech, 296
the sound of an oar slapping the waves / chills my bowels through / this night . . .
     tears, 63
the sound of a water jar / cracking on this icy night / as I lie awake, 144
the sound of hail— / I remain, as before, / an old oak, 92
spider—what is it, / what is it you are crying? / autumn wind, 54
spring begins— / new year, old rice / ten quarts, 98
spring goes away— / with the people of Ōmi / I share the sorrow, 288
spring rain— / down along a wasps' nest, water / leaking through the roof, 378
spring that people / do not notice—plum blossoms / on the back of a mirror, 335
still alive / they are frozen in one lump / sea slugs, 373
the stillness— / seeping into the rocks / cicadas' screech, 249
sting the fool / given to the moon and blossoms! / the coldest season starts, 350
the stone's smell / summer grasses look red, / dewdrops warm, 235
a Suma fisherman / ready to shoot an arrow— / a hototogisu's cry?, 198

summer grasses / where stalwart soldiers / once dreamed a dream, 242
the summer moon / coming out of Goyu—/ into Akasaka already!, 37
the Suruga road—/ orange blossoms also / smell like tea, 384

the temple bell too / seems to start ringing—/ cicadas' screech, 204
there too was a night / when a robber visited my home—/ the year's end, 375
this autumn / why am I aging so? / to the clouds, a bird, 407
those who have heard a monkey's cry: / how about this abandoned child / in the
    autumn wind?, 103
though the autumn wind / has begun to blow, it is green—/ a chestnut bur, 319
a tiny crab / crawls up my leg . . . / clear water, 161
to Kyoto / still half the sky to go—/ snowy clouds, 168
toward the brushwood gate / it sweeps the tea leaves—/ stormy wind, 62
toward the sun's path / hollyhock flowers turning / in the seasonal rain, 293
town where I was born—/ as I weep over my umbilical cord / the year comes to a
    close, 178
"traveler" / shall be my name—/ first winter shower, 166
try to emulate / a traveler's heart, / pasania blossoms!, 356
twilight of dawn / a whitefish, with an inch / of whiteness, 117

under the crescent moon / the earth looms hazily—/ buckwheat flowers, 339
under the same roof / courtesans, too, are asleep—/ bush clover and the moon,
    261
under the tree / soup, fish salad, and all—/ cherry blossoms, 286
under the waterweeds / whitefish swarm . . . they would fade away / if put on my
    palm, 69
unlike anything / it has been compared to: / the third-day-moon, 207

village has grown old—/ not a single house without / persimmon trees, 395
village where they ring / no bells—how do they live? / nightfall in spring, 230

waft your fragrance! / on a hill where they mine coal / plum blossoms, 179
was it spring that came / or was it the year that went? / the Second Last Day, 19
weatherbeaten skeleton / haunting my mind, how the wind / pierces my body!,
    100
what makes this bird / hurry to the year-end fair? / a crow, 282
whereabout is / Kasashima? this rainy month, / this muddy road, 240
where is the moon? / the temple bell is sunk / at the bottom of the sea, 269
where is the shower? / with an umbrella in his hand / a monk returns, 61
where peaks of the clouds / have crumbled one after another / the moon's moun-
    tain, 255

Index of Bashō's Hokku in Japanese

fūryū no hajime ya oku no taueuta, 238
fuyogomori mata yorisowan kono hashira, 215
fuyuniwa ya tsuki mo ito naru mushi no gin, 277
fuyu no hi ya bajō ni kōru kagebōshi, 170

ganjitsu wa tagoto no hi koso koishikere, 224
ganjitsu ya omoeba sabishi aki no kure, 87
gu ni kuraku ibara wo tsukamu hotaru kana, 74

hai ide yo kaiya ga shita no hiki no koe, 248
hana ni asobu abu na kurai so tomosuzume, 153
hana no kage utai ni nitaru tabine kana, 189
hana no kao ni hareute shite ya oborozuki, 27
hana no kumo kane wa Ueno ka Asakusa ka, 154
haranaka ya mono ni mo tsukazu naku hibari, 156
haremono ni sawaru yanagi no shinae kana, 377
haru nare ya na mo naki yama no usugasumi, 126
harusame ya hachi no su tsutau yane no mori, 378
haru tatsu ya shinnen furuki kome goshō, 98
haru ya koshi toshi ya yukiken kotsugomori, 19
hatsuaki ya umi mo aota no hitomidori, 208
hatsushigure saru mo komino wo hoshigenari, 275
hatsuyuki ya suisen no ha no tawamu made, 148
hibari naku naka no hyōshi ya kiji no koe, 227
hibari yori sora ni yasurau tōge kana, 187
higoro nikuki karasu mo yuki no ashita kana, 308
hi no michi ya aui katamuku satsuki-ame, 293
hito mo minu haru ya kagami no ura no ume, 335
hitotsuya ni yūjo mo netari hagi to tsuki, 261
hiyahiya to kabe wo fumaete hirune kana, 392
horohoro to yamabuki chiru ka taki no oto, 191
hototogisu kie yuku kata ya shima hitotsu, 199
hototogisu koe yokotau ya mizu no ue, 354
hototogisu naku ya goshaku no ayamegusa, 338
hototogisu ōtakeyabu wo moru tsukiyo, 314

iki nagara hitotsu ni kōru namako kana, 373
inazuma ya kao no tokoro ga susuki no ho, 391
inazuma ya yami no kata yuku goi no koe, 394
ishi no ka ya natsugusa akaku tsuyu atsushi, 235
Ishiyama no ishi yori shiroshi aki no kaze, 267

iza kodomo hashiri arikan tamaarare, 278
iza saraba yukimi ni korobu tokoro made, 177
izuku shigure kasa wo te ni sagete kaeru sō, 61

kabitan mo tsukubawasekeri kimi ga haru, 46
kagerō no waga kata ni tatsu kamiko kana, 225
kakehashi ya inochi wo karamu tsutakazura, 210
kakurega ya tsuki to kiku to ni ta san-tan, 273
kame waruru yoru no kōri no nezame kana, 144
kami haete yōgan aoshi satsukiame, 158
kane tsukanu sato wa nani wo ka haru no kure, 230
kangiku ya konuka no kakaru usu no hata, 368
ka ni nioe uni horu oka no ume no hana, 179
Karasaki no matsu wa hana yori oboro nite, 129
karazake mo Kūya no yase mo kan no uchi, 306
kareeda ni karasu no tomarikeri aki no kure, 57
kareshiba ya yaya kagerō no ichi ni-sun, 180
Kasashima wa izuko satsuki no nukarimichi, 240
kaze no ka mo minami ni chikashi Mogami-gawa, 253
kazu naranu mi to na omoiso tamamatsuri, 393
kiku keitō kiri tsukushikeri omeikō, 214
kiku no hana saku ya ishiya no ishi no ai, 364
kiku no ka ya Nara ni wa furuki hotoketachi, 400
kiku no ka ya niwa ni kiretaru kutsu no soko, 367
kimi hi wo take yoki mono misen yukimaruge, 151
kinbyō no matsu no furusa yo fuyugomori, 365
ki no moto ni shiru mo namasu mo sakura kana, 286
kirishigure Fuji wo minu hi zo omoshiroki, 102
Kisagata ya ame ni Seishi ga nebu no hana, 257
Kiso no tochi ukiyo no hito no miyage kana, 211
Kiso no yase mo mada naoranu ni nochi no tsuki, 213
kite mo miyo Jinbe ga haori hanagoromo, 30
ki wo kirite motokuchi miru ya kyō no tsuki, 41
kochira muke ware mo sabishiki aki no kure, 298
kochō ni mo narade aki furu namushi kana, 271
kodomo-ra yo hirugao sakinu uri mukan, 359
kogarashi ni iwa fuki togaru sugima kana, 327
kogarashi ya hohobare itamu hito no kao, 303
komo wo kite tarebito imasu hana no haru, 284
kono aki wa nande toshiyoru kumo ni tori, 407
kono michi ya yuku hito nashi ni aki no kure, 406

kono yama no kanashisa tsugeyo tokoro hori, 183
kōri nigaku enso ga nodo wo uruoseri, 78
kumo nani to ne wo nani to naku aki no kaze, 54
kumo no mine ikutsu kuzurete tsuki no yama, 255
kumo oriori hito wo yasumeru tsukimi kana, 137
kumo to hedatsu tomo ka ya kari no ikiwakare, 31
kutabirete yado karu koro ya fuji no hana, 195
kyō bakari hito mo toshiyore hatsushigure, 344
kyōku kogarashi no mi wa Chikusai ni nitaru kana, 120
Kyō made wa mada nakazora ya yuki no kumo, 168
Kyō nite mo Kyō natsukashi ya hototogisu, 294
Kyō wa kuman-kusen kunju no hanami kana, 24

machi-ishi ya yashikigata yori komamukae, 33
masu kōte funbetsu kawaru tsukimi kana, 403
matsudake ya shiranu ki no ha no hebaritsuku, 323
mazu tanomu shii no ki mo ari natsu kodachi, 291
meigetsu no hana ka to miete watabatake, 397
meigetsu ya hokkoku biyori sadame naki, 268
meigetsu ya ike wo megurite yomosugara, 143
meigetsu ya mon ni sashi kuru shiogashira, 340
michinobe no mukuge wa uma ni kuwarekeri, 105
Miidera no mon tataka baya kyō no tsuki, 321
mikazuki ni chi wa oboronari soba no hana, 339
mikazuki ya asagao no yūbe tsubomu ran, 82
misoka tsuki nashi chitose no sugi wo daku arashi, 108
mo ni sudaku shirauo ya toraba kienu beki, 69
mononofu no daikon nigaki hanashi kana, 369
mugi no ho wo chikara ni tsukamu wakare kana, 381
Musashino ya issun hodo no shika no koe, 34
muzan ya na kabuto no shita no kirigirisu, 265

nagaki hi mo saezuri taranu hibari kana, 155
namagusashi konagi ga ue no hae no wata, 362
nami no hana to yuki mo ya mizu no kaeribana, 78
nami no ma ya kogai ni majiru hagi no chiri, 270
nanigoto no mitate ni mo nizu mika no tsuki, 207
nani ni kono shiwasu no ichi ni yuku karasu, 282
nani no ki no hana to wa shirazu nioi kana, 181
nao mitashi hana ni ake yuku kami no kao, 193
natsugoromo imada shirami wo tori tsukusazu, 135

natsugusa ya tsuwamono-domo ga yume no ato, 242
natsu no tsuki Goyu yori idete Akasaka ya, 37
nebuka shiroku arai agetaru samusa kana, 324
neko no koi yamu toki neya no oborozuki, 337
neko no tsuma hetsui no kuzure yori kayoikeri, 39
niwa hakite yuki wo wasururu hahaki kana, 346
nomi shirami uma no shitosuru makuramoto, 246
no wo yoko ni uma hiki muke yo hototogisu, 234
nozarashi wo kokoro ni kaze no shimu mi kana, 100
nusubito ni ōta yo mo ari toshi no kure, 375

omoshirōte yagate kanashiki ubune kana, 205
Oranda mo hana ni kinikeri uma ni kura, 50
otoroi ya ha ni kui ateshi nori no suna, 312

ran no ka ya chō no tsubasa ni takimono su, 110
rokugatsu ya mine ni kumo oku Arashiyama, 387
ro no koe nami wo utte harawata kōru yo ya namida, 63

sake nomeba itodo nerarene yoru no yuki, 150
samazamano koto omoidasu sakura kana, 185
samidare ni kakurenu mono ya Seta no hashi, 203
samidare ni nio no ukisu wo mi ni yukan, 160
samidare ni tsuru no ashi mijikaku nareri, 73
samidare no furi nokoshite ya hikaridō, 244
samidare no sora fuki otose Ōigawa, 385
samidare wo atsumete hayashi Mogami-gawa, 251, 385
samidare ya kaiko wazurau kuwa no hata, 383
samidare ya ryūtō aguru bantarō, 40
samidare ya shikishi hegitaru kabe no ato, 318
sarabachi mo honokani yami no yoisuzumi, 389
saru wo kiku hito sutego ni aki no kaze ikani, 103
sato furite kaki no ki motanu ie mo nashi, 395
sazaregani ashi hainoboru shimizu kana, 161
shiba no to ni cha wo konoha kaku arashi kana, 62
shibaraku wa hana no ue naru tsukiyo kana, 311
shibaraku wa taki ni komoru ya ge no hajime, 232
shini mo senu tabine no hate yo aki no kure, 116
shiodai no haguki mo samushi uo no tana, 345
shiogoshi ya tsuru hagi nurete umi suzushi, 259
shiore fusu ya yo wa sakasama no yuki no take, 26

shirageshi ni hane mogu chō no katami kana, 134
shiragiku no me ni tatete miru chiri mo nashi, 408
shirauo ya kuroki me wo aku nori no ami, 353
shizukasa ya iwa ni shimiiru semi no koe, 249
shizu no ko ya ine suri kakete tsuki wo miru, 162
sōkai no nami sake kusashi kyō no tsuki, 52
suisen ya shiroki shōji no tomoutsuri, 325
Suma no ama no yasaki ni naku ka hototogisu, 198
Surugaji ya hanatachibana mo cha no nioi, 384
susuhaki wa ono ga tana tsuru daiku kana, 374
suzushisa ya hono mikazuki no Haguro-yama, 254
suzushisa ya suguni nomatsu no eda no nari, 386

tabibito no kokoro ni mo niyo shii no hana, 356
tabibito to waga na yobaren hatsushigure, 166
tabi ni yande yume wa kareno wo kake meguru, 413
ta ichimai uete tachisaru yanagi kana, 236
taka hitotsu mitsukete ureshi Iragosaki, 171
takotsubo ya hakanaki yume wo natsu no tsuki, 201
tenbin ya Kyō Edo kakete chiyo no haru, 36
te ni toraba kien namida zo atsuki aki no shimo, 112
te wo uteba kodama ni akuru natsu no tsuki, 317
tōgan ya tagai ni kawaru kao no nari, 396
togi naosu kagami mo kiyoshi yuki no hana, 173
tomokakumo narade ya yuki no kareobana, 328
tonbō ya toritsuki kaneshi kusa no ue, 297
toshidoshi ya saru ni kisetaru saru no men, 351
toshi kurenu kasa kite waraji hakinagara, 125
tsuka mo ugoke waga naku koe wa aki no kaze, 263
tsukigane mo hibiku yō nari semi no koe, 204
tsuki hana no gu ni hari taten kan no iri, 350
tsuki hayashi kozue wa ame wo mochi nagara, 163
tsuki izuku kane wa shizumeru umi no soko, 269
tsukimi suru za ni utsukushiki kao mo nashi, 299
tsuki sumu ya kitsune kowagaru chigo no tomo, 409
tsuki wa are do rusu no yō nari Suma no natsu, 197
tsuki zo shirube konata e irase tabi no yado, 21
tsuru naku ya sono koe ni bashō yarenubeshi, 233
tsutsuji ikete sono kage ni hidara saku onna, 132

ubazakura saku ya rōgo no omoiide, 22

uguisu wo tama ni nemuru ka taoyanagi, 88
uguisu ya mochi ni funsuru en no saki, 336
uki fushi ya take no ko to naru hito no hate, 313
uki ware wo sabishi garase yo kankodori, 315
uma bokuboku ware wo e ni miru natsuno kana, 90
uma wo sae nagamuru yuki no ashita kana, 118
ume ga ka ni notto hi no deru yamaji kana, 376
umi kurete kamo no koe honokani shiroshi, 123
uo tori no kokoro wa shirazu toshiwasure, 333
ushibeya ni ka no koe kuraki zansho kana, 320
uzumibi mo kiyu ya namida no niyuro oto, 217

ware ni niru na futatsu ni wareshi makuwauri, 295

yagete shinu keshiki wa miezu semi no koe, 296
yamaji kite naniyara yukashi sumiregusa, 127
yamazato wa Manzai ososhi ume no hana, 309
yase nagara wari naki kiku no tsubomi kana, 165
yoku mireba nazuna hana saku kakine kana, 139
yo ni furu mo sarani Sōgi no yadori kana, 83
yo no hito no mitsukenu hana ya noki no kuri, 239
yoru hisokani mushi wa gekka no kuri wo ugatsu, 56
yūgao no shiroku yoru no kōka ni shisoku torite, 75
yūgao ya yōte kao dasu mado no ana, 358
yuki no ashita hitori karazake wo kami etari, 65
yuki wo matsu jōgo no kao ya inabikari, 326
yuku aki no nao tanomoshi ya aomikan, 343
yuku aki ya te wo hirogetaru kuri no iga, 398
yuku haru wo Ōmi no hito to oshimikeru, 288
yuku haru ya tori naki uo no me wa namida, 119, 228, 381

Index of Names

In this index "f" after a number indicates a separate reference on the next page, and "ff" indicates separate references on the next two pages. A continuous discussion over two or more pages is indicated by a span of numbers. *Passim* is used for a cluster of references in close but not consecutive sequence. Italicized page numbers indicate commentary on Bashō's hokku.

—poetic ideals: *fūga*, 4, 85, 103f, 111, 177, 237, 326, 331, 335, 342, 356; *sabi*, 61, 78, 248, 285, 299, 306, 316, 362, 365, 400, 414; *wabi*, 62f, 65, 76f, 85, 132, 184, 225, 247, 272, 357, 361; *karumi*, 91, 279, 286, 323, 336, 339, 357, 365, 370–80 *passim*, 414; *atarashimi*, 138; *fūryū*, 160, 189, 234, 238, 273, 290, 367, 410; *nioi*, 239, 261, 402
—works: *Kai ōi*, 6, 29f; *Edo ryōgin shū*, 35; *Edo sangin*, 38; *Jiin*, 67, 80; *Minashiguri*, 85, 92, 95, 112, 121f; *Nozarashi kikō*, 95f, 100, 105, 115, 122, 135; "Genjūan no ki," 135, 279, 291; *Sarumino*, 135, 275, 279, 300, 304, 307, 355; *Hatsukaishi hyōchū*, 138; *Kashima mōde*, 145; *Atsume ku*, 145; *Oi no kobumi*, 147, 166, 170f, 174f, 197f; *Tsuzuki no hara*, 147; *Sarashina kikō*, 174, 176; *Oku no hosomichi*, 221–23, 228–29, 236, 243, 255, 268; *Saga nikki*, 304, 315; *Sumidawara*, 365–66, 371; *Betsuzashiki*, 371
—commentary on his own hokku: written by himself, 30, 37, 214, 284, 336, 355; cited by Dohō, 98, 110, 117, 160, 166, 282, 286, 306, 345, 351; cited by Kyorai, 130, 288, 300; cited by others, 380, 392, 413
Baudelaire, Charles Pierre, 4
Biji (Takayama Biji), 80, 85
Bokugen (Terashima Bokugen), 168 69
Bokuin (Tani Bokuin), 95, 116, 121, 273
Bokusetsu (Mochizuki Bokusetsu), 390
Bonchō (Nozawa Bonchō), 300, 304

Bōsui (Katano Bōsui), 395
Bōtō (Makino Bōtō), *230, 248, 282*
Buson (Yosa Buson), 2, 127–28, 243, *259, 345, 376, 388, 410, 414*
Butchō, 68, 105, 124, 145
Byron, George Gordon, 4

Chamberlain, Basil Hall, 9, 10n
Chang Tu, 61
Ch'eng Ming-tao, 139, 153, 273n
Chia Tao, 321–22
Chikurei (Kakuta Chikurei), *39, 47, 54, 149, 191, 228, 267, 291, 299, 364, 367*
Chiri (Naemura Chiri), 95, 122
Chishū (Tomoda Chishū), 278
Chou Mao-shu, 273
Chuang-tzu, 67, 74, 78f, 88f, 101, 133, 271, 391
cummings, e. e., 11

Dante Alighieri, 373
Dohō (Hattori Dohō), 7, *98, 110, 111, 117, 160, 166, 173, 181, 227, 278, 282, 286, 306, 309, 345, 349, 351, 365, 387*
Donshū, 413
Donto (Tōkai Donto), 37, *50, 57, 65, 74f, 84, 98, 100, 102, 118, 123, 132f, 135, 149, 153, 161, 177f, 180, 191, 193, 198f, 204–15 passim, 224f, 240, 248, 263, 275, 296, 299, 318, 323f, 333, 338, 350, 358, 374, 376, 386, 394, 411*

Ebara Taizō, 8, *21, 40, 50, 61, 72f, 81, 87, 91, 107, 109, 112, 121, 126f, 132, 155, 158, 163, 170, 173, 184, 187, 189, 210, 214, 241f, 244, 248f, 253–61 passim, 265, 269f, 273, 282, 311f, 316f, 320, 335,*

342, 359f, 378, 381, 383, 387, 394,
398, 410
Eisenstein, Sergei M., 4
Eliot, T. S., 128, 275
Etsujin (Ochi Etsujin), 147, 176, 210,
212f, 223

Fujiwara Hidehira, 242
Fujiwara Norinaga, 76
Fujiwara Sanekata, 240–41
Fujiwara Yoshitsune, 114f
Fūko (Naitō Yoshimune), 32, 38, 160
Fu Wen, 56

Gautama Buddha, 229, 264
Gomizunoo, Emperor, 199
Gosodō (Raisetsuan Gosodō), 267
Gotoba, Emperor, 130, 338
Gozan (Aida Gozan), 140, 315, 335
Gyōki, 192, 239

Hagiwara Sakutarō, 8, 59, 240, 264,
282
Hakuin, 140
Handa Ryōhei, 59, 91, 124, 127, 133,
139, 143, 158, 160, 171, 178, 192,
200, 206, 210, 215, 231, 235, 251,
254, 278, 286f, 297, 311, 316, 319,
325, 355, 368, 373, 389, 394, 400,
406, 410f
Han Shan, 85, 346
Hanzan (Yamagishi Hanzan), 278
Hearn, Lafcadio, 9, 10n
Henderson, Harold G., 10
Higuchi Isao, 71, 92, 108, 111, 125,
132, 154, 160, 171, 203, 208, 215,
229, 257, 265–70 passim, 284,
301, 310, 340, 353, 365, 388, 414
Higuchi Jirō, 265
Hokushi (Tachibana Hokushi), 221
Hōnen, 81

Honma Shume, 391
Hori Nobuo, 22, 61, 66, 72, 75, 79,
101, 107, 115, 121, 125, 133, 153,
161, 165, 172, 184, 186, 188, 196,
203, 206, 211f, 216
Hsi Shih, 257–58
Huntley, Frank Livingstone, 10
Hyōroku (Asai Hyōroku), 409

Ikkyū, 273
Imoto Nōichi, 9, 30f, 36, 50, 56, 64,
66, 69, 79, 84, 104, 115, 121, 124,
131, 139, 142, 160, 184, 196, 206,
212, 229, 231, 237f, 243–48 passim, 256, 261, 267, 276, 285, 290f,
296, 320, 350, 352, 362, 368, 374,
378, 392f, 405f, 412, 414
Issa (Kobayashi Issa), 2
Isshō (Kosugi Isshō), 263–64
Iwata Kurō, 21, 27, 41, 89, 113, 117,
124, 131, 143, 154, 164, 179f, 187,
192, 196f, 211, 213, 216, 232, 235,
266, 274, 285ff, 299, 310, 313,
318f, 322, 326, 358, 361, 363, 369,
373, 379, 382, 384, 395, 402, 405

Jirōbei, 348, 370–72
Jō Magodayū, 31
Jutei, 348, 370–71, 390, 392f

Kaempfer, Engelbert, 50
Kakei (Nakajima Kakei), 31, 155
Kakinomoto Hitomaro, 192
Kashin, 239
Keion (Nunami Keion), 31, 47, 88,
127, 130, 134, 139, 183, 187, 207,
234, 284, 294, 313f, 341, 394
Keishi (Hasegawa Keishi), 403–4, 409
Kigin (Kitamura Kigin), 17, 29, 38, 57
Kikaku (Takarai Kikaku), 32, 53, 85,
138, 141, 145, 147, 176, 331, 355,

Ninkō (Saiganji Ninkō), 38, 40
Nobutane (Shinten-ō Nobutane), 39,
76, 118, 126, 139f, 143, 151, 158,
165, 171, 178–83 passim, 187, 189,
191, 199, 204, 224, 232, 242, 249,
251, 261, 265, 272, 306, 312f, 321,
333, 339, 344, 380, 384
Noguchi Yonejirō, 8, 102, 127, 195,
314
Nōin, 230
Nose Tomoji, 77, 99, 307, 352

Ogata Tsutomu, 9, 77, 91, 101, 124,
126, 131, 186, 237, 255, 303, 307,
310, 355, 377, 382, 399
Ōmi, Prince, 172
Ōmori Shirō, 238
Ono no Komachi, 391
Ōsha (Imura Ōsha), 25, 41, 150, 278,
393
Ōtani Tokuzō, 36, 82, 317, 338, 397,
404
Otokuni (Kawai Otokuni), 342
Ōtomo Yakamochi, 155

Po Chü-i, 53, 85, 103, 215, 253
Pound, Ezra, 4

Ranran (Matsukura Ranran), 363
Ransetsu (Hattori Ransetsu), 53, 145,
331
Renard, Jules, 308
Rika (Bashō's disciple), 67, 71, 408
Rika (Fun'ya Rika), 26f, 61, 64, 144,
150, 191, 204, 251, 263
Rikyū (Sen Rikyū), 166, 167n
Ritō (Sakurai Ritō), 57
Riyū (Kōno Riyū), 300–301
Rohan (Kōda Rohan), 47, 77, 108,
111, 127, 130, 139, 141, 156, 192,

202, 231, 239, 256, 291, 299, 302,
306, 316, 338, 340f, 351, 353,
361ff, 376, 381, 385, 400, 411, 414
Romaru (Kondō Romaru), 129
Rosen (Naitō Rosen), 160, 354n
Rossetti, Dante Gabriel, 195
Rotsū (Inbe Rotsū), 223, 279
Ryōbon (Tomoda Kakuzaemon), 278
Ryōta (Ōshima Ryōta), 88, 98, 193,
236, 273, 356

Saigyō, 83, 85, 121, 166, 274, 284;
waka cited for comparison, 57, 137,
156, 181–82, 211, 236–37, 240–
41, 261–62, 292, 315, 408
Saisei (Murō Saisei), 8, 46, 100, 130,
137, 158, 302, 364, 406
Saitō Sanemori, 22, 265–66
San'en, 278
Sanga (Horoan Sanga), 81, 123, 130,
163, 171, 187, 249, 269, 275, 302,
328, 359, 365
Sanpū (Sugiyama Sanpū), 29, 32, 53,
176f, 213, 331, 348, 354
San'u (Shoshian San'u), 7, 83, 105,
137, 156, 408
Sanuki, Lady, 83f
Seihō (Shimada Seihō), 56, 59, 69,
116, 135, 151, 202, 264, 314, 362,
368, 410
Seisensui (Ogiwara Seisensui), 8, 42,
56, 75, 78, 132, 134, 225, 229, 238,
240, 244, 246, 250–59 passim,
268, 285
Seishi (Yamaguchi Seishi), 52, 115,
131, 136, 226, 247, 251, 308, 312,
379
Seishin (Shibuya Kurōbei), 253
Sei Shōnagon, 328
Sekisui (Ishiko Sekisui), 7, 198, 228

Tokugawa Tsunayoshi, 46
Tōkyū (Sagara Tōkyū), 238
Tōrin (Matsuo Tōrin), 305
Tosai (Chijitsuan Tosai), *50, 59, 61,
63, 74, 78, 88, 90, 103, 108–17
passim, 132, 134, 139f, 144, 149–
54 passim, 163, 166, 168, 177, 185,
193, 199, 203, 207–13 passim,
224–35 passim, 239, 246, 256,
260, 265, 269, 271, 277, 291, 293,
295, 311, 315, 325, 328, 333, 336,
345, 358, 377, 379, 387, 393, 395,
397, 403, 409*
Tōsai (Kanbe Tōsai), 223
Tōyō (Hayashi Tōyō), 118f
Tōzan, 225
Tu Fu, 63, 83, 85, 103, 110, 121, 249,
301
Tu Wu-lang, 348

Unchiku, 298
Utsubo (Kubota Utsubo), *101, 107,
126, 128, 134, 139, 149f, 157, 161,
164f, 172, 177–85 passim, 202,
206, 217, 226, 235, 247, 264, 278,
286, 312, 337, 339, 383, 389, 400,
408*

Van Gogh, Vincent, 158

Wang Hsin-min, 65f, 369
Wang Wei, 414
Watsuji Tetsurō, *7, 41, 77, 81, 91,
107, 151, 166, 170, 200f, 236, 249,
251, 257, 263, 298–306 passim,
314f, 317, 333, 339, 346, 363, 378,
390, 411, 414*
Williams, William Carlos, 11
Wordsworth, William, 4

Yaba (Shida Yaba), 365–66
Yakumu (Roppeisai Yakumu), 40
Yamamoto Kenkichi, *8–9, 26, 33, 37,
40, 51, 55, 60, 64, 66, 72–77 passim, 84, 91f, 101–11 passim, 115–
21 passim, 126, 128, 134, 139, 142,
149f, 150, 155, 157, 159, 165, 169f,
172, 178f, 187–96 passim, 200,
202, 213, 224, 229, 234–46 passim, 254–75 passim, 282, 285,
290–94 passim, 301, 307, 314,
323, 328, 334, 336, 340, 342, 345,
357, 380–90 passim, 398, 400,
406–14 passim*
Yasuyoshi (Ozaki Yasuyoshi), 63,
228
Yūzan (Takano Yūzan), 29, 32, 38,
45

LIBRARY OF CONGRESS CATALOGING-IN-PUBLICATION DATA

Ueda, Makoto, 1931–
  Bashō and his interpreters : selected hokku with commentary /
compiled, translated, and with an introduction by Makoto Ueda.
    p.   cm.
  ISBN 0-8047-1916-0 :
    1. Matsuo, Bashō, 1644–1694—Criticism and interpretation.
I. Matsuo, Bashō, 1644–1694. Poems. English. Selections. 1992.
II. Title.
PL794.4.Z5U39   1991
895.6′132—dc20   91-14035
                                                        CIP
                                                        Rev.

  ⊗ This book is printed on acid-free paper.